FREE ENTERPRISE

LAWRENCE B. GLICKMAN

Free Enterprise

AN AMERICAN HISTORY

Yale
UNIVERSITY PRESS

NEW HAVEN & LONDON

Published with assistance from the Louis Stern Memorial Fund.

Yale University Press books may be purchased in quantity for educational, business, or promotional use. For information, please e-mail sales.press@yale. edu (U.S. office) or sales@yaleup.co.uk (U.K. office).

Set in Times Roman type by Integrated Publishing Solutions, Grand Rapids, Michigan.
Printed in the United States of America.

Library of Congress Control Number: 2019931295
ISBN 978-0-300-23825-9 (hardcover : alk. paper)

A catalogue record for this book is available from the British Library.

This paper meets the requirements of ANSI/NISO Z39.48-1992 (Permanence of Paper).

10 9 8 7 6 5 4 3 2 1

To Jill Frank, Sandra Glickman, and Ronald Glickman

CONTENTS

ACKNOWLEDGMENTS

IN THE ESSAY "I, PENCIL" (the subject of chapter 6), Leonard Read speaks with awe of the pencil's "innumerable antecedents." As with Read's pencil, behind this book is an impossibly long line of people who have helped bring the project to fruition, and I am extremely grateful to them all. Although it is, to quote Read, "impossible for me to name and explain all of my antecedents," I would like to credit some small fraction of the people and institutions that made this book possible.

I'd like to start with the historians who inspired me. I would not have thought to write this book if it were not for the intriguing mentions of *free enterprise* in the works of Angus Burgin, Nathan Connolly, Darren Dochuk, Elizabeth Fones-Wolf, Howell John Harris, Katherine Rye Jewell, Kevin M. Kruse, Bethany Moreton, Kathryn S. Olmstead, Kim Phillips-Fein, Wendy L. Wall, and many others cited in the endnotes. Thanks also to the dozens of librarians and archivists who helped me along the way, with a special shout-out to Lucas R. Clawson, the reference archivist at the Hagley Museum and Library who helped me during my research visits and patiently responded to my many email queries. I am also tremendously grateful to the extraordinary librarians at Cornell, including Virginia Cole, Lynn Thitchenor, and especially Heather Furnas, who went way above and beyond the call of duty many times, doggedly tracking down obscure sources that I'd given up on ever finding. Many other scholars generously answered my queries, shared information with me, and/or agreed to write letters on my behalf, including Leon Fink, Eric Foner, Gary Gerstle, Howell John Harris, Richard John, the late Ann Johnson, Michael Kazin, Pamela Walker

Laird, Sue Levine, Nelson Lichtenstein, Noam Maggor, Heather Cox Richardson, Daniel T. Rodgers, Sam Rosenfeld, David Stebenne, Benjamin Waterhouse, Sean Wilentz, and Kyle Williams.

I began this book as a faculty member at the University of South Carolina and completed it at Cornell University, where I have taught since 2014. At both institutions, I've been extremely fortunate to have supportive, friendly, and brilliant colleagues. At South Carolina, I'd like to thank Lacy Ford, my chair, and the former dean, Mary Ann Fitzpatrick, who provided much-appreciated support as I was launching the research. Thanks also to three excellent (now former) graduate students, Laura Foxworth, Robert Greene, and Caroline Peyton, who provided superb research assistance. Derek K. O'Leary did me a huge favor by scanning key articles from the *San Francisco News*. At Cornell, I am grateful to my chairs, Barry Strauss and Sandra Greene, and to the dean, Gretchen Ritter, who hired me. I am especially indebted to the extraordinary generosity of Stephen and Evalyn Milman, who fund the endowed chair that I have held since 2016. Thanks also to colleagues and students who have participated in the History of Capitalism Initiative at Cornell, and to all those who attended our conferences in 2014 and 2016 and our reading group and colloquia. Ed Baptist, Jefferson Cowie, and Louis Hyman invited me to be a part of this group when I arrived at Cornell, and it has opened a new world of scholarly and personal connections. My former colleague Victor Seow co-taught a graduate course with me on the comparative history of capitalism, and he and the students in that class—from disciplines as varied as anthropology, comparative literature, government, history, and science and technology studies—taught me a great deal in the process. Although I haven't been able to attend often, I've been motivated by the members of Historians Are Writers! at Cornell, who once even inspired me to compose a poem about the writing of this book.

I have been fortunate to present parts of this book at a number of fantastic conferences and seminars where I benefited from extremely helpful feedback. Special thanks to Nelson Lichtenstein, who invited me to two conferences at UC–Santa Barbara; the first, in 2011, provided impetus for me to conceptualize this book. I found the 2015 "Beyond the New Deal Order" conference extremely inspiring, and I am grateful to all of the attendees, especially K. Sabeel Rahman, who offered helpful comments on my paper. I was lucky to present at the Newberry Library Seminar in the History of Capitalism at an early stage in the writing of this book, and I thank Leon Fink and Jeff Sklansky for the opportunity and the feedback. Thanks to Kevin Kruse and Julian Zelizer for the invitation to present at the Princeton University Political History Seminar, where Stephen Macedo offered helpful suggestions as commenter. A 2014 session at the Organization of American Historians on the meaning of *free enterprise* with Nathan Connolly, Louis Hyman, and Wendy Wall helped me think about alternative perceptions of the concept that I thought I understood. Thanks to Holly Case, who invited me to speak at the Cornell University History Department Colloquium shortly after I arrived, and to all those who braved the (what seemed to me then as an Ithaca newbie) bitter cold that evening to attend and discuss. Richard John, who invited me to participate in a plenary session at the 2017 Business History Conference, helped me think about ways to frame this book, and also generously sent me leads when he found them. I am grateful to Jefferson Cowie for inviting me to the Vanderbilt University American History Seminar and for inspiring me as a historian and encouraging me as a friend. At Vandy, I got extraordinarily helpful feedback from Brandon Byrd, Heath Carter, Sarah Igo, Paul Kramer, Daniel Scharfstein, Ganesh Sitaraman, and the bonus guests: my old friends Ann Powers and Eric Weisbard. At the Society for U.S. Intellectual History conference in 2015, I learned a lot from my co-panelists, Angus Burgin and Andrina Tran, the commenter Elizabeth Tandy Shermer, and members of the audience, especially Andrew Seal. Attendees at the Johns Hopkins Institute Seminar provided helpful feedback on my first iteration of the book's introduction. Thanks to Burgin and Louis Galambos for the invitation and to Christy Ford Chapin for encouragement and constructive criticism.

I was fortunate to be able to publish essays on issues related to this book for a broad public audience in some amazing outlets, including *Aeon, Bloomberg View, Boston Review, Process: A Blog for American History*, and the blog of the Society for U.S. Intellectual History. I am thankful for permission to reproduce here some material that appeared in these periodicals in earlier form. Thanks also to my editors, Andrew Hartman, Sam Haselby, Colin Kinniburgh, Avni Majithia-Sejpal, Adam McGee, Stephen Mihm, Andrew Seal, and Jonathan D. Warner, for helping me clarify my thoughts.

I owe special thanks to Adina Berk, my editor at Yale University Press, who not only got what I was trying to do but insisted that I actually do it by sending me back to the manuscript after I thought I was done (twice), helping to make this a far stronger book as a result. The rest of the team at Yale University Press has been a pleasure to work with, including Kristy Leonard and Eva Skewes.

Thanks also to Robin DuBlanc for excellent copyediting, Suzie Tibor for expertly handling the visuals, and to Kurt Newman for his work on the index. Much gratitude also to two historians I respect enormously, Pamela Walker Laird and Kim Phillips-Fein, the referees for the Press, who both provided a perfect mix of encouragement and thorough, extremely helpful critiques of the manuscript. (Special thanks to Kim for also reading a revised chapter at the last minute.) I am very thankful to Jill Frank and Marc Schachter, who offered incisive readings of the manuscript and pointed out inconsistencies and infelicities.

Many other friends and colleagues asked me questions and/or listened to me hash out my arguments, and I'm grateful to them all. I owe special thanks to Bonnie Honig, who always took the time to engage and offer sharp suggestions. So many other friends, most of them far flung, stayed in touch, showed an interest in my research, and simply showed me they cared, which means more than I can say. I'm so grateful to these people, even though I don't get to see them as often as I'd like. But when I see them—on visits to my place, ski trips, while traveling, or at conferences—my intellectual batteries are refreshed and my soul revived. Many people that I do not know irl, as they say, engaged with me and encouraged me on Twitter and Facebook, and I'm grateful especially to all the #Twitterstorians, especially the brilliant, mostly younger, scholars of conservativism, who weighed in in various ways.

My extended family (on both sides) is full of generous, supportive, and talented people, many of whom offered encouragement and support. My parents, Sandra and Ronald Glickman, have always loved and encouraged me, and their active engagement in politics and the world of ideas remains an inspiration, as does their generosity of spirit. Abigail and Alexander, who were children when I began this book, are now young adults who inspire me with their curiosity, humor, kindness, and impressive engagements of their own. Jill Frank is an amazing partner in every way who models intellectual and emotional generosity. I am so lucky.

FREE ENTERPRISE

Introduction

"A GREAT MANY OF OUR AMERICAN PEOPLE talk lovingly of what they call 'The Free Enterprise System,'" began a five-part series of editorials in the *Des Moines Register* in February and March 1940. "They insist that they want it preserved. They make devotion to it the acid test of 'Americanism' itself. They revere it. They virtually worship it. They make it sort of a god."[1] Although the editorial emphasized that free enterprise was an authentic American religion *revered* with *devotion* and *worshipped* like a *god*, the editorialist's quizzical rather than celebratory tone as well as the reiteration of fidelity to this "system," like the overwrought protestations of a doubting parishioner, worked to undermine rather than reinforce the professed faith in free enterprise that supposedly lay deep in the American psyche and soul.

The editorials described that system as freedom for business firms, which was best promoted when government "takes its hands off." The opposite of "free enterprise" was "regimentation," which portended that "freedom of other kinds will go, with very little lag." Less a set of positive ideas than a negative imperative, the practice of free enterprise amounted to "resisting the onslaughts on American freedom," as Ogden Mills, the secretary of the treasury under Herbert Hoover, claimed in 1936.[2] It was a preventive impulse, a protector of freedom not by virtue of what it did but because of what it opposed.

The second editorial in the *Register*'s series claimed: "We can best understand the Free Enterprise System if we approach it historically."[3] That is the task of this book: to interpret this apparently straightforward but perplexing term that has been deemed central to the American experience but has rarely been treated as a historical phenomenon. While this is probably not the book "devoted to the theme of the beneficent purpose of our free enterprise system" that the anti–New Dealer Samuel B. Pettengill wished for in 1940, it explores at length his widely shared view that free enterprise was an essential American ideal. It also examines his fear, generally embraced by free enterprise advocates, that under the New Deal, "your freedom is being stolen from you right under your eyes," and that free enterprise was a vital resource in the battle to restore that pilfered liberty.[4]

An American Myth

When I began this study of "the free enterprise system" as an American myth, I thought that the term *free enterprise*, which I mistakenly understood to be roughly synonymous to *free market*, was false as a description of the American economy and its relationship to the government. I believed that it perpetuated what the historian Oscar Handlin had discovered in the 1940s: that the idea of the United States as a laissez-faire society was a "misconception," even though it could be "found not only in the pretty publications of the National Association of Manufacturers where it might be expected, but also in the serious works of our most careful scholars into which it obtrudes almost automatically."[5] I believe I was correct in assuming that "glib mythologies of free enterprise" were an inaccurate depiction of the nature of American economic development, which has always been a product of a combination of government and the private sector or, as it came to be known, the "mixed economy."[6] Celebrants of free enterprise seemed like hypocrites or prevaricators.[7]

However, I discovered that the idea of free enterprise is also a myth in another, more important sense: a set of assumptions, narratives, and attitudes that has guided our common sense and, regardless of empirical accuracy, has dramatically shaped how Americans have understood and engaged in politics. In what Henry Hazlitt, the *Newsweek* economics columnist, called in 1949 "the ideological war for free enterprise," the creation of guiding narratives was pivotal.[8] To take one example, free enterprisers developed a populist language in which they described prerogatives of the business firm as a source of individual freedom. "Talk to the average man and he'll tell you free enterprise means the right of corporate enterprises to make profits," declared a 1944 advertisement for Baltimore's First National Bank.[9] Speaking on behalf of the "average man" and identifying his interests with banks and other businesses and against the government crucially shaped the political landscape of the twentieth century and beyond.

Free enterprise advocates invoked myth in still another way when they described it as a custom. Those who from the 1920s through the 1970s reinvented the phrase and gave it an entirely new meaning as an anti–New Deal slogan almost immediately portrayed it as an old-fashioned verity. They referred to it as "the traditional American free enterprise system" and called it "the realization of the hopes and aims and aspirations of man as far back as we have recorded history."[10] Converting a nineteenth-century term with fluid and clashing connotations into an age-old custom required retroactively reading a new conception of the term into the past, thus denying the right of others to claim it in the present. Free enterprise, according to Ogden Mills, stood for "the maintenance of our economic and political system as it developed over a century and a half of amazing progress." Like other opponents of the New Deal, Mills feared that attacks on free enterprise, "the light that guided western civilization for over 100 years," would lead to civilizational collapse.[11]

Finally, myth inoculated against incorrect predictions. Most of the disasters predicted by free enterprisers failed to materialize. The Social Security Act did not destroy the free enterprise system in the 1930s, as opponents claimed it would. But the power of the discourse did not inhere in its predictive capacity or its truth claims but in its repetitive familiarity. Believers treated it as a secular religion requiring and rewarding faith.[12] Political defeat only emboldened them to call for what the Republican Indiana senator Raymond E. Willis termed in 1943 "a rebirth" of faith in "our philosophy of free enterprise" that was necessary to combat the future possibility of statist tyranny.[13] In 1977, Ronald Reagan, the once and future Republican presidential candidate, argued that the free enterprise system "has never failed us once." On the contrary, "we have failed the system, usually by lacking faith in it."[14] Like other faith-based doctrines, it could be maddeningly opaque or unpersuasive to its critics. Yet the merger of faith with myth proved enduring and powerful.

The commonly used phrase *free enterprise system*, first coined in 1924 (*system of free enterprise* was first used in 1919) suggested a capaciousness of meaning. Just as advocates of the "free labor system" of the nineteenth century took it to be the building block of a democratic and prosperous society, those who spoke of free enterprise conceived of it as a complete civilizational ecosystem. The word *system* suggested both that free enterprise comprised an organic whole and that it was incompatible with other systems. It was also a language of naturalization; advocates treated free enterprise as a self-governing force endangered most of all by "artificial" efforts, such as state intervention, to interfere with it. Believers in this idea suspected that, no matter how benign, efforts to reform the system would have dangerous consequences. Throughout this period, the advocates of free enterprise treated proposed modifications, even seemingly minor ones, as "an assault on the free enterprise system."[15] Advocates of free enterprise thus emerged as jealous protectors of a system that they viewed as both uniquely powerful and perpetually vulnerable. The tone that followed from this view—fearful, aggrieved, even apocalyptic—became as central to free enterprise thought as did the substance of its proponents' ideas, and the psychology of what I call "elite victimization" shaped the nature of American conservatism.

Free enterprise has long been a part of the American political vocabulary. It played a central role in the defining clash in the nineteenth-century between the "free labor system," with which it was paired, and the system of chattel slavery. In the twentieth century, it served as a key concept in the war between the New Deal and its enemies. Free enterprisers took their agenda to be a necessary moral crusade. That first set of debates, rooted in the nineteenth century, morphed into the second set in the twentieth and came to shape modern political culture. Far from being merely economic disputes, these were fundamental debates over the meaning of morality, society, and politics. Just as free laborites believed that the nation could not endure being half slaveholding and half free, twentieth-century free enterprisers draw a similar conclusion about the dangers of a mixed economy in which government and private business worked together.

Starting in the 1920s, through capitalism's ups and downs, advocates of free enterprise focused on a compelling set of fears about the dangers of government power. This metamorphosis was largely the work of an energetic group of politicians, business leaders, lobbyists, pundits, and leaders of trade organizations. As one proponent said in 1941, "The story of free enterprise in America should be told and retold."[16] This book tells how one version of that story became dominant and how this narrative constrained and transformed politics in the United States, even during the height of the period from the 1930s to the 1970s that historians call the "New Deal order," when it appeared to be on the losing side of history.[17] Long after Franklin Roosevelt's death, this vocabulary endured as the linchpin in the battle against the welfare state, the Great Society and, eventually, postwar liberalism itself.

In its most important twentieth-century incarnation, then, free enterprise became a mirror of the New Deal, and the clash between the two is a leitmotif shaping every chapter of this book. The free enterprise backlash against the New Deal occurred almost immediately and continued unabated for many decades. Long after Roosevelt was gone, free enterprisers drew repeatedly on the lessons of their attempt to undo his legacy. They reduced almost every political debate to this defining binary. Free enterprisers provided the template for the "party of opposition to the threat of the New Deal" that Pettengill demanded in 1944.[18] Eventually, the Republican Party became that "party of opposition," but initially many free enterprisers were, like Pettengill, disgruntled Democrats. In this process, free enterprise discourse served as a bridge, providing a home for New Deal critics, many of whom remained in the Democratic Party for decades, before the slow process of political realignment sorted conservatives into the Republican Party.

Free enterprisers fought a New Deal that existed largely in their imaginations. The actual New Deal, however radical, was also racially exclusive, ideologically promiscuous and, at least by some measures, over well before the end of Franklin Roosevelt's second term in office.[19] Yet free enterprisers assigned it both ideological coherence and supernatural power. They treated it not as it actually existed but as the most dangerous American vector of a global movement toward "collectivism" that was bound to metamorphose into totalitarianism.

Similarly, the "free enterprise system" was an abstraction. Its supporters saw it as all-encompassing, but they variously singled out the corporation, the small business firm, and the lightly regulated market itself as the essence of the system. Although they often represented or championed business interests, free enterprisers rarely acknowledged a partisan perspective or even a self-interested economic standpoint. They spoke instead in the name of ideals such as "freedom" and they believed that the promotion of business interests, as they understood them, would best promote individual liberty.

In a parallel fashion, the free enterprise critique of "statism" did not extend to all or even most functions of the government. Free enterprise advocates especially disliked what came to be called the "welfare state," the government's powers of redistribution, taxation, and spending on social programs. Yet they distinguished free enterprise from laissez-faire, and were not averse to employing the state to promote their interests and to punish those they opposed. Free enterprise supporters of segregation, for example, wanted the government to enforce Jim Crow, claiming it was a dereliction of duty not to do so. Similarly, business free enterprisers fought hard to promote legislation that made certain forms of union activity illegal. Those who embraced free enterprise, then, put the "New Deal" and "statism" to ideological use. As Bruce Bliven, the editor of the *New Republic*, noted in 1943, those who want free enterprise "are glad to have government interference when it works in their direction."[20]

"Who's Killing Free Enterprise?"

My interest in the topic of free enterprise began with a conundrum, a gaping chasm between primary and secondary sources. Whereas users of the term recognized its malleability, scholars have generally taken its meaning for granted. In the nineteenth century, Americans invoked the phrase for a variety of purposes— usually to signify the importance of the government unleashing "the free enterprise of our citizens," as President Andrew Jackson said in his "President's Message" of 1832—a meaning distinct from the dominant modern one in which business interests take precedence over the state.[21] Evidence abounds that, throughout the twentieth century, advocates of "free enterprise" recognized the phrase to be as "vague as it is generic," debated its meaning vigorously, expressed frustration at their inability to disseminate it, and even periodically sought to replace it with a more easily understood term.[22] "There are few words that have so many different interpretations as free enterprise," wrote one of the phrase's biggest champions, the conservative publisher Raymond C. Hoiles, in 1947.[23] In 1958, the U.S. Chamber of Commerce even spearheaded a program to help clarify the phrase, and the inability of the business community to define the term and to effectively "sell" the phrase set off periodic waves of confusion and panic from the 1930s to the 1970s.[24]

In the end, as the *Des Moines Register* editorialist suggested, one dominant meaning for free enterprise proved triumphant: the autonomy of the business firm, free from government restriction. Free enterprise advocates treated business freedom and power as a precondition for individual liberty and a defense against the ever-present danger of "statism." In 1938, Glenn Frank, a rising star in the GOP, described free enterprise as "the right of business to act without restraint, depending on its own good judgement." Although he, like most proponents of this new conception of the term, conceded that the government should provide what he called "decent economic traffic laws," the essence of free enterprise was, in the final analysis, the autonomy of the business firm, which meant freedom from government "dictation."[25] Strong business and compliant (though not necessarily weak or small) government spelled the formula for economic and political liberty by preventing the modern version of slavery, whose most likely cause was overly powerful government.

From the start of the New Deal, free enterprise advocates feared that the supposedly sturdy tradition was under threat.[26] They worried that, as a group of bankers claimed in 1940, the country was "moving away from the system of free enterprise."[27] The story of dispossession was endlessly retold. It went like this: in the past, we had complete free enterprise. But in the present, it is being undermined and faces the danger of disappearing altogether, along with the freedom that it underwrites.

It did not matter when "the present" was. During the period between the 1930s and 1970s, advocates described the free enterprise system as perpetually under siege. The theme of Wendell Willkie's presidential campaign of 1940 was that the New Deal was "killing free enterprise."[28] Advocates interpreted even seemingly benign extensions of the state as mechanisms designed to destroy free enterprise. Lou R. Maxon, the head of the eponymous advertising agency, said in 1943 at the meeting of the Sales Executive Club that grade labeling of canned goods marked "the first step in the eventual destruction of the American system of free enterprise by government standardization and regimentation."[29] One year later, James J. Davis, Republican senator from Pennsylvania, argued that the "New Deal had stripped America almost entirely of free enterprise."[30] The theme was so popular that "Who's Killing Free Enterprise?" was the discussion topic for a meeting of the Illini Toastmasters in 1949.[31]

Throughout the era of the widespread invocation of the "free enterprise system," its champions perceived it as being on the brink of collapse. Although many commentators accused free enterprisers of crying wolf, the declarations of war continued unabated. As early as 1948, columnist James Marlow urged Americans not to "be kidded into getting excited every time you hear someone scream that free enterprise is in danger of being destroyed," advice that Marlow himself sometimes disregarded.[32] Free enterprisers did not heed such warnings, nor could they, given the degree to which predictions of imminent threat imbued their favored phrase with meaning. In 1962, Donald I. Rogers, the author of *The End of Free Enterprise*, claimed that "we are now in imminent danger of losing" the system that "once lost," would be "irretrievable."[33] Champions of free enterprise as the rock upon which the United States stood specialized in mourning its imminent disappearance and in calling, as the National Association of Manufacturers (NAM) did in 1940, for a "crusade" to save the indispensable system that was "the base and bulwark of all the freedoms of the common people."[34] They described such crusades as necessary and desperate responses to the unfair "attacks" that they discerned all around them. "The principle of free enterprise . . . is under constant attack," proclaimed the trade journal the *American Builder* in 1954. "What are you doing to fight back?"[35]

Although what we might call the "age of free enterprise," the era when the phrase was in near-constant use as a foil to the New Deal, coincided almost precisely with the Cold War battle against Soviet communism, proponents described the dire threats to the system as primarily domestic, not foreign. Free enterprisers imagined the mechanism of subversion as the slippery slope of social reform, not the bloody revolution or the violent military coup. New Deal liberalism, they believed, had laid the groundwork for socialist totalitarianism. As one critic said of the 1936 Republican presidential candidate, Alf Landon saw "a salaam to Stalin in every New Deal act or utterance."[36] Advocates of free enterprise took the process by which a welfare state became a police state to be unstoppable, which lent the battle against even minimal additions to the safety net the flavor of existential warfare. Free enterprisers refused to distinguish liberal New Dealers from socialists and other radicals. Since, in her free enterprise teleology, New Deal liberalism was fated to become totalitarianism, the conservative commentator Ruth Alexander, like many of her peers, felt obliged to use the terms *welfare state* and *socialism* "interchangeably."[37] Not everyone went as far as E. F. Scoutten, a vice president of Maytag, who wrote in 1964, "There is no essential difference between an absolute monarchy, a dictatorship, a fascist form of government and a Welfare State."[38] But free enterprisers described the choice as binary and claimed that reforms, no matter how mild, could have devastating consequences. Indeed, they questioned the very idea of liberal reform, labeling it as an illusory category fated, by the slippery slope process they took to be inevitable, to transform into some version of statist tyranny.

Once introduced in the late 1920s, the new version of free enterprise discourse hung in a kind of suspended animation. The dominant rhetorical patterns and even specific language that first appeared at that time changed little over the next fifty years. In 1940, Wendell Willkie said that it was "five minutes to midnight" for free enterprise as the nation sank into a "totalitarian pit."[39] Thirty-eight years later, Ronald Reagan, aspiring for the presidency he would gain in two years, worried that the Democrats had "led us down the road of collectivism" and fretted that "it is five minutes till midnight for this wonderful, unique free enterprise system of ours."[40] In the free enterprise discourse that reigned from the 1930s through the 1970s, time literally stood still. (Although Ruth Alexander set the alarmist clock forward in 1952 to "past midnight.")[41] Central to free enterprise ideology was the view that the present moment represented a last stand.[42] Walter Trohan's dramatic description of "the American institution of free enterprise standing wounded and bleeding with its back to the wall in a life or death struggle with collectivism" was echoed two decades before the *Chicago Tribune* published these particular words in 1952 and for many years afterward.[43]

But redundancy had its costs. As early as 1949, journalist and sociologist Daniel Bell complained that the phrase "free enterprise" had become a cliché, "frayed in its dull repetitiveness."[44] Many understood what Bell took to be a defect as a virtue. Werner Gullander, the new president of the National Association of Manufacturers, reflecting on his long career in a 1963 speech to the Public Relations Society of America, confessed that he "had been concerned about threats, challenges, and yes—inroads on our Free Enterprise" since his time as a management trainee more than thirty years earlier. He reminded his audience that "this pretty well coincides with the initiation of the 'New Deal.'" Although that episode in political history had passed, his priorities had not changed and he remained, he said, "still concerned about a challenge to Free Enterprise."[45] Among advocates, Gullander was in the majority in believing that repetition of the free enterprise mantra was a necessary bulwark against the dangers that the New Deal and its successor regimes represented.

Using language born in the crisis of the 1930s and World War II, free enterprisers cultivated the perception of emergency. As early as 1938, Senator Arthur Vandenberg declared, in what became a favored metaphor, that there was a "war on business."[46] "We are close to the line where government expansion must stop, or our free enterprise system is lost," declared Senator Robert Taft in 1949.[47] The idea that the "hour is late" for free enterprise was the premise of the famous "Powell memo" of 1971, which described an "attack on the American free enterprise system."[48] Reagan, pondering a run for the presidency in 1974, claimed, much as Alf Landon had in 1936, that "capitalism and free enterprise are under assault."[49] In 1980, he won the presidency with much the same message, now increasingly popular, in spite of the manifest weakness of the putative assaulter, New Deal liberalism.

If the free enterprise text from the 1920s through the 1980s remained remarkably stable, the context did not. The description "New Deal order," applied retrospectively by historians to this era, imposes a stability that did not exist. Free enterprise language rarely changed, but its meaning and impact varied widely depending on circumstances. In spite of the frozenness of free enterprise discourse throughout the period from the election of Franklin Roosevelt through the election of Ronald Reagan, advocates responded flexibly and effectively to their changing roster of foes, from the New Deal to the height of postwar liberalism to the conservative turn in the "age of Reagan," which it helped usher in.[50] There was also cumulative power to this rhetoric, which led Powell's memo, published as the New Deal order was falling apart in 1971, to have a far greater real-world impact than the hundreds of eerily similar statements that had preceded it in the previous four decades.

It is noteworthy that when the leadership of the Republican National Committee (RNC) launched a journal of "thought and opinion" in 1978, its founders chose to call it *Common Sense*, evoking not just Tom Paine's revolutionary tract but the more recent conservative claims to the phrase as an antidote to an out-of-touch bureaucratic worldview that they associated with postwar liberalism.[51] In the opening issue, the RNC chair, William Brock, called the battle between political parties a "contest of ideas." But, in keeping with what was at that moment a nearly four-decade tradition of free enterprise common sense, Brock proposed no new ideas. Instead, he highlighted a very old one, a warning about the dangers of an "activist federal government."[52] In 1984, a *Los Angeles Times* correspondent described the new ideas celebrated by the Reagan-era party at the Republican Convention as "a thorough rejection of big government and an unbounded optimism about the nation's future."[53] These were hardly new ideas; rather they were the essence of the free enterprise vision. But Brock's timing (and Reagan's) was propitious, and he spoke to a receptive audience that extended well beyond the usual purveyors of this vision.

One such enthusiastic observer was the Democratic senator from New York Daniel Patrick Moynihan, who praised the RNC's journal and did far more than Brock to amplify the notion that the GOP had become "the party of ideas."

Moynihan made this claim in a much-discussed opinion piece in July 1980, the year that, with the election of Ronald Reagan, many historians view as marking the end of the "New Deal order." Moynihan and other Democrats who praised the Republicans in this era did not cite any novel ideas, but rather embraced long-standing free enterprise talking points. Moynihan, for example, urged the Democrats to stop being seen as "the party of Government" and to support tax cuts. Invoking language first used in the 1930s in opposition to the New Deal, he claimed that government had become "tyrannical" and "exorbitantly expensive." Versions of his claim that Democrats believe that "government should be strong and America should be weak" had been said many times before.[54] None of these ideas was in the least bit novel; what was new was that some Democrats were now trumpeting them. In Moynihan's celebration of old free enterprise ideas, we can see them in the process of migrating from oppositional to dominant. In 1984, Norman Ornstein, a political analyst at the American Enterprise Institute, put his finger on what was new about the reception of GOP beliefs when he said, "The Republican Party has gotten on the rising tide of changing fashions in ideas. In the '50s and '60s, Republican ideas were pretty much out of the mainstream. But clearly, that's all different now."[55] Free enterprisers played a central role in mainstreaming these ideas.

"Sturdy Common Sense"

The battle over free enterprise was a fight over faith, common sense, and moderation. Common sense works as an anti-method that avoids calling attention to its claims as anything other than statements of the obvious—"life in a nutshell," in the words of Clifford Geertz.[56] It is constructed gradually, largely through the power of continuity and repetition. Free enterprise discourse operated not via the articulation of precise formulations or through the marshaling of empirical support but by way of repeating a reinforcing set of assumptions, claims, and catchphrases, among them the vague, ill-defined term *free enterprise* itself.[57] Free enterprisers did not understand their discourse as extreme or radical or even necessarily conservative. It was, in their view, simply American, a type of "sturdy common sense," according to Frank Knox, the Republican candidate for the vice presidency in 1936.[58] Reinforcing common sense remained the mission of free enterprisers.

Free enterprisers framed their down-to-earth common sense as the polar opposite of dangerous utopian statism. "We are engaged in a bitter political campaign," editorialized the anti–New Deal *Chicago Tribune* in 1936, "in which men of common sense are doing their utmost to check the dangerous trend of our public policy toward state socialism, or something resembling it."[59] Free enterprisers proclaimed themselves to be the party of common sense, thus branding their opponents as, ipso facto, unreasonable. "To combat the New Deal, we must restore common sense in government," said Landon, the presidential candidate in 1936. Common sense, to Landon, as to nearly every Republican nominee for the presidency through Mitt Romney in 2012, meant reversing the welfare state: "The shackles must be taken from American free enterprise."[60] Turning a deeply contested ideological set of practices and beliefs into common sense may have been the greatest achievement of the free enterprisers. It is no accident that the phrase appeared in a memo, "Language: A Key Mechanism of Control," produced in 1990 by the future Republican Speaker of the House Newt Gingrich, wherein he contrasted common sense with what he called "contrasting words" such as "red tape," "welfare," "taxes," "spend[ing]," and "liberal."[61]

Dismissing New Dealers as elitists, free enterprisers, by contrast, appealed, as a 1949 NAM advertisement claimed, "to the common sense of the American people," giving their economic program a kind of democratic sanction that, they claimed, the New Deal lacked, in spite of its manifest popularity.[62] Free enterprise common sense, sometimes called "horse sense," signified democratic opposition to overambitious government that came "at great cost to taxpayers," as critics of the New Deal were already saying in 1933.[63] It was also described as a "sixth sense" that told free enterprisers that "capitalism, whatever its faults has proven to be the most practical benefactor of the human race," as the *Nation's Business* editorialized in 1940.[64] Common sense would, in this view, rescue the country from dangerous statist schemes that, unless stymied, would enhance the dictatorial power of agents of the state, undermine managerial prerogatives, and threaten individual freedom.

The denigration of expertise was central to the language of free enterprise common sense. "What this country needs is less intelligentsia and more commonsensia," the Reverend Norman Vincent Peale said in 1936.[65] Politicians who advocated free enterprise often criticized the outsized role of intellectuals in public life, which they blamed for the disparagement of commonsense business leaders. Free enterprisers preferred to follow the humble path of custom, which for them meant tasking the market with answering questions that no human, especially a government "bureaucrat," could grasp.

When in 2004 Peggy Noonan, the former speechwriter for Ronald Reagan, penned an ode to President George W. Bush as a man of plain talk and common sense, she was invoking a venerable persona. "Mr. Bush is the triumph of the seemingly average American man," she wrote. "He's normal. He thinks in a common-sense way. He speaks the language of business and sports and politics."[66] Her judgment was not that different from that of the columnist who declared of the Republican vice presidential candidate in 1944, "Governor Bricker thinks and talks good Americanism" or that of H. W. Prentis, the leader of NAM, who in 1940 spoke of the need to "reawaken America to the value of private enterprise for the 'man in the street.'"[67] Liberty resulted from following popular rather than elite counsel and free enterprise custom rather than statist experimentation. Underlying these celebrations of normality was a feeling that intellectuals deliberately misled the people. Donald J. Trump's self-description as a person with a "very high IQ" as well as "strong common sense," in a 2013 tweet fits into this tradition. Reverend Peale, who officiated at the first of the future president's weddings, could not have said it any better.

Over time, one particular interpretation of the contested concept of "free enterprise" became common sense, first in opposition to the New Deal order and then as guiding light of the Reagan Revolution. In this process, competing understandings narrowed and hardened into what was variously called "virulent free enterprise" or "the NAM version of free enterprise." Proponents soon proposed these radically new, and deeply reactionary, adaptations of the phrase as simply widely shared American customs.[68] Despite their stress on consensus, anti–New Deal free enterprise advocates took free enterprise to be a fighting faith. They emphasized the need for "a full revival of the American gospel [of free enterprise]," as Thomas C. Boushall, the president of a Virginia bank, demanded in 1939.[69] That gospel, which linked a rollback of the New Deal to democratic freedom, remained remarkably consistent and eventually became the core of modern conservatism.

As part of their embrace of common sense, free enterprisers often portrayed themselves as purveyors of what Wendell Willkie called a "moderate middle of the road course" who stood in stark opposition to dangerous ideological extremists and utopians on both the left and right. Their rhetoric, assumptions, and logic, however, were anything but moderate. Filled with binary choices and apocalyptic metaphors (*road to serfdom, five minutes till midnight*), the new free enterprisers employed a language of extremes. Arthur Larson, Eisenhower advisor and promoter of "modern Republicanism," used the phrase "middle-of-the-road extremists" to refer to resolute moderation, but others took the middle way to be the last firewall between communism and fascism.[70] Free enterprise was a reactionary discourse that clothed itself in the respectability of the business community.

While claiming the mantle of moderation, free enterprisers like Herbert Hoover "scoffed at talk of a 'middle of the road' course," suggesting that compromise with the New Deal was really defeat.[71] Indeed, one of the first writers to introduce the idea of the "middle of the road" highlighted the "difficulties inherent in the great ideal" itself.[72] Conservative columnist and economic popularizer Henry Hazlitt condemned those who "complacently" spoke of a "middle way." "What they overlooked," he claimed, is the "inevitable tendency of Government" to grow in "ever widening circles."[73] Emphasizing the slippery slope from reform to totalitarianism, free enterprisers held that "any step toward socialism is a step away from free enterprise and the American Way of Life."[74] In the view of many free enterprise advocates, the middle way was a dangerous fantasy, made possible only by ignoring the inexorable and, they believed, indisputable law of statism, which held that small doses of government would automatically grow bigger until state control was nearly absolute. Hazlitt was not alone among free enterprise proponents in his predictions that despotic power was the destiny of statism.[75] Like other free enterprisers, he did not extend this concern to corporate power or concentrated wealth, no matter how vast.

If the language of free enterprise made conservative moderation difficult, it also framed the opposition, those who supported the New Deal, as inherently radical. Free enterprisers aimed the bulk of their criticism at New Dealers and their descendants, advocates for regulated capitalism, progressive taxation, and a welfare state that protected the needy and the vulnerable. Although there were people to the left of the New Dealers, free enterprisers, for the most part, not only aimed their venom at liberals, not socialists or communists, but conflated these distinct groups. They did this by depicting New Deal liberalism as a disguised version of the dangerous "statism" and "collectivism" that would eventually ensue if they were not vigorously opposed. James J. Kilpatrick, conservative columnist, spoke in 1972 of the need to "get on the offensive" against "socialist-liberal forces whose avowed objective is to destroy the private enterprise system."[76]

The tale of how "free enterprise" transmuted is anything but straightforward: a phrase championed by free laborers, abolitionists, proponents of government-sponsored infrastructure development, and free traders (among many others) in the nineteenth century ultimately became the political mantra of business conservatives in the twentieth century. As we will see, others with very different politics, including Democratic presidents, trade unionists, civil rights activists and, for a brief period, even the leader of the Communist Party of the United States, claimed the term. But these groups failed to do so successfully, and their political visions were generally seen as the danger against which free enterprise needed to stand. In spite of their best efforts, these claimants were rejected as pretenders who "perverted" its meaning.[77] Anti–New Deal free enterprise proponents claimed sole ownership of the phrase, stripping it of its evolving connotations through history and ignoring the vagueness that plagued it in the present. It is part of the genius of the free enterprisers that previous and competing meanings as well as the definitional self-doubt that led some to call for jettisoning the term were, at some point, forgotten, replaced by the widely shared view that free enterprise needs no modification or definition because it is part of the air we breathe.

This book builds on a remarkable wave of historical scholarship that has highlighted the importance of "free enterprise" in a wide variety of twentieth-century political battles.[78] These works have shown the centrality of the term in campaigns against the New Deal, the labor movement, and the civil rights movement; in battles over "slum clearance"; and in the formation of white suburbia and Christian conservatism. Yet historians have, by and large, underexplored the history of the phrase itself. (To be fair, pollsters and political scientists have generally assumed that the term speaks for itself. In their 1967 study of American political beliefs, for example, Lloyd Free and Hadley Cantril asked citizens to rate the importance of "Preserving Our Free Enterprise System," with no explanation of what the pollsters meant by these words.)[79] Although the profession typically interrogates almost every term and concept, historians have by and large taken the meaning of the term for granted. We have studied the mechanisms of the postwar free enterprise crusade but left unaddressed the main success of the effort, the normalization of a radically new worldview. Rather

than treating it as both a vague and hotly contested term whose meaning was far
from stable, we have accepted it as a phrase that requires little by way of definition, clarification, or contextualization. We employ the phrase as a rough synonym for *free market* or *laissez-faire*. Historical figures are said to advocate
"free enterprise" or to champion "free enterprise politics," as if the meaning of
these phrases were self-explanatory. Yet history shows that Hoiles was spot-on:
the term was one of the most debated of the twentieth century. Therefore, in
this book, I take up Matthew D. Lassiter's suggestion that free enterprise was
"a discursive fiction wielded as a form of power."[80]

Free enterprise's ambiguity and its taken-for-grantedness existed as part of a
tense whole; the inexactness of "free enterprise" was essential to its centrality.
We should not confuse vagueness with political tentativeness. Over time, and
despite many setbacks, nebulousness metamorphosed into common sense and
a diffuse set of meanings congealed into a single tradition that shaped popular
views of the role of government and the meaning of freedom.

"Apostles of Free Enterprise"

"The greatest shortcomings of capitalism have not been in production or
distribution of goods, but in the dissemination of ideas." So believed author and
psychologist Henry C. Link, who spoke before the National Association of Advertisers in 1946, at the onset of the Cold War. "Capitalism has completely
failed to develop its own ideology," he told the audience. Its proponents had not,
Link said, adequately demonstrated "the merits" of the "free enterprise system." Nor had they combated "the relentless campaign of ridicule and defama-
tion waged against all business men." Business leaders, Link believed, needed
"to tell their story to the public" because "it's a great story that everybody ought
to hear."[81]

It is not a stretch to say that the idea of "free enterprise," as it developed in
the years before Link's speech to the advertising convention, represented the
development of the "ideology of capitalism" he demanded. It was an ideology
revealed through narrative, claims to common sense, and assertions of faith. Free
enterprise discourse is an important component in the history—and victory—of
a particular version of capitalism in the twentieth century. It worked in part by
labeling alternatives and modifications as not just inferior but deadly. Notwithstanding the claims of its supporters that it was imperiled and on the verge of

extinction, the free enterprise worldview triumphed by setting the limits of political discourse.[82]

The term *free enterprise* appeared frequently in public discourse in the United States in the years between the 1930s and 1970s, although, ironically, it did so much more rarely in the decades prior to that period, which were often described as the "golden age of free enterprise." Advocates debated and explained it not only in the halls of academia (where Harvard's Society for the Preservation of Free Enterprise, founded in 1947, and other Ivy League student groups emphasized the importance of the idea for future leaders) but in newspaper columns, on pulpits, and in political speeches, trade publications, pamphlets, educational films, and after-dinner talks.[83] *Free enterprise* did not have a single coiner. Notwithstanding the consistency of its central premises, it was a flexible language employed by a large group of people over a long period of time. Members of this cohort, born between the late nineteenth century and early twentieth century, reinvented the term in the 1920s and consistently and effectively promoted it, even when their political fortunes seemed bleak.[84]

The creation of modern free enterprise was a collective endeavor. But pride of place should be given to the group that I call, following contemporary usage, the "apostles of free enterprise."[85] This cohort was constituted by people born between the two Republican presidents who bookended the New Deal order, Herbert Hoover (born 1874) and Ronald Reagan (1911). Alf Landon (1887), Wendell Willkie (1892), Thomas E. Dewey (1902), the Republican presidential candidates from 1936 to 1948, helped associate the phrase with opposition to the New Deal. Glenn Frank (1887), magazine editor, university president, and rising Republican political hopeful, popularized the phrase as the enemy of "planning" and collectivism. Ruth Alexander (1899), right-wing libertarian columnist and friend of Ayn Rand (1905), emphasized the binary, apocalyptic tone that came to characterize free enterprise discourse. Lewis F. Powell Jr. (1907), Richmond lawyer and later U.S. Supreme Court justice, emphasized an "attack on the American Free Enterprise system" in an influential memo of 1971.

Even more important than these individuals were the groups that made "selling free enterprise" their mission.[86] Two such organizations, the U.S. Chamber of Commerce and NAM, played particularly long-term and prominent roles in shaping free enterprise discourse. They did this in part through the work of key individuals, such as Merle Thorpe (1879), the editor of *Nation's Business*, the monthly journal of the chamber, and H. W. Prentis (1884), the president of the

Armstrong Cork Company and, for a time, leader of NAM. These groups also used their publications and lobbying to shape the views of their membership and the public at large. Other organizations achieved prominence due largely to the energy and passion of their leaders, who figure prominently in this study. DeWitt Emery (1896), the president of the National Small Business Man's Association, fought to promulgate the phrase. Leonard Read (1898), the founder of the Foundation for Economic Education (FEE), highlighted the system as a domain of human freedom. Thurman Sensing (1899), the executive vice president of the Southern States Industrial Council, sought to link business freedom to "states' rights."

As important as these people and organizations were in spreading the free enterprise gospel, they were joined by thousands of others—many of them unnamed editorialists or long-forgotten community leaders—who echoed this language, put their own spin on it, and boosted its power through repetition. These people, from the worlds of business, advertising, public relations, religion, politics, and academics, were primarily responsible, beginning in the 1920s, for reinventing "free enterprise." They developed the genre that I call the businessmen's jeremiad, characterized by alarmist language that posited the simultaneous centrality and precariousness of the free enterprise system, an enduring style that remains central to conservative politics.[87] Although scholars tend to assume that prominent public intellectuals such as Walter Lippmann, the popular columnist and author of the influential 1937 book *The Good Society*, initiated the attack on the dangers of "planning," the onslaughts of NAM, anti–New Deal politicians, and many editorialists were well under way by that time.[88] Lippmann's admirer Friedrich Hayek, the author of the best-selling critique of collectivism *The Road to Serfdom*, published in 1944, condemned the burgeoning welfare state, but as the Austrian émigré himself acknowledged, an army of mostly anonymous free enterprise publicists and propagandists challenged the New Deal order as effectively as did intellectuals, and their efforts to delegitimize it began long before the publication of his classic book.[89] When Hayek called people like Leonard Read "second hand traders in ideas," he meant it as a compliment, believing, as he did, that free enterprise needed popularizers as much if not more than theorists.[90] The "neoliberals" of Hayek's Mont Pelerin Society in the early postwar years were not, at least in the United States, the first or most influential venerators of the market and denouncers of the state.

This group of popularizers shaped American political language through numerous channels: campaign speeches, editorials, radio programs, school curriculum materials, and tips for employers in trade magazines.[91] Therefore, my sources are largely drawn from newspaper columns, pamphlets, trade association journals, and records of political speeches that traffic well below the stratosphere of high intellectual thought. The sentiments expressed in these quotidian documents provided Americans with a vocabulary that influenced political culture even—we might even say *especially*—when they were on the losing end of political battles.

Significant differences existed among the free enterprisers who helped transform American political culture. Over time, the target of their battles changed. Yet this book is distinctly a work of "lumping," not "splitting," since it puts disparate people who lived at different times into a single overarching category. To borrow Isaiah Berlin's famous terms, I define the free enterprisers, in spite of their diversity, as hedgehogs, who know "one important thing," rather than foxes, who know many things.[92] This is not to suggest that the views of Reagan and of Landon, who attended the Progressive Party convention the year after the fortieth president was born, are identical in all respects. NAM and the U.S. Chamber of Commerce represented different constituencies and had different mandates, they both evolved over time, and each of their leaders had a different emphasis. Regarding the key matters treated in this book, however, far more holds these individuals and groups together than separates them. Of course attention should also be paid to the variances among the apostles of free enterprise.[93] But it should not come at the cost of the bottom line, which is that the apostles of free enterprise—made up of a few famous political and business leaders but mostly of figures largely unknown today—collectively shaped political culture in a way that has not yet been fully acknowledged or documented, and they did so with a message that remained remarkably durable.

The success of the anti–New Deal free enterprisers, notwithstanding their suspicion of intellectuals and valorization of common sense, challenges pundit George F. Will's judgment that the roots of modern conservatism were "remarkably bookish" and emerged only in the 1950s.[94] The not particularly bookish apostles of free enterprise shaped conservativism, even if they did not generally use that term, soon after the New Deal began in their natural habitat of after-dinner talks, advertisements, newspaper columns, trade journals, sermons, and political speeches. Although their arguments were typically less than original, they influenced American political culture by virtue of their assertions, narratives, and aphorisms, repeated and reinforced over a long period.

The following pages tell the story of how the idea of "the free enterprise system" became conservative common sense. Like most invented traditions, free enterprise discourse worked not only through its links to the American past but by defining itself in opposition to the dominant political regime at the time of its initial emergence. Therefore, this book also examines the rise of free enterprise as an "other" to the New Deal order, a keyword—to borrow Raymond Williams's term for what he calls "binding words" whose history of contestation is often ideologically "masked"—in the battle against government as public purpose.[95]

Free Enterprise is structured both chronologically and thematically. But the first chapter starts at the end of the story, focusing on the 1971 "Powell memo," which came at the close of the New Deal era. It argues that Powell's missive recapitulated arguments that had been made since the 1930s and shows the document to have been the culmination of trends that the rest of the book traces. The second chapter takes us back to the beginning, as it traces the development of free enterprise thinking from its inception as a subset of the "free labor ideology" in the nineteenth century through the 1920s, when it began to take independent shape in its recognizably modern form. Each of chapters 3–7 focuses on a specific theme or topic in the crucial years of the so-called New Deal order, between the 1930s and the 1970s, when free enterprise was largely an oppositional ideology, and thus the chapters overlap significantly in chronology. Chapter 3 shows how advocates of free enterprise defined their ideas in contrast to the New Deal, which they viewed as a dangerous deviation from American customs, even though the "traditional free enterprise system" they celebrated was one that they had only recently invented. Chapter 4 examines the quandaries and frustrations of free enterprisers, who repeatedly but unsuccessfully tried to define the term that they took to be foundational, and shows how they resolved these problems. Chapter 5 explores how free enterprise served as a holding bin for ideas—and, just as important, attitudes—that later came to be called "conservative" and how advocates of the term foreshadowed and catalyzed the political realignment that ultimately made the Republican Party the representative of these ideas and attitudes, which I describe as "inverted populism." Chapter 6, through a close reading of Leonard Read's influential 1958 essay "I, Pencil," demonstrates the ways in which free enterprisers embraced a mystical faith in markets that led them to ignore or underestimate the fact that business firms possessed enormous power. Chapter 7 shows that, notwithstanding the efforts of business conservatives to claim the phrase for themselves, civil rights and labor activists briefly took advantage of the term's nebulousness to try to deploy it in the service of progressive politics. Chapter 8 explains how free enterprise proponents worked to delegitimize the most basic functions of government with their critique of public spending and taxation as not only inefficient but immoral. The epilogue explores the mixed legacy of free enterprise after its seeming triumph in the late twentieth century and examines the way in which the presidency of Donald Trump represented a new phase in the history of free enterprise, since it is a term that Trump rarely employed, in stark contrast to every previous Republican president or aspirant since Herbert Hoover. At the same time, it shows that the Trump presidency represented the triumph of "elite victimization" that has long been the characteristic tone of free enterprise proponents. It speculates that the presidential election of 2016 and its aftermath may have represented the triumph of grievance politics and celebrations of corporate power, unconnected to free enterprise's characteristically redemptive stories about freedom and the magic of the marketplace, thus sundering the two halves of a discourse that had existed previously in a sometimes uneasy whole.

It has been said that "free enterprise does not exist, but America still believes in it anyway."[96] In these pages, I hope to show that "free enterprise" not only "exists" in the United States—and has for almost two centuries—but that its long history reveals a tale of ambiguity, contestation, and transformation. But it is equally a history of how such debates have been forgotten, of how free enterprise came to be taken for granted and thus shielded from scrutiny. At the dawn of the "new cultural history," Robert Darnton claimed in his influential book *The Great Cat Massacre*, there was a rich bounty for historians in exploring what befuddles us: the jokes, proverbs, and rituals of the past that we do not "get."[97] If this book accomplishes anything, I hope it is to reveal that the history of what we think we already know, like the concept of free enterprise, can be equally enlightening, especially if we explore the processes by which it became common sense.

1

"A Memo That Changed the Course of History"

ON A SATURDAY EVENING in August 1971, Lewis F. Powell Jr. was working in his Richmond office to complete a last-minute favor. The sixty-three-year-old Powell, a partner in Virginia's biggest law firm and a past president of the American Bar Association (ABA), had spent the morning attending to his firm's clients, among them the nation's largest businesses. Dictating to his secretary, Sally Smith, he now aimed to put on paper the thoughts he had shared over a recent lunch with his friend and neighbor Charles Sydnor about an acute but ill-understood crisis in American society: the embattled state and diminished status of American capitalism. The day before, Sydnor, the head of the Southern Department Store chain, a former member of the Virginia House of Delegates and the General Assembly, and the recently appointed chair of the Education Committee of the United States Chamber of Commerce, had telephoned Powell and asked him to formulate his ideas in a memo that Sydnor could share at a Monday meeting at the chamber's office in Washington, DC. In Powell's understanding, Sydnor sought "ideas as to what they might do to improve the climate of public opinion with regard to the free enterprise system," and Powell had many such thoughts to share.[1]

The writing took longer than the "hour or two" that Powell expected and, as his thoughts expanded on the diagnosis and solutions, he and Smith called it quits for the night and resumed work on it Sunday morning. By early that afternoon, Powell had drafted and Smith had typed a thirty-four-page "Confidential Memorandum" that he titled "Attack on American Free Enterprise System."[2] The martial language of the title captured the tone of the entire essay, as meta-

Lewis F. Powell Jr. (Courtesy of Library of Congress,
Prints & Photographs Division [LC-USZ62-60140].)

phors of battle punctuated the document. There was a war against free enterprise and Powell believed that the business community had to engage aggressively in a defensive fight of its own in order to survive; the attack *on* American
free enterprise needed to be repulsed by an attack *of* American free enterprise.[3]
"No thoughtful person can question that the American economic system is under
broad attack," Powell observed, urging business leaders, like generals scouting
the field of battle, to recognize the seriousness of the threat. He described various dimensions of the assault and offered a comprehensive plan for a counterattack in, among other domains, advertising, the media, the educational system,
the courts, and politics. The multidimensional campaign required many types
of responses, and his memo's subsections spelled them out in some detail.

The normally unflappable lawyer believed that time was short, that business
faced a legitimation crisis requiring not only a powerful response but an immediate one. Although the ostensible target may have been business, Powell

believed that nothing less than American freedom hung in the balance. "There seems to be little awareness that the only alternatives to free enterprise are varying degrees of bureaucratic regulation of individual freedom—ranging from that under moderate socialism to the iron heel of the leftist or rightist dictatorship," Powell concluded in frustration, echoing the binary thinking that had become standard among free enterprisers. Powell urged not only quick action but sustained commitment because, he warned, the action plan he proposed "is a long road and not one for the fainthearted." The busy lawyer had done his job, giving the Chamber of Commerce much to consider in its quest to "improve the climate of public opinion."

Such were the origins of the so-called Powell memorandum, which became, in the twenty-first century, one of the most notorious documents in modern U.S. history. Or at least, this was Powell's modest narrative of how he came to compose the memorandum "quite by accident," as he claimed in a 1973 letter to his three law clerks. He never publicly discussed the memo.[4]

For several months after Powell drafted the memo, this document served exactly the purpose that Powell and Sydnor expected, as it circulated among the leadership of the chamber and among the select clients and contacts with whom Powell eagerly shared it. But the memorandum remained unknown and unpublicized during his confirmation hearings for Supreme Court justice, which he sailed through, and for most of his first year on the bench. This changed suddenly in late September 1972, when Jack Anderson broke the story of the memo in three of his widely syndicated "Washington Merry-Go-Round" columns. Anderson called it "a blueprint for an assault by big business on its critics" that reflected a "militant political action program." The columnist condemned the Senate and the FBI for an incomplete investigation of Powell's record, and argued that Powell should recuse himself from cases involving "business interests" since, in writing the memo, he had established himself as a partisan of those interests.[5]

Anderson's disclosure of Powell's role as free enterprise defender and strategist initially elicited few criticisms of the justice. Rather than outrage at Powell's forthright defense of business and his counsel of aggressive action, the immediate round of responses to Anderson's revelations enthusiastically endorsed both Powell and his call to action. Letters of praise poured in to Powell's office at the Supreme Court and to Sydnor. Editorials condemning Anderson and supporting Powell appeared in newspapers and on the radio. Letters to the editor in newspapers all over the country overwhelmingly defended Powell and lambasted Anderson for having, in the words of one correspondent to the *Washington Post*, "mudraked Mr. Powell up one side and down the other."[6] Business leaders praised Powell for urging them to "wake up and tell their story and that of the free enterprise system in clear and forceful fashion," as Sydnor wrote in a long letter to the *Richmond Times-Dispatch*.[7] The radio station WARM of Wilkes-Barre and Scranton, Pennsylvania, broadcast a series of four editorials in January 1973, claiming the memo "just might be the most important single document regarding the free enterprise system ever written" and commending Powell's "all-out fight against apathy."[8] "It is not illegal to defend the free enterprise system and the concept of individual liberty on which this country was founded," wrote Henry J. Cappello, the general counsel of the National Small Business Association, the organization that the pioneering free enterprise proponent DeWitt Emery had founded in the 1930s, in an unpublished letter to the *Washington Post* that he copied to Powell.[9]

Business leaders took the memo's message to be that they should "stop behaving like the Caspar Milquetoast of the American society," as Powell's hometown newspaper editorialized in a piece defending Powell's missive.[10] (Milquetoast was the sad-sack protagonist of H. T. Webster's *Timid Soul*, a long-running comic strip and briefly a television show, whose motto was: "Speak softly and get hit with a big stick.")[11] Longtime senator Harry F. Byrd Jr. even took to the Senate floor to defend his fellow Virginian and friend, and the *Richmond Times-Dispatch* cheered Powell's "program to defend the nation's free enterprise system against unfair, unfounded, and malicious criticism."[12] Powell's words had clearly struck a chord, particularly the idea that business should use what Cappello called "all legitimate means" to fight for its rights and to publicize its views as if they were articulations of American freedom itself.

While Powell never made any public statements about his memo, he did defend it once in private, in the 1973 letter to his law clerks, written in response to an article in the *Washington Post* about the ways in which the Chamber of Commerce was considering how to implement what it called the "Powell Plan."[13] Enclosing the *Post* article as well as the memo itself, Powell explained to his clerks that "it might be helpful if you knew exactly what I said and under what circumstances."[14]

Downplaying the significance of the document, Powell explained that he composed it "merely to comply with a friend's request," not for a client, and for private, not public, purposes. Expressing no remorse over his voluntary work for the chamber, he highlighted the violation of his privacy rather than the content of the document, which he did not discuss. "But, thanks to the new morality with respect of private papers and the availability of Xerox machines," the memo was leaked to the columnist Anderson, "who ran a couple of fairly inflammatory columns on it without getting in touch with me or inquiring as to the circumstances under which it had been written." "I am glad," he wryly concluded, "that I retained my small investment in Xerox stock."[15] Powell also confided to his clerks that Sydnor told him that the memo "fell almost 'like a lead balloon'" when he discussed it with his committee, which feared the costs of implementing his ambitious plan and the possible unpopularity of aggressively promoting the discredited idea of free enterprise. Powell concluded by assuring his clerks that "I have not discussed any aspect of the memorandum's contents with any representative of the Chamber since coming to the Court."

Powell's explanation of how he came to prepare the memo—as a one-off favor for a friend—misrepresents his commitment to the cause of free enterprise, which had been an ongoing passion. He may have written the document in a weekend but, like many other representatives of the business community, he had long been pondering how to rescue free enterprise, which he was not alone in seeing as dangerously embattled. He did not dash off the memo from scratch, as we will see, but referenced an extensive set of clippings that he and Sydnor had collected and discussed over the years, and amplified talking points that had been articulated in the previous decade by the U.S. Chamber of Commerce leadership.[16]

Nor did his efforts conclude, as he implied in his letter to the clerks, with the crafting of the memo. His lawyerly language to his clerks left the possibility that he had discussed the memo with members of the chamber before he became a Supreme Court justice and with others even after he joined the court, and Powell, in fact, had taken time out of his busy schedule to accompany Sydnor to Washington to meet with the leadership of the chamber to discuss his plan. At a time when photographic reproductions were difficult to obtain, Powell asked Arch Booth, the vice president of the chamber, for Xeroxes of the memo so that he could share it with "a client or two." When Booth sent him only two copies, he instructed Sally Smith to make five more, which he mailed to clients and friends, including Ross Malone, the general counsel for General Motors. He urged Malone to encourage the Chamber of Commerce to "become a vital force to defend the enterprise system and the freedom which it sustains."[17] He implored another client, K. A. Randall, the president of United Virginia Bankshares, to push the chamber to play "a much larger and more dynamic role in defense—aggressively—of the enterprise system."[18] No wonder Sydnor wrote with optimism to Powell upon the announcement of his appointment to the court, "I hope it may be possible, and ethical, for me to have the benefit of your advice on this project in what form it may develop."[19]

In an opinion piece published in October 1971, Arch Booth conveyed the gist of Powell's "confidential" recommendations. "Business is under attack," Booth began, sounding very much like Powell. Without attribution, Booth quoted or paraphrased key sections of Powell's memo, and he concluded, like Powell, by urging "the thinking people of the country to recognize that the ultimate issue may be the survival of the free enterprise system." Thus Powell's ideas were quickly disseminated, as he wished, little more than a week before Richard Nixon nominated him for a seat on the Supreme Court.[20]

Powell continued to promote the message of his memo even after he joined the court. His friend Bernard Segal, a prominent Philadelphia lawyer, wrote to Powell in November 1972 thanking the new justice for sending him copies of three (positive) editorials about the message of the memo.[21] After he was nominated to the court in November 1971, Powell published a critical analysis of the Left's claims that the United States was a politically repressive society, in which he dismissed the outcry against wiretapping as "a tempest in a teapot."[22] Later, after he joined the court (but before Anderson revealed the existence of the memo), Powell made public comments with a similar message at the Prayer Breakfast of the ABA annual meeting. In this speech, he condemned the "excess self-flagellation" of the "establishment" and observed that "business management has been unwilling to make a massive effort to protect itself and the system which it represents."[23] This was not a neutral observation but a call to action, much as his memo offered not just a diagnosis but an urgently needed therapy. For his part, Sydnor gratefully wrote Powell in October 1972 to thank him for sending copies of his correspondence about the memo and to report that "your very cogent ideas have been presented in a manner which is most fitting and conducive to their implementation, and all of us involved in the effort are most grateful to you." This seemed in tension with Powell's report to his clerks a year later that "there was not great enthusiasm" for the program that he had recommended.[24]

In spite of the passion it aroused in the fall of 1972, the memo itself was the topic of public discussion only briefly and it soon disappeared from public discourse, seemingly for good. Indeed, the 1973 *Washington Post* article that prompted Powell to write to his clerks marked the last mention of the Powell memo in a major American newspaper for many years.[25] Lost in the tide of the Watergate scandal, the close of the Vietnam War, and the general chaos of the 1970s, the Powell memo appeared to recede from memory. Anderson's discovery of the memo was not even mentioned in his obituaries in 2005.[26] The standard biography of Powell, published in 1994, omits it, in spite of the fact that the book's author, John C. Jeffries, happened to be one of the Supreme Court clerks who received Powell's November 1973 ex post facto explanation letter. "At the time, I did not see the Powell Memo as the important document that it is widely thought today," Jeffries recalled in 2014.[27]

An "Unlikely Paul Revere" of the "Business Rebellion"

And yet the memo, forgotten for a generation, has had an unusual afterlife. It came to be seen by many commentators in the twenty-first century as the key to the conservative resurgence of the last quarter of the twentieth century. Whereas in the immediate aftermath of Anderson's revelations, conservatives celebrated Powell's memo as significant because of its forthright counsel of a pugnacious response to widespread criticism by liberals and radicals, a later generation of journalists, politicians, and scholars on the left highlighted it as a portent of the country's conservative turn. (Conservatives, for their part, have paid far less attention to the document.)[28] Agreeing with Powell's long-forgotten initial defenders in the wake of Jack Anderson's revelations that it was an important and original defense of free enterprise but disagreeing with their conservative politics, twenty-first-century critics read in the document a "master plan" for a right-wing triumph that uncannily portended what the radical geographer David Harvey has called the "neoliberal turn."[29] What Powell described as a quick favor for a friend offers, in this view, an explanation of America's conservative transformation.

For others, the memo was a causal force and an origins story, what one writer in 2014 called "the one catalyzing event" that precipitated "the vast power and control which business holds in today's America."[30] "The class war appeared to begin in earnest in August, 1971, with Lewis Powell's now famous memo urging the GOP to go on the offensive to promote and defend big business," writes historian David L. Chappell, though Powell was a lifelong Democrat who did not mention either political party in his memo.[31] "History often has hidden beginnings," explained the journalist Hedrick Smith in 2012. "One such beginning, with a powerful impact on our lives today, occurred in 1971 with the 'Powell memorandum.'" Attributing tremendous predictive power to Powell, Smith called him "an unlikely Paul Revere" of the "Business Rebellion" who set off nothing less than "a brilliantly executed coup." With a misapprehension shared by Powell and his cronies, progressive radio host Thom Hartman said that "up to that point, business hadn't been influencing culture." One journalist surmised in 2012 that it "may or may not have been the first shot fired in the nation's late twentieth century right-wing revolution." A progressive blogger claimed that it marked "the intellectual genesis of the American Corporatocracy." Robert Kuttner tells us that it stimulated a "counter-revolution," leading the business class to "rediscover its latent power as a ruling elite." For Bill Moyers, it marked "a call to arms for class war waged from the top down," and for Katrina vanden Heuvel, the editor of the *Nation*, "it was a blueprint for what is now coming to fruition with the phenomenon of the Koch brothers, Citizens United, and a right-wing activist Supreme Court ready to roll back decades of New Deal jurisprudence." Jeffrey D. Clements claims that "the success of the Powell Chamber of Commerce Plan transformed American law, government, and society." Focusing on the person as much as the memo, Egberto Willies, liberal radio host and blogger, labeled Powell "the man who told the GOP How to Destroy America's Middle Class," and captioned a photo of the justice with the words, "This man is the father of the GOP misinformation machine. He laid out the blueprint." A 2016 letter writer claimed that the memo "financially unstabilized the middle class."[32] Few documents or individuals have been granted such talismanic force, as both augur and agent. Remarkable results for a weekend's work.

It is understandable that, in the aftermath of the undeniable conservative transformation in American politics, readers of the Powell memo would attribute to it both originality and predictive power.[33] Placing the Powell memo in the context of twentieth-century free enterprise rhetoric, however, puts it in a different light. The document is important less because it was original than because it synthesized so many components of a pervasive free enterprise discourse that had long dominated American political culture. It is an important link in a long chain that extends back to Herbert Hoover, DeWitt Emery, Leonard Read, and others who developed free enterprise discourse in response to what they saw as the threat of the New Deal regime. Particularly important in this chain were the efforts of trade associations, advertisers, and lobbying groups, beginning in the 1930s and periodically revived for the next two decades, to "sell" free enterprise to the American people. What changed was less what the Powell memo said than how it was received. Powell wrote in the midst of a changing political climate, many of whose features aligned with the long-term goals of free enterprisers: the decline in the labor movement, decreasing trust in public spending policies, a resurgence in free market thought, a revolt against regulation, and the clustering of people who increasingly called themselves conservative into one party (though many southern whites, like Powell, continued to promote free enterprise as Democrats).

Although these changes were under way, albeit far from complete, in 1971 when Powell wrote his memo, most advocates of free enterprise in the early 1970s took little heed of these momentous but inchoate transformations. Like Powell, and indeed like most free enterprise advocates since the New Deal, they believed that their philosophy, and with it the country, was endangered. John Connally, the head of Democrats for Nixon, said in a 1972 speech to the Veterans of Foreign Wars, "You and I are seeing today the most bitter attack on the free enterprise system ever launched in the history of the United States."[34] An investment banker expressed alarm in 1974 about "the rapid rise of anti-business sentiment in this country."[35]

With the benefit of hindsight, we can more clearly observe what Powell, Connally, and the banker did not foresee, but which came sharply into focus in the coming decades: that Powell wrote his memorandum at a time of a dramatic decline in the relative power of the New Deal coalition. One of the most perceptive seers of that change was the 1968 Republican candidate for the presidency, Richard Nixon. In a nationwide radio address in May of that year, he announced that "a totally different grouping" in politics was emerging. "Without most of us realizing it, a new alignment has been formed, and is already a majority," Nixon declared. He called this new majority the "silent center." The majority may have been new, but there was nothing novel about what it stood for. The beliefs of the silent majority as Nixon described them were essentially identical to the free enterprise message that had circulated since the 1930s: "The more centralized and domineering a government gets, the less personal freedom there is for the individual." Nixon's point was that the message was old but that the coalition of people receptive to this message constituted, for the first time, a majority.[36] Nixon was prescient. A decade later, a Gallup poll confirmed increasing agreement with the claim that "the government has gone too far in regulating business and interfering with the free enterprise system."[37] Like so many earlier free enterprisers, Nixon mixed his proclamation of the new "alignment" with concerns very similar to Powell's.

Capitalism and Free Enterprise under Assault

The Powell memo followed the well-established conventions of a genre that we can call the businessman's jeremiad. The seemingly peculiar characteristics of Powell's memo—the diagnosis and declaration of war, the linking of business freedom with political liberty, the co-optation of the language of minority rights, the self-pity, the fear of imminent collapse, the faith in public relations— had long been the constituent elements of the rhetoric of free enterprise. This genre was simultaneously aggressive and defensive, hopeful and fearful, positive and negative. On the offensive side was the desire to "resell the American System to America," as the U.S. Chamber of Commerce announced it would do in July 1938. (The use of the word *resell* suggested that previous such sales had been unsuccessful.) Business, according to the chamber, also needed "to combat attacks on American business and the American system of free enterprise." The counterattack, the chamber claimed, "cannot safely be delayed."[38] Powell's claims along these lines thus followed a well-worn trail. Born in 1907, he was one of the younger members of a chain of free enterprisers that dated back to Herbert Hoover, and his message didn't depart significantly from that of previous free enterprise "apostles."

Yet despite the continuity of this free enterprise tradition, the connotation of this seemingly self-evident phrase has been anything but transparent, even to its fiercest advocates, who fretted over their inability to develop a vocabulary consisting of what the financier E. F. Hutton called "words that bounce along the sidewalk" rather than the prevailing "conference room language" that he and many others scorned.[39] Since the 1930s, periodic crises of meaning had led its frustrated proponents to attempt to redefine free enterprise and even to rename it. Throughout this period, free enterprise essay contests were a staple of high school curricula and corporate public relations, and so too were debates about its meaning in the trade magazines and management journals. Everyone, it seemed, was waiting for the perfect, concise, and widely accepted definition that ordinary Americans could understand and embrace. As we will see in chapter 4, such a consensus never emerged and, tiring of definitional turmoil, advocates of free enterprise tried to explain it in terms of its essential characteristics and benefits rather than its precise meaning. Americans were told it was something they couldn't live without and that the growing state apparatus marked a threat to its existence.

From the 1930s to the end of the century, free enterprise advocates described it as a tradition that was being torn from its moorings. "The heritage of generations of American people," proclaimed the introduction to a series of three award-winning essays published by the Kearney and Trecker Corporation of Milwaukee in 1945, was in danger of being "legislated out of existence."[40] This juxtaposition of deep foundations and constant threat—of preciousness and precariousness—gave free enterprise its dualistic qualities, claims of rapture and rupture existing side by side. Alongside the ever-present threat of destruction was a strange lassitude of those best positioned to defend it, what Senator Barry Goldwater called an "apathetic attitude" in a 1953 address to retailers. This "may be the last go-around," warned the retailer-turned-politician; "next time we may not have another chance to preserve our freedoms."[41] In the anxious mind of the free enterpriser, it was always five minutes till midnight.

What made matters tricky is that no declarations of war were ever announced. Many groups that business free enterprisers saw as enemies—including most prominent New Dealers, labor and civil rights leaders, and consumer advocates—claimed to support the system as well: indeed, to be the true free enterprisers. This made vigilance and reading between the lines all the more important. The job of free enterprisers was to highlight the "magnitude of the challenge to free enterprise" that the American people "have failed to comprehend," said William Jackson of the U.S. Chamber of Commerce in 1947. Frustrated by their inability to understand, Jackson believed that "Americans need to be aroused to the dangers of the attack upon capitalism and profits to employers by the Philip Murrays and the Reuthers," his argument connecting profits, corporations, and freedom, and highlighting labor leaders as the chief enemies.[42] Like Powell, Jackson believed that the chamber and its allies needed to arouse the public to offset the actions of their enemies. In 1954, Nathan Shefferman, a labor relations consultant who had worked for Sears, called on Americans to recognize the undeclared "war on free enterprise from many radical sources" that posed "a threat to the liberties of every man, woman, and child in our country."[43] Sixty years later, Bruce Rauner, the Republican candidate for the governorship of Illinois, claimed that "we have to compete and go to battle for free enterprise," which to him meant to destroy the social safety net and the public spending regime.[44] Free enterprisers became experts at scouting rumors of war.

Telling the tale of free enterprise necessitated rehabituating Americans to their "traditional" system and challenging the popularity of competing claims by refuting them, positioning them as not just suboptimal but deadly. The chamber's Jackson posited that "because of the long tenure of the New Deal, a new generation of Americans is coming to maturity, which has no personal memory of the time when the free enterprise system was taken for granted." The goal of free enterprise advocates was to ensure that it became taken for granted again, to make it once again common sense. As Jackson exhorted, "This generation and those to follow must be reconditioned to the American way."[45] That Powell's memo to the chamber addressed the generation that followed with language strikingly similar to Jackson's of 1947 reveals that the phrases and the logic of free enterprise, if not the reality, was consistent over the period from the 1930s to the 1970s. If the Powell memo had been as groundbreaking as its critics claim, it would not have been nearly as effective as it was. Free enterprise was not a fact-based discourse but a narrative one, and Powell's story worked by reference to familiar hopes and fears rather than original ideas.

"The American Business Executive Is Truly the 'Forgotten Man'"

What did the Powell memo say? We have already seen the premise: the free enterprise system was under attack and without an immediate, multifaceted, and forceful response by business leaders and their political allies, its days were numbered. Powell identified the "chilling" tone set by a disparate group of celebrity radicals—admittedly, he wrote, "varied and diffused"— including counterculture prophet Charles Reich, Black Panther Eldridge Cleaver, radical lawyer William Kuntsler, Marxist professor Herbert Marcuse, and consumer advocate Ralph Nader. While Powell acknowledged that "there always have been some who opposed the American system," he worried that "the media accord unique publicity to these attackers." As a result, these outlying views were "gaining momentum and converts" among "perfectly respectable elements of society: from the college campus, the pulpit, the media, the intellectual and literary journals, the arts and sciences, and from politicians." Ordinary "misguided Americans," Powell feared, were now "parroting" the arguments of the "revolutionaries who would destroy the entire system."[46] What was at stake, he claimed, was the "survival of what we call the free enterprise system, and all that this means for the strength and prosperity of America and the freedom of our people." Free enterprise, in this view, served as the basis of all democratic freedoms.[47]

Yet the rejoinder of leaders in the areas of business, law, the media, and politics, according to Powell, was, in fact, a nonresponse, an inexplicable passivity. "One of the most bewildering paradoxes of our time is the extent to which the enterprise system tolerates, if not participates, in its own destruction," he despaired, sounding much as Goldwater had in his address to retailers eighteen years earlier. To Powell and many others, it seemed that the war on free enterprise was a one-sided battle, whether because business leaders underestimated the problem, were too busy selling their own widgets to be concerned about broader political questions, or simply lacked "guts."[48]

Like other free enterprisers, Powell imagined a topsy-turvy world in which business had "little influence" in the political arena. On top of its own ineffectuality, business had become, Powell claimed, using an image favored by free enterprisers since the New Deal, the "favorite whipping-boy of many politicians for many years."[49] Business had, incredibly, sunk to the level of a minority group, a hated and despised "other" whose interests were not represented in the nation's corridors of power. Indeed, Powell claimed that "few elements of American society today have as little influence in government." As evidence, Powell highlighted "the stampedes by politicians to support almost any legislation related to 'consumerism' or to the 'environment'" and the widespread condemnation of corporations by that year's presidential candidates. Moreover, Powell observed a growing class war aimed at the well-to-do that served to "undermine confidence and confuse the public." He detected in the attacks on free enterprise a new form of "political demagoguery" that consisted of "setting of the 'rich' against the 'poor,' of business against the people" and that represented, he believed, "the cheapest and most dangerous kind of politics." Given business's status as a "whipping boy," Powell understood these juxtapositions as perverse because it was class warfare misdirected against a group lacking prestige or power. It was a war on the weak, who responded meekly, if it all.

Drawing from and adding to an older stream of political rhetoric that, as we will see in chapter 5, had long been embraced by free enterprisers, Powell claimed that "the American business executive is truly the 'forgotten man.'" His conception of the forgotten man residing at the apogee rather than, as FDR had understood him, the bottom of the economic pyramid, his depiction of business firms as weak and lacking political representation, was the essence of top-down populism, but it was not a new development in free enterprise discourse. His statement built upon years of free enterprise claims that the taxpayer or the businessman was the true forgotten man, but it upped the ante by placing "executives" in this category for the first time. (As Thomas J. Donohue, the president of the U.S. Chamber of Commerce, declared in 2015, "American free enterprise is the economic populism we need and must support.")[50] It also evoked an even earlier use of the phrase by the Gilded Age classical liberal and social Darwinist William Graham Sumner, for whom the "forgotten man" was person A, coerced into relieving the "suffering" of person X. Just as person A was "the victim of the reformer" for Sumner, so too, for Powell, was business the victim of modern liberals.[51]

Drawing on this inversion—with business concurrently despised, mocked, and coerced—and on the "rights revolution," which he otherwise condemned, Powell built an edifice out of two not entirely compatible languages: populism and interest-group liberalism. This was not new either: for decades, free enterprise advocates had been treating business as both a despised representative of the people and an interest ignored in politics. As early as 1939, H. W. Prentis, the president of the Armstrong Cork Corporation and the leader of the National Association of Manufacturers, denounced the "growing tendency to disregard minority rights," a formulation that treated business as an outsider group that lacked a place in the seats of power.[52] In 1963, George Champion of Chase Manhattan Bank referred to business leaders as a "muted minority," an interest whose voice was not heard.[53] Both comments also adopted the language of the less powerful to establish both sympathy and institutional power for business leaders.

In defining themselves as dispossessed, free enterprisers displayed a key characteristic of what historian Richard Hofstadter labeled the "paranoid style in American politics."[54] Hofstadter meant to characterize an enduring stream of rhetoric of those who believed that "America had largely been taken away from them" and felt that the fate of the nation depended on regaining the power that had been unjustly stolen. At the time that he wrote, Hofstadter identified this style among the John Birch Society and among other groups that depicted themselves as both fearful and powerless, not among corporate lawyers and bank presidents. And yet well-to-do free enterprisers in positions of undeniable power, like Powell, also prophesied doom and projected impotence, which, as we will see in chapter 2, they had been doing since they repurposed the phrase *free enterprise* in the 1920s.

In Powell's vision, business had taken the place of FDR's "forgotten man" at the bottom of the (political, if not economic) pyramid and needed to borrow the techniques of social movements that traditionally had represented outsiders. Powell highlighted, as models, the "civil rights movement" and the "labor unions" as well as "interested citizens groups," all of which, in stark contrast to business, had been successful in promoting their interests. Here, too, as we will see, Powell drew from a long-standing pattern in which free enterprisers mocked reformers as "wild eyed radicals," "long haired orators," "wooly-headed liberals," and "ultraliberals," but also paid grudging respect to their effectiveness.[55] Frank Chodorov, a pioneering conservative thinker of the postwar years, described leftists as masters of engaged and effective lobbying, even as he despised their message. Socialists "got what they wanted because they fought for it." In contrast, he claimed, free enterprisers have been "strangely apologetic and timid."[56] Writing in the pioneering conservative journal *Human Events*, James Brewbaker marveled at the effectiveness of his enemies in the labor movement. He believed that "business needs dedicated men—a Walter Reuther or a John L. Lewis and men like the late Phil Murray—willing to do whatever it takes without fear of criticism, physical harm or the outside chance of prison."[57] In the view of free enterprisers, their enemies, unconstrained by the timidity that business leaders exhibited, avidly and effectively pursued their self-interest. Powell too thought that business should learn from progressive social movements, adopting a "more aggressive attitude" in politics. "There should not be the slightest hesitation to press vigorously in all political arenas for support of the enterprise system," Powell wrote. "Nor should there be reluctance to penalize politically those who oppose it." In the process of becoming an effective pressure group, Powell claimed, business should avoid the "irresponsible tactics of some pressure groups." Still, he argued, free enterprisers should, like their opponents, commit to effective lobbying "at all levels and every opportunity."

The issue was not just electoral politics. With the phrase "all political arenas," Powell called for remaking a large number of organizations, branches of government, and the general culture so that business could more favorably position itself. Powell saw possibilities in the courts and in "stockholder power," both of which he claimed had been "neglected" by business. One main arena of concern for Powell was the university, especially "the social science faculties" that "usually include members who are unsympathetic to the enterprise system." Powell counseled the promotion of "balance," which was "conspicuous by its absence on many campuses, with relatively few numbers being conservatives." He called for a critical examination of textbooks and the promotion of a more ideologically diverse faculty. Moreover, he supported the expansion of conservative "think tanks" that would have a staff of scholars and speakers who could promote free enterprise and challenge its critics on campus, in the public realm, and in "scholarly journals." This model had already been well established by the Foundation for Economic Education founded by Leonard Read, one of the leading free enterprise propagandists of the postwar era, in 1946.

Powell also focused on the need for rethinking advertising and public relations, calling on businesses to support the free enterprise system rather than only the "specific products" they sold. "If American business devoted only 10% of its total annual advertising budget to this overall purpose, it would be a statesman-like expenditure," he advised. He pushed for free enterprise education in television, radio, and other media. This was not a new idea. Fundamental to these campaigns to sell free enterprise was the desire to tell the story of free enterprise more effectively and in a variety of media. Selling meant telling (highlighting the virtues of free enterprise), but it also meant yelling (condemning those out to undermine it). Indeed, the two could not be separated since critics seemed always to be gaining ground.

From the perspective of free enterprisers, the task should have been easy. Writing in 1939, public relations executive Stephen H. Fifeld believed that "because of free enterprise, America has advanced more in the last 150 years than Europe has advanced in the last 1,000 years." Business advocates needed to convey this causal chain, Fifeld believed, to show that free enterprise not only accompanies prosperity and democracy, it catalyzes it. "It is up to us public relations men and women to tell the story, and by doing so we will help to ensure" the continued triumph of the system.[58] Business "Boswells" could publicize

these gains, leaving no fair-minded American with any choice other than un-
questioned support for free enterprise.[59] "While at heart the average American
wants to believe in the superiority over all other systems of the American free
enterprise way of life, yet so many aspersions have been cast on it that he is bewildered," asserted the Reverend Norman Vincent Peale in a speech before the
fifty-third annual meeting of the Congress of American Industry in 1948. This
partisan of "positive thinking," whose book on that subject would soon make
him famous, claimed that "those who believe in the free enterprise system" must
do more than "grumble and complain" and take a page from the book of the
diligent and effective "advocates of collectivism." Each "industrialist and businessman" needed "to correct muddled thinking and erroneous ideas in his own
community," Peale claimed.[60] Decades later, Powell echoed this message.

The promotion of free enterprise, Powell believed, was best handled by institutions such as the U.S. Chamber of Commerce. While individual business
leaders had a role to play, the job required a degree of coordination possible
only in a mass membership lobbying group. Although free enterprise advocates
praised corporate freedom and disdained economic planning, they had also argued, at least since Merle Thorpe in the 1920s, that they could win the ideological struggle only through planning and organization. "Strength lies in organization, in careful long-range planning and implementation, in consistency of
action over an indefinite period of years, in the scale of financing available only
through joint effort, and in the political power available only through united
action and national organizations." Only coordinated action could overcome a
history of "appeasement, ineptitude, and ignoring the program." The critics of
free enterprise had, in Powell's view, benefited from a slow evolution to their
point of view, "from a gradualism that provoked little awareness much less
any real reaction." However, "the ideological attack on the system itself" had
reached a dangerous tipping point. And although he labeled his ideas "tentative
and suggestive" and called for the chamber to engage in further study, he also
said it "would be an exercise in futility" if the organization were to reject his
main premises that business power was in decline, time was short, and coordinated action was needed. Powell did not hide the fact that his suggestions were
going to tug at the pocketbooks of business leaders. Implementation "would
require far more generous financial support from American corporations than
the Chamber has ever received in the past." But the investment, he believed,
would more than pay for itself.

Despite his confidence in his plan, Powell, like his predecessors, recognized that the obstacles to victory were many and proliferating. Enemies both at home and abroad undermined free enterprise. Executives were often narrow-minded in their conception of what needed to be sold, advertising specific goods without highlighting the system that made those goods possible. Business was reluctant either to celebrate or to defend itself. The New Deal system of business regulation and public spending had become normalized. (Daniel Bell observed in *The Coming of Post-industrial Society* [1973] that the United States was "moving away from a society based on a private-enterprise market system" in favor of one in which economic decisions were made at the "political level.")[61] With each passing year—first in economic crisis, then in war, then in a Cold War environment punctuated by what Powell called an "ideological attack on the system"—critics had increasingly institutionalized and normalized antibusiness ideas. This presented a dangerous problem since free enterprise, as he and many others conceived it, was an either/or proposition that was fundamentally threatened by seemingly minor governmental incursions in law, regulation, and tax policy as well as the low estimation of business in popular culture.

One final element of the Powell memo worth highlighting was an omission, one common among other defenders of the "American Way." Powell did not define the object of attack and the system in need of rescue, namely, "free enterprise." He placed an asterisk next to the phrase "American economic system" in the first sentence of the document. The footnote, meant to explain the meaning of the term, read in its entirety: "Variously called: the 'free enterprise system,' 'capitalism,' and the 'profit system.'" This list may have been meant to suggest, as free enterprisers had done for decades, that the terms were equivalents and that the name was not particularly important. Yet Powell did not use the latter two phrases in the remainder of the essay. "Free enterprise," however, appeared four times in the text as well as in the title, suggesting that it took pride of place. If it encompassed the "profit system," the idea of the "free enterprise system" also stood for a broader conception of political freedom, which included representative democracy, the veneration of the risk-taking individual, the celebration of mass production and consumption, the renunciation of state-sponsored solutions to social problems, and a skepticism about dissent as expressed by radicals (though not by business). For Powell, as for so many free enterprisers, no other term covered this range of political, economic, moral, and social goods.

"We Are Losing a Proper Perspective on History"

The Powell memo, which has been called "a memo that changed the course of history," thus actually said very little that had not been said many times before.[62] It encouraged business leaders to enter politics, as had NAM in 1949, when it urged "the nation's economic leaders to take an active part in public affairs."[63] If it was a "blueprint for corporate dominance," Powell was far from the original draftsman.[64] If it responded to a "war" on free enterprise, battles of this sort had been proclaimed in every decade since the 1930s. If it lamented a decline in civic power, this was hardly different from James Brewbaker's 1958 claim that "business associations today have no political influence whatsoever."[65] If it pointed to universities as sites of subversion, so too did H. W. Prentis in 1940 when he said, "In many of the colleges of America creeping collectivism is rampant."[66] If it called for efforts to promote the popularity of business, this was precisely the goal of every campaign to "sell" free enterprise since the 1930s.[67]

Anyone conversant with the missives of NAM or the Chamber of Commerce, anyone who had listened to Republican campaign speeches or perused *Vital Speeches of the Day*, a monthly magazine of speeches and lectures, often by business leaders and politicians, over the preceding four decades would have found the diagnosis familiar. Even those outside the direct orbit of the business lobby would have seen and heard claims and proposals similar to Powell's expressed in advertisements, radio programs, political speeches, and newspaper editorials. Students would likely have seen them in their issues of *My Weekly Reader* and in filmstrips or in the dozens of documentary movies and cartoons celebrating free enterprise produced by Harding College in Searcy, Arkansas.[68] Most of what Powell said about free enterprise had become the common sense of the business community and its defenders, familiar to the vast majority of the American people. As historian Benjamin Waterhouse has noted, "Conceptually the document broke little new ground; business leaders had been voicing many of these same concerns for years, if not as eloquently or persuasively."[69]

Well before that fateful August 1971 weekend during which Powell wrote his memo, changes were in the air for advocates of free enterprise. "Business leaders 'must wade into politics from the precinct level up,'" said Phillip M. Talbott, the chair of the U.S. Chamber of Commerce, in 1958, foreshadowing language that Powell was to use more than a decade later.[70] Beginning in the mid-1960s, business leaders and conservative politicians, feeling besieged by Lyndon Johnson's Great Society, the civil rights movement, and the New Left, called on free enterprisers to develop a more vigorous public voice. This renewed call for action began at least half a decade before Powell prepared his memo. As early as 1966, the chamber's leader, Arch Booth, renounced the "political apathy of the business community" and highlighted the organization's "great positive program for strengthening private business" as well as its opposition to public spending, truth in packaging laws, and regulation more generally, which he condemned as "repetitions of ideas that didn't work in the 1930s." For Booth the defining enemy of free enterprisers remained what it had been for decades, the legacy of the New Deal.[71] The proclamations of Booth and others in the years before Powell's memo suggest that the common view—that before that momentous weekend in 1971 the U.S. Chamber of Commerce had become "lackluster" or "asleep"—is in need of revision. They also underscore that Powell's memo is best understood as a catalogue of long-standing free enterprise views and tactics rather than a sharp departure from the past.[72]

Powell's debt to earlier free enterprise discourse took many forms. The most direct influences were the clippings, collected between 1969 and the time he wrote the document, that he quoted from or paraphrased, such as Jeffrey St. John's op-ed piece recommending that General Motors "fight back" against critics and an article from his local newspaper that referred to a poll showing that roughly half of the American student population "favored socialization of basic U.S. industries" and that more than half "would choose surrender rather than war with the Soviet Union."[73] Several months before Powell set pen to paper, James Roche, the chairman of General Motors, accused critics of "threatening the entire free enterprise system, assaulting America's reputation and creating an unfairly negative image of American business."[74] In 1971, Powell was not alone in judging the present moment a crisis.

Far more important than these direct influences, however, were the indirect ones, based on the accretion and repetition of claims over the course of forty years. Powell drew on a familiar set of rhetorical patterns and economic and political understandings framed around opposition to the "New Deal Order."[75] Almost every claim and argument in the Powell memo had been made previously, starting with the idea that something called a "free enterprise system" existed, that it was uniquely and fundamentally American, and that it needed vigorous defending lest American freedom recede. The doomsday scenario was an old trope of free enterprise discourse, even if the agents of subversion changed over time. Chodorov wrote in 1950 that "it should be evident that further compromise now means . . . the ultimate extinction of capitalism and the ultimate is only a generation away."[76] Eight years later, the conservative journalist James L. Wick wrote, "Socialism will soon complete its conquest of America if businessmen do not organize immediately."[77] Such fears were omnipresent, and Chodorov and Wick, like Powell, saw the imminent collapse of capitalism to be a function of internal weakness rather than Soviet aggression.

Another reason to question the groundbreaking qualities of the Powell memo lies in the nature of the man who has been dubbed the agent of the "business rebellion." Powell was a brilliant lawyer, and as an associate justice he practiced, contrary to Jack Anderson's fears, what the legal scholar Mark Tushnet calls a "jurisprudence of centrism." This comports with the recollection of an associate at his law firm who recalled him as a "big fan of balance" and the "most responsible human I've ever met."[78] Hardworking, earnest, and thorough, he also held conventional views for a person of his class, race, region, and gender.[79] In a profile of Powell published soon after Nixon nominated him to the high court, journalist John Darnton emphasized "the moderation of his ideas and approach to integration."[80] Powell's moderation, however, was in keeping with what Walter F. Carey, a Michigan trucking executive and the Chamber of Commerce president in 1964, characterized as "militant moderation" or what Arthur Larson called "middle of the road extremism."[81] His commitment to pluralism buffered the radicalism of his view that business was an embattled minority. (Indeed, the conservative columnist James. J. Kilpatrick argued that just as Justice Thurgood Marshall was an advocate for "integration" and former justice Arthur Goldberg was a supporter of "labor," it was perfectly legitimate for Powell to do the same for business interests.)[82] Like other free enterprisers from the South, Powell was "prone to thinking of white southerners as an embattled minority," and he saw business, in spite of its power and influence, very much the same way.[83]

At the Senate confirmation hearings, held jointly with William Rehnquist, the other nominee Nixon proposed (there were two vacancies on the high court), it was the latter who was portrayed as a "right-wing zealot" and who endured three days of contentious interrogation, compared to Powell's one day of largely perfunctory questioning.[84] Powell is the last person we should expect to have originated a revolutionary new doctrine. He hewed closely to conservative conventional wisdom on political, economic, and ethical matters. He opened his speech at the 1972 ABA Prayer Breakfast with the confession that he would say nothing that was "original or profound," a pledge that no one in the audience could have doubted that he kept. In this talk, the associate justice observed that it "had become increasingly fashionable to question and attack the most basic elements of our society." These were fashions he found easy to eschew and rebuke. "It is said that religion is irrelevant, our democracy is a sham, the free-enterprise system has failed, and that somehow America has become a wholly selfish, materialistic, racist society—with unworthy goals and warped priorities." It went without saying that Powell vehemently rejected all of these claims. While he acknowledged that "we have witnessed racial injustice in the past," he claimed that "no one can fairly question the present national commitment to full equality and justice." This view strikingly paralleled the free enterprise view of the necessity of government intervention in the economy in the past but the danger of such action in the present.

While Powell believed in the wonders of free enterprise as much as Leonard Read, he also recognized the need for collective action and lobbying in order to save that system. He was at heart an institutionalist who posited that the interests of business, far from representing the narrow "self-interest" he denounced, advanced the good of society.[85] Powell rejected the "highly individualized self-interest" among "large segments of our people"—what he condemned as "unanchored individualism." He especially targeted those who expressed "hostile attitudes toward existing institutions," noting that they were often the same people who held "excessively tolerant views toward personal conduct—sexual morality, use of drugs, and disobedience of laws believed by the individual to be unjust." Powell's version of the free enterprise system, unlike Read's, which, as we will see in chapter 6, highlighted discrete individuals connected by the free market, was one that foregrounded the business firm as the model of a good society.

While Powell's ABA speech put forward little in the way of new ideas, it did offer an important, if inadvertent, clue for how best to interpret his memo. "It may be that, in our concern with the present and our serious social problems, we are losing a proper perspective on history," he told the audience members, encouraging them not to blow the current moment out of proportion. Powell concluded these reflections by noting that history "immortalizes all of us in the sense that we are not seen solely as the products of the present day, but as links in an ageless chain of human struggle and progress." While the chain backward from the Powell memo may not have been "ageless," it was also not the product of the "present day" in August 1971 when Powell composed it. Powell's biographer, John Jeffries, has claimed that he omitted the memo from Powell's life story because "its content was not different from other things he was saying at the time."[86] Perhaps more important, what Powell was saying at the time was not fundamentally different from what his like-minded predecessors had been declaiming for the previous two generations.

"Many Fine Things That Can Be Said about the Free Enterprise System Have Been Left Unsaid"

The phrase *free enterprise* has a long and complicated history in the United States. The dominant form of the term emerged in the 1930s as a critical response to the New Deal and the threat formed by the expansion of the welfare state. In a 1943 pamphlet, the leaders of NAM claimed to have recently "taken it out of the category of technical phrases used only by economists" and made free enterprise "part of the American vocabulary."[87] For many business leaders and politicians, free enterprise served as a shorthand for the kind of political economy that they preferred, one with minimal government interference in the form of laws, taxes, and regulations and maximal freedom for firms to do as they wished. As the business journal *Fortune* editorialized in 1949, the most important job of the corporation was "to stop the encroachment of government on its prerogatives" and, in a passage that could have been written by Powell, to "justify its profits, not apologize for them."[88]

Free enterprisers understood their system in moral terms, believing that the bottom line was not the self-interest of businesses but the good of society. "The threat to the enterprise system is not merely a matter of economics," Powell wrote. "It is also a threat to individual freedom." Thus business leaders believed that they had an important—indeed, heroic—role to play in promoting this system, which hinged on their ability to do their jobs unimpeded by an adversarial state or by powerful social movements. H. W. Prentis flattered the members of his audience at a NAM convention in 1940 by labeling them the vanguard of liberty: "Freedom for the ordinary run of mankind has almost invariably developed under the leadership of middle class business men, such as we who are here tonight."[89] Perhaps in compensation for their perceived unpopularity, such self-congratulation was the order of the day in free enterprise rhetoric. As R. E.

Daley, an executive at Union Carbide, told the Sheffield, Alabama, Board of Commerce in 1947, "You men of business have made great contributions to the common welfare."[90] Their mission, as George Benson, the president of Harding College and a leading free enterprise evangelist, put it, was to "re-educate the masses to the value of free enterprise and constitutional government."[91] Some critics of the business community might have taken the references to the "ordinary" or "common" "masses" to be a form of elitism, but free enterprisers saw it as their solemn duty to instill what one group of advertisers called in 1938 "a better understanding of the system of free enterprise."[92]

Free enterprisers rarely conceived of the business firm as powerful and never, in spite of their defense of corporate profits, described their demands as partisan or narrowly self-interested. They displaced business interests and corporate power by defining the free enterprise system as one that primarily benefited consumers and citizens—and only incidentally executives and managers. While profits were the essence of business, these were properly understood as the down payment that enabled goods and services to flow freely and individual liberty to flourish.[93] "Our enterprise system is far more than just a way of doing business," said Daley. This was so because, of all political and economic systems, it maximized both material wealth and morality. Daley, speaking in Alabama on the cusp of the civil rights movement, urged "business men to come to the defense of our American system of free enterprise and equal opportunity," by which he meant not racial equality but the freedom of business to continue to produce prodigious amounts of goods. As support for his claim, he argued, "The truth is that under our system we have accomplished the outstanding feat of producing approximately 93,000,000 tons of steel annually, and more aluminum, magnesium, phosphates, and everything of use than have been produced under any other forms of government in the world." For its advocates, free enterprise was the system that made the American cornucopia as well as political freedom possible.[94]

Regulation was harmful, in this rhetoric, not because of the damage it did to business but due to the shackles it placed on consumers. "The entire success of free enterprise can be traced to the vitality it gains by competitive striving to satisfy the discriminating consumer," declared GM's Roche in 1971. "To destroy the concept of consumer sovereignty is to destroy free enterprise." Moreover, free enterprise was not simply a synonym for "free markets." It was rather a crucial aspect of the civic whole that made up the American nation. In the same speech in which he highlighted the importance of business leaders, Prentis called free enterprise an essential and indivisible leg of the "tripod of freedom" that also included representative democracy and religious freedom. Prentis feared that "creeping collectivism" might soon destroy private enterprise, with the "resultant collapse of the whole tripod of individual freedom." The threat to freedom could take many forms, Prentis believed. The collectivist might "call himself a Socialist, Communist, Nazi, Fascist, or New Liberal," and in some sense Prentis saw these as equivalents, in that all would undercut "individual liberty," which he saw as the essence of a free society.[95]

Balancing self-congratulation and self-flagellation, free enterprisers maintained an ethic of elite victimization marked by defensiveness, bafflement, and righteous anger. Like Prentis and Powell, they saw free enterprise as both foundational and endangered at the same time. How, they often wondered, could a system that made individual freedom and national prosperity possible be called into question? "The most important problem business faces today, if you want to get down to brass tacks, is the fact that business isn't out of the doghouse yet," as an editorial in *Fortune* proclaimed in 1949. "Every U.S. businessman, consciously or unconsciously, is on the defensive."[96] Shifting from defense to offense remained the goal of free enterprisers, who described the shackles placed on capitalism by government and the unpopularity of business as the primary obstacles facing the country.

The attacks on business, as free enterprisers understood it, made launching the offensive that they believed was necessary easier said than done. Too many people viewed business, said Philip Reed, chairman of General Electric, in 1940, as a "convenient political whipping boy," and as a result it "continues to be in the doghouse"—the same metaphor *Fortune* employed almost a decade later.[97] The problem, free enterprisers believed, was that ordinary, well-meaning Americans—the segment Powell called the "perfectly respectable elements of society"—were increasingly accepting radical ideas, making those ideas dangerously mainstream. The "assault on free enterprise," Powell worried at the outset of his memo, "is gaining momentum and converts." The domino theory of business vilification befuddled Powell and his predecessors as much as it angered them. Unable to account for arguments against capitalism, Richard F. Sentner, a U. S. Steel executive, in 1958 highlighted what he called an "unconscious campaign—or perhaps a conscious one—of misinterpretation." These "continuing and recurrent" attacks on free enterprise had "numerous heads and as soon as one is whacked off another is promptly grown."[98] Saving free enterprise was a lot like playing the "whack-a-mole" game at the state fair.

The danger, free enterprisers believed, inhered less in the frontal assault of the radicals then in the insidious, seemingly mild reforms of the liberals. This is why Powell expressed less concern with the actions of what he called the "socialist cadre" than with the ordinary American who had been won over to some elements of the attack on business. Even before F. A. Hayek's *The Road to Serfdom* was published in 1944 and long afterward, free enterprisers argued that incremental expansions of the welfare state represented dangerous portents of totalitarianism.[99] In this view, all political and economic decisions inevitably had binary outcomes; either they reinforced free enterprise or they undermined it. There was no middle ground. Free enterprise equaled freedom, and the welfare state ultimately led to unfreedom. Thomas R. Shepard Jr., the publisher of *Look* magazine, authored a pamphlet in 1971 called *The Disaster Lobby*, in which he treated the mandate to install seat belts in automobiles as one of a series of opening wedges in a broader attack on individual freedom concocted by liberal alarmists.[100] Powell, who kept a well-underlined copy of this treatise in his files as he worked on his memo, most likely agreed with Shepard's conclusion that "once free enterprise succumbs to the attacks of the consumerists and the ecologists and the rest of the Disaster Lobby, the freedom of the consumer goes with it." Shepard longed to return to the days when the unencumbered citizen had the "freedom to live the way he wants and to buy the things he wants without some Big Brother in Washington telling him he can't." Jeffrey St. John, in another article that Powell highlighted, worried that Ralph Nader "seems to want to go radically beyond the New Deal," which into the 1970s represented the primary enemy for free enterprisers.[101] Reform could quietly spiral out of control, destroying free enterprise by slowly, imperceptibly, and relentlessly chipping away at its edifice. The fear that liberal reform could morph into political extremism led Powell and many other free enterprisers, in turn, to endorse conspiracy theories that took the regulatory state to be portents of Orwellian totalitarianism.

Some proponents of free enterprise, particularly those in advertising and public relations, suggested that the solution was straightforward: to tell the story that business leaders were reluctant to recount. The battles of the postwar years, claimed W. G. Paul, the head of the Los Angeles Stock Exchange, in 1949, could be reduced to a "conflict of free enterprise versus statism." Paul urged his audience to see this ideological battle as "a situation of two business rivals competing for public favor." Business leaders, however, too often "lack the courage or initiative to meet the challenge and defend themselves." As a result, he feared, "the very existence of free enterprise is challenged."[102] Because free enterprise was essential but undefended, Prentis urged his colleagues to "become sentinels and missionaries in behalf of free private enterprise."[103] Several years later, the *Saturday Evening Post* concurred: "What free enterprise needs is a new and better propaganda technique."[104] Business leaders needed to overcome their tunnel vision and reticence and begin to celebrate not just their goods and services but the system as a whole. As Harold B. Dorsey, the founder of the Argus Research Corporation, an investment research firm, declaimed in 1961, with a frustration that was both familiar and baffling, given how hard free enterprise had been sold for going on three decades, "Many fine things that can be said about the free enterprise system have been left unsaid."[105] Offering these previously unspoken testimonials to the system remained the mission of free enterprisers. In 1963, the president of NAM, W. P. Gullander, said that business "had done everything to sell the goods to the public and all too little to explain the traditional American values that made it possible."[106]

Even after the publicizing of the Powell memo, business leaders continued to express the view that, as Douglass Harvey, the vice president of Kodak, put it, "People in business have been slow to share what they have learned from experience about the economic facts of life." Harvey was no doubt sincere in his view that "it is time for business people to present a brief for free enterprise."[107] From the point of view of free enterprisers, the time for this brief, whether in the decade of the 1930s or the 1970s, was always past due. John Davenport, a former editor of *Barron's* and a member of the board of editors of *Fortune*, identified a "paradox" in 1973. "Businessmen are master salesmen of automobiles, refrigerators, and widgets. They are something less than articulate spokesmen for basic economic, political, and moral principles."[108] The paradox, from the free enterprise point of view, was that business freedom made possible affluence, democracy, and the good society, but this truth was not only unrecognized but distrusted and even rejected by the broader public.

"Our Merchandise Is and Must Be Enterprise"

In late 1937, another future Supreme Court justice, Robert H. Jackson, addressed the annual meeting of the American Political Science Association in a speech entitled "The Menace of Free Enterprise." At the time, Jackson was serving as the assistant attorney general of the United States in charge of the Antitrust Division. As a New Dealer, he thought the best way to defend free enterprise was to keep business power in check.[109] "As students of political science we must try to understand the philosophy of big business," he told the audience. "Unfortunately," he lamented, "no acknowledged business leader has formulated its doctrine or been its spokesman in the sense that Marx spoke for socialism, Lenin for communism and Jackson and Roosevelt for democracy." Certainly business had its publicizers but, he noted, "manifestoes, such as those of the Manufacturers Association, like political platforms, are patchworks that do not add up to a coherent philosophy." Jackson suggested that the philosophy of big business could be conjured "only in its conduct and in the editorials of those close to it who from day to day defend its conduct." Perhaps reconsidering the idea that such a "philosophy" could be discerned at all, he observed that "business adheres to an attitude rather than a doctrine," astutely identifying the centrality of the psychological components of free enterprise agitation.

Jackson shared with the political scientists a second concern related to the first. Why was business, the beneficiary of so many New Deal reforms, the Roosevelt administration's leading and most vociferous opponent? And why, he wondered, quoting his colleague in government Joseph P. Kennedy, were business leaders engaged in "a chronic bellyache"? (The next year, Leon Davis, in a typical example of this bellyaching, denounced the "business baiting" that had become, he said, characteristic of the new class of "politician bureaucrat," like Jackson, enshrined by the New Deal.)[110] Given "the unvarnished truth . . . that the government's recovery program has succeeded nowhere else so effectively as restoring the profits of big business," Jackson wondered why business was perpetually in a "rich man's panic" and constantly adopting "threatening tactics." What, he wondered, reversing himself once again and acknowledging that business did, in fact, profess a philosophy of a sort, "can be the underlying, and probably unconscious, philosophy of big business to cause its bitter opposition to every reform in whatever shape it may be proposed, and its uncompromising opposition to those like myself who suggest reforms, with the motive of placing business on a firmer, sounder financed, and more honest basis of operation?" In attempting to "liquidate the New Deal" and to "throw off all government interference," business philosophy, such as it was, amounted to a declaration of war against the government and the reforms it embodied. Busi-

ness, Jackson concluded, "has merely been saved from ruin and restored to arro-
gance," a sense of self-importance that made the clear articulation of a philosophy unnecessary. Jackson again identified the affective nature of free enterprise
discourse.

As if in confirmation of Jackson's fear, Powell declared in his memo that
there had been a "massive assault" on the "philosophy" of business. He did not,
however, flesh out the meaning of this philosophy other than upholding "its
right to continue to manage its affairs" and to practice "its fundamental economics," which he did not elucidate. (Elsewhere in the memo, he condemned
"economic illiteracy," which he also did not define.) But what Jackson perceived as an arrogant refusal to spell out a philosophy may well have been
motivated by fear and insecurity. Elite victimization, Jackson discerned in
1937, had already become the essence of free enterprise discourse. Operating
in an atmosphere of threats that free enterprisers analogized to war made crisis
management, not philosophizing, their primary mode of operation, and grievance, not policy, their main expression. Getting out of the doghouse and breaking the shackles were the top priorities.

Advocates of free enterprise seemed to best articulate their "business philosophy" when they engaged in a pitch in which the object of sale was what they
called "the free enterprise system" itself, which was at war with the New Deal
state. "Advertising's job is not merely finding customers for soap, automobiles,
and a thousand other commodities," as an advertising trade group noted in
1940; "it includes 'selling' the American public on the value of business itself,
and of free enterprise in general."[111] Two years later, James Selvage, the public
relations counsel of the Lee and Selvage firm in New York, speaking before the
Advertising Club of Worcester, Massachusetts, went even further. "Ours is not
a job of selling merchandise," Selvage began bluntly. Indeed, he added, in a
statement with which many manufacturers might not have agreed, "The life or
death of a single corporation, regardless of its size, does not matter in the future
of this country." Instead, "Our merchandise is and must be enterprise," which he
defined as "the American system of individual initiative and profit as contrasted
with a regimented economy." The definition was typical in that it explained the
system only vaguely and mostly by distinguishing it from other, competing economic systems, in this case a "regimented" one, and also in conflating corporate
profits with individual liberty. Selvage highlighted the relationship between war
and enterprise. "We are selling America itself to Americans who have forgotten

what America has symbolized in the past as the envy of every other nation in the world—and what it must continue to symbolize—else freedom and its blood brother free enterprise will perish from the earth."[112] Selvage's wartime push to sell free enterprise included several characteristic arguments: the claim that Americans had forgotten the true meaning of free enterprise, that free enterprise and freedom are twinned, and that something like a preemptive war against "governmental bondage" must continually be fought. The job of free enterprise was to reintroduce, with force if necessary, the norms damaged and in danger of being destroyed by grasping government as well as by popular apathy and business passivity.

The metaphor of war was particularly timely for Selvage, who gave his speech one year after the Japanese attack on Pearl Harbor. Like other free enterprisers, Selvage deemed the war for free enterprise as important as the war against fascism. As he told his audience, "This is no sham battle that is going on behind the battlefront." While conceding that "our opponents in economic philosophy want to win the fighting war just as we do," he feared that these opponents would use the exigencies of war as a pretext for permanent and dangerous forms of government power. Invoking the slippery slope via a pre-Hayekian road metaphor, he called statism "an easy road to long-incubated objectives for remaking America—and even the world." He worried in particular that "we hear a multitudinous twaddle about fighting this war for almost everything under the sun except to preserve the American way of life, representative government, and enterprise that our boys can come back to." Selvage claimed that he thought it was "the wish of every person in this room" that they should "lay aside" what he called "bickering" and in unified fashion "devote ourselves to winning the war." And he acknowledged that "we have got to lick the Japs and Nazis." But he also wanted the audience to recognize and vanquish what he called the "chains of Fascism" inherent in wartime controls. To "regain private enterprise," he claimed, "we will demand the casting off of our shackles and return the American people to the American Way of representative free government and honest free enterprise." As we will see in chapter 3, selling free enterprise, then, meant opening a second, internal front in the war against totalitarianism, adding a civil war against the enemies of free enterprise to the war against the Axis powers.

Selling free enterprise remained a serious business in the postwar years. On the one hand, the United States, as the Chamber of Commerce and NAM never tired of pointing out, was the envy of the world as by far the biggest producer and consumer of homes, cars, radios, and every other good imaginable in these years.[113] At the same time, an atmosphere of crisis reigned as oppositional ideologies seemed to be knocking free enterprise off its pedestal. Hence the need to "dress up our system-selling" just "as we do our day-to-day product selling," as R. E. Daley said in his 1947 speech to Alabama businessmen. An official of NAM was even blunter at a regional conference in Los Angeles in 1946, calling out his members as "lousy salesmen" who pitched their chief product—free enterprise—with "as much appeal as a chorus girl in a flannel nightgown."[114] Interestingly, Daley used the same gendered simile: "When it comes to selling the system we get as drab as a crutch, as unexciting as a chorus girl in a flannel nightgown."[115] Whereas most advertisers would not miss the opportunity to promote, even exaggerate, the sex appeal of their goods, business leaders were neutering their naturally alluring product.

In 1948 Harvard Business School professor Edward C. Bursk became the first academic to assess the campaign to sell free enterprise, which was then entering its second decade.[116] Unlike Robert Jackson, he believed it was possible to grasp the philosophy of business. Indeed, it could be found precisely in the pronouncements of the trade associations that Jackson had dismissed. "Although the word 'sell' when used in this way is generally enclosed in quotation marks, I should like to take it at face value," he began. For him, following the claims of business leaders since the war, free enterprise was the "product" business aimed to peddle. Bursk pointed to the same issue identified by Jackson a decade earlier. "Actually what management wants to sell is its own philosophy, rather than an economic system as such." Yet this philosophy was hard to pin down since the term that emerged from the sales pitches he examined was "a subjective concept that is inevitably rather fuzzy." This was so because "much of the feeling or attitude that I have called a philosophy has never been made explicit by those who hold it, if indeed they are conscious of it themselves." Furthermore, the attempt to articulate such a philosophy is always "in danger of resulting in platitudes." It was, therefore, perhaps best to think of the term as a "brand" and to understand efforts to promote free enterprise less as a battle of philosophies than as a marketing campaign. Like many others, Bursk wondered whether the term itself, rather than the failure to sell the system vigorously, was the problem. He proposed a rebranding with the "forthright" term *private management*. Like Jackson, Bursk noticed the identity politics of free enterprisers.

Powell's memo was not the first statement to contain the "bellyaching" Jackson observed, the selling campaign Bursk discerned, and the free enterprise philosophizing both desired. Nor would it be the last. A thread running through this language was the urgency in selling free enterprise.

A paranoid way of thinking that conservative intellectual and former official in the George W. Bush administration Peter Wehner identified as novel in 2015—"an apocalyptic view of American life" that, he claimed, began "during the Obama era"—has a history that extends back to the New Deal or earlier, and owes a significant debt to the deep patterns of free enterprise discourse.[117] Such ominous rhetoric is often associated with the radical Right. But business leaders and mainstream politicians have frequently championed the pessimistic view that "the foundations of freedom are slipping away," as Prentis told the forty-sixth annual Congress of American Industry in 1941.[118] That same year, Alan Arthur Stockdale worried that free enterprise was at the end of its rope, with "the complete surrender of individual freedom" inevitably to follow.[119] This was not a perspective limited to wartime: in a 1961 speech opposing what came to be known as Medicare, the General Electric spokesman, Ronald Reagan, warned of the danger that "under the name of liberalism the American people would adopt every fragment of the socialist program" and thus obliterate freedom.[120] Powell, respected attorney and director of several Fortune 500 companies, exhibited what a previous justice of the Supreme Court, Robert H. Jackson, called "rich man's panic" in his fear not just of political defeat but of the loss of freedom.

An apocalyptic worldview that represented free enterprise as endangered and totalitarianism as on the march has been a central feature of the business-oriented conservatism championed by most free enterprisers, like Powell, who warned in his memo that "we in America already have moved very far indeed toward some aspects of state socialism."[121] Nor did such fears end with the Cold War. In 2010, Donohue of the Chamber of Commerce, for example, condemned the "general attack on our free-enterprise system," which put the system "truly at risk."[122] "With Obamacare fully installed," Mitt Romney predicted in April 2012 as he campaigned for the Republican nomination for the presidency, "we will have effectively ceased to be a free-enterprise society."[123] His running mate, the vice presidential hopeful Paul Ryan, called it a "dangerous moment" and worried, as had generations of free enterprisers before him, that "we're running out of time."[124] NAM's 1946 pamphlet *The Eleventh Hour for American Enterprise* had expressed similar sentiments.[125]

In 1998, President Bill Clinton, addressing the World Trade Organization in Geneva, claimed that "the argument over which is better, free enterprise or state socialism, has been won."[126] Since the 1920s, as we will see in the next chapter, business free enterprisers have refused to accept this victory as anything other than provisional or illusory. "So many non-radical Americans," Powell worried, "unwittingly weaken the very institutions of freedom they wish to sustain," and which "may hasten the day when the heel of repression is a reality." Reminding Americans of the free enterprise message, Powell claimed that the alternative to free enterprise was tyranny. On the cusp of the conservative transformation in American politics, Powell warned that eternal vigilance was necessary to protect against "the greatest danger to liberty in America."[127] Powell's alarmist conclusion in his memo that "business and the enterprise system are in deep trouble, and the hour is late" was the essence of the businessman's jeremiad, a diagnosis that echoed thousands of other statements by business leaders, lobbyists, public relations experts, and politicians from the New Deal to the present. In this worldview, fear of imminent subversion and the demand for perpetual warfare were not obstacles to free enterprise common sense but the essence of it.

The Powell memo marked the culmination of nearly four decades of the development of a particular version of free enterprise thought that emerged in the late 1920s and became dominant in opposition to the New Deal. But the term *free enterprise* has had many meanings, a number of them quite at odds with the commonsense type that Lewis Powell defended in 1971. The next chapter examines the term's emergence in the nineteenth century as a quality associated with the virtues of "free labor" abetted by the state and explores how it evolved in the early twentieth century into a "system" associated with big business and weak government.

2

From "Free Labor" to "Free Enterprise"

IN 1820, THE INAUGURAL ISSUE OF ONE of the first abolitionist newspapers in the United States, the *Emancipator*, proposed the "free labor system" as the remedy to the evil of an economy based on slave labor. By the 1830s, abolitionists regularly employed this phrase to describe a system that was both more efficient and more just than slave-based enterprises.[1] In 1851, the *New York Daily Tribune* described the "two antagonist social systems" in oppositional terms, and later in the decade, the founders of the Republican Party championed "free labor."[2] African Americans and many white northerners viewed slavery as "the deadly enemy of free labor and free enterprise" and they saw the Civil War as the final battle between these antagonistic systems. They viewed the triumph of the free labor system as a victory of the good society itself.[3]

Little more than a century after the phrase *free labor system* started appearing regularly in the pages of abolitionist newspapers, opponents of the New Deal began to describe what they called "the free enterprise system" as a key alternative to the New Deal.[4] Treating the New Deal as the antithesis of the free enterprise system, they compared the former to the slave system of the Old South. The United States was, once again, a "house divided." For its champions, "free enterprise" had replaced "free labor" as a guiding principle of opposition to tyranny and even enslavement caused by the concentration of power and also as a formula for the good society. Preserving the nation required a victory for the free enterprise system, including its promotion of individual liberty and economic well-being.

"Free enterprise" was a subset of a broader "free labor ideology" in the nineteenth century. The "free labor" rallying cry became dominant in the antebellum North both as a critique of the political economy of the slaveholding South and as a backbone of the good society. After the Civil War, the free labor vision became hegemonic in the nation as a whole, even as it transformed again into a defense of business prerogatives rather than of a liberated interracial working class. Without slavery as an "other," business propagandists deemed free labor triumphant, even as debt peonage, labor exploitation, Jim Crow segregation, and violent repression of the labor movement became the norm.

In the twentieth century, free enterprise became an ideological force of its own, as it both transformed and replaced the earlier free labor vision. By the 1920s, when the idea of a "system" of free enterprise was first promoted, "free labor" was no longer a nation-defining phrase. When the Progressive Party ("Bull Moose") platform in 1912 celebrated the previous generation of heroes who had in the Civil War era promoted the transformation "from slavery to a free labor system," it sounded more like a last hurrah for a venerated ideal than a building block of contemporary liberation.[5] At the same time, Progressives, believing that they were fighting analogous battles against present-day forms of slavery, were more likely to invoke free enterprise than free labor as their fighting motto and, as we will see, they contributed significantly to the transformation of the term.

In a great reversal, "free labor," once a stand-alone concept, became a relatively minor constituent component of the free enterprise vision. Free laborers had depicted the independent producer as the heart of society. Free enterprisers replaced labor with business as the core of the free and just society, and "free labor" became subordinate to "free management."[6] The term that had once signaled primarily an attribute—a "spirit of enterprise"—reified into a noun that stood for the business firm, the corporation or, more generally, the capitalist economic system as a whole.[7]

The idea of "free enterprise" served as the main counterpoint to the dominant "New Deal order" for the crucial half century from the Great Depression through the presidency of Ronald Reagan.[8] During this period, free enterprisers won many battles, especially in establishing an equivalence between business and political freedom. Reckoning with the battle between two encompassing ideas is key to understanding modern political culture in the United States.

A prehistory of that story, focusing on the evolution of free enterprise from its first appearances as a term in the early nineteenth century through the 1920s, when it began to be reshaped into its modern sense, is critical because only by understanding how the idea developed can we understood how it acquired its power. How did free enterprise morph from an individual virtue into a social, economic, and political "system"? How did it come to shape a set of oppositions and binaries that continue to govern how we think not just about economic arrangements but about the good society, the just polity, and individual freedom?

Tracking free enterprise's evolution offers insights into fundamental changes in the history of capitalism from a time when "free laborers" defined themselves in opposition to "slave power" to the period when "free enterprisers" contrasted their liberating vision of business autonomy and miraculous markets with naïve and potentially totalitarian "statists." Both antebellum "free labor" advocates and twentieth-century "free enterprise" proponents served as political defenders of capitalism; both tied economic efficiency and power to justice and liberty. But they differed in their conception of the proper relations among state, markets, and the business firm. Nineteenth-century advocates generally saw the promotion of free enterprise as a state project. In contrast, later promoters of free enterprise described the genius of free enterprise capitalism as its reliance on the "automatic workings of the market," which made "central planning" not only unnecessary but counterproductive and dangerous.[9] Although free enterprisers from the 1920s onward claimed to be invoking a nearly continuous chain of thought dating back to the Founders, their ideas were radically new, developed in the context of an urbanizing, industrializing society, large business firms, and a global economic power but cloaked in the language of individual proprietors and small businesses popularized by nineteenth-century free labor advocates. As the Free Enterprise Alliance, a small business lobby founded in 2008, put it, assuming a straight line from the late eighteenth century to the present day, American prosperity "is the direct result of our Founding Fathers," who "created a society based upon the principles of free enterprise."[10] But the line between the Founders (who, in fact, did not use the phrase) and the present was crooked; nineteenth-century advocates of free enterprise would not have recognized the term as it developed in the twentieth century.

"Free Enterprise and Untamed Energy"

In the 1830s abolitionists began to speak of a "free labor system" that somehow defined the true spirit of the United States but also opposed a powerful and antithetical system—chattel slavery—that threatened to dominate and undermine this framework and the nation itself. They described the clash between these two systems as the hinge upon which the fate of the nation would be determined. What did free labor mean? Eric Foner, the most careful analyst of antebellum "free labor ideology," calls it a product of an "expanding, enterprising, competitive society." Antebellum Americans in the North described "enterprise" as an attribute: they spoke of "citizens of enterprise," "the spirit of enterprise," and "the virtues of the enterprising life." They favored economic independence in a world of independent proprietors, and viewed both the slave economy and concentrated business entities as the antithesis of a free labor society. They championed the small entrepreneur—famously apotheosized by Abraham Lincoln as the free laborer made good—as the embodiment of the democratic polity. Free labor was not just an economic system; as Foner notes, it "represented a model of the good society."[11]

The idea of free labor was a political-economic hybrid, promoting democracy, affluence, and civilization itself. "Of the future, it may be predicted with certainty, that unless we of the slave States shall, by emancipation, give a fair chance to free labor and free enterprise," declared a Louisville editorialist in 1848, "we must see our towns grow slowly." This antislavery editor claimed that urban growth was the result not of "mere accidents" but was made possible by the conscious cultivation of "artisans" and commerce, not by slavery, which was "antagonistical to the growth of large cities."[12] "Free labor and free enterprise" would provide "freedom and the energy which freedom creates," claimed an Oshkosh newspaper, suggesting the political benefits of this economic system.[13] Here, the newspaper characteristically linked free labor and free enterprise, but with the former understood as a catalyst for the latter.

Even in the nineteenth century, free enterprise had multiple meanings and was employed by advocates of internal improvements, abolitionists, free traders, and urban boosters. For all of them, however, the term connoted, above all, what made the United States (at least the parts of it that rejected chattel slavery) the home of an energetic, entrepreneurial, democratic people who seamlessly produced economic abundance and political liberty. This, we will see, was exactly the formula that free enterprise proponents espoused in the twentieth century. Celebrants of the free enterprise system, despite its differences from the free labor system, assured the public it would deliver an analogous set of social and economic benefits.

Americans described the United States as "a land of free enterprise" as early as 1856, but what they meant by this description connoted something quite different from twentieth-century understandings of this idea.[14] For antebellum Americans, government, especially its capacity to develop infrastructure, made free enterprise possible. They saw the state and free enterprise as symbiotic, not antagonistic. For example, in 1843, the citizens of Detroit petitioned Congress to build a canal "to connect the lower lakes with Lake Superior." This act, the petitioners claimed, would open the rich natural resources of the lake for commercial gain. Residents believed that government was necessary to unleash what they called "the free enterprise of the people of the United States." A decade earlier in a message to Congress, Andrew Jackson became the first president to invoke the term, making a similar claim. He described "the free enterprize of our citizens" as a capacity that was necessarily "aided by the State sovereignties." What Jackson called the "machinery in government" promoted both "self government" and free enterprise. Jackson was describing what legal historian J. Willard Hurst later called the key organizing principle of the nineteenth-century state, that a "legal order should protect and promote the release of individual creative energy."[15] Using the metaphor of waves of water, a Kansas newspaper in 1855 described the slave state of Missouri as "a Dam across the great channel of free enterprise." The editor was confident that free enterprise, "in its accumulation," would submerge "the cursed institution of slavery," which was both inefficient and immoral.[16] Free enterprisers believed the inefficiency and immorality were of a piece and that free labor produced the opposite: abundance and an ethical civilization.

Notably, Jackson and the Detroit petitioners described government (both national and state) as a facilitator rather than an enemy of free enterprise. Historian Richard White notes that "Whiggish free labor" in the nineteenth century was "dependent upon government subsidies, tariffs, and other interventions; it was far from liberal laissez-faire."[17] Free enterprise was not a synonym for business firms but rather a characteristic of citizens, one necessarily abetted by state policy.

In antebellum America, the words *free enterprise* also characterized businesses that relied upon free rather than slave labor, which northern advocates saw as a morally and economically superior "system." For abolitionists, in particular those involved with the "free produce" movement that aimed to promote stores that eschewed goods made by slave labor, "free enterprise," businesses that relied upon free labor, contrasted with "slave enterprise." Antislavery activists condemned a government that served to "prostrate free enterprize of the country at the foot of the slave power," as a Vermont newspaper asserted in 1845.[18]

Free enterprise also became synonymous with free trade arguments, which similarly celebrated an economy "unshackled by the thousand barriers to free enterprise" produced by "unnecessary restrictions on trade."[19] This was a new meaning that posited government, at least in the form of import taxes, as an obstacle to the freeing of enterprise. As the *New York Tribune* editorialized in 1845, "The course of free enterprise and individual energy by which alone the prosperity of the whole People can be enhanced, are crushed beneath the weight" of the tariff.[20] In answer to the question "What is free enterprise?" a Detroit editor described it as "enterprise without restriction, without tariff." He called for the removal of "every artificial restriction" to enterprise.[21]

Long after the Civil War, "free enterprise" continued to be described as an attribute of individuals and communities. In 1880, a writer attributed "American ingenuity" to "free speech, free thought, free enterprise, and free schools." This list evoked the "free soil, free labor, free men" mantra of the early Republican Party.[22] Through the end of the nineteenth century, then, Americans understood free enterprise as a characteristic of a hard-working, democratic, free laboring nation benefiting from government policies that nurtured these attributes. A look at Republican Party presidential platforms before the New Deal gives us a sense of the shift in meaning that subsequently occurred. In 1896, the Republican platform accused the Democrats of "halting enterprise" and, as late as 1920, it criticized taxation policies that "needlessly repress enterprise and thrift." After the New Deal, as we will see, the GOP invoked the term as a noun, another way of describing an economic system rooted in the primacy of the business corporation and the weakness of the regulatory state.[23]

The "Effort to Throttle Free Enterprise"

The Progressive Era marked a liminal moment in free enterprise discourse, the period during which the idea of "free labor" as a dominant political ideology waned but before the emergence of the modern conception of free enterprise. Although the term maintained many of its older significations, important changes in the meaning of free enterprise began in this period. In the decades after the period ended, a large number of former Progressives formed a key contingent opposing the New Deal on the grounds that it violated free enterprise principles.

Progressives had an ambivalent attitude toward business. In response to the unregulated and violent capitalism of the Gilded Age, they sought to ensure the survival of American democracy by limiting the power of private economic groups. While they feared that business could "corrupt politics," they also posited that businessmen were especially suited to make government more effective and efficient. Even as they condemned the practices of Standard Oil, as Ida Tarbell's popular muckraking articles in *McClure's* did, they celebrated the well-run business as a model for good governance. Moreover, business leaders shaped and staffed the new government offices responsible for regulation.[24]

Even those Progressives who promoted regulation of business in the interest of the public good reconceived the nature of the business firm in ways that ultimately contributed to a redefinition of free enterprise. In a speech before the Economic Club of New York at the Hotel Astor during his campaign for the presidency in 1912, Woodrow Wilson emphasized that circumstances "have put the question of the relation between politics and business before every other question." While they might have had different answers, his successors agreed that the relationship between business and politics was the crucial question. Over time, many Progressives came to see the government as the enemy and business as the engine of freedom.[25]

By the time Wilson became president in 1913, the balancing act between criticism and emulation of business was already well under way. Wilson understood that government needed to employ appropriate regulations to suit a dynamic economic world in which big business had become a formidable power and to which traditional limited government responses were no longer effective.[26] But Wilson also called for the "emancipation of the rank and file of business men in this country . . . from irresponsible, central Government" and condemned "every effort to throttle free enterprise and break down the initiative of the average man."[27] Wilson's framing of the "rank and file" businessperson, rather than the corporation, as the norm and the state as the throttler of the ambitions of ordinary people anticipated two key elements of anti–New Deal free enterprise discourse.

In 1912, after Wilson was elected but before he took office, he told the American people, "We're all caught in a great economic system that is heartless." But

Wilson's message was not targeted primarily at the little person. Indeed, Wilson aimed throughout this speech to assuage the fear of those he called "some of the biggest men in the US, in the field of commerce and manufacture," who "are afraid of something." The president-elect expressed concern that "American industry is not free, American enterprise is not free" and, while he sympathized with "the man with little capital" who "finds it more and more impossible to compete with the big fellow, because our laws do not prevent the strong from crushing the weak," what resonated in his speech was the claim that American business and enterprise were constrained and unfree. Presaging future free enterprise rhetoric, Wilson compared powerful corporations to a person (the "big fellow"), rather than placing them in a different category from ordinary people.[28] Wilson made similar remarks in his nomination speech about the need to make the "business system more free, more equitable, more open to ordinary men, practicable to live under, tolerable to work under." This critique of a business system that made people unfree could be read as a denunciation of a system that hindered business. Wilson left ambiguous whether the flaws of the "business system" were internal, external, or some combination of the two.[29]

During the 1912 presidential campaign, Wilson's most extensive comments about the relationship among business, government, and freedom came at the annual Jackson dinner, typically an opportunity for Democratic politicians to announce their solidarity with the people. Co-opting and modernizing the founding Republican triplet of "free soil, free labor, free men," Wilson called for the "the promotion of free thought, free action, free enterprise," which he labeled symbols of "the Democratic ideal itself." Wilson's use of "free enterprise" was ambiguous, hinting both at the nineteenth-century idea of an attribute and the modern notion of the autonomous business firm. The candidate pronounced government and business equally victimized by what he called "private control" and claimed that freeing both was his "present political object." While noting that government "had been controlled by those whose power in business was greatest" and that this harmed "the free action of Government," he also claimed that in such a system "the free development of business" was also "impossible." He complained about "small groups of men" who controlled both business and government and unjustly dominated the rest of society.[30]

After Wilson took office, he described his goal as "a battle against monopoly, against control, against the concentration of power in our economic development, against all those things that interfere with absolutely free enterprise."[31]

Business could mobilize these sentiments in its own direction, especially as it employed a new conception of free enterprise against the state. It portrayed itself, consistent with Wilson's framing, as the little man victimized and dominated by the state, reversing the terms of the original Progressive critique.

In the late nineteenth century, business leaders, lobbyists, lawyers, and politicians understood business prerogatives in terms of "liberty of contract," that is, the right of firms to contract individually with employees. Beginning in the Progressive Era, they began to change their frame of reference. Rather than describing freedom of the firm in terms of its relationship with employees, business leaders and politicians began to speak about the primary importance for the firm of autonomy from regulation by the state.

The idea that government should be run like a business eventually became a free enterprise cliché, but it emerged initially in characteristic Progressive wrestling with the relationship between justice and efficiency. Populist leader Charles Macune wished to see government act like "a business organization for carrying on the public business in a common sense, businesslike manner."[32] Although often corrupt, Macune and other Populists believed that honest business methods provided resources that could rescue politics.[33] An admiring profile in 1904 of the new Republican mayor of Baltimore, E. Clay Timanus, noted that as a "business man," he "naturally applies business principles to his administration."[34] Progressives praised the replacement of cronyism and graft with one of their favored principles, "efficiency," which many of them associated, above all, with the business firm.[35] Commentators also praised the way in which the commission form of government that was widely adopted during this period was leading many municipal governments to be run "like a business office."[36] The key question of the age was how to "eliminate politics" from governing, according to the *Hartford Courant* in 1909, which posited as a solution the effort to conduct urban government "on business principles."[37] When William Howard Taft became president, the *Wall Street Journal* expressed hope that he would administer the federal government "upon something more nearly like a business basis."[38] Although Progressives regularly condemned the illegal and immoral doings of many corporations and individual leaders, many of them sought the solution for sclerotic and corrupt government in the efficiency of the modern business firm.

This attitude not only outlasted the Progressive Era but accelerated after the Great War. In 1920, the Illinois governor, Frank O. Lowden, emphasized the "business of government" as "the great incisive issue" of the day. He promised to "modernize Uncle Sam's machinery, to scrap the ramshackle methods which have grown up haphazard and to put the government's business on a sound, up-to-date basis—in other words, to apply to the government's business the methods which in the last hundred years have revolutionized private enterprise."[39] In this view, "private enterprise" was a model for public enterprise to emulate, rather than an out-of-control power to regulate.

In the 1920s, many of the most praised governmental leaders were those who had experience in applying business methods. Referring to Leonard Wood's experience as governor-general of Cuba, Governor Henry Allen of Kansas, candidate for the Republican nomination for the presidency, said in 1920: "He taught us that Government should be run like a business." Allen feared that unless domestic politicians learned the lessons that Wood applied in Cuba, "business may come to be run like Government," an inversion that remained the nightmare of critics (who often single out the Post Office) well into the twenty-first century.[40] Two years later, as he left his position as the first director of the Bureau of the Budget, Charles Dawes claimed, "The government can be run not only as economically as a private business but more economically than a private business." While in government, Dawes hired successful business leaders to reorganize their departments according to "business methods." Dawes gave credit to President Harding for being "determined to overhaul the antiquated government machinery, eliminate wastefulness, and save the taxpayers billions of dollars." Dawes was praised for cutting "red tape" with "ruthless efficiency," a project that he continued as Calvin Coolidge's vice president from 1925 to 1929.[41]

Business leaders complained about the dangers of government in business, and they emphasized the value of bringing what Julius H. Barnes, the president of the U.S. Chamber of Commerce, called "business judgement" into the world of politics.[42] Moreover, in an enduring formulation that marked an inversion of Progressive Era thinking, they described government as the domain of the elite and powerful and business as the home of ordinary men and women. Very often they represented the bureaucrat as the symbol of out-of-touch, overweening elitism. By contrast, they described the small businessman—in the person of the peanut vendor, "the boot black, the corner grocer"—as the very soul of the nation.[43] This entrepreneur needed minimal government to protect the rules of fair trade but otherwise the market should be allowed to operate in as much freedom as possible. The populist celebration of ordinary Americans was increasingly applied to the business firm, which replaced the ordinary farmer or worker as the carrier of virtuous producerist values.

Progressives generally treated state power and corporate power as dual threats. Through their ambiguous language, however, they opened the possibility that government represented the more enduring and formidable threat to human freedom. In the 1920s, with the Progressive Era over and business once again as dominant as it was in the Gilded Age, the critique of government continued apace. By 1934, it had become common for free enterprisers to denounce "the tendency of government to hem in the individual, to restrict his liberty of action and expression of initiative," while remaining silent about the problem of business corruption and power, which had only decades earlier been at the top of the nation's political agenda.[44]

"Business Is the Very Essence and Mainspring of Modern Life"

Although the modern idea of "free enterprise" coalesced in opposition to the New Deal, the reformulation built on Progressive fears of government as a force for domination began in the 1920s, well before the onset of the Great Depression. In this period, free enterprise began its migration from an attribute (the "spirit" of "free enterprise") to a noun (the "free enterprise system"). Far from an unchanging custom—"the traditional American concept of free enterprise," as it was often described—this version of free enterprise was a dramatically new one.[45] Notwithstanding its claims to tradition, the modern conception of free enterprise emerged in a particular historical moment and, to a remarkable degree, the concerns of business at that time set the terms of free enterprise discourse.

One important element of this new conception was the view that government and free enterprise were mortal enemies rather than close allies. Another was a new understanding of free enterprise as a synonym for business and an unencumbered market, what came to be popularized in the post–World War II years as the "free market." As early as 1923, the National Association of Manufacturers recognized that the "regulation of free enterprise"—an early formulation equating the concept with business itself—was "justified by necessity when for the common good," but this group also condemned what it deemed the bigger problem of overregulation that was harmful to the public.[46] In 1920, a Scranton newspaper described the need to curb the "incubus" and complexity of federal taxes in order "to free enterprise from the exasperating influences by which it is hampered under current conditions."[47] Here the newspaper conceived of "enterprise" as the collective business community that needed freeing from overregulation by greedy government, rather than as a communal spirit that was abetted by state action.

In the 1920s, advocates began to describe free enterprise as a system of business autonomy that worked automatically and efficiently, but only if the government played a limited role in aiding, rather than restricting, the firm. No longer understanding markets as creations of the state, free enterprisers began to treat them as autonomous, miraculous, and the best guide not only to economic efficiency but also political freedom. Benjamin Anderson, a Chase Manhattan economist, claimed that the heavy hand of government "would pervert and distort the price mechanism and the market machinery, which under a system of free enterprise and private property work to create an industrial balance."[48] Anderson's "system of free enterprise" is one of the first references to *free enterprise* as a noun, and one of the first uses of the wording "free enterprise system" that became standard in the 1930s. Using language that became common in the postwar years, the conservative *Chicago Tribune* columnist Scrutator hailed in 1925 what he called the "genius of enterprise" precisely as its ability to catalyze the "automatic regulation of the price system," as opposed to the "juridical processes" of the state, which hampered it.[49] Rather than government regulation being necessary to prevent domination, a growing number of free enterprisers now dismissed it as not only unnecessary but as a cause of domination itself, with its dangerous "prying into private business" as a *Lancaster Eagle* columnist wrote, that portended an assault on freedom writ large. The price mechanism, on the other hand, meant not just freedom from stifling regulation but freedom itself. Foreshadowing the future of free enterprise rhetoric, the *Lancaster Eagle* columnist also described markets as natural, operating automatically and independently, and the state as artificial, operating by "prying," or entering into areas where it did not belong.[50] Free enterprisers thus celebrated actions in the market as the essence of political freedom, framing each such action as a "vote" that was far more effective—more frequent, more responsive, more efficient— than the traditional franchise.[51]

Free enterprise was reborn at a time of business confidence and political power. The language that matured in opposition to FDR first developed during the era of Calvin Coolidge and Herbert Hoover, a time when the popular chronicler of business James Truslow Adams observed that "the business man finds himself the dominant power in the life of the nation," which he called "a situation unique in history." In his best-selling book of 1929, Adams labeled the moment "our business civilization."[52] The free enterprise vocabulary was thus as central to the business offensive of the 1920s as it was to the business counteroffensive of the New Deal era.

Business was in the saddle in the 1920s, but it still felt uneasy. "The chief business of the American people is business," Coolidge famously announced in 1925.[53] Most sectors of the economy flourished and journalists looked upon business leaders like Henry Ford as prophets of modernity. Progressivism, with its suspicion of business, had been thoroughly renounced in the 1920 presidential election. Moreover, the wartime repression of the Left and the labor movement as well as disillusionment with the outcome of the Russian Revolution all weakened alternatives to the popular celebration of business leaders as folk heroes.[54]

At the same time, satirists and writers mocked business culture. No man "stood more staunchly for common sense and enterprise than good old George" Babbitt, the protagonist of Sinclair Lewis's 1922 satiric novel of modern business.[55] This combination of power and mockery bequeathed to business leaders and lobbyists a unique combination of attitudes that they maintained throughout the free enterprise era: power and entitlement coupled with defensiveness and the feeling of being outsiders, underdogs, victims. The discourse born in the 1920s reflected this simultaneously aggressive and aggrieved stance and became characteristic first of free enterprise discourse and, eventually of conservatism. Writing for the magazine of the U.S. Chamber of Commerce in 1925, journalist Harper Leech, who had been public relations director for Harding's Railroad Labor Board, added another important element that was to remain a distinguishing characteristic of free enterprise discourse: the representation of business leaders as besieged, underappreciated, and in need of aggressive tactics to defend and explain themselves. After noting with the boastful tone in keeping with the spirit of the era that "a system of comparatively free enterprise has done more for humanity in one century and a half than all the intellectual ancestors of our Babbitt-haters accomplished in forty centuries before," Leech complained that business leaders were too "apologetic" and "are ashamed to live like capitalists." Rather than being passive and embarrassed, he counseled, business should "quit taking insult 'lying down.'" Free enterprise needed to act aggressively, to "wield permanently" the "political influence commensurate with its importance in the social scheme." Like other advocates of business in this period, Leech urged business leaders to "stand together" in the face of literary and cultural denigration.[56]

Business writers of the 1920s, then, celebrated not just the individual entrepreneur or the innovative company but what Adams called "business civilization" as a whole. In 1926, Leech, quoting a British writer, lamented that "what is called capitalism is almost without a literature" (unless one counted the mocking satire of writers like Lewis and Upton Sinclair). The only way to combat what he called the "hostility" to business in the culture industry was to unite under "a regime of free enterprise." This aspirational regime, he believed, would have to be counter-hegemonic since "plain hostility to, or outspoken contempt for, business marks a large amount of our fiction, our drama and our moving pictures." Business needed to respond to the "constant sniping of humor and sarcasm" because the hostility "may turn out to be something worth worrying about." There was a need to align the culture with the economy, and free enterprise could lead the way, Leech suggested.[57] Depicting business leaders as besieged underdogs has been a characteristic of free enterprise discourse ever since, but it was a particularly remarkable assessment in the "Roaring Twenties," when three successive presidential elections resulted in business-friendly presidents. Leech's conception of business as lacking power remained central to free enterprise discourse in the New Deal era. In this vision, business was under either implicit or explicit attack and needed to correct for its inherent passivity by responding aggressively and immediately. Crucially, it needed to do so not just in economic terms but in the arena of culture.

Business leaders and politicians took the lead in reconceiving free enterprise. But it was an uneven process, as older ideas of free enterprise commingled with new ones throughout the decade. As they lurched toward what one writer in 1925 called the "the economic order of free enterprise," business champions were ambiguous about the precise composition of that order.[58] On the campaign trail in 1928, for example, Herbert Hoover, who had been the highly successful secretary of commerce under Warren Harding and Coolidge, highlighted the importance of "individual enterprise" and spoke, in terms that would have been familiar to an antebellum audience, of the need to "unshackle initiative and free the spirit of American enterprise." In the next sentence, however, Hoover proposed a program to achieve these ends that would have made little sense to a first-generation Republican, calling for liberation from "excessive expenditures and crippling taxation."[59] Government, in this new view, imprisoned rather than freed enterprise.

Even before the full range of ideas associated with free enterprise became fully explicit in the 1930s, one striking change became notable immediately after the close of World War I, the idea that it was, among other things, a synonym for the business community. Advocates of this new vision, building on the Progressive legacy, began to see business as an interest group in a pluralistic society in need of organization. This thinking accelerated in the 1930s when the monumental growth of the labor movement became a sort of negative role model for business. Calling for the need for "one big union for business" in a 1938 article for the Chamber of Commerce magazine, Luther Bell, a lobbyist for the aeronautical industry, proclaimed that the "preservation of free enterprise calls for a type of action that requires far greater unity among business interests than we have yet achieved." Notwithstanding the lionization of Ford and other celebrity business titans, many business lobbyists believed that the United States had evolved beyond the era of the charismatic inventor or company president. "The successful leader today is no Napoleon of Commerce," as Bell wrote. "The logic of the situation" calls for a "more closely-knit congress of American industry, trade, commerce, agriculture, and finance."[60]

There was also a change in the expectations of government, which was increasingly seen as an undermining rival rather than a symbiotic promoter of free enterprise. Government's task was to promote "liberty of free enterprise," which now meant the autonomy of business from government constraint, austerity, and an identification of business well-being with the public good.[61] Advocates of this new conception of free enterprise promoted a new view of the government as a neutral "umpire." In 1935, Bainbridge Colby, a founder of the Progressive Party who had been, briefly, Woodrow Wilson's secretary of state but had developed, like many former Progressives, an animus to the New Deal, claimed that his former boss believed that the federal state should be an "umpire, never a master."[62] (Similarly, after calling in 1940 for "free enterprise with reasonable government umpiring," NAM's H. W. Prentis reminded these referees that they don't "get into the game" themselves.)[63] Government had an obligation to "preserve decency" and "prevent violence" but beyond these functions, it should support business, said Frank Knox, the Republican vice presidential candidate in 1936, another former Progressive. He held that the free enterprise system—the "richest, happiest, and kindest social order the world has ever known"—depended upon the autonomy of entrepreneurs from the state apparatus.[64] Although Colby, Knox, and most other ex-Progressive advocates of free enterprise disclaimed laissez-faire, they placed strict limits on the acceptable role of government in a democratic society. Government should limit itself to "interpreting the rules of the game" rather than "assuming a dictation position over either business or labor," said Edward A. Hayes, a national commander of the American Legion and Republican candidate for governor of Illinois, in 1939.[65] In this view, as expressed by Wendell Willkie, the Republican presidential candidate in 1940, under "our old system of free enterprise," government was a "servant" rather than a "master."[66] In reality, the "old system" that Willkie valorized was the product not of the distant past but of the 1920s.

If the key figures in an era that valorized independent proprietorship were the free laborer, the independent proprietor, and/or the heroic inventor (often assumed to be one and the same), the 1920s placed business civilization on a pedestal and demanded freedom for the firm. John Corbin's 1921 profile of Hoover, the new secretary of commerce, highlighted these "tantalizing" new ideas about business that had thus far, he believed, "only trickled" to the public. Among them was the recognition that "business is the very essence and mainspring of modern life." Hoover, who had performed heroically as head of the U.S. Food Administration during World War I, possessed precisely the kind of business savvy needed to make government effective. Corbin asked, "Why, then, should we make a virtue of taking business out of politics and politics out of business?"[67] Although Hoover did not employ the phrase *free enterprise* at this date, he did articulate many of the ideas that characterized his post-presidential career as a critic of the New Deal order.

The first post–Progressive Era president, Warren G. Harding, condemned what he took to be the business-bashing ethos of that earlier period. Indeed, the essence of the "normalcy" that he promoted meant the cessation and reversal of the Progressive war on business. "We have seen during nearly eight years, indeed, a nearly reckless governmental obstructing and harassing of business" that would lead, he feared, to "business stagnancy." Business, Harding averred, was not a "selfish privilege-seeking monster," and anyone who held this view (not uncommon in the previous decades) could be dismissed as an "agitator." Rather than an all-powerful bloc, he described what he called "enterprise"—what soon came to be labeled "free enterprise"—as a collection of individual entrepreneurs. "Business in America is not big business," he declared, in a refrain often repeated by free enterprise advocates ever since. "It is little businesses—all the units of production, even the single machine in the shop and the farm and the home," which made up the "magnificent tapestry" of American civilization. Minimizing the power of the business firm by erasing the differences of scale between a corporation and a mom-and-pop store became a characteristic of free enterprise language, especially popular among representatives of the large firms in the Chamber of Commerce and elsewhere. Finally, Harding called for "less government in business and more business in government," beginning the free enterprise tradition of ranking business above government rather than viewing them as coequals, each with an important and unique role.[68]

The business offensive of the 1920s can be understood as part of a broader backlash against the political Left at home and abroad. With labor weakened, the Socialist Party diminished, and Progressivism exhausted, business leaders and conservative politicians proclaimed capitalism "triumphant" and held out the unencumbered businessman as the exemplar of the new era.[69] As president, Calvin Coolidge, like Harding, articulated a post-Progressive vision that valorized business at the expense of government. "I believe in the American system of individual enterprise," he claimed, "and I am opposed to any general extension of Government ownership and control." That, along with exercising "economy" in public spending, was what Coolidge called "Common Sense in Government." In making lax regulation, lower taxes, and government austerity characteristic of "common sense," Coolidge foreshadowed an influential way of thinking about this new not-yet-named system of free enterprise as a form of customary wisdom.

Another element added in the 1920s was the celebration of business profits as not merely necessary but virtuous. The popular economic journalists William Trufant Foster and Waddill Catchings, early adopters of the phrase *free enterprise* in what came to be its modern sense, similarly praised business civilization and profits as "the pulsating force that drives the life-sustaining blood to every part of the economic body. The blood is money."[70] The free market economist Milton Friedman's claim in 1970 that "the social responsibility of business is to increase its profits" may have been controversial but it was hardly original.[71]

Along with the celebration of profits, free enterprise advocates in the 1920s developed another element that became standard: an attack on organized labor. Business must "learn to stand together," Harper Leech wrote in 1925, "to meet organized labor with organized attack."[72] This was an important formulation and marked a break from the nineteenth-century discourse of free labor. Rather than celebrating "free labor" as their Republican ancestors had done in the age of Lincoln, the advocates of business free enterprise framed trade unionism as an enemy potentially as dangerous as the modern bureaucratic state itself. Figuring business in individualistic terms even as it strived for collective organization, free enterprisers condemned trade unions and the state as powerful collective forces—joined during the Cold War by international communism—that served to limit individual freedom.

The conservative Democratic governor of Maryland Albert C. Ritchie became the first politician to put forward a version of free enterprise that became the norm by the mid-1930s. Speaking at the 1926 U.S. Chamber of Commerce meeting, he declared, "Business should be free to work out its own destiny." Ritchie condemned "anything that chills the free enterprise out of business," a formulation that showed that the term had not totally transformed meaning, since it took free enterprise to be a characteristic of business rather than business itself, whereas a later generation would view them as synonymous. At the same time, his anti-government perspective foretold future free enterprise discourse. "Too much government," he claimed, constrained business creativity, which was the engine not only of economic growth but of social progress. It was also a problem because government was uniquely dangerous, "the most imperfect of human institutions." This was a new view positing that "the antagonism between business and government" was one-sided, with government threats to business the main danger.[73] Ritchie and others focused very little on the business threat to government, a topic that had been a major concern of the Progressives.

Criticism of government functionaries became central to anti–New Deal politics, but this too was foreshadowed when in 1931 the *Chicago Tribune* identified the problem "of expanding bureaucracy." "Shall we steadily expand the role of government in American life?" asked the *Tribune* editorialist rhetorically. The answer was no because bureaucracy would only "further narrow the limits of free enterprise." The paper called for "resistance" to the dangerous tendency "for solving all our problems by putting them in the hands of government agencies."[74] In this passage, we can glimpse the beginning of a modern language of free enterprise understood as the aggressive defense of American business values arrayed against a paternalistic and overempowered government understood as the enemy of individual liberty.

"The Enemy Now Is Regimentation Attempted by the Government"

Former Progressives played a major role in reinventing free enterprise in the 1920s and 1930s. They increasingly limited their fears of concentrated power to government (and organized labor) and largely abandoned their prior concern with the dangers of corporate power. "I am on the same side now that I was back in the old Colliers days," wrote Mark Sullivan, journalist and author, in a 1935 letter to Albert Shaw explaining his anti-Roosevelt posture. Rather than seeing a contradiction between his Progressivism and his anti–New Dealism, he described continuity. "The fight was for individualism then and it is for individualism now." Whereas at one time "the enemy was regimentation attempted by big business," Sullivan wrote, "the enemy now is regimentation attempted by the government."[75] "Some of us look back with satisfaction upon the valiant men who, in the Congress of three decades ago, fought vigorously against the malpractices and threats of big business," wrote Republican Party leader and former president of the University of Wisconsin Glenn Frank in 1939. Frank concluded that, at the present moment, "the gravest danger lies" with "big government." "Economic autocracy" was preferable to "political autocracy," Frank averred. While big government as a countervailing power to big business "sounds plausible," in practice it would mean "the end of the rights of man."[76] Implied in this defense of one kind of "autocracy" was that even unconstrained business power was a friend of the people.

Other Progressives also flipped their views on the relationship between government and business. In 1907, for example, Senator Albert J. Beveridge (R-IN) celebrated the necessity of a strong national government. The individual states "acting separately could not end slavery," he noted, and it also would take a powerful federal government to "end the piracies of capital in 1907." Without a strong government, "the buccaneers of business" would run rampant. Recalling the nineteenth-century conception of the government's role in making free enterprise possible, Beveridge highlighted the importance of the national government in promoting internal improvements, regulating food and drugs, preserving forests, and ending child labor. A robust government would serve to "free the hands of the American people and not to shackle them" and would work for the "benefit of the enormous majority of all business men who are not buccaneers."[77]

Within two decades, Beveridge, like many other former Progressives, had totally reversed his views. In a speech to the Sons of the Revolution's annual dinner in Boston in June 1923, Beveridge condemned the state as an enemy rather than an accomplice of freedom and labeled his previous confidence in government a "fatal error." "America would be better off as a country and Americans happier and more prosperous as a people," he proclaimed, in language that Ronald Reagan was to echo almost precisely half a century later, "if half of our Government boards, bureaus and commissions were abolished, hundreds of thousands of our Government officials, agents and employees were discharged and two-thirds of our Government regulations, restrictions and inhibitions were removed." Highlighting the dangers of bureaucracy and an expanding mission of government, Beveridge applauded the "spirit of revolt" that, he claimed, was "spreading against governmental regimentation of everybody and everything." Another portent of the future of free enterprise discourse came in the senator's call for a return to "the plane of common sense," which he opposed to the "faddists and experimenters" in government.[78] For Beveridge, as for many other former champions of a strong state, a concern with out-of-control government had displaced a fear of piratical capitalists as the new common sense.

Looking for retroactive support from the leading Progressive icon, in 1945 John Temple Graves, a southern newspaper editor, described Woodrow Wilson as the architect of modern free enterprise. Wilson rejected a "superstate" in either domestic or foreign policy, Graves said. Wilson's "New Freedom was a freedom of men, business and regions to compete on an equal basis, with government umpiring." For Graves the lesson of Progressivism was that men and business ranked above the state, whose only job was to quietly referee but not to insert itself into the economy.[79]

It is notable that the notoriously anti–New Deal 1936 Republican ticket, Alf Landon and Frank Knox, consisted of two former Progressives. Knox, the Republican vice presidential nominee in 1936, described his views as consistent with the Progressivism he had championed as a young journalist and politician. His 1936 campaign biography is laced with affirmations of his lifelong commitment to the cause. A chapter called "Knox—Progressive" noted that he "has always prided himself on being a progressive." Indeed, he invoked his Progressive roots to condemn "the hidden menace in the New Deal." In August 1933, barely after the completion of the first "hundred days" of the Roosevelt administration, which were widely seen as rescuing American capitalism, Knox demanded in a front-page editorial a massive reduction in government so as "to create conditions under which confidence can be restored and private initiative and enterprise given a chance to function."[80] By this time, the language of the state as an umpire, not an actor, a servant, not a master, a subordinate, not a ruler of business, had become commonplace.

Republicans had constituted the majority of the Progressive movement and many of them, like Herbert Hoover, later compared the battle against the New Deal with the Civil War fight against slavery—and themselves with Abraham Lincoln. The binary choice between "Lincoln's Republic or New Deal dictatorship" (in the Republican senator Robert A. Taft's words) was for many of them a battle for the preservation of free enterprise.[81] "Whatever the New Deal system is, it is certain that it did not come from Abraham Lincoln," proclaimed Hoover. Claiming continuity with the Republican Party during the era of the Civil War and the Progressive movement during the battle against corruption, advocates of the new sense of free enterprise sought the sanction of America's venerated moral and political traditions, including the free labor system. This enabled them to claim the mantle of custom even as they embraced a radically new notion of free enterprise.

No one in the business world did more to modernize free enterprise discourse prior to the New Deal than Merle Thorpe, the longtime editor of the Chamber of Commerce magazine, the *Nation's Business*. After his death in 1955, he was remembered, accurately, as the "consistent voice of embattled free enterprise," and he was one of the business leaders in the 1920s who crafted that embattled voice and transformed "free enterprise" into a thing, a "system," as it began to be called.[82] Thorpe set the template for modern free enterprise discourse in a series of articles, "Our Vanishing Economic Freedom," published in the *Saturday Evening Post* in 1931, well after the Great Depression began but more than a year before the election that brought Franklin Roosevelt to power. In this series, Thorpe took his talking points from the specialized readership of the *Nation's Business* to a national audience. In spite of what seemed to be bad timing for such an argument about the virtues of autonomous business and weakened government, precisely the conditions that many Americans saw as the cause of the Great Depression, Thorpe directed his ire at the state. His diagnosis of the many dangers of the growth of government—bureaucracy, paternalism, spending run amuck, planning versus freedom—became the standard lines of attack of free enterprisers through the rest of the century.[83]

Thorpe believed that there had been a recent and abrupt departure from what he called the "original purposes of government," which he defined in the typically narrow terms of the 1920s business community. "We have added a thousand ungainly leans-tos" to the "simple edifice" of traditional American government, Thorpe said. With this growth in the state came increasing taxes and regulation that served to limit "the area left to private enterprise." As a result, the "elbow room" for business was "perceptibly shrinking." Thorpe portrayed a zero-sum game in which the strengthening of government inevitably meant the weakening of business. Needless to say, he did not view the opposite to be true; indeed, he demanded a world in which growing business power left a smaller "area" to government. Business autonomy, of which "the first Americans made much as a national heritage," had been "preempted for another enterprise— government." What Thorpe called "private enterprise" had, he said, "built up the greatest economic commonwealth the world has ever seen." But business, he said at what was nearly the trough of the Great Depression, was now "outrun" by what he called "public enterprise."

Critiquing the metastasizing state in the era of Herbert Hoover—who later, for his part, criticized the rampant statism of the New Deal—Thorpe claimed that "so stupendous has become the burden it lays upon productive enterprise, so widely has it extended its ramifications into every field of activity, that it has paved the way for the imminent question of whether private enterprise is to survive or give ground entirely to the flowing tide of public administration." To Thorpe, the question was existential, the very survival of the system of business enterprise that had been around for 150 years, and time was short: "the need of making a decision is nearer at hand than we suspect." Thorpe's dire and urgent language became characteristic of free enterprise language and politics during the era of the New Deal and beyond. "Either state enterprise must give ground or private enterprise must succumb," he wrote. "The parting of the ways seems to have been reached."[84] Such binary framing preempted any discussion of a proper role for the state (even a "businesslike" one) or for adjusting policies of regulation. By casting the state as an enemy of business, Thorpe proposed a policy of complete opposition, and he set the terms for future conservative interpretations of the government as, if not the only cause of the Great Depression, a principal extender of it, as reflected in the Republican congressman Mike Pence's comment, shortly after the economic meltdown of 2007, that "it was the spending and taxing policies of 1932 and 1936 that exacerbated the situation."[85] The characteristics of government, in Thorpe's telling, were not just an obstacle to business but a threat to liberty. Allying business with American freedom and positioning the state against that freedom were enduringly important elements of Thorpe's claims.

By pronouncing a rupture with contemporary trends and calling for a return to traditional values, Thorpe's novel free enterprise vision benefited from its association with custom. Conversely, he delegitimized what came to be called "statism" as a new and dangerous force that undermined not just business but liberty. Ultimately, the cost of public enterprise statism, Thorpe argued, was the weakening of "political freedom." By linking the autonomy of enterprise with freedom itself and by calling government action the enemy of both, Thorpe installed the key elements of free enterprise discourse. When the New Deal began, its opponents turned increasingly to this language, which served as an alternative to the New Deal order until, in the age of Reagan, free enterprise language and logic began to overtake it.

Although he didn't use the words "free enterprise" in this series of articles, Thorpe presciently laid out many of the defining elements of what became in the next decade a widely used language of opposition to the New Deal. In a book coauthored with James M. Beck in 1936—by which time "free enterprise" had become a commonly employed weapon in the war against the New Deal—he further developed the idea that America had always been a free enterprise society. The Founding Fathers, they suggested, were free enterprisers, not essentially different from contemporary critics of the New Deal in their hatred of "despotic government." They were, they wrote, "capitalists and business men" who "devised a plan of government that would protect and promote the capitalistic system." Rather than viewing them as virtuous farmers, they were, they said, more accurately understood as representing "the 'Wall Street' of their day." For Thorpe and Beck, overweening government challenged what they called "the spirit of free enterprise," which entailed "the wherewithal to take risks" and "permitted the American nation to dare to speculate, as no other nation could dare to do." The weakening of this spirit resulted in a dangerous "decay of American individualism."[86]

Thorpe and Beck, then, imparted a radically new meaning to the idea of free enterprise even as they proclaimed it to be a long-standing, fundamental, and largely unchanging American custom. Yet they did draw on custom as they modified the old political language of the "free labor system," especially by carrying forward the binary view that slavery and freedom could not long coexist. The spirit of "free enterprise" had been central to that free labor vision. Along with many others in the early twentieth century, Thorpe and Beck turned free enterprise, now usually understood as a synonym for both the business community and the freedom-producing world of market relations only minimally connected to the "artificial" schemes of bureaucratic statists, into a very different kind of system, but one that nonetheless had the sanction of tradition.[87]

Free enterprise, as it came to be understood in the mid-twentieth century, was built by the simultaneous rebranding of an already existing multivalent term, by the flattening of its complex history and, above all, by repetition. To speak of the invention of free enterprise in the early twentieth century, then, is to challenge both the assumption that it was invented by anti–New Dealers in the 1930s as well as the view that the phrase is simply "traditional," and to recognize that the same term meant something different in the nineteenth century than it did in the twentieth. It is to the construction of the dominant modern meaning that we next turn, when free enterprise emerged in its most enduring form in opposition to the New Deal.

3

Free Enterprise versus the New Deal Order

THE HISTORY OUTLINED IN THIS BOOK helps explain an incident that went viral on the Internet in 2015. An Okanogan, Washington, man, wearing a T-shirt reading, "Lower Taxes + Less Government = More Freedom," thanked a group of firefighters for saving his home. The men and women who did so, however, were government workers, employed by many different federal and state agencies carrying out emergency response efforts in the area.[1] The template for this pattern of vocal ideological hostility to the welfare state combined with an appreciation for its benefits was laid in the 1930s. In that era, proponents of *free enterprise,* an old term that had recently taken on new significations, employed that phrase to attack the New Deal, introducing an enduring political and emotional vocabulary that continues to dominate our civic life well into the twenty-first century. Since the 1930s, *free enterprise* has served as shorthand for opposition to the welfare state in whatever form it existed or threatened to become.

For more than eighty years, the idea of free enterprise, despite being ill defined, tussled with the New Deal order, animating the central tension of modern political culture in the United States. The words *free enterprise* came to stand for the fear of overweening government, the dangers of excessive public spending, and the threat of "red tape" and bureaucratization that marked most debates about the expansion of the welfare and regulatory state. The free enterprise vision proved to be an extraordinarily compelling alternative. An examination of the success of free enterprisers reveals the fierce and often effective challenges that the New Deal faced from the very beginning. Although the opposition took many forms, the call for "free enterprise" was a common denominator of most criticism, and under this rubric, critics shaped conceptions of the proper role of government even during the acme of the New Deal. The belief that "the traditional free enterprise philosophy" and New Dealism "are locked in a death struggle," as a Colorado politician said in 1956, was widely shared and framed how many Americans thought about the meaning of freedom for several generations.[2]

During the New Deal years, a new conception of free enterprise, less than a decade old, was invented as an American custom. Anti-Rooseveltians went to great lengths to construct a tradition from which they claimed the New Deal radically diverged, backdating the idea many decades or even centuries. New York congressman Bertram Snell asserted in 1935, "America has always been the land of free enterprise."[3] Anachronistically reading the presidential heroes recently carved into Mt. Rushmore, a *Los Angeles Times* columnist proclaimed it "inconceivable that either Washington or Lincoln" would have stood for "the destruction or curbing of free enterprise by giving government autocratic power over trade and industry."[4] Pushing the story even further back in time, others described Christopher Columbus, the "Puritans of New England," and the "Cavaliers of Virginia and Maryland" as free enterprisers.[5]

Although the modern free enterprise political vision emerged shortly before the election of Franklin D. Roosevelt in 1932, it coalesced in opposition to the "New Deal order" that his presidency initiated, and the term was widely popularized in this period.[6] Just as the New Deal coalition was a jerry-rigged, often tense union of disparate groups with competing and overlapping interests, what we can call the "free enterprise coalition" also consisted of diverse groups. If the New Deal coalition included African Americans, white southerners, and a large number of working-class "ethnics," each of whom had their own distinct interests, those who celebrated free enterprise in opposition to the New Deal included combinations of small businesses represented by the National Association of Manufacturers, the larger firms united in the U.S. Chamber of Commerce, moderate Republicans, conservative Democrats, reactionary newspaper publishers, libertarians, and many others. Although fissures appeared among the advocates of free enterprise, as they did in the "Roosevelt coalition," what stands out is the coherence of the anti–New Deal free enterprise worldview. The success was largely due to the common enemy all of these groups shared, the New Deal, which was the primary target of free enterprise wrath.

While rarely referred to as such, the coalition of anti–New Dealers united under the banner of free enterprise proved, in many ways, a more enduring political bloc than the far more widely discussed "Roosevelt coalition" that dominated politics into the 1960s. In an important sense it also emerged first: the phrase "anti–New Deal coalition" appeared in 1935, long before commentators spoke of the "New Deal coalition." In 1937, the former president Herbert Hoover urged this coalition to form "around ideas and ideals," and "free enterprise" served as shorthand for this set of principles of opposition.[7] Critics understood the New Deal as "a chilling substitute for the former American free enterprise system" that needed to be stemmed and reversed.[8]

What united free enterprisers was a deep suspicion of the New Deal not only as a set of policies but as a dangerous philosophy, on a spectrum with the nefarious forces of fascism and communism that were gaining popularity in Europe in this period. Free enterprise opponents of the New Deal invoked a binary political language in which they figured the New Deal as an incipient form of totalitarianism. Faced with an either/or political choice, the diversity of the free enterprise coalition melted away as members of this group, notwithstanding their differences, united in fierce opposition to the New Deal, which they understood as a threat to liberty. Free enterprise critics of the New Deal spoke in a psychological register of loss and alarm that proved to be perhaps their most consequential political legacy. They called for nothing less than a preemptive counterrevolution, one made necessary by what they took to be the collectivist teleology of the New Deal.

In seeking to define the New Deal as beyond the pale politically, opponents described Franklin D. Roosevelt and his administration as, in the *Baltimore Sun*'s words, dangerously "power loving," updating long-standing republican fears of monarchy and slavery.[9] They labeled the democratically elected president and Congress as power-hungry would-be dictators. "Never before have we seen demagoguery on such a gigantic and dangerous scale as that presented by the New Dealers," said Senator Robert A. Taft in a speech to the Women's National Republican Club in 1936.[10] The same year, another Republican senator called Roosevelt a "New Deal Caesar" who had "ruthlessly attacked" free enterprise.[11] In 1938, Glenn Frank denounced the "fascist program of the New Deal," a phrase that minimized the political differences between the United States and the governments of Germany, Italy, and Japan, with which the country would soon be at war.[12] Referring to the other end of the political spectrum, a 1940 editorial in the *Nation's Business* dismissed a national health insurance proposal as "not essentially different from that conceived by Lenin and Stalin in the Russian Five-Year Plans."[13] Others compared the "government dictation" of the New Deal to slavery.[14] Rather than depicting the New Deal as an outgrowth of democratic processes, they treated "New Deal totalitarianism" as a dictatorial and dangerous imposition.[15]

While statism came in many shapes, from the binary point of view of the anti–New Deal free enterprisers the form it initially took mattered little, since all collectivisms tended inexorably in the same dictatorial direction. It was, as Congressman Richard Nixon said when he announced his candidacy for the Senate in 1949, the "same old Socialist boloney no matter how you slice it." Hoover and other free enterprisers employed "road" metaphors well before Friedrich A. Hayek's 1944 manifesto *The Road to Serfdom* to describe the slippery slope to which the weakening of free enterprise inescapably led. "By stifling progress in a strait-jacket of governmental control, the New Deal has started this nation on the road to totalitarianism," said Dr. Melchior Palyi, an economist, in 1939.[16] Free enterprisers also charted New Deal roads to "chaos" (Herbert Hoover), "dictatorship" and "defeatism" (Thomas E. Dewey), "statism" (former secretary of state James F. Byrnes), and "communism" (H. E. Humphreys, the president of U.S. Rubber).[17]

Employing alarmist rhetoric and depicting freedom when exposed to statism as voluble and evanescent, free enterprise critics of the New Deal feared that the "system" they celebrated was on its last legs. "Is the free enterprise system doomed?" was the subject of a radio roundtable in Chicago in 1943.[18] Advocates of free enterprise pondered the same alarmist question throughout the period of the New Deal order. We "may be the last generation of Americans to receive and cherish the legacy of liberty," warned Indiana congressman Samuel B. Pettengill in 1936.[19] In this view, what became known in the late 1940s as the "welfare state" was merely a transitional moment, and a brief one, on the "road to dictatorship."[20] Such apocalyptic language became a cornerstone of modern conservatism. When Ronald Reagan, the increasingly politicized spokesperson for General Electric, criticized the proposed Medicare plan in 1961, he drew directly from the anti–New Deal rhetorical repertoire: he expressed concern that "our children and our children's children" would learn "what it once was like in America when men were free" only from the fading memories of their grandparents, the last generation to grow up in a regime of free enterprise.[21] Free enterprisers adapted old civic republican concern about the evanescence of democracy by defining state interference in the private economy as the fundamen-

tal source of political corruption and devolution. Over time republican apprehension about the fragility of virtue morphed into fear about the evanescence of
free enterprise.[22]

Facing what they viewed as a dire threat, opponents of the New Deal latched
onto *free enterprise* as the phrase that best expressed their firm opposition. An
examination of Republican presidential platforms provides evidence that this
version of free enterprise was an invention of the long New Deal era. Indeed,
the history of Republican presidential platforms provides insight into the transformation of the term. As we saw in chapter 2, when the phrase appeared on the
GOP platform in the nineteenth century, it referred to the attribute of being enterprising. The term, in the process of transforming, went unmentioned in the
1932 Republican platform. In 1936, several years after it had become familiar
to millions of Americans as the opposite of the New Deal, it emerged front and
center, appearing five times as the central framing device. "Two economic systems are contending for the votes of the American people," declared the Republican Party platform of that year. "One is the historic American system of free
enterprise and the other is called the New Deal, which is a system of centralized
bureaucratic control." In two sentences, the GOP laid out the stark choice of
"systems" that they put before the American people well into the twenty-first
century, one representing tradition and democracy and the other standing for
dangerous forms of statism. The Republican National Committee described
the New Deal as being "in basic conflict" with "American principles of democracy."[23] Thereafter, mentions of "free enterprise" and variants of the phrase
became an obligatory part of the GOP platform. This was so long after the New
Deal itself ended; indeed, the platforms of 1964 (eleven mentions in the year
of Barry Goldwater's candidacy), 1968 (thirteen affirmations), 1984 (a record
twenty-one uses of the term at the height of the "age of Reagan"), and 2012
(seven mentions in the first presidential campaign after the passage of Obamacare, widely seen as a threat to "the proven values of the American free enterprise system") demonstrate the continued staying power of the phrase as a point
of distinction with the post-Roosevelt Democratic Party.[24]

The juxtaposition of free enterprise freedom and New Deal statism was not
confined to GOP platforms but became a regular talking point of Republican
candidates during the era of the New Deal order. "Whatever you choose to call
it," as the Republican presidential candidate Wendell Willkie declared on the
campaign trail in 1940, referring to the New Deal reforms, "these are merely
different names for the same thing—absolute and arbitrary power in the hands

of the government." Willkie's campaign book of that year, an encapsulation of his political philosophy, was one of the first to be titled *Free Enterprise*.[25] That same year, in *The Case against the New Deal*, Thomas E. Dewey claimed that in the coming presidential election for which he was, for a time, the Republican frontrunner, "the American people will be called upon to make the most critical decision they have faced in eighty years." As in the election of 1860, voters faced a fateful choice between two conflicting and opposing systems. Dewey was far from alone in evoking the Civil War era and especially Abraham Lincoln's framing of the fateful choice between competing and opposing economic systems. In a world of momentous binary choices, the only option, according to Dewey, was to revive free enterprise, "the system which made American great."[26]

That the Republican presidential candidates of 1936 through 1948, all understood as political moderates whose views stood "well to the left of the Republican center" and who were regularly denounced by conservative publications like the *Chicago Tribune* for being insufficiently "real Republicans," embraced the dualistic and dire language of free enterprise suggests that on the question of the legitimacy of the New Deal, there was not significant daylight between their views and those of the more extreme conservatives.[27] Self-identified moderate Republicans did not merely mimic a free enterprise rhetoric created by others; they helped invent it. For example, Glenn Frank, university president and magazine editor, was one of the first people to frame the New Deal as a "war on business." In his 1940 campaign, Willkie approvingly repeated Winston Churchill's claim from three years previously, that FDR had waged "a ruthless war on private enterprise."[28] Conceiving of politics as a choice between "the retention of our traditional capitalistic individualism and the collectivism envisaged by the New Deal," the moderates felt they had no option but to cast their lot with the traditions undermined by the New Deal.[29] Most moderate critics of the New Deal fundamentally accepted the view that "the only known alternative to the private free enterprise system is first, collectivism and then, totalitarianism."[30] It was difficult to square moderation with the binary, slippery-slope language of free enterprise that most moderates embraced and amplified.

Free enterprisers described the New Deal as not only unnecessary but counterproductive and dangerous. Employing what the economic historian Albert Hirschman has called the "perversity thesis," they argued that government intervention intended to save the economy only prolonged and deepened rather than ameliorated the Depression.[31] Free enterprisers claimed that reforms that increased the power of the welfare state, however well meaning, were destined to backfire. Attempts to promote security threatened to denude the system of its risk-based core. Planning would undermine the magic of the market, substituting the rule of the few for the wisdom of the consuming masses. Taxes would diminish the initiative and profits on which the system depended. Regulation would choke innovation and add the "bureaucracy" about which they constantly complained. Government spending would crowd out private investment and undermine consumer sovereignty. Any of these things, even in little doses, threatened to undermine the entire system of free enterprise. They saw even the modest precursors to the "welfare state" (a term first popularized in 1949) as "a prelude to the total state."[32]

In the free enterprise worldview, the "collectivism" represented by the New Deal was not something to debate at face value but to suspect "no matter in what form it masquerades," as a group of Republicans said in 1935.[33] Free enterprisers differed as to whether the New Dealers and their supporters were naïve or devious, but they shared a concern about the slippery-slope dangers of statism. "Unless the present trend is reversed," declared the Congress of American Industry in 1935, political devastation would be "the inevitable result."[34] Misleadingly advertising itself as offering a pragmatic effort to save capitalism, American collectivism would inevitably lead to totalitarianism. Planning, according to the *Wall Street Journal* in 1942, is nothing more than an "innocent-seeming invasion of the private enterprise domain by the government."[35] In this context, erring in the direction of limited government regulation and business autonomy seemed the prudent choice to most free enterprisers.

Free enterprisers suspected incremental reform on the theory that, as a group of businessmen declared just before the onset of World War II, "government does not readily give up powers, once acquired."[36] Indeed, many free enterprisers viewed liberal reform as more dangerous than out-and-out socialism because it pretended to be something that it was not. They regularly described the New Deal as "a wolf in sheep's clothing," a statist program dangerous precisely because of its humanitarian cover.[37] Free enterprisers feared that New Dealers were lulling the American people into a gradual acceptance of growing government power.

The idea that the nascent welfare state was catalyzing a stealth revolution lingered long after Roosevelt's death. "We can peer through the smokescreen . . . we know all [the enemy's] tricks of camouflage," according to the "The Free

Man's Manifesto," a widely publicized statement in favor of "private free enterprise" by movie star Robert Montgomery presented at the annual dinner of the Congress of American Industry in 1951 and performed around the country for the next few years.[38] In this view, New Dealers and welfare statists either had a hidden agenda or were naïvely unaware of the dangerous trajectory of their policy prescriptions, which were setting the country on a dangerous and unstoppable path.[39] Some critics, using the martial metaphors often favored by free enterprisers, described the liberal camouflaged path to statism as an undeclared war that necessitated a fierce counterattack. In 1952, for example, a former Commerce Department official condemned what he described as the "secret battle being waged against American business men by government employers trying to substitute soviet style commerce for the American free enterprise system."[40] Other free enterprise advocates feared that liberals were winning this war by duping the population. This gradualist path to serfdom was, one critic said in 1955, "if anything, worse than all-out Communism."[41] Whether statism accrued power by secrecy or seduction, the free enterprise bottom line was the same. No matter how well intentioned, "government intervention in the market economy always results in a worse situation than would otherwise have existed," as the popular conservative economics writer Henry Hazlitt wrote.[42] However pragmatic its mission, the New Deal (and its successor administrations), in this conception, was as dangerous as the collectivist dictatorship it was fated to become. "It is said that Harry Truman is no socialist," declared Taft in 1950. "That makes little difference if all his policies lead to socialism."[43] In this view, the slippery slope turned avowed liberals into de facto demagogues.

In these respects and many others, free enterprisers developed a counterpoint to the New Deal order, perpetually challenging not only its program but its assumptions, ultimately derailing both. For many decades, they took as their duty a pledge "to continuous opposition to nearly every New Deal measure and proposal affecting business," as the Congress of American Industry promised in 1935.[44] Even in the affluent 1950s, General Electric executive Lemuel Boulware, friend and mentor to Ronald Reagan, who was his employee before he became a politician, claimed, "Never in our history has our freedom and material well-being been in such peril." Though Boulware made this claim during a time of Cold War anxiety, the peril, he believed, came not from the Soviet Union but from the internal threat posed by "public or government enterprise, as opposed to private enterprise," which was dangerously accelerating "the trend toward collectivism."[45]

In the conflict between free enterprise and the welfare state, the New Dealers and their descendants won many programmatic and electoral battles but they generally lost the broader ideological wars. Many government programs from the New Deal era through the Great Society, which free enterprise critics dismissed as "repetitions of ideas that didn't work in the 1930s," remained popular into the twenty-first century.[46] In important ways, the 1949 observation of economic journalist and, later, Michigan senator Blair Moody remains true: "Most of the New Deal reforms are knit so deeply into the national fabric that they have become generally accepted."[47]

In spite of the popularity of programs like Social Security that date back to the New Deal, it is hard to take issue with Milton Friedman's view that conservatives "have largely won the battle of ideas."[48] The general anti-statist view promulgated by the anti–New Deal free enterprisers, one that they anachronistically labeled traditional, eventually became common sense. In 1967, at what was arguably the acme of the New Deal order, Lloyd Free and Hadley Cantril's groundbreaking book *The Political Beliefs of Americans* identified American citizens as "ideological conservatives" but "operational liberals," meaning that, like the man wearing the "Less Government = More Freedom" T-shirt, they disliked government in the abstract, believing that the welfare state threatened to impinge on freedom, even as they enjoyed its benefits. In a discrepancy the puzzled authors labeled as "schizoid," half of their respondents described themselves as ideological conservatives (with only 16 percent calling themselves liberal), but 65 percent qualified as liberal in their views of government programs.[49] This set of seemingly contradictory beliefs can be explained, at least in part, by the success of free enterprisers in making anti-statism common sense. Ever since the 1936 Republican candidate Alf Landon said that "we must restore common sense in government" by removing the "shackles" placed on "American free enterprise," conservative free enterprisers have used this phrase to suggest the New Deal marked an impractical and dangerous departure from American norms and traditions.[50] This common sense was rooted in the new version of "free enterprise" that emerged in the late 1920s, was fortified during the Second World War, and became increasingly mainstream even at the peak of the supposed New Deal consensus.

Throughout this era, advocates of free enterprise viewed expansions of the welfare state with suspicion because they understood government intervention in the economy as un-American, ineffective, and dangerous. As the British political scientist and socialist Harold Laski observed with some puzzlement in 1948, most Americans look "upon the state as an enemy." Laski did not explain the source of what he called Americans' "deep discomfort when they are asked to support the positive state," but part of the answer surely lies in the nearly continuous campaign against the New Deal that launched almost as soon as FDR was inaugurated.[51] The perception that public spending, progressive taxation, and regulation threaten the very existence of liberty has been a constant chorus since the New Deal.[52] Similarly, free enterprisers framed every extension of the welfare state or any government initiative they disliked—from the New Deal to the "War on Poverty" to Obamacare—as an "attack on business."[53] One congressman even described U.S. participation in the celebration of the International Women's Year of 1977, using the exact language that NAM's H. W. Prentis employed more than two decades previously, as a "wolf in sheep's clothing" and a threat to "the free enterprise system" that "makes America great."[54]

In the view of the New Deal's critics, modifications to what business leaders and politicians referred to as the "system" of free enterprise could be deadly, especially those that privileged government at the expense of business. They equated free enterprise with "the muscle and bone of America," as an editor wrote in 1940, which, by extension, made the undermining of business tantamount to the weakening of the nation.[55] As the political scientist Alpheus Thomas Mason wrote in 1950, free enterprisers understood the welfare state as "a diabolical prelude to totalitarianism and despotism" rather than as a safety net that protected the poor, the infirm, and the unlucky and that stabilized the capitalist system.[56]

"A Contest between Regimentation and Free Enterprise"

The *Washington Post* in 1951 characterized the United States as a "hybrid" economy, "partly free and partly control[ed]," in which "business is regulated but not owned by Government."[57] Despite the reality of a mixed economy, free enterprisers described it as untenable over the long—or even the medium—term. Although they sometimes acknowledged that modifications had been necessary in the past and they regularly disclaimed the idea of laissez-faire, they saw great danger in government intervention. In 1939, an editorial in *Bankers Magazine*, for example, called the upcoming presidential election "a contest between regimentation and free enterprise." After quoting from Abraham Lincoln's famous "house divided" speech, the editors wondered, "Can our economic structure function effectively half one thing and half the other?"[58] Similarly, the president of Baldwin Locomotive Works, an advocate of what he called (but characteristically did not define) the "traditional American concept of free enterprise," declared that "America cannot be organized simultaneously as individualistic and collective." Like others who understood the New Deal and the American Way as opposing rather than reinforcing, he drew the Manichean conclusion, "We must choose one or the other."[59]

The invocation of the Lincolnian idea of an unsustainable "house divided" was so prevalent that in 1936 the *New York Times* editorialized against the overuse of the analogy between an economy made up of free and slave labor and the mixed economy. "A good maxim, like any other good tool, requires judicious handling. Abraham Lincoln's 'half slave and half free' is no exception to this rule," noted the editorialist. "Obviously not all half-and-half combinations are fatal," including the hybrid economy.[60] Franklin D. Roosevelt agreed. Although he famously declared in his acceptance of the Democratic presidential nomination in 1936 that freedom is "no half-and-half affair," his conception of freedom included a government powerful enough to constrain those he called "the economic royalists" and to provide jobs for the needy.[61]

This commonsense caution did nothing to stem the tide of "house divided" references, comparisons to the blunt economic choices of the Civil War era, and assertions about the inviolability and fragility of freedom, which was compatible only with pure free enterprise. Referring to the origins of the Republican Party as "a great liberal movement on behalf of human freedom," Ogden Mills, the former secretary of the treasury, worried in 1937 that overly powerful government could make "men slaves," paying no heed to the *Times'* warning of the previous year.[62] Similarly, newspaper publisher Frank Gannett observed in 1940 that a free nation could not sustain a system "half collectivist and half free enterprise."[63] Denying the possibility of a mixed economy, even during World War II when this description was manifestly a description of reality, the *Wall Street Journal* editorialized in 1942, "A planned economy and free enterprise cannot live in the same country at the same time."[64] After the war, the binary thinking continued. "No economy can be part socialist and part free enterprise," asserted the editorialist at the *Fort Lauderdale News* in 1947, as Congress considered significant expansions in the areas of unemployment insurance and Social Security.[65]

The language of "half" free enterprise and "half" state control did not provide an accurate account of the nature of the economic problem, as the free enterprisers understood it. For them, the tipping point for the ruin of free enterprise came not when the mix was equal but at the margins, with the first appearance of government intervention. Even a society 95 percent "free" and 5 percent "regimented" was, in their view, doomed to implode. "There is no half way ground," Herbert Hoover wrote in 1936. "The American system of freedom" and "a planned society," the former president declared, "cannot be mixed."[66] Free enterprisers thus proposed a "one-drop" rule: free enterprise could potentially be fatally infected with even small acts of government intervention. Free enterprise advocates condemned small expansions of the welfare state as portents of doom, "endangering our political as well as our economic freedom," as NAM resolved at its 1944 annual meeting.[67] A "hybrid system, partly of free enterprise and partly of government dictatorship," the *Los Angeles Times* editorialized in 1949, is "an impossible system."[68] Americans faced a choice, according to C. B. Alexander, president of the Bemis Bag Company of Indianapolis, in 1949: either "servitude under a regime doctored with a socialistic panacea, or free enterprise under the sound old American democratic system."[69] In this view, the so-called mixed economy would soon prove to be a dangerous illusion. Over time, in this understanding, the government would strangle any semblance of private enterprise, and freedom would be lost. Free enterprise, for all its centrality, required purity to survive; even a touch of planning would eventually destroy it.

Stressing the power and autonomy of individuals, in part by downplaying corporate strength, free enterprisers positioned themselves as enemies of all forms of "collectivism" and expressed frustration at what Ogden Mills, Hoover's former cabinet secretary turned fierce New Deal critic, called the "present state of public confusion" that conceived of the New Deal as consistent with democracy and free enterprise. "As opposed to collectivism," claimed Mills, evoking the original Republican slogan of "free soil, free labor, and free men," "we stand for free government, free men, and free enterprise."[70] In this vision, the New Deal was akin to the Slave Power, a corrupt political rump supporting an economic system that would inevitably undermine democratic government and political freedom. By the same logic, free enterprisers analogized themselves to modern-day abolitionists, rooting out the modern enemy of liberty, which was not expanding slavery but intrusive government.

Comparing their times to the crisis of the Union in the Civil War era, free enterprisers pronounced politics as usual as insufficiently suited to the task of rescuing the nation. "The fundamental issue is now clear," editorialized the *Lewiston Daily Sun* in 1936. Whereas the concern in the Civil War era had been the preservation of the free labor system, now, the editorial argued, "the issue before the country is the preservation of free enterprise." And in spite of the fact that "no one can define the new deal or even describe it," facing "the end of free enterprise in America" meant contemplating the demise of the nation itself. The newspaper continued in a Lincolnian vein that "there is no half-way house" for free enterprise, and counseled that important decisions needed to be made quickly. "The country must choose between the regimentation of the economic life of 130,000,000 people by politically appointed Federal bureaucrats and the continuance of the American system of free enterprise." The choice: regimentation imposed from above leading to dictatorship or individual autonomy and freedom.[71]

"In the Long Run Freedom Is the Best Planner of All"

World War II marked a key period in free enterprisers' battle against the state. Free enterprisers did not declare a cease-fire in their campaign against the New Deal during the war. Instead, they intensified their critique of the federal government in a constant barrage occasionally punctuated by conditional expressions of support. Those entrusted to oversee "freedom's forge," the arsenal that produced miraculous levels of wartime production, feared that the tentative efforts of the New Deal would morph, during a time of total war, into a permanent and widely legitimized form of statism.[72] In 1944, James Fifield, the head of the conservative religious organization Spiritual Mobilization, wrote to his friend the Reverend Norman Vincent Peale expressing concern that free enterprise had suffered a "serious setback" because it seemed "un-American to do anything but applaud everything that was said or done in Washington."[73] Many free enterprisers, however, overcame their reluctance and roundly condemned the wartime government in hopes of delivering a preemptive strike against the postwar welfare state. As historian Mark R. Wilson has written, "Business leaders and associations worked deliberately—and spent lavishly—to frame the war as a contest between totalitarianism and economic liberty."[74] Many business leaders took up this battle against the dangers of statism at home even as the war against global fascism raged, the outcome still uncertain.

From the onset of the American effort, business leaders viewed the war as an opportunity to vanquish homegrown collectivism alongside foreign fascism. One day after the Pearl Harbor attack, an article in the *Pittsburgh Post-Gazette*, whose front page highlighted in a huge font Roosevelt's call for Congress to declare war, noted that the "managers of American industry" were fighting to "preserve free enterprise." Business leaders, the newspaper claimed, "fear regimentation above all else." As free enterprisers often did before the war, these leaders denied that they were "opposed to all forms of central planning." They acknowledged that the war must be fought but urged that it be done in a way that kept business free. Already looking beyond the war, they declared that maintaining "free enterprise and individual initiative" would be "the crucial problem of the post-war period." It "won't be easy," they concluded, because government "does not readily give up powers, once acquired." Even though the American war effort was just commencing, they viewed with suspicion the government charged with carrying out that mission. Alfred P. Sloan, the head of General Motors, feared that government officials would "look upon the present emergency as a 'heaven sent' opportunity to alter . . . the American system of free enterprise." Sloan conceded, "Winning the war is one paramount job." But "winning the peace," by which he meant restoring free enterprise, was an equally urgent and important task.[75] From literally the first day of the American entrance into World War II, business leaders feared that the war effort and its seeming vindication of the powerful state would further erode free enterprise.

The wartime fear of growing state power marked a direct extension of the prewar fears of free enterprisers. Before the Pearl Harbor attack, NAM developed an "eight-point program" designed to "win the post-war crisis," which it defined as defending free enterprise from its critics and from a government sure to gain power relative to industry during the war.[76] The leader of a bankers' group expressed concern that wartime preparation was hastening the pace of statism and thus "slowly stifling the way of life which is the rightful and automatic heritage of Americans."[77] Others worried that excessive taxation to fund rearmament was a "scheme," perhaps "treasonable," rather than a practical necessity.[78]

Once the war began, business leaders boasted that "free private enterprise"

NAM president H. W. Prentis.
(Courtesy of the National
Association of Manufacturers.)

produced the "battleships and planes and guns" that would "mean the difference between victory and defeat for Hitler, the dictator."[79] The use of the word
dictator highlighted the danger of dictatorship of any kind. The kind they feared
the most was internal. Detecting that "a shift from the free private enterprise
kind of private spending toward the totalitarian kind of government spending
has been steadily in progress," John Bricker, Ohio governor and Republican
candidate for vice president in 1944, stressed the need for vigilance.[80] During
the war, Bricker and many other conservative politicians denounced their own
government for its "totalitarian tendencies" in the midst of a war against fascism and dictatorships. For them, what William Mullendore called the domestic
"war against free enterprise and for the Socialist state" was as dangerous as the
foreign foe, an enemy that, they claimed, would be defeated by free enterprise,
understood as private business firms, and not government.[81]

Many free enterprisers applied the language of slippery slopes and "Trojan
horses" that they had used during the early days of the New Deal to the war.[82]
"If we ever do lose our freedom in America," said Prentis, the NAM leader, in
1945, "I predict that it will be due to planned economy coming as a wolf in
sheep's clothing." As World War II raged, Prentis believed that regimentation
meant the "doom of personal liberty" and he feared that "we are far closer to it

than most of us realize."[83] For Prentis, the wartime government's threat to freedom was far greater than that posed by the Nazis. One year earlier, Alf Landon had expressed concern that "authoritarianism stalks our land today like a grim, grisly ghost."[84] The former presidential candidate was referring not to the threat of Nazism but to the dangers of big government.

Free enterprisers thus fought a two-front war: one external in support of the Allied battle against Germany, Italy, and Japan, and one internal, what one columnist in 1943 called a "civil war" to retain "free enterprise in its entirety" against enemies from "within."[85] Business leaders and representatives forthrightly and aggressively placed the fight for free enterprise on par with the war effort, and often before it. "Were we in any way to surrender our past heritage of free enterprise, as a consequence of the demands of the present war effort then the war itself would become a mockery, defeating, as the price to be paid for victory, the very objective for the preservation of which we fought," said John Costello, a California congressman and later the general counsel of the Los Angeles Chamber of Commerce. In 1943 Costello and the LA Chamber expressed concern that wartime acquiescence to planning might lead to postwar defeat for free enterprisers. They cautioned against trusting that the government would of its own volition allow a return to what they saw as the free enterprise norm.[86] An editorial in the Salt Lake City newspaper claimed, with concern, that "freedom appears to be in the middle of a losing fight," referring not to the Allied armed forces but to government-imposed constraints on business autonomy.[87]

Many business leaders improbably claimed that wartime production levels proved the superiority of the free market. Frederick Crawford, the president of NAM, described the war effort in a full-page ad that ran in many newspapers as proof that "in the long run freedom is the best planner of all." Before the war, Crawford claimed, "there was much wringing of the hands and wailing over the planlessness of our American life and free enterprise system." But business's success in building the wartime arsenal resulted from the fact that what he called "our alleged planless, aimless, chaotic, cut-throat, competitive system" had "answered the blitz" with spectacular results. Crawford saw this planless success as a rebuke to the "totalitarian planners who for years planned and plotted their assault on freedom and happiness."[88] In this ad, NAM appeared to be targeting both the foreign enemy of fascism and the internal enemy of statism. Echoing the business lobby, Bricker was not the only politician to proclaim, "The American system of free enterprise is winning the war."[89] Lobbyists like Crawford and politicians like Bricker rarely emphasized the government-sponsored boost to business in their celebrations of wartime enterprise.

These same leaders also worried that the war was legitimating the New Deal state, in whose employ millions of soldiers and defense workers toiled. They claimed, against abundant evidence to the contrary, that the wartime and postwar interests of business and the American people were identical. Business theorist Peter Drucker hailed the businessman's emergence from "the doghouse" during the war but warned that "bureaucratic power must be overcome if we are to have a free country after the war."[90] The threat of a bureaucratic and intrusive government was, according to Bourke B. Hickenlooper, the governor of Iowa, "a most ominous threat to the basic American principle of free enterprise."[91] In 1943, the Chamber of Commerce's leader Eric Johnston warned, "There is some danger that our country may go totalitarian" unless "the free enterprise system, which has worked so well in the war, is allowed to function without governmental domination in peacetime." Johnston feared that an all-powerful "super-state" might emerge out of the warfare state.[92] The same year, with the war's outcome still uncertain, Wilfred Sykes, the president of the Inland Steel Company, told attendees at a NAM conference that it was the "duty of government immediately to set enterprise free" after the war.[93] These leaders urged ordinary Americans to cast their lot with the businesses that were helping soldiers win the war rather than with the government that threatened to stifle them in peacetime.[94] The alliance with government had to be temporary, in the view of many business leaders and representatives.

Rarely speaking on their own behalf, free enterprisers set the interests of the people and especially the ordinary soldier against those of the state. "While our fighters are smashing through to victory," said Lawrence Sullivan, the author of *Bureaucracy Runs Amuck*, a 1944 screed against statism, "the federal bureaus are digging in for postwar permanency."[95] Government power "has set the stage for the loss of the very freedom for which American men are fighting," declared Senator Albert W. Hawkes, who feared that "the free enterprise system that has made this nation great no longer will exist."[96] Free enterprisers expressed concern that "under the guise of emergency," wartime leaders are "taking advantage of the stress we are now in to promote and advance their scheme of collectivism," as the Georgia congressman Eugene E. Cox said in March 1942, very early in the U.S. war effort.[97] Washington, he feared, had ulterior motives beyond winning the war. The oilman J. Howard Pew agreed, claiming in 1942, "At times

the aim seems to be not winning the war but the substitution of political domination for industrial self-government."[98] Others worried that the government's
wartime message of collective sacrifice might weaken support for the "profit
and loss system."[99] Free enterprisers feared that the statists might use the war,
however justifiable it was, as an excuse to expand their powers, leading to a loss
of liberty on the home front.

Business leaders assumed that ordinary Americans, particularly soldiers,
shared their conception of the goal of the war as preserving free enterprise and
opposing "dictation." The planners, in this view, were not just challenging business interests, they directly contradicted the wishes of the populace. "By and
large, the American people do not wish to see their government turned general
employer," said the Georgia senator Walter F. George in 1943, telling the "people" what they believed. "The vast majority of the American people are willing
to rely upon our system of free enterprise as the surest means of preserving
essential human values and freedoms with which we are blessed."[100] Speaking
in the name of the American people, free enterprisers assumed an identity of
interest with them. In advertising and speeches, the most common voice in
favor of free enterprise was not the corporate executive but the average GI, on
whose behalf they spoke but rarely quoted. In a 1943 advertisement, the United
Gas Line Company claimed "our job" is to assure soldiers "that they will have
a place . . . in preserving and expanding the free enterprise system that made
America great."[101] Frank Branch Riley, a Portland lawyer, confidently proclaimed in a 1944 speech to a business group that returning soldiers "will want
a job—in private industry—not government dole, no leaf-raking project." Furthermore, he claimed, they "will not want to sell their liberties, one by one, for
the false promises of economic security."[102] Riley, like other free enterprisers,
assumed that the soldiers shared his values.

Just as some criticized the ideological uses of the long-dead Abraham Lincoln as a champion of business free enterprise, others condemned those conservatives who spoke on behalf of the soldier as an ideological ally in "speeches,
articles, editorials, books, pamphlets and confidential reports telling us what
this legendary character thinks, feels, wants, needs and plans." "Oddly enough,"
wrote Charles G. Bolte, the chairman of the American Veterans Committee,
"the business men say he needs free enterprise in big doses." The "courses of
action they recommend" tend to "parallel their own professional bents," Bolte
noted dryly in 1945, shortly before the end of the war.[103] "If he reads up on de-

velopments at home," the solider "must shake his head at times," wrote Bruce
Crawford in 1943. He criticized the "propaganda assembly line of Patriots for
Profit," which claimed that soldiers wanted "a pre-New Deal peace," a "Hoover-
ism" that "ignores the lessons of a dozen years or more."[104] These critiques did
little to stem the tide of homilies that identified the interests of business and
soldiers as perfectly coincident and in which both groups equally rejected the
use of the war as an opportunity to expand statism. Free enterprisers treated the
threat from the wartime state as if it presented a danger on a par with fascism
and in some ways actually more ominous, since they were more confident about
their ability to vanquish the Axis powers than they were about their capacity to
rein in government.

When not representing soldiers, advertisers spoke on behalf of children or
the population as a whole in favor of free enterprise. The Kansas Electric Power
Company's 1944 ad took the point of view of a child who wondered, "Would it
be asking too much of the folks at home to vigorously fight to protect my Country's basic rules of living, including that all important principle of Free Enterprise?"[105] The Chamber of Commerce's Merle Thorpe predicted in 1942 that
the unpleasant "taste of State control" would reinforce the people's free enterprise sensibilities and shape their postwar desires. Ordinary Americans, he said,
"see little difference between such a life and the authoritarian way they are
sending their sons to fight against."[106] Given the evils that the soldiers fought
against, this was a remarkable claim.

Fearing that victory in war would come at the cost of an empowered state,
business leaders and politicians requested assurances and guarantees. Notwithstanding their dislike of security as a guiding concept of governance, they demanded commitments that government controls would be loosened as soon as
the fighting ended. Business free enterprisers might have celebrated risk in the
abstract as the essence of freedom but they often wished to avoid it in their own
economic dealings.[107] "Restoration of free enterprise must be insured," declared
the Indiana Republican Party's "win war" platform of 1942. "It must be restored
to insure a victory that has not been fought in vain."[108] Sykes, the president of
Inland Steel, dismissed "public works panaceas" since "government jobs do not
create jobs" and said it was the "duty of government to set enterprise free," lest
"self-appointed reformers . . . turn free enterprise into something else."[109] Sykes
and other business leaders depicted business autonomy as a symbol of postwar
freedom writ large. Although free enterprisers condemned the New Deal prom-

ise of security for ordinary Americans, they demanded it for themselves. Crawford of NAM called for "a true affirmation free of weasel words and mental reservations, of full faith and confidence in our free economic system, as the only secure foundation of a free political system." Crawford did not specify whom he wanted to declare this affirmation, but he claimed that it would lead to "a rebirth of faith in the system of free enterprise," which had been damaged by "the uncertainty of government's real attitude toward private enterprise."[110] A year after the war ended, Pennsylvania's Republican candidate for governor, Edward Martin, said, "Free enterprise will not live if that vast concentration of power is left unchanged in Washington." Calling for a "speedy return to the American system of free enterprise and free action," Martin said, "The towering structure of agencies, bureaus, commissions, authorities, and federal tycoons must be pulled down." Disliking "phony promises of security for all," Martin demanded a secure business climate for firms in his state and the country, but disclaimed the goal of economic security for the masses.[111]

Notwithstanding the incontestable fact that government contracts bought business out of the Depression, creating demand that the private sector had been unable to generate, business leaders often described the main goal of the war as a renewal of free enterprise, by which they meant less spending on public welfare, weakened trade unionism, and empowered businesses.[112] In a 1944 speech, Governor E. P. Carville of Nevada claimed that citizens who wished to preserve liberty should call for the return to free enterprise "as rapidly as possible after the cessation of hostilities." As was often the case in free enterprise rhetoric, Carville claimed, without supporting evidence, that "the people" demanded the removal of "the shackles of excessive government control."[113] A reporter for the *Washington Post*, assuming that voters were also looking beyond the war, described the upcoming election of 1944 as "a struggle between so-called New Deal elements" and those who sought "a return to free enterprise at the earliest possible moment."[114] The reporter framed a binary opposition between the New Deal and free enterprise as the key issue of a wartime election.

During World War II, the term *bureaucracy* (or, in the spelling of the *Chicago Tribune*, the leading anti–New Deal organ, "burocracy") emerged as a symbol of a dangerous new force, anathema to free enterprise. Fearing "increased postwar regimentation," Senator Hawkes condemned "unreasonable and unnecessary restraints placed upon free enterprise" in 1944.[115] The same year, Bricker used the same phrase ("post-war regimentation") to discuss his fear that "New

Deal leaders" were accelerating their plan to "change our system of free enterprise" by bureaucratic means.[116] Free enterprisers described the regimented
economy not as a necessary temporary expedient to win the war but as a portent
of totalitarianism that could be vanquished only with a battle against the New
Deal state as vigorous as the war effort against the Nazis.

Free enterprisers often described the Roosevelt administration as an untrust-
worthy ally. Their desire to eliminate "controls" and their apprehension that the
war effort legitimized "statism" led them to question the motives of the country's elected leaders. In 1942, former president Hoover and a coauthor highlighted what they called a "widespread fear" that "under cover of the war emergency interested groups are doubly active in attempts to socialize industry."
Anxious about the diminution of "economic freedom" and wondering whether
the "peacemakers" would "continue the methods of the war emergency, half-
Fascist and half-Socialist," they rejected the legitimacy of a mixed economy,
even when events seemed to be demonstrating its efficacy. When, they wondered,
would the leadership of the nation "grant free enterprise" its due, as if that were
an urgent political matter in the midst of war.[117] In a 1943 speech to the Georgia
Bankers Association, Eugene Cox, who the previous year had expressed concern about "collectivism," claimed, "There are too many who are trying to win
the war with one hand and overthrow the system of free enterprise and democracy with the other."[118] Free enterprisers often suspected the nation's wartime
leaders of sending mixed messages, if not of having dual loyalties. An even
more extreme example of the critique of the administration came the following
year from Richard J. Lyons, the Republican nominee for the U.S. Senate in
Illinois. In Lyons's narrative, the war was being won "by American industry
under the system of free enterprise." Lyons believed that the war had forced
New Dealers to do an about-face and to "call in the leaders of free enterprise
they had been denouncing." He dismissed "the false premise that they are winning the war." His fear was that "now with victory in sight the New Deal communists and collectivists are hurrying their schemes for more complete regimentation." He praised the soldiers and generals, whom the free enterprise
system had "supplied abundantly," but not the nation's political leaders. In an
astonishing conclusion, Lyons claimed that credit for the successful war effort
should not go "to the man who loves to call himself the commander in chief,"
President Roosevelt. He justified this belief on the ground that free enterprise,
not the government, was responsible for the coming victory.[119]

It did not take long for business leaders and some politicians to redefine the war as one for free enterprise, against not only fascism but also what they often called "collectivism," by which they meant the revivified New Deal state. They took President Roosevelt's war aims articulated in 1941, known as the "Four Freedoms," to be incomplete and even dangerous. In his State of the Union address that year, Roosevelt presented his reasons for the American people to reject isolationism and to support Great Britain and its allies in the fight against the Axis forces. He made an ethical argument, claiming that the war against fascism was also a fight for four universal freedoms: freedom of speech and expression; freedom of religion; freedom from want; and freedom from fear. For many free enterprisers this list of war aims omitted what they took to be the fundamental freedom from which all others sprang.[120]

By 1942 Roosevelt's critics, worried that the Four Freedoms might provide the basis for a postwar welfare state, began to describe free enterprise as "a fifth freedom for which Americans should fight," as C. C. Carr, the advertising manager of Alcoa, told the Southern Newspaper Publishers Association in Hot Springs, Arkansas. Without this Fifth Freedom, Carr warned, it was entirely possible that "we can win the war and lose our American way of life." He worried that a group he termed "statists," temporarily empowered by the war, might seek to expand their foothold when the war ended. Free enterprisers needed to defeat these statists on the home front.[121] A 1943 ad for the Northern States Power Company, one of many such corporate pronouncements that sought to transform the Four Freedoms into a celebration of American business, called for "a fifth freedom to tie them together and make them work."[122] The same year, in a thinly veiled critique of FDR, an advertisement for the Kemper Insurance Company, after noting that "free enterprise isn't mentioned in the famous Four Freedoms," claimed that "without it there is no free America."[123]

The idea that free enterprisers needed to be vigilant during the war and assertive after it was over also appeared in a famous advertising campaign by the Republic Steel Company. One of their 1944 ads, celebrating the free enterprise system as the "American way of doing things," included the following threat, which matched the serious visual imagery of an apron-clad shopkeeper behind an old-fashioned counter, a wood-burning stove, and a few unsmiling patrons listening to a briefcase-carrying businessman, who appears to be explaining the meaning of free enterprise to them. "Sure, we're willing to put up with a lot of irritating things right now—in order to win the war—but I don't believe we'll

"Boys, I'll tell you what Free Enterprise really is!"

"It's a lot of little things—and some mighty big things, too.

"But in a nutshell, it's our right to live our own lives, run our own jobs and our own businesses in our own way—without needless interference.

"It's our right to criticize the government, bawl out the umpire, or make a speech on the public square. It's our right to travel when and where we choose—to work or not, as we please.

"It offers *opportunity* to anyone who really wants it. It rewards thrift, hard work and ingenuity. It thrives on competition and raises our standard of living. It encourages invention, stimulates research and promotes progress.

"It offers us a chance to save and invest and build and grow.

"Under Free Enterprise men who have faith in an idea can take risks to develop it. Our railways started that way. So did the motor car industry—and oil and steel and aviation and scientific mechanized farming.

"Free Enterprise made small shops and factories into big ones—and then started more small ones. And now, fighting a desperate war in which production will turn the scale, America is out-producing every other country in the world, hands down—and is doing it faster and better.

"Yet in spite of all this, some folks would like to change our American way of doing things—and rebuild our whole country under a *new* and *different* system.

"If they had their way, Tom here, wouldn't own this store. He'd be regimented with a lot of other storekeepers and told how to run his business by some bureaucrat who probably never tended store in his life.

"Ed's farm would belong to the state, and Ed would be told how to run it and what to raise by someone he wouldn't even know.

"Jim would be working for a state-owned factory—with his job and wages frozen. And I don't know *where* we country doctors would be.

"We fellows aren't rich—and probably never will be. But we've got a lot of self-respect and religion and decency and common sense. We own our own homes and farms, send our kids to college, have cars, radios, and a lot more of the luxuries of life than millions of people living under fancy political systems and 'planned economies' in other countries.

"Sure, we're willing to put up with a lot of irritating things right now—in order to win the war—but I don't believe we'll stand for being pushed around much after it's over.

"Frankly, I don't like the name Free Enterprise for the system under which this country has grown great. I'd rather call it *American* Enterprise, because it's the most American thing we have. It really *is* America. Let's *keep* it."

BUY WAR BONDS AND STAMPS —AND **KEEP** THEM!

The Army-Navy E flag waves over seven Republic plants and the Maritime M floats over the Cleveland District plant.

REPUBLIC STEEL

GENERAL OFFICES: CLEVELAND 1, OHIO
Export Department: Chrysler Building, New York 17, New York

ALLOY, CARBON, STAINLESS STEELS · COLD FINISHED STEELS · PLATES · BARS · SHAPES · STRIP · SHEETS · PIPE · TUBING
TIN PLATE · NUTS · BOLTS · RIVETS · NAILS · PIG IRON · FARM FENCE · WIRE · FABRICATED STEEL PRODUCTS

Some people would like to see us lose our right to live our own lives like free men. They'd rather see us governed by bureaucrats. *Keeping our freedom is worth all the work and fight that's in us.* And millions who see this message in the April 22 Saturday Evening Post are fighting beside us to *keep* America *American*.

This 1944 ad for Republic Steel espoused views typical of many wartime businesses in its celebration of free enterprise and its deep suspicion of government. (American war posters from the Second World War, BANC PIC 2005.004:0213—D. Courtesy of The Bancroft Library, University of California, Berkeley.)

stand for being pushed around much after it's over."[124] The copywriters left the question of who the "we" was ambiguous: was it the Republic Steel Company? The business community? The American people? The ad articulated the perspective that wartime rationing and regulation were not just "irritating" but dangerously coercive ("being pushed around") and that, come the end of the war, statism would no longer be acceptable.

Advocates of the "Fifth Freedom," like other free enterprisers in wartime, often claimed to speak on behalf of ordinary Americans. A 1943 ad for the Puget Sound Power and Light Company that appeared in the *Ellensburg Daily Record* suggested a pledge that Americans should make "to her fighting men." Assuming once again that advertisers knew what the soldiers wanted and that their desires coincided with the aims of business leaders, they pledged, "We'll make no changes in the American Way of Life while you are gone. We will not lose for you here at home the things you are fighting abroad to keep," which was "our Fifth Freedom—FREE ENTERPRISE."[125] The assumption, frequently repeated, was that soldiers were self-consciously fighting for free enterprise understood as business autonomy. A wartime ad for Tiedtkes, "Toledo's One-Stop Shopping Center," called free enterprise "as American as the Thanksgiving turkey—Old Glory—and 'e pluribus unum.'" It claimed, as Fifth Freedom advocates often did, that free enterprise "can make a jeep and a 'P-40' and a battleship," suggesting that armaments and materiel were primarily the product of private businesses.[126] Fifth Freedom advocates often elided the positive role of the state that FDR claimed was at the root of the Four Freedoms. The same year in a speech to the Lawrence Rotary Club, R. W. McClure, the president of the Kansas Electric Power Company, worried that free enterprise "is now on its way out unless real red-blooded Americans are more alert than they have been for the past decade," dating America's lethargy in battling on behalf of freedom to the early days of the New Deal. In spite of the urgency of the ongoing war effort, he encouraged citizens to be wary of their government representatives, whom he described not as patriots but as "totalization agents, now actively engaged in doing away with the American Way of Life." He rejected Roosevelt's Four Freedoms as "glib" but described the Fifth Freedom as the base "upon which all the other freedoms must rest if they are to endure." To McClure, it was by no means clear that these other freedoms would last since they were "being threatened with extinction," not so much by Hitler as by bureaucrats who were fighting for the Four Freedoms at the expense of the Fifth. In this vision, victory in war was most important as a prerequisite for the battle to save free enterprise, which had, he claimed, "made America great," but which only thrived when it ruled, preeminent and unchallenged.[127]

During the war, proponents of the Fifth Freedom emphasized the contributions of free enterprise at every opportunity. "Too many people seem to forget that America was built by free enterprise," according to the president of the National Association of Real Estate Boards two years into the war effort. Cyrus Crane Wilmore, a St. Louis builder, argued in 1943 that "without free enterprise this war would have been lost months ago," calling on his colleagues to remind Americans of this fact.[128] Moreover, free enterprisers believed that the "Four Freedoms" were misconceived, an inappropriate justification for the war effort. The Fifth Freedom, rather than an add-on, was fundamental, "the cornerstone of the foundation upon which the other four freedoms must rest," as Nicholas Murray Butler, president of Columbia University, called it in a 1943 speech.[129] They thought Roosevelt's omission of this essential freedom telling, an indication of his lack of commitment to free enterprise, and claimed there was broad support for this position. "Almost everyone who has given any thought at all to the now famous 'four freedoms' of President Roosevelt has either wondered to himself or wondered out loud why in these freedoms the very cornerstone of American freedom and progress is not mentioned," claimed an editorial in the *Milwaukee Sentinel*. "The freedom that is strangely missing from the celebrated four is FREE ENTERPRISE and its concomitant, OPPORTUNITY for all." This "grave omission" of "business freedom" threatened to "de-Americanize" the war effort, according to the newspaper. In this view, the Four Freedoms were not just secondary to the all-important Fifth one but un-American, if not explicitly linked to free enterprise. The problem was that the Four Freedoms seemed to favor collectivism over individualism and stability over risk, and therefore did not promote the free enterprise system. "SECURITY is overemphasized and SELF-RELIANCE—the very core of the American way—is not mentioned at all as either a national or universal virtue."[130] Conservative radio commentator Fulton Lewis Jr. claimed that "without this Fifth Freedom, the other four would be of small worth," and that therefore free enterprise stood above those other freedoms enumerated by the president. "It is freedom of enterprise which alone can create the conditions under which the Four Freedoms . . . can come to fruition."[131] Lewis, like other advocates of the Fifth Freedom, saw the war as a battle to preserve free enterprise as much as democracy.

Proponents of free enterprise did not pretend to form a united front with the president and his allies during the war. The U.S. military may have been saving the world, but the government that employed those soldiers still threatened to undermine freedom at home. S. S. Humphreys, in a 1944 letter to the editor of the *Newmarket News* endorsing the Republican Party in the upcoming presidential election, reflected on the "disturbing fact" that "while we are securing liberty to peoples and nations all over the world, we are steadily losing our liberties at home." Humphreys criticized the wartime commander in chief and his administration as "Sinister, Unamerican forces" who "are at work devising and planning new ways of replacing our constitutional form of government with many more initialed bureaucracies."[132] For Humphreys, as for many free enterprisers, the primary danger, the sapping of freedom by means of bureaucracy, was internal.

Free enterprisers called for a reassertion of their preferred ideals to save the country. Eddie Rickenbacker, World War I flying ace turned airline executive and longtime critic of FDR, argued in a 1944 article about his preferred characteristics of the next president that the nation needed "a man who believes in free enterprise," which he took to mean pro-business and anti–civil rights. Further, he wanted "a man who will not cater to or coddle minorities or pressure groups," one "who will eliminate bureaucracy" and "respect states' rights."[133] Rickenbacker rejected the premise of the war effort as African Americans and many others understood it: as a battle against both Nazism and white supremacy. Speaking of the American government, not the Nazi regime, the Salt Lake City newspaper editorialized in 1944 that "freedom appears to be in the middle of a losing fight." Instead of promoting the Fifth Freedom, the newspaper complained, "there are those in high places who seem determined to take it away." In reality, it concluded, there is only "one freedom, not four," since free enterprise was the "very foundation of all individual freedom, political, social, and economic."[134]

This pattern of free enterprise thinking continued after the Allied victory. Just days after the conclusion of the war, Herbert Hoover implied that the United States had won a Pyrrhic victory. He brought together arguments that had developed before and during the war and highlighted the danger with alarmist language that foreshadowed Ronald Reagan's 1961 anti-Medicare speech: "You and I must not be marked as the generation who surrendered the heritage of America!" With the Depression over and the war effort successful, Hoover might have been expected to celebrate. Instead, he warned his compatriots of the need for a "great decision" about the future, not just of the nation but also of the world. He particularly highlighted what he called "the decoy term planned economy" which, like communism and socialism, meant a constraining collectivism. He feared the rise of "bureaucratic power over the liberties and economic life of the people."[135] Rather than a lesson about the compatibility of a strong state, democracy, and a free economy, Hoover took a different moral from the war: the fear of an emboldened state in which planners hampered personal freedom.

This generalized fear colored the views of free enterprisers even as they celebrated the triumph of unprecedented affluence and choice in the postwar United States. Although the "possibility of socialism or fascism in this country seems remote, perhaps absurd," as syndicated columnist James Marlow noted in 1946, a good number of people feared this unlikely outcome. If they did share this anxiety, it may have had to do with Marlow's warning that "these next five or ten or 20 years may be the most important in the history of the United States," a claim widely echoed. This immediate postwar future, he said, "may, in fact, decide whether free enterprise is to continue to be the way of life in this country." Spelling out the source of the problem, Marlow explained that free enterprise meant "freedom from government dictation," which needed to be eliminated as soon as possible. Forgetting the fuss that his colleagues put up during the New Deal period, he claimed that "we had such free enterprise before the war." Now the challenge was to reawaken free enterprise from the threat posed by the "opposite way of living." In order to avoid a "death blow," free enterprise had to pass the test posed not only by socialism in England and communism in the Soviet Union but by bureaucrats and planners at home.[136]

Even during the height of the Cold War, free enterprisers pronounced the danger of internal enemies much more pressing than the threat posed by foreign enemies. In 1949, the Vermont representative Charles A. Plumley labeled a range of activities that he called "soft socialism," which he took to mean the welfare state and a government unafraid to spend on behalf of the public purpose, "the greatest menaces confronting us today, not excluding Russia."[137] For this reason, free enterprise advocates also continued to push for the "Fifth Freedom" after the war. The United States Junior Chamber of Commerce embarked in 1947 on a "Fifth Freedom Flight," a "sustained campaign to strengthen Democracy and the free enterprise system that [American soldiers] so gallantly and unselfishly defended on the battlefield."[138] Even in 1949 during the height of the Cold War, John Flynn, a fierce anti–New Dealer, former member of the American First Committee, and vitriolic anticommunist, called "the socialist takeover of the Democratic Party" a much more pressing danger than Soviet communism.[139] As Ethel Lyman Stannard, a regular letter writer to the *Hartford Courant*, warned in 1953, one month after Eisenhower's inauguration, "super-state tyranny" could "as easily be imposed upon us as by an outside power."[140] The source of that imposition, she and many other free enterprisers believed, was the welfare state, which threatened to constrict freedom even in the first Republican presidency since Herbert Hoover's.

"A Revolution to Bring Back the Freedoms We Have Lost"

Supporters of the New Deal spoke of a "Roosevelt Revolution," a positive transformation in the philosophy of governance. They termed it an unusual revolution, however, one that restored rather than destroyed capitalism. In his 1959 book *The Roosevelt Revolution*, political scientist Mario Einaudi stressed "the extent to which the New Deal remained within the framework of what has been loosely called the capitalistic system."[141] New Dealers themselves recognized their philosophy's lack of ideological coherence, and critics ever since have noted that it was, in Jennifer Mittelstadt's words, "exclusionary and inequitable."[142] From this perspective, the New Deal, rather than a totalized force, was "inconsistent and confused," as a 1935 assessment had it.[143]

Critics of the New Deal, however, described it not as contradictory but as unitary, not as reformist but as radical, not as continuous with previous progressive reforms but as a dangerous departure from age-old norms. In the very early days of the New Deal, the *Chicago Tribune* labeled it "a complete makeover of the American system."[144] The following year, the same newspaper warned of "the revolutionary implications of the New Deal." Although Roosevelt claimed otherwise, the New Deal was, according to the *Tribune*, taking the country on the path of "European radicalism."[145] The fear that the New Deal might dangerously transform the country, that it might unleash an unwanted revolution, long outlasted the early, uncertain years of Roosevelt's first term.

Free enterprisers proposed a preemptive counterrevolution made necessary by what they took to be the inevitable logic of the New Deal. They feared, as business journalist Samuel Crowther wrote in 1941, that the nation was "giving way to social revolution of controlled economy."[146] As we have seen, free enterprisers differed about exactly how long the process of "giving way" would take, but all agreed on the need for action to forestall the growth of statism and planning under the New Deal. In this context, James Lincoln, a Cleveland utility executive, called in 1947 for "a revolution to bring back the freedom we have lost."[147] This was the counterrevolution free enterprisers had in mind, one that would stem and reverse the tide of the New Deal state, which they believed was in the process of metamorphosing into a form of totalitarianism that they took to be its destiny. Such language continued into the Cold War years, when many free enterprisers continued to see the communist threat as primarily internal. In 1952, General Douglas MacArthur denounced the politicians "leading us toward a communist state with as dreadful certainty as though the leaders of the Kremlin were charting our course."[148] As during World War II, fighting the Cold War meant being as vigilant against the domestic threats to free enterprise as against global communism.

Some free enterprisers unapologetically used the word *counterrevolution* to describe their goals in the postwar years.[149] Using slightly different language in 1947, Friedrich A. Hayek told the manufacturing and industries committee of the Chamber of Commerce, "Those who believe in free enterprise should open a counteroffensive against the forces seeking to drive this country toward socialism and excessive government controls."[150] Hayek was not telling those in his audience something they did not already believe. The chamber and other business groups had argued since before the war that the path of the counteroffensive lay in the aggressive selling of free enterprise.

The battle between free enterprisers and New Dealers was not symmetrical. Free enterprisers, for all their defensiveness and defining sense of victimization, declared and fought a one-sided war. Yet ever since the New Deal, they have claimed to be under siege. Larry Kudlow, conservative television commentator and later top economic advisor to President Donald Trump, accurately expressed their perspective when he said in 2006 that, "capitalism in this country has been under assault ever since FDR's New Deal 1930s."[151] The description of the New Deal as, in the words of the Fox News managing editor Brit Hume, "a jihad against free enterprise" reverses the valence of the nature of the war by projecting the accommodators as the aggressors, and by describing those who carried out the war on the welfare state as defenders of a civilization under siege.[152] The war *of* free enterprisers was often depicted as a war *on* free enterprisers, who viewed themselves as undermatched "babes in the woods" facing powerful forces of "state-coercion," to borrow the 1939 words of Merle Thorpe.[153] From this perspective, vigilance required that free enterprisers be prepared for the necessary counterrevolutionary war that needed to be fought to prevent the "assaults" on their beloved system that New Dealers and their descendants regularly launched.

For their part, New Dealers and their supporters claimed to believe in the free enterprise system. They held that government was necessary to preserve and expand it, and believed that the history of the 1930s bore out this claim. They argued for what Rexford Tugwell called "the necessity for government interference when a free enterprise system finds itself in trouble beyond its self-repairing capabilities."[154] A group of Keynesian economists in 1938 described the goal of the New Deal as propping up a free enterprise system that, "left to its own devices, is no longer capable of achieving anything approaching full employment" by "restoring the demand for the products of private industry through a vigorous expansion of the public sector."[155] For free enterprisers, however, self-correction was the essence of the capitalist system, and the suggestion that state intervention was necessary to save capitalism counted as an attack rather than a statement of support, proof of the irreconcilable nature of their differences.

The free enterprise critique of the New Deal became the default position and conventional wisdom not just of conservatism but of a good chunk of the broader political culture. Its basic premise is strikingly reactionary: that in the long run, there is no such thing as moderate reform, since all regulatory proposals tend inevitably toward overwhelming statism. If one believed, as Ogden Mills argued in 1935, that the New Deal fostered "authoritarian government and an economic system based on coercion," then any accommodation to it appeared unwise and irrational.[156] When one holds, as did the *Wall Street Journal* in 1942 in the midst of the war effort, that "planning is the direct antithesis of liberty," then it is difficult to justify government intervention in any form.[157]

Examining the leading counternarrative to the New Deal allows us to see how partial and tentative the consolidation of the New Deal was and how a vocal and powerful minority weakened and challenged it, even during its supposed years of triumph. Those who viewed the halting growth of a welfare state as the negation of American freedom have had an outsized influence on American political culture. Free enterprisers understood freedom as indivisible and endangered, and they took the threat to be fundamentally political. Mills set the template for future responses to liberal reform when he said in 1935 that Roosevelt's proposed reforms "cut so deep as to threaten not only the form but the spirit of our institutions."[158] Year after year, free enterprisers framed elections, legislative debates, and regulatory battles as stark—usually binary—choices with potentially devastating consequences to democracy in America. Failed predictions of apocalypse did not stop them from predicting disaster every time expansions of the welfare state were debated. Although New Dealers and their successors succeeded on many fronts, they spent a surprising amount of time during the era of the New Deal order on the defensive, confronting the charge that they were in the process of undermining basic American principles in a way that proponents of tax cuts in any and all circumstances rarely, if ever, did.

Yet we should not be too quick to grant the free enterprisers victory in their war on the New Deal and the welfare state. We should not forget that, in spite of fierce opposition, the New Deal succeeded in transforming the political landscape of the United States. If Henry Steele Commager's 1949 proclamation "If it can ever be said that anything is permanent in American politics, it can be said that the New Deal is permanent" seems overly definitive, it is undeniable that many of the New Deal's core elements endure.[159] Conservatives have generally agreed with this assessment; they have tended to see the New Deal order as winning and free enterprise as under threat or defeated. Indeed, Alfred Jay Nock claimed the New Deal "was here to stay" in 1934, long before most New Dealers would have made this statement with any confidence. Garet Garrett's influential 1944 essay *The Revolution Was* held that the New Deal's victory was irreversible.[160] Even in the wake of the undeniable successes of the conservative counterrevolution in American politics that began in the 1970s, the statist innovations of the New Deal era have by and large survived. In 2011, conservative writer Matthew Continetti, reflecting on the "end of the New Deal order," claimed that the "house that FDR built sits on a wobbly base," suggesting that the basic edifice still stood, however precariously.[161] Indeed, free enterprisers have often depicted themselves as the vanquished party. During the Obama administration, everything from an increase in the minimum wage to the legal enforcement of nondiscrimination was labeled "the death of free enterprise."[162] The Heritage Foundation's Norbert J. Michel claimed in 2015 that "people who believe in the power of individual liberty and free enterprise have had a rough time lately," reflecting a sense of being embattled that is a hardy perennial in free enterprise discourse.[163] Andrew Hartman is likely correct that the 1970s "signaled the beginning of the end of the New Deal order," but that process has been gradual and the project remains incomplete.[164]

Rather than treating the New Deal order and the conservative backlash as serial events, it is more historically accurate to view what New Deal apostate James P. Warburg called "a free enterprise order" and the New Deal order as competing forces, in tension with each other, neither totally dominant even during their periods of relative hegemony.[165] Tracking the battle between free enterprise and the New Deal shows that the pundits were premature to declare a permanent victory for the New Deal in the immediate postwar years. But it also suggests that scholars are equally incorrect to pronounce its defeat in the 1970s or 1980s. In their influential book that introduced the concept of the "New Deal order," Steve Fraser and Gary Gerstle frame its history as one of a "rise and fall."[166] It is more accurate to speak of a continual dialectic rather than a period of victory followed by defeat. For every Alfred Sloan, who announced in 1934 that the "spell of regimentation and a planned economy has been broken" and the stage set for the return of free enterprise, there was the claim, as an editorial cartoonist had it in 1944, that "the death of the New Deal has been greatly exaggerated."[167] This tension is best explained by the persistence and acceptance of the version of free enterprise that was introduced in the late 1920s and remains an immensely popular mode of political discourse. If it did not succeed in fully vanquishing the New Deal order, it helped make free enterprise the dominant political language of the late twentieth and early twenty-first centuries. For a term of such significance, however, it was surprisingly ambiguous. It is to the slippery efforts to define the phase, and ultimately the abandonment of those attempts, that we next turn.

4

A "Beautiful but Much-Abused Phrase"

"IF ONE CAN FOLLOW THE TRAIL OF A telling phrase," wrote conservative columnist John Chamberlain in 1964, "one can often find the key to a social movement."[1] The phrase *free enterprise*, as anti–New Dealers employed it, spawned such a significant movement. Yet following the trail of free enterprise is tricky because of the difficulty of defining what Felix Morley called the "beautiful but much-abused phrase."[2]

Consider DeWitt Emery, the founder and president of the American Small Business Man's Association, who felt frustrated in the fall of 1948 and wanted his fellow citizens to know why. The six foot six, 245-pound Emery, the self-proclaimed "biggest advocate of small business," branded himself "a salesman for free enterprise." After more than a decade spent promulgating "free enterprise" as the fundamental American value—indispensable in the battle against what he saw as the dangers of New Deal statism and the totalitarianism that it threatened to become—Emery experienced an incident close to home that suggested how much work remained to be done. As he explained in his syndicated column, his son James, a high school freshman, had recently been assigned to write an essay on "free enterprise," a common topic for secondary school students in the post–World War II years. Following his dad's suggestion, James began his research by seeking a definition of the term. James perused the family's encyclopedia to no avail, then he checked other reference books in the house, "including three dictionaries, without finding anything." After satisfying himself that his son had searched assiduously, Emery discussed with him the

DeWitt Emery, the "biggest advocate of small business" and an ardent free enterpriser. (Historical Images/ Acme/Newspictures.)

meaning of the term and together they came up with a definition that worked well enough to earn James an A on the assignment.[3]

"Not being able to find a definition in our encyclopedia," Emery confessed, "worried me." So the next morning he sent his secretary to the Chicago Public Library, confident that the many thousands of reference works in one of the nation's best municipal libraries would contain a definition of this fundamental American term. Three reference librarians gamely but unsuccessfully took up the challenge. For Emery, the lack of a readily available definition represented a crisis. "For more than one hundred fifty years, 'freedom of enterprise' has been the very backbone of the economic life of the country," he wrote, "yet three highly skilled professional librarians working with as large and complete a collection of reference books as there is to be found any place in the country were unable to find a definition of this commonly used term." Emery's history may have been dubious, but his statement accurately reflected the panic of those who believed that a fundamental American term appeared to have been left out of the most basic of all sources of information, the dictionary.

Emery's column, reprinted in hundreds of newspapers around the country, "stirred up quite a rumpus."[4] Inspired by it, the *San Francisco News* ran a multipart series about the meaning of free enterprise. John Piper, the newspaper's business editor, decided to investigate, wondering why, notwithstanding the fact that "business leaders talk constantly about 'free enterprise,'" this "battle cry of the National Association of Manufacturers" lacked the imprimatur of a dictionary entry. After sending a reporter to the San Francisco Public Library, whose day-long search for a definition proved as fruitless as the one in Chicago, Piper invited his readers to define the term. Over the course of several weeks, the newspaper received dozens of definitions.[5] Business leaders echoed Emery's concern that a ready definition of what they took to be a central American idea was not widely available.

That concern was also mocked. *Detroit Free Press* editor Malcolm Bingay called the phrase "meaningless and tautological" and was unsurprised "that you will not find such poor English in any good dictionary." He recommended abandoning the substanceless term altogether. "When our business leaders quit worshipping catch phrases a good many of our national problems will solve themselves," he concluded.[6] Pat Frayne, a labor journalist, was equally dismissive: "A nationwide hunt is on for the definition of 'free enterprise,' with the recent discovery that no one has yet set down an authoritative meaning for that phrase," he wrote. "Used for years as a cliché-club over the head of organized labor and cliché-cloak for management, it is now revealed that 'free enterprise' has neither a dictionary for a father nor an encyclopedia for a mother."[7] Frayne saw the lack of definition as undermining the entire business free enterprise project because it showed the claims by its advocates of a long genealogy to be false. He hoped the revelation about what he took to be the fraudulence of the phrase as used by business and political leaders would weaken the political power of its advocates.

The wisest response to Piper's quest for the term's definition on behalf of the *San Francisco News* came from a reference librarian: "If there was any definition for it," she told him, "there would be no need for all those books concerning it to be written." As the librarian recognized, the ambiguity of free enterprise was a key to its staying power. In 1939, the *Washington Post* denounced the "general run of vague and often meaningless tributes to the spirit of free enterprise."[8] While undoubtedly vague, the tributes to free enterprise were anything but meaningless. Although the difficulties defining the phrase persisted, it did not follow that, as one commentator said in 1944, it is "a word that from the very beginning anyone is free to give it any interpretation one wishes."[9] Indeed, definitional confusion did little to stem the tide of the "social movement" that business free enterprisers built. This is so in large measure because free enterprise acquired meaning as an opposite to, and rejection of, what free enterprisers took to be the dominant threat facing the nation, the expansion of government power under Roosevelt and successor governments. In defining these threats as acts of war, they imparted "free enterprise" with meaning, above all, as the linchpin of the heroic battle against the enemies of free enterprise. They took the great dictionary fiasco to be further evidence of the need to expand this war.

The definitional crisis threatened for a time to undermine the "free enterprise" cause just as it seemed to be emerging as a viable counterpoint to, and constraint on, the New Deal. Ultimately, many advocates decided that a definition was not the best or even a necessary way to explain the "nature of free enterprise."[10] But the path to understandings of the "free enterprise system" as common sense, as tradition, and as the "American Way" was tortuous and included a long period of wrestling with the phrase. Was the phrase itself inadequate? Or was the lack of a ready definition an easily correctable oversight? For a time, advocates searched for alternative definitions and even some of its strongest supporters proposed abandoning the term. Ultimately, free enterprisers, in spite of their angst about the lack of consensus about what the term meant, deemed definitions relatively unimportant. Even without successfully promulgating a consensus definition, they successfully made the term one that we take for granted, a condition that shields it from critical scrutiny. The irony is that from the late 1930s through the 1950s, free enterprisers themselves scrutinized the phrase relentlessly as they tried to fine-tune its meaning and spread its message in an atmosphere of crisis. By relentlessly turning it into the widely adopted label for enemies of the New Deal, however, they also made the work of definitions relatively unimportant.

"The Trail of a Telling Phrase"

Emery's anxiety about the failure of the term to appear in reference books was one of several periodic episodes in which free enterprisers worried about the effectiveness of the term upon which the "system" rested. Although they wished it to enter the popular lexicon unambiguously, it remained deeply contested, with business leaders, editorialists, and politicians devoting tremendous energy to solving what they perceived as a definitional crisis. The first of several well-publicized reminders that advocates' attempts to explain the term had been unsuccessful, a Gallup poll of 1943, five years before Emery's column, found that most Americans could not define the phrase.

Despite the absence of a definition, the first profile of Emery to appear in a major newspaper, early in 1938, shortly after he had traveled to New York to promote his "movement" of small businessmen, showed that Emery had nonetheless imbibed key elements of the emerging free enterprise discourse. In a talk at the Hotel Pennsylvania, he highlighted what had already become and would remain the central idea of free enterprise discourse, the negation of what he took to be dangerous initiatives of the New Deal. The "tall, genial bespectacled Ohioan" and "lifelong Republican" "attacked the New Deal and all of its works." He called for deregulation (ending "government meddling in business"), tax cuts ("equitable and just tax laws"), and austerity ("some real old-fashioned political economy"). He also extolled the political wisdom of the "corner grocer," a figure already becoming a cliché of free enterprisers, who underemphasized the political power of large business firms by assimilating them with grocers and other small proprietors.[11] Like other free enterprisers, he regularly condemned government "bureaucracy" and organized labor. As Lewis F. Powell Jr. was to do decades later, he called for a strong counterattack against what he saw as the prevailing trends, which were all moving, as far as he was concerned, in a negative direction. Naming the enemy, far more than constructing definitions, proved to be the preferred path for free enterprisers, and the more enduring one. Without offering a definition, Emery laid out something more important for a discourse that worked by repetition: a series of talking points that he hoped to make common sense.

Like other free enterprise apostles, Emery never veered from the ideas he publicized in 1938; as one 1947 profile noted, his "tune is always the same."[12] Just as important, he consistently employed an aggrieved tone and a sense of urgency that were just as central to free enterprise discourse as his preferred policies. Small business, he claimed in 1945, was in a "life or death struggle for existence."[13] The New Deal, in his view, was a form of snobbery, since it not only empowered elites to tell ordinary people what to do, it spent (and wasted) their money in the process. Emery denigrated the "planned economy" as an illusion concocted by "long haired boys" who were convinced that "if we will just turn everything over to them, they'll be able to plan everything so that we will, at last, actually have in this country, the land of milk and honey the world has been searching for since the beginning of time." These elitist, unmanly utopians, he claimed, viewed the people as "nothing more than the poor dumb saps who pay the taxes." Arrogantly, they believed that they "can plan our individual lives for us infinitely better than we can do for ourselves."[14] Treating the New Deal as a form of theft in which one group took from another and haughtily imposed its unwelcome and alien ideas, Emery insisted that, as the 1947 profile put it, "what business wants is what the country ought to have." Emery, like most free enterprisers, took business's representatives' desire to serve the needs of the country as evidence that they should run it. Whereas government planners arrogantly foisted their views onto the citizenry, Emery assumed that business leaders spoke for the people and that their preferred policies, in contrast to those of the arrogant statists, would best serve them.

Over his long career, Emery championed free enterprise without ever defining it. He was far from alone. "Americans need no definition of the free enterprise system," wrote Virginia senator Harry Byrd in 1957. For Byrd, as for many others, the results of the system spoke for themselves. "It is the system that, within a span of some 160 years, has brought us from the impotency of thirteen colonies to our present position of world leadership. It has enabled us, with only 6 per cent of the world's population, to out produce the rest of the world."[15] In this view, the fruits of the free enterprise system, the abundance it unleashed, were sufficient proof of its value. It was to be understood not by words but by virtue of the material wealth and political liberties it produced.

Emery was not the first to note that *free enterprise* did not appear in reference books. In 1944, syndicated writer Susan Thayer reflected on "how many people don't know the meaning of that phrase we see so often—'free enterprise.'" Realizing that her dictionary did not contain a definition, she reported, "Just for fun I looked up 'free' and 'enterprise.'" Then, playing "the old game, how many words can you make out of it?" she proposed multiple definitions and argued that the term was inherently ambiguous.[16] In 1947, in a well-publicized forum on free enterprise, A. D. H. Kaplan noted that the term did not appear even in "the unabridged Webster."[17] In 1943, Emery himself had participated in a radio discussion about the meaning of free enterprise. The moderator, Ben Grauer, opened the program by reading a letter from a listener who was "puzzled by the term free enterprise." One of the other panelists, William Benton, called it a "very tough question." He reported that New York governor and soon to be presidential candidate Thomas Dewey "has been trying to get a good definition of free enterprise for years, and I don't think Mr. Emery and Mr. Crawford and I are going to answer it in a minute or two." Benton concluded that "its meaning changes from generation to generation."[18] Emery didn't disagree, although he did not mention this incident when, five years later, he reported on the inadequacies of the Chicago Public Library's reference works and implied that this episode is what shocked him into awareness about the lack of a readily findable definition.

The reality, as Elisha Douglass wrote in his historical survey of "free enterprise," was that "practical businessmen" by and large "do not ponder deeply about its meaning," although they firmly rejected the idea that the phrase was a "delusive euphemism." For them, it was what he called "an honorific term" and an "emotion laden phrase," important for "guardians of the conservative tradition" who sought to battle the encroachments of statism.[19] As one Creston Wolfe noted in a letter to the editor of the *St. Louis Star and Times*, confusions about the meaning of the term hadn't weakened people's devotion to the idea. Quite the opposite: "The seeming devotion often lavished on this little-understood concept frequently has the appearance of worship."[20] Wolfe implied that the need for faith followed from the lack of definition. But the reverse was also true: declarations of faith rendered the search for a definition immaterial.

By the late 1940s, then, what we might call the "free enterprise freak-out" that Emery initiated when he expressed his shock at the lack of a consensus definition was already a well-established genre. "Unnumbered millions of men have given their lives for slogans, mere words, that they did not understand, could not define, nor translate into action," wrote Michael O'Shaughnessy in 1945 in a book chapter titled "Free Enterprise—What Is it?"[21] The ongoing crises of definition did remarkably little, however, to stem the power of free enterprise discourse. Instead, they abetted its power by encouraging free enterprisers to invoke faith, adopt the language of common sense, and engage in massive campaigns to "sell free enterprise" to the American public.

Although advocates periodically proposed replacing free enterprise with a new label, they ultimately settled on another approach in which they substituted myth for linguistic precision, abandoned definitional purity for a catalogue of the beneficial characteristics of the free enterprise system, called on custom for legitimation, and proclaimed the term the crucial ammunition needed in the war to save American capitalism and liberty. Acknowledging in 1944 that free enterprise was "easy to speak, but very hard to define," for example, an editorialist in Oregon claimed that the term had value because it stood for opposition to the government's efforts "to regulate everybody and everything."[22] Opponents of the New Deal knew what it meant even if they had a hard time defining it. A 1940 editorial published in Scripps Howard newspapers noting that "various G.O.P. hopefuls in their Lincoln Day speeches dwelt on a fine and glittering phrase, 'free enterprise,'" and predicting that "it is apt to become something of a Republican slogan" but only "if they define it," was half correct: "free enterprise" became a GOP slogan but it remained undefined.[23] Indeed, not defining it proved to be less of an impediment than the free enterprisers predicted. As Henry Wriston, the president of Brown University, pointed out in December 1943, "Free enterprise is a subject upon which, when definitions are avoided, nearly everyone can agree."[24] Eventually, most anti–New Deal advocates of free enterprise took Wriston's advice and avoided offering definitions in their hopes of achieving consensus.

"A Lot of Woids"

We can date modern free enterprise's crisis of meaning with some precision. It followed the release of the findings of a Gallup poll in 1943, mentioned above, the results of which stunned business leaders and politicians. The headline in the *Washington Post* and many other newspapers on November 6 of that year told the story: "Only Three in Every Ten Are Able to Give Correct Definition of 'Free Enterprise.'"[25] How was it possible, wondered George Gallup, as well as those who had promoted the slogan relentlessly for the previous decade, that the vast majority of Americans did not comprehend the phrase that was, they believed, the bulwark of American prosperity and democracy? Gallup argued that "if proponents of 'free enterprise' hope to enlist widespread public support under this banner, they have first to do some work in educating the public on the meaning of the term itself." On the basis of his survey, he was quite certain that "the great majority are either without any idea or with an erroneous one." This represented a serious problem for an idea that proponents described as deeply embedded in the consciousness of ordinary Americans.

Tellingly, Gallup did not himself define the phrase. But this did not stop him from asserting that knowledge about free enterprise varied by class and gender, with professional men possessing the most acute understanding. He noted that only a quarter of women could define the phrase, while a third of men could do so, and that those "best able to define the term from a percentage point of view, are professional and business people." In highlighting the worst definitions,

Gallup cited only working-class people—"a printer in Queens County, NY," a "truck driver from Holdenville, OK," "a New York City drug clerk," and "a soldier"—whom he reported to be "bewildered," suggesting that their honesty about their ignorance was worse than the assertions of understanding voiced by business leaders. He quoted their confused statements, including "I don't know what it means. Why not tax it?" to comic effect. The fact that, according to Gallup, "only one in six among unskilled laboring groups know what the term means" indicated to him that proponents of free enterprise had not successfully explained why it might matter to the "rank and file." This should be "disturbing to those fighting on behalf of free enterprise," whom Gallup understood, correctly, to be the business and political elite.

Gallup's martial phrasing here was ambiguous: was he referring to business's fight against the New Deal or to the war effort? Free enterprisers fought a two-front war: educating citizens about the meaning of the term while also convincing a suspicious public that the term was worth defending in the first place. According to the columnist H. R. Baukhage in 1944, the campaign for free enterprise was meant to answer the question "What are we fighting for?"[26] Some critics of the phrase, emboldened by the poll, questioned the notion that free enterprise lay at the root of the American war effort. "Of all the baloney being passed around about what we're fighting for, free enterprise takes the cake," Bruce Bliven, the editor of the *New Republic*, claimed in a 1943 radio debate held at Cleveland's Carnegie Hall on the question "What Is Free Enterprise?"[27]

What might have been more disturbing to business free enterprisers was not the confusion but the perceptiveness with which some of the supposedly clueless workers understood the phrase. One reported to Gallup, "Free enterprise is what the Republicans haven't got under Roosevelt," a statement more lucid, concise, and insightful than any definition offered by business leaders. The worker's comment brilliantly, if inadvertently, pointed out that the fundamental reference point for business free enterprisers was the New Deal that they vehemently opposed. Free enterprise was precisely a fighting phrase; it made sense and acquired meaning only in opposition.

Business leaders and politicians feared that the lack of understanding of free enterprise, underlined by the findings of the Gallup poll, "may explain a good deal about the astonishing success of the economic quackery that has been in circulation the last few years," as an editorial in the *Salisbury Times* claimed shortly after the release of the poll. For free enterprisers, the New Deal qualified as quackery. Admitting that it was an "oversight" that Gallup had failed to "submit a pat definition," the editorialist claimed that a profession of belief in free enterprise, if not a definition, was "necessary to safeguard the national welfare."[28] If free enterprise were seen as unimportant or unclear, business leaders and politicians feared that radical alternatives might take its place and that the traditional moorings of the nation might be displaced.

For anxious free enterprisers, the definitional deficit foretold a political crisis. Just days after the release of the Gallup poll, the trade journal *Advertising Age* echoed the themes of public ignorance and business responsibility. Advertisers, an editorial in the magazine claimed, "ought to start working hard on the vital problem of presenting the story of the enterprise system in such a way as to sell the 70 per cent who either don't understand it or are opposed now to what they think it means." Those charged with building "favorable public attitudes toward the system" had their work cut out for them, and the stakes were high, since the editors interpreted the lack of understanding to be a form of hostility.[29] For example, in early 1945, H. W. Prentis, president of Armstrong Cork Company and former leader of NAM, told the Business and Professional Men's Group at the University of Cincinnati that in light of the Gallup poll, "only three in ten Americans understand the differences between state socialism and our republican form of government."[30] This was a telling comment because it revealed that underlying the definitional quandaries was less a fear that Americans didn't understand free enterprise so much as the concern that they continued to support the positive view of government initiated by the New Deal. Prentis took free enterprise to be equivalent to "our republican form of government" and the New Deal tantamount to "state socialism."

One of the most instructive responses to the crisis of free enterprise came in March 1944 when Leonard Dreyfuss, the longtime president of the United Advertising Corporation, initiated a free enterprise definition contest. Concerned that free enterprise "has come into as bad repute as the phrase capitalism was some years ago," and that "unless American business prevails, democracy hasn't a chance," Dreyfuss, like others in his industry, associated understanding free enterprise with endorsing it. This was not just an issue of definition but of legitimacy. To solve both issues—definition and legitimation—Dreyfuss encouraged readers of *Printers' Ink*, an advertising trade journal, to submit definitions of free enterprise that "John Q. Public can absorb." Dreyfuss looked eagerly to a future in which the term would "never be used on any platform or in conversation, unless a four second explanation goes with it." Perhaps overoptimistic about the power of the advertising trade group to dictate meanings, he proposed that the editor select a jury to pick the three best accounts and "pledge everybody to use them."[31]

In response to Dreyfuss's solicitation, several dozen readers submitted definitions that the editors published throughout the spring of 1944.[32] One businessman even submitted a poem explaining what the system meant to "Mr. and Mrs. John Q. American." The poem appeared on a poster that explained for business owners "in a very to-the-point fashion the value of private enterprise to their employees and the public." The suggested definitions ranged in length from a few sentences to many paragraphs and rarely strayed from a decade of well-worn clichés long articulated by Emery and others, such as the lines of the free enterprise poem noted above that read, "To be no chattel of the State / To be the master of our fate."[33] Ralph S. Dunne, a coal-coke fuel oil retailer from Pennsylvania, said that free enterprise "stands for freedom of opportunity." Bernard Craven of the Craven & Hedrick advertising firm emphasized "the free play of competition without undue government regulation." It was a "social system under which individual ambition is limited only by one's self," offered Robert R. Brown of Outserts, Inc.[34] No new ground was broken and no one definition emerged triumphant.

An editor's postscript to Dreyfuss's call for a definition contest held out the possibility that the problem might inhere in the term: "It may be the phrase itself that should be altered, or perhaps discarded entirely and another one substituted for it—one that is more readily understood by the rank and file of people." The use of the same phrase that Gallup employed, rank and file, was telling, suggesting that advocates took the problem to lie with the consumers rather than the disseminators of the phrase. At about the same time, an internal NAM memo claimed that free enterprise was one of those terms that "somehow fails to register . . . to readily, snappily convey their meaning."[35] This seeming willingness to abandon the phrase (about which more below) suggests the degree to which free enterprisers felt incapable of persuading Americans of the phrase's importance and of their consequent inability to "sell" it. "Our Free Enterprise system is facing one of the greatest challenges in its history," claimed a pamphlet produced by NAM in 1945.[36] While, as we have seen, it was not at all unusual for advocates to declare free enterprise imperiled—indeed, they depicted it as being in a state of continual crisis—the lack of definition temporarily set off consternation about the term's very utility. Writing in *Printers' Ink*, Lifford Murragh sounded as critical as the liberal editor of the *New Republic* when he declaimed that "'believing' in something with a meaning as hazy and undefinable as the meaning of free enterprise seems to be, is just superstition."[37] Rather than counseling faith, Murragh suggested that reliance on the term was not a strategy for success. If advertising men, the free enterprise shock troops, found the supposedly foundational phrase to be vague and ineffectual, the fight for free enterprise appeared lost.

Some accentuated the positive in the floundering efforts to define free enterprise. The editors of the *Annapolis Capitol* described the numerous and diverse submissions as "an encouraging sign of the times" that proved the term was not "outmoded."[38] Most observers, however, took a negative view. Even *Printers' Ink*, the journal that sponsored the definition contest, published mostly negative commentary about the effort. Typical was the letter writer who called the effort "a notable failure."[39] Similarly, John Orr Young, the founder of the Young and Rubicam ad agency, wrote that "the variety of the definitions submitted to *Printers' Ink* indicates a good deal of uncertainty about what 'free enterprise' means." Thinking pragmatically, Young claimed that "the test of an expression of this kind, an often used generality, for advertising purposes should be the reaction of the reader. If it has only a vague meaning for people, if it doesn't suggest they ought to do something about it, or if it may be applied in quite the reverse of the advertiser's intention, some other slogan or related idea had better be chosen." Young stated that "there is undoubtedly an idea that businessmen really need to sell to the American people," and he was confident that they could sell it "in terms of the people's felt wants and common understanding."[40] What exactly those were, he was not prepared to say.

The nadir of the contest came when a wounded soldier, Erwin H. Klaus, predicted in a letter to the journal that "the overwhelming majority of the men now fighting for America will reject these definitions." Doubtless to the chagrin of the free enterprisers, who saw themselves as the voice of the war's larger meanings and who frequently claimed to speak on behalf of ordinary servicemen, Klaus wrote, "It seems that many leaders of business and industry have taken no account of the thoughts and ideas of the men who may be called upon to spend their lives for the free enterprise of post-war America." Referring to the shortcomings of specific definitions submitted, he wrote, "They will tell Bernard N. Craven, who asserts that 'the right of an American to work and earn is not guaranteed by any business system,' that that is not what they are fighting for," and "They will ask L. L. Brastow, who defines free enterprise as 'a chance to take a chance,' if he means to imply a denial of responsibility for the common good."[41] Klaus believed that regular soldiers disclaimed the anti–New Deal cause on whose behalf they were regularly said to be fighting.

Weighing in grumpily on the definitions published in *Printers' Ink* at his behest, Leonard Dreyfuss labeled all of them unacceptable. "I contended that businessmen had a fairly good idea of 'Free enterprise' but the public had no definition which they could easily understand," he began, reminding readers of the impetus for the contest. Continuing to believe that free enterprise "is one of the foundation stones of the American way of living," Dreyfuss claimed that no submission had hit the mark he had set: concision and common sense. "It shouldn't be necessary ... to read four pages of technical language to grasp what we mean by two simple American words," he wrote in frustration.[42] Dreyfuss concluded that the contest he initiated had failed.

When Eric A. Johnston, head of the U.S. Chamber of Commerce, described the situation for free enterprisers in April 1944 as one of "crisis and opportunity," he could have been accused of seeking to turn lemons into lemonade. A few months later, Johnston admitted, "Ask any ten businessmen what a free, private, competitive enterprise system means or involves, and you are likely to get as many different answers, some wrong, some right, some ambiguous, and some confused." As was the case with many other proponents, Johnston never himself explained what the "right" answer was.[43] Johnston chose instead to emphasize the opportunities available to proponents of free enterprise, mostly by focusing on what they opposed.

A coda to this story of definitional crisis came after the war when *Business Week*, using terms remarkably similar to those that Gallup had employed two and a half years earlier, published an article early in 1946 lamenting that the group the reporter for *Business Week* interviewed—"the wage-earning element of the population" in a number of eastern cities—still did not understand free enterprise. The reporter mocked their supposedly inane misunderstandings. Much like Gallup, the magazine concluded, on the basis of a "field investigation" into the lives of "the common man, whose century some say this is," that "the term free private enterprise means nothing at all." The author quoted a "New York City subway guard" who, when asked to define the phrase, said, "It's just a lot of woids."[44]

To *Business Week*, "the moral of our little study" was that in spite of the confusion it generated, the term free enterprise served "the common welfare better than any other that is likely to be devised." The solution was for business leaders to provide "a far better opportunity" to understand the term. Like Gallup, *Business Week* turned the definitional confusion into a class issue; the problem was less the wealthy purveyors than ordinary Americans, who failed to grasp this essential concept. And, once again, it was hard not to read the sarcastic comments of working people as critique rather than incomprehension. The idea that working people took the phrase to have no meaning or cynically assumed it to be merely self-serving rhetoric of the ruling class continued to concern free enterprisers. As Paul H. Griffith, the national commander of the American Legion, said in a speech in December 1946, one half of the population has "no idea at all of its meaning" and, more dangerously, those who thought they knew what the term meant often assign "it highly original and individualized interpretations having nothing to do with the orthodox conception of the phrase."[45] Like Gallup and the *Business Week* reporter, however, Griffith did not define this "orthodox conception."

"Free Enterprise Is Not Laissez Faire"

Free enterprisers, as we have seen, had a hard time saying what exactly it was. They were much clearer about what it was not. By far, the most important negative landmark was the New Deal. But, perhaps surprisingly, they also went to great lengths to distinguish free enterprise from laissez-faire. If they rejected the statism of the New Deal, they also regularly asserted that they did not condemn government entirely. When the *Business Week* reporter visited the public library to "discover the nature of free private enterprise," he appeared shocked that the reference librarian "explained that we could become enlightened about free private enterprise by reading, of all things, about laissez faire!" The reporter was offended that the librarian treated free enterprise and laissez-faire as equivalents. Since, as the *Economist* reported the previous year, the *Readers' Guide to Periodical Literature* treated free enterprise as a synonym for laissez-faire, the reporter should not have been surprised.[46] Yet free enterprisers vehemently rejected this connection, arguing that laissez-faire, as Herbert Hoover said in 1934, "has been dead in America for generations," and claimed that they had no desire to revive it.[47]

Advocates rejected laissez-faire not just because it was out date but because it was unrealistic in the modern world. "Free enterprise is not laissez faire," declared a discussant in a 1944 debate, echoing a point that had already become a truism.[48] When he ran for president that year as the Republican nominee, Thomas E. Dewey "pledged his devotion" to free enterprise. But alongside this fealty, he declared, "The U.S. never will return to the days of unchecked operation of laws of supply and demand, starvation wages and ruinous farm prices." The "era of dog-eat-dog is ended," Dewey proclaimed.[49] Free enterprisers walked a fine line, proclaiming simultaneously that government intervention had once been necessary and that even a small expansion of the state could lead to the downfall of the republic.

Recognizing the unpopularity of a totally unregulated economy, even a rare unabashed supporter of the idea, the conservative journalist and economics writer John Chamberlain, claimed that it need to be rebranded, "scrubbed clean of its past associations." The term, he said in 1950, "conjures up pictures of . . . tenements, of the Pinkertons shooting down strikers at Homestead," all images of class warfare.[50] In 1943, in the midst of World War II, Henry Wriston complained, "Whenever one speaks about reducing the restrictions and regulations now applied to our economy, the finger of scorn is waggled at him; he is accused of wanting to return to 'laissez faire.'" No "modern indictment . . . could be more damning."[51] Most free enterprisers, however, did not wish to reclaim the term, scrubbed of past associations or not. Like Hoover, they believed that it was "outmoded."[52]

Despite the repeated claims that the germ of government intervention would produce "a virus of creeping socialism," free enterprise advocates rejected the ideology of laissez-faire.[53] They followed a long-term pattern of claiming that they accepted some previous forms of government intervention but adamantly rejected the need to consider any further extension of statism. As *Fortune* magazine declared in 1942, with admirable forthrightness: "The counterrevolution we propose is not a return to laissez faire."[54] Believing that the "traditional" system had been subverted by the revolutionary New Deal, free enterprise advocates believed in a particular limited kind of counterrevolution. They preferred to articulate a theory of containment that accepted most of the previous gains of the Progressive Era and even some of the New Deal, rather than a rollback that would wipe them out entirely.

Free enterprisers almost universally acknowledged a theoretical place for government in the economic life of the nation. Nevertheless, in practical terms, they rarely identified what such a proper role might be. "No one of any sense proposes a system of free enterprise without corresponding government regulation," said Alf Landon, the Republican presidential nominee in 1936. "No one really wants complete laissez faire."[55] Landon was silent about what forms of regulation were appropriate. Even the virulently anti–New Deal H. W. Prentis, the president of the Armstrong Cork Corporation and leader of NAM, claimed in 1940 that the free enterprise system differed from "the laissez faire of Adam Smith." Introducing a metaphor favored ever since by conservatives, Prentis endorsed "reasonable umpiring on the part of government to insure fair play." Straightaway, however, he worried about situations in which "government ceases to be an umpire" and instead indulged "the full strength of its dominating authority."[56] Like others who disclaimed laissez-faire, he refused to define the line between legitimate and illegitimate government action. No specific case seemed to meet the criteria for the general principle of government intervention, although he and others recognized that such cases did exist in theory.

The rhetorical dance that free enterprisers perfected was a two-step: first, admit that government intervention had been necessary in the past, and second, claim that further intervention was not just unnecessary but dangerous. Strom Thurmond, the governor of South Carolina, demonstrated the pas de deux in 1949, when he conceded that "there are, of course, many fields in which government can and should operate to provide improved living conditions, health, and security for unfortunate citizens."[57] Yet his overall message was that totalitarian dangers lurked behind every social welfare or civil rights scheme orchestrated by the government.

The discussion of laissez-faire among free enterprisers almost always took a "yes . . . but" form. "Obviously, some functions of government are both necessary and desirable," said Robert Liebenow, president of the Chicago Board of Trade in 1959, in a typical statement of the genre, "but wouldn't you agree with me in saying that for government to continue to expand until it is the mainspring of our national economy is both unsafe and unwise?"[58] Rarely did the free enterprise critics of laissez-faire mention a proposed form of government intervention that they supported. Their approval of regulation was almost always backward looking. "Don't leap to the conclusion that [I am against] regulation, or that I think free enterprise should be unfettered," said Alan Boyd in a 1974 speech on the challenges to free enterprise. "That would be far off the mark." Unlike most free enterprisers, Boyd enumerated regulatory policies that he endorsed, all of them well in the past. The examples he gave—pure food and drugs, weights and standards, the "safe use of deposited funds in public banks"—were no longer controversial topics at the time that he spoke, most having been addressed during the Progressive Era.[59]

Senator Robert A. Taft disclaimed the similarity of laissez-faire to his preferred ideal, noting that "free enterprise has never been completely free." Taft asked the question that was central to free enterprisers: "how far can the government go without in effect destroying the substantial freedom of private enterprise."[60] For most free enterprisers the answer was: not far at all. Although Taft maintained, "No one can rightly claim that he should not be regulated in the public interest, or taxed to support necessary government activities," he did not specify what qualified as a public interest worth regulating or a necessary government expenditure. Although they differentiated free enterprise from laissez-faire, proponents rarely linked it with any welfare or public spending programs other than those that were long ago legitimated.

A good example of this theoretical opposition to laissez-faire combined with hyperbolic fear of actual government programs came from Harold D. Koontz in his 1951 article "Government Control: The Road to Serfdom?" Despite employing the phrase made famous by F. A. Hayek in his title, Koontz began by claiming that laissez-faire was unsuited to the times. "It is perfectly natural that, as our economic system has become more complex, we should increasingly assign the responsibilities of control to our Federal government," Koontz wrote. Rather than enumerating these responsibilities, he worried that the "extension of collectivism in such free nations as Great Britain would eventually bring an end to political and economic freedom."[61] Koontz left unclear what category of government action was both necessary and unlikely to lead to "serfdom."

Into the 1970s, free enterprisers paradoxically claimed both to have moved beyond free market fundamentalism and to oppose social welfare programs, public spending, and government regulation. "Please don't misunderstand!" declared Richard Lesher, head of the U.S. Chamber of Commerce and a principal architect of the deregulation movement of the 1970s. "Most of the business community has come to applaud progress in many areas of human activity—human rights, environmental protection, consumerism, and others!" Lesher insisted, "Those objectives are no longer questioned."[62] Several years later, however, his organization led the fight against a proposed cabinet-level Consumer

Protection Agency. Although business leaders applauded "progress," very few of them saw regulation as a path to progress. Instead, they understood it as a road to serfdom. The mode of free enterprisers was to praise no-longer-controversial governmental action in the past and to denounce any form of regulation under consideration in the present. Laissez-faire was unacceptable in the contemporary world, but so too was the more dangerous threat of super-statism. In this context, claiming that free enterprise was not the same as laissez-faire had very few real-world implications, since the recognition of the limits of free markets applied only to the past.

"Only a Term"

As the debates over the term's definitions show, free enterprisers viewed their ideal as both foundational and fragile, and the two were intimately related. They understood free enterprise, born and raised in a perpetual atmosphere of (often imagined) crisis, as vulnerable. Its time of peak use and political salience coincided with the New Deal order, a period during which free enterprisers described themselves as under near-constant attack and the system as under duress. "The theory of free enterprise was forced to take a back seat . . . during the depression years of the 1930s," claimed the *Washington Post* in 1951.[63] But this common enough assertion gets the timing almost precisely backward. For the decade of the 1930s is when the idea of free enterprise, in its modern sense, moved into the front seat alongside its nemesis, the New Deal, where it remained for the rest of the century. Free enterprise was treated as a tradition and a bulwark against the New Deal threat, and its advocates invented a mythical past for the term. Frequently referring to the "period of free enterprise, 1920–1932" or the "free enterprise era of 1920 through 1932," proponents described a golden age in which the idea supposedly reigned unchallenged.[64] Yet even in the late 1920s, advocates stressed not their triumphs but the obstacles that the free enterprise system faced. As we have seen, there was no time during which free enterprisers did not claim that their ideal was endangered.

Proof that free enterprise's meaning emerged in opposition can be found by examining when the term was widely deployed. Although advocates described the period from 1920 to 1932 as the golden age, in fact the phrase appeared only 50 times in twelve of the nation's leading newspapers in those years. By contrast, during the era when advocates described it as most endangered, 1933 to

1972, the period from the election of Franklin Roosevelt to the publication of the Powell memo, it appeared 44,293 times in those same publications.[65] The real "era of free enterprise," then, came in the four decades or so after the election of Franklin D. Roosevelt, when the phrase flourished as an oppositional concept, an antidote to the New Deal. Although it was commonly held that, as columnist Ernest L. Meyer wrote, "The anti–New Dealers are plucking slightly moldy chestnuts from the political dustbin," the term, as they used it, was novel.[66]

In the period when free enterprise emerged as the New Deal's "other," there was considerable confusion about its origin, with advocates calling it traditional and opponents highlighting its novelty. The explosion in its use led many people to assume that it was new; indeed, "free enterprise" made it into the annual *Dictionary of Neologisms* in both 1947 and 1949.[67] One journalist wrote in 1948 that the term had been recently invented and promoted by "one of the bright young men then working for the National Association of Manufacturers," the business lobby led by Prentis, archcritic of the New Deal.[68] This idea continued to be articulated in the twenty-first century, when a well-known political scientist claimed the phrase "was only invented in the late 1930s." In 2008, two other writers claimed, with even more specificity, "The American lexicon was expanded in 1942, never before had the term 'free enterprise' been used."[69] Those who called *free enterprise* a newfangled term of the 1930s were technically incorrect, since the compound word had been employed almost continually for more than a century. In important ways, however, they were correct to note that the term, in its modern sense as a fighting phrase against the welfare state, had its origins in that period. Their claims are no more misleading than the more narrowly accurate statement of Arthur Brooks of the American Enterprise Institute, who wrote in 2011 that free enterprise "has been integral to American culture from our nation's earliest days."[70] The assumption of continuity of meaning does at least as much injustice to the contested history of the term as do the false claims of novelty, not least because the idea that there was a deep tradition of free enterprise dating back centuries was central to anti–New Deal politics.

During the era of the New Deal order, free enterprisers pronounced their favored system an endangered idea that required unconditional support to survive. "The era of free enterprise which has made the United States a leader among nations is drawing to a close," editorialized the *Arizona Republic* in 1941.[71] A few months later, Florence Fisher Perry wondered, "Who is to say how long the system of free enterprise will endure?"[72] "Unless our ears and eyes deceive us completely the era of 'free enterprise' is just about ended," predicted a Kansas editorialist in 1944.[73] "Give us about 20 years of this and there will not be enough people who will remember what it is or was like to live in the age of free enterprise," wrote W. Jay Hunston in a letter to the editor in 1959.[74] One commentator in this period referred to the "permanent war to save free enterprise."[75] In this emergency context, advocates repeatedly argued that "there was no middle ground," that even minor alterations to free enterprise were potentially lethal.[76] Highlighting this binary understanding in 1943, NAM called upon politicians to declare whether "they are for free enterprise or against it."[77] Free enterprise was always on the brink of defeat because, it was alleged, even small reforms were tantamount to self-destruction.

The binary idea that free enterprise was something you were for or against made the question of definitional niceties moot. Instead of a definition, free enterprise required an ever-present and powerful enemy. In this context, Hayek's *Road to Serfdom*, with its argument about the inherent dangers of "planning" and the real possibility of a well-intentioned slippage to totalitarianism, was very much in keeping with free enterprise rhetoric, not a new departure. As early as 1945, shortly after the publication of Hayek's book, NAM's president Ira Mosher called for "manufacturers great and small" to begin "huddling" to respond to the "unmitigated warfare that has been waged for a decade against the free competitive enterprise system."[78] Well into the postwar years, this discourse persisted, as when the conservative economic analyst and soon-to-be Fed chair Alan Greenspan worried in the late 1970s that "there are limits to the durability of a Free Enterprise system" and that even limited forms of government intervention "can bring a Free Enterprise economy on its knees."[79]

Only a few months before he realized that the phrase didn't appear in dictionaries, Emery expressed annoyance in his syndicated column that "terms and concepts, once associated with the progress and dynamic growth of our nation and our business system, have fallen into disuse or disrepute." He voiced concern that words like *management* and *businessman* had become a "couple of new curse words in our language." Furthermore, he complained that "'Capitalist' is now an outright epithet and even 'free enterprise' is taking on a tarnish."[80] Putting a shine back on free enterprise was not only his life's mission but the urgent assignment for think tanks, ministers, politicians, and business leaders. Definitions, in spite of the occasional urgent demand from Emery and others, ultimately turned out to be largely tangential to this process, and for all the fuss he raised briefly in late 1948 and early 1949, Emery, who remained a vocal free enterpriser until his death in 1955, quietly dropped this concern. Defining this phrase could wait, but ensuring that it remained in the good graces of the people was urgent.

For all their concern about the term's ambiguity, Emery and other free enterprisers fought not so much for a precise or official definition of the phrase as for the exclusive right to determine its meaning and associate it with freedom itself.[81] On those rare occasions when free enterprise advocates did propose a definition, it was typically anodyne to the point of meaninglessness. "What is free enterprise?" asked the columnist Gilcrafter in 1944. His answer managed to be illuminating without being particularly specific. "It's a lot of little things— and some mighty big things too. But in a nutshell, it's our right to live our own lives, run our farms and businesses in our own way—without needless interference."[82] Indeed, Emery himself offered one such vague and open-ended definition, which the retailer, J. C. Penney found "especially apt." Sounding much like Gilcrafter, Emery said free enterprise was "made up of many things—bath tubs and automobiles, big cities and small towns; farms and victory gardens, mammoth steel mills and village shops . . . laughter and sorrow; eagerness and despair, and people."[83] Although Penney found this definition "down-to-earth," free enterprise came to life not in the hackneyed narratives of Americana that attracted Penney but in opposition to the New Deal order.

Still, the pattern of not defining the term or offering vague tributes continued. For example, a 1964 statement by the Ohio Manufacturers Association titled "Free Enterprise Defined" strikingly offered no definition whatsoever. Indeed, the statement began by asserting that free enterprise "has nothing to do with politics or wealth or business or class." That claim eliminated quite a lot, and was remarkable given how central the term had been to political and economic debates for the previous thirty years and considering that the group also expressed concern that lack of knowledge of the term's meaning was leading to support for "government ownership or government control," which are obviously political matters. The positive definition the organization mentioned was characteristically vague: "It is a way of living in which you and I, as individuals, are important." The manufacturers' group also offered examples of free enterprise at work as a set of "rights." It "is the right to open a gas station or grocery store"; "the right to lock your door at night"; "the right to save money if you wish, or blow it all on a good time if that is what you want to do." Finally, the association asked readers to ponder "how miserable we'd be if someone stole it from us."[84] In this conception, free enterprise was indispensable but nonpolitical, a set of rights and a "way of living" that made freedom possible. Although the title promised a definition, what the text offered was, like the descriptions of Gilcrafter and Emery, a set of patriotic clichés and a vision of abundance and classlessness ("how much money you have" doesn't matter) that obscured the central message, the brief against "government control."

"The Words, Not the System"

Throughout this period, many advocates of free enterprise who believed the concept was a bulwark of American society evinced a surprising willingness to jettison the phrase. Gilcrafter, the author of the paean to free enterprise as "lots of little things," confessed, "I'd rather call it American enterprise." Even NAM, the group accused by critics of foisting the term on the public just after the election of FDR, equivocated about the term.[85] Indeed, NAM's 1947 two-volume study of the topic by the group's "economic principles commission" referred to what it called the "American individual enterprise system" and included a section on "other terms currently in use." Damning "free enterprise" with faint praise, NAM offered weakly that, when "properly interpreted," free enterprise was a "reasonably accurate" phrase—not exactly the stuff of persuasive campaigns to sell free enterprise. The group considered and rejected other terms, including the "private enterprise system," the "competitive enterprise system," and the "American system." The section on synonyms for free enterprise concluded that "no mere term and no formal definition can adequately present those qualities which have made the American economic system so successful."[86] Despite their concerns about the lack of a consensus definition, free enterprisers worried that such a definition would narrow and freeze the meaning of a dynamic term that stood firmly against the great danger to liberty in the modern world: statism.

Many free enterprise proponents took a different approach to the phrase's ambiguity. Rather than demanding a consensus definition, they argued that the term itself had outlived its usefulness. "We sometimes think the friends of free enterprise—and we include ourselves among that number—might serve their cause better by giving the phrase a rest," editorialized the *Pittsburgh Post-*

Gazette in 1944. "A slogan is useful as long as it summarizes tersely an idea everyone understands," the editorialist noted. "When the time comes that everyone who uses it has to explain what he means by it, he better start putting his own ideas into his own words."[87] This was a remarkable confession in the midst of the wartime apotheosis of free enterprise. In an editorial that appeared shortly before the end of World War II, the *Deseret News* similarly proclaimed, "We're ready to scrap 'free enterprise.'"[88] "These columns have used the term free enterprise or private enterprise probably as frequently as anyone else," the editorialist candidly admitted. "But we are ready to scrap" it since *free enterprise* has become "one of the most abused terms in our language today." The newspaper was careful to note that it was ready to "scrap the words not the system." Since it is "only a term, we are perfectly willing to permit its elimination." Noting that "the term has been so smeared by communists, travelers, new dealers and so-called liberals that it has acquired a stigma in many minds," it argued that the "words of free enterprise register" with most Americans "like water on a duck's back." Moreover, the phrase had become poisoned not as a result of any fault in the system but because "it has become progressively more clear that these expressions are irrevocably associated in the minds of many men with the big depression, with bread lines and soup kitchens, with veterans vending apples, and with many big business abuses." Rather than evoking images of abundance, the newspaper feared, the phrase too often reminded ordinary Americans of business's biggest systemic failure, the Great Depression.

Blunt and clinical in justifying their decision, the Utah editors wrote, "We are perfectly willing to permit its elimination" in favor of 'freedom of choice.'" They insisted that this decision was purely instrumental and not an indictment of the "system" that "free enterprise" stood for: "Regardless of words and phrases we insist that the American system is the best in the world and that it holds the only hope of our survival as a nation of free men." Saving the "system" was urgent even if the term to describe it was no longer salient, since it remained necessary to halt the threat of statism that had dramatically expanded during the New Deal and World War II.

"Freedom of choice" was also the preference of Henry R. Johnston, a member of the Committee for Economic Development Board of Directors. Writing in the trade paper the *American Druggist* in 1945, he claimed, "American business must find a more popular phrase than free enterprise to describe what they stand for." But, like many others, he was not wowed by the popular alternatives.

Johnston ruled out "The American Way of Life" as "another foggy and undefinable phrase," rejected "private enterprise" ("too exclusive"), and eliminated "capitalism" (not understood by "the "average citizen"). By contrast, "free choice," he thought, could be easily understood: "It means the right to choose a newspaper, a radio program, a brand of toothpaste or breakfast food."[89] Highlighting only abundance and consumer choice, Johnston's favorite significantly narrowed the robust political meanings that free enterprisers claimed to promote.

Advocates of free enterprise proposed a variety of other terms as substitutes. As Nathan Shefferman had written in 1954, "We call this the American Way, or freedom of enterprise, or any one of a dozen names," as if the label mattered little.[90] Leonard Read of the Los Angeles Chamber of Commerce suggested "free competitive enterprise" in 1944.[91] B. Brewster Jennings, the chairman of the Board of Socony Mobil Oil Company, disliked the term "private enterprise" for its "suggestion of exclusiveness" and proposed instead "responsible enterprise" in 1957.[92] Arthur Larson, a member of Eisenhower's cabinet and a champion of "modern Republicanism," put forward "enterprise democracy," which he said represented "neither statism nor free enterprise."[93] N. D. Alper recommended "the competitive price system."[94]

In spite of the proliferating options, most advocates stuck with the original term, agreeing with Emery, as he wrote in 1944, that, whatever its faults, "there is a degree of magic in the expression 'free enterprise.'"[95] Emery was correct. All of the alternatives to free enterprise had limitations. In a survey of American attitudes toward economic concepts, the British publication the *Economist*, agreeing that "free enterprise" was problematic, dismissed the alternatives: capitalism" (because "it reminds too many people that they own no capital"), "private enterprise" ("sounds too exclusive"), "free competition" ("sounds a little ruthless"), "rugged individualism" (which "seems too harsh in an era committed to expansion of social services"), and "individual enterprise" ("too grotesque in the shadow of mammoth corporations").[96] Nor did these alternatives marry well with the idea of a "system"; they lacked the combination of political, economic, and psychological attributes captured by "free enterprise." Despite the push for alternatives, the definitional quandaries, and the discouragement of some of its leading champions, "free enterprise" remained ubiquitous. It would be hard to imagine any other phrase appearing in the headline of two different syndicated columns as "free enterprise" did in the opinion page of the *Beckley*

Post-Herald on May 19, 1959. Sandwiched between a lamentation that the "art of penmanship has all but vanished," readers could find Ray Tucker's piece on "socialism vs. free enterprise" and Thurmond Sensing's critique of intellectuals for being "ignorant about free enterprise."[97] Like democracy, free enterprise, it turned out, was the worst name except for all of the others.

Defenders of the term explained that free enterprise derived its meaning from its effects rather than a shared definition. In an editorial titled "A Rose by Any Other Name Is Just as Sweet," the *Central New Jersey Home News* criticized a New York newspaper for "asking its readers to suggest a new name for American capitalism 'less opprobrious' than free enterprise." While acknowledging that "what things are called is surely important," the Jersey paper asked its readers to "look beyond the name." The key instead, it advised, was to consider what free enterprise "is doing, and has done." It mentioned the aggregate income of the state and the benefits of a system that relied on "self-interest, not the noblest of human instincts but the most reliable." In contrast, it noted, socialist states tended to "become dictatorships."[98] Here was the bottom line: free enterprise was a proven weapon in the battle against socialism. The moment of crisis was not the time for an untested term.

Titled "The Name Doesn't Matter—Only the Meaning of Free Enterprise," a 1952 advertisement for the Rockland Light and Power Company also argued that confusion about the term should not lead to uncertainty about its meaning. "Some people say we should get a new name for free enterprise. Perhaps," the ad began. "But what does the name matter as long as we preserve its meaning." The ad elucidated its meaning. It stood for hope, decency, home, courage, dignity, and education. And the copy concluded, "Free enterprise—Americanism—profit-and-loss-system . . . the name doesn't matter so long as you're on alert against the people who are trying change and destroy its meaning."[99] In this view, only those trying to transform its meaning were dangerous. The danger lay not in the vagueness of the phrase or the alternatives being offered but in the nefarious aims of the statists and collectivists seeking to undermine the system.

In the end, free enterprise won out precisely because definitions and synonyms were peripheral to its main function. Labeling free enterprise a key element of the American "way of life," when that way was defined as anti-statist, made it both central and undefinable.[100] In a speech before the Rotary Club of Los Angeles in the mid-1950s, W. C. Mullendore, chairman of the board of Southern California Edison, highlighted the "elements of danger to the American way of life when the economy is dependent on Big Government and not upon traditional free enterprise."[101] Turning free enterprise into a defining American tradition, one unalterably opposed to statism, made the quest for definitions superfluous. Its value lay in what it prevented.

Free enterprise outlasted competing terms as the essence of opposition to the New Deal. It was telling that in a 1938 speech advertised as "defining free enterprise," Herbert Hoover made minimal gestures toward a definition (he called it a key to the American "standard of living"). His talk came to life, however, when he claimed that the New Deal leads to "complete fascism, complete socialism" or "economic nonsense" and that it "coerced and regimented" citizens.[102] Free enterprise for Hoover, as for Mullendore, represented above all a barrier preventing these unhappy outcomes.

The tentativeness and confusion about the meaning of free enterprise, the degree to which it had sunk into popular consciousness, and the questioning of the terminology itself stood in stark contrast to the way that advocates presented the "free enterprise system," which they often described as the rock-solid and traditional foundation of the United States. Proponents frequently described the founding of the nation and the free enterprise system as coterminous acts. In 1937, Merle Thorpe, the editor of the U.S. Chamber of Commerce magazine, proclaimed the need to "defend a system which since its establishment in 1776 has provided people with a standard of living that transcends even the imagination of Jules Verne."[103] What the *Wall Street Journal* called in 1948 the interchangeable "American system" or "the free enterprise system" served as the "political and economic order which permits every citizen to acquire property ownership in proportion to industry, thrift, and intelligence."[104] These synonymous terms stood for traditional individualism as against statism. Notwithstanding the insecurities and concerns about the phrase that free enterprisers mostly shared internally, to the outside world they told a story of a firmly rooted "system."

The "Genius of American Free Enterprise"

More than a definition of free enterprise, Emery and his colleagues sought to promulgate a conception of a system that was both timeless and traditional— and a timely weapon against the New Deal. They posited a commonsense philosophy that they contrasted with the newfangled and untested experiments of the New Deal and the welfare state. Well aware that others—including FDR himself—employed the term for different purposes, they aimed—and, it must be granted, succeeded—in developing the dominant understanding of free enterprise and in passing off their invented tradition as authentic.

Emery and his cohort popularized the idea that a "genius of American free enterprise" was a long-standing national characteristic and that Americans had long lived in political and economic conditions best understood as a "free enterprise system."[105] Crucially, as we have seen, they also consistently maintained that this system was threatened by the New Deal and its liberal successor administrations. "Ask any business man just what he means by the American system, by free enterprise and he is hard put to answer," noted Merle Thorpe. "Yet these same business men believe in and most of them are fighting for, the American way of free enterprise." According to Thorpe, they were guided by what he called "a sixth sense" that "tells them capitalism, whatever its faults, has proved to be the most practical benefactor of the human race."[106] They perpetuated this sixth sense through repetition and in defensive war against the state. Free enterprise came to life in the fight to preserve it.

This repetition often involved misdirection and embellishment, through the embrace of free enterprise as the source of the accreted customs and practices increasingly known as the "American Way of Life," a phrase whose popularity tracked closely with it.[107] Emery, who demanded a precise dictionary definition in late 1948, claimed in early 1949, by which time he had seemingly abandoned the quest, that free enterprise "is a way of life, the American way of life."[108] Others made similarly vague and grandiose claims. Free enterprise was the traditional "base and bulwark of all the freedoms of the common people," according to NAM's H. W. Prentis in 1940.[109]

The vague versions of free enterprise as a way of life, although they aroused episodic self-criticism and concern, proved immensely useful. They cloaked the quest for business autonomy and the war against the New Deal in platitudes of Americanness. In 1952, Robert Taft confessed that he was uncomfortable with a narrow, more strictly defined meaning of the phrase that was becoming increasingly popular. "I have never really liked the term 'free enterprise' because it seems to refer only to business liberty and we are interested in something more than that," Taft said. Hearkening back to its earliest meaning, the Ohio senator preferred the view that the free enterprise spirit had helped produce the freedoms we "have enjoyed for the last 165 years," which he nonetheless mobilized for political purposes more in synch with later understandings of the term. The utility of the phrase, Taft admitted, was that it stood against the "European philosophy of today that only more Government operation and control can improve the life of the people." Taft did not disclaim the importance of "business liberty" but framed the quest for it in terms of long-standing and widely embraced traditions rather than the self-interested desires of corporate executives and their political supporters.[110]

Although free enterprisers flagellated themselves for their inability to define the term and they condemned the public for not grasping its meaning, in the end they believed that the New Deal state, not the lack of entries in reference works, proved the biggest threat. New Dealers do not believe "in our form of government or system of free enterprise," said the conservative newspaper publisher Frank Gannett in 1940.[111] Although advocates had trouble defining the term, they thought of free enterprise as a self-correcting system that made government intervention not only unnecessary but counterproductive. "If we had a full understanding of free enterprise," claimed Prentis in 1940, "we could get everybody back to work in a very reasonable time—say a year or so."[112] Prentis did not specify what that understanding entailed.

"It Is Not Big Business That We Have to Fear"

Another Gallup poll, this one released in April 1945 with the end of the war in sight, brought more seemingly disconcerting news to free enterprise advocates. The poll, as Gallup interpreted it, revealed that Americans did not consider the preservation of free enterprise as among the top challenges they faced. In answer to the question "Aside from winning the war, what is the most important problem facing the country?" respondents ranked the issue of "how to reduce Government control or interference and stimulate free enterprise" sixth out of ten questions in order of priority, with only 5 percent saying it was important.[113] It is notable that Gallup tacitly accepted the conservative free enterprisers' viewpoint in formulating his question. Rather than asking what free enterprise was, as he had done in 1943, Gallup this time assumed its primary meaning to be anti-statism. For anxious free enterprisers, Gallup's findings, like those of his earlier poll, were cause for concern and an impetus to sell free enterprise more vigorously. Yet the 1945 poll was actually a sign of how much free enterprisers had achieved in a short period of time. Even though NAM was likely incorrect in 1938 when it asserted that "public opinion has shifted its favor from government 'control' to free 'enterprise,'" the group and its allies had made this dichotomy, if not NAM's preferred policy position, seem common-sensical.[114] For a long time thereafter, the binary between New Deal statism and free enterprise became the lens through which ordinary Americans interpreted politics.

Cold War exigencies made the art of formulating precise definitions seem like dangerous lollygagging. In describing the motivation for her satirical 1951 song "Free Enterprise," folk singer Malvina Reynolds called it "one of the razzle-dazzle phrases of our time that needs a little critical examination," but free enterprisers rejected introspection in favor of dissemination.[115] Acknowledging that "free Enterprise is a much abused term," George Peck in 1944 argued that "the phrase should be amplified."[116] Amplification, however, is not the same as definition. The need was urgent since if free enterprisers did not succeed, "we will really have to go back to the history of the good old days to read about what free enterprise was like."[117] Even during the war itself, what the Guarantee Trust Company of New York called in 1944 the "growing realization that serious thought must be given now to the preservation of the free enterprise system" led many business leaders to claim that survival trumped semantics.[118] Even after the war, maintaining the durable but fragile system in the face of manifold threats remained their priority.

But definitional quandaries persisted. "We Americans are often given to hap-hazard uses of general terms about which we are far from being of one mind on a definition," editorialized an Oklahoma newspaper in 1945. "Take for in-stance this thing we loosely call free enterprise. Just what do we mean by it? Are we in definite agreement as to what it implies?"[119] The answer, according to the editor and many other observers, was no. The evidence seemed to be on the side of those agnostic about its meaning. A clear definition of the term was not effectively reaching its intended audience, nor was it well understood by the business leaders and politicians promoting it. "I have noticed that whenever a group of Big Business reps get together they worry about the failure of the guy in the factory to understand" the term, as the *Detroit Free Press* editor Malcolm Bingay wrote in 1944. "They forget that they do not understand it either."[120] For advocates of free enterprise, an atmosphere of crisis rather than complacency reigned. For this group, free enterprise was always under threat, endangered not only by public ignorance of its meaning and by the failure of its advocates to provide a compelling definition of the term but by the actions of government that threatened to undermine the "system" that had made America great.

The sellers of free enterprise merchandized not definitions but an invented tradition of anti-statism and celebrations of business interests as popular ones. Free enterprisers suggested that, until the very recent past, individuals and business had operated with minimal government interference. Thus Wendell Willkie, one of the first politicians to use the phrase in its modern anti–New Deal signature, spoke in February 1933, one month before Roosevelt took office, of "that faith in free American enterprise which was so acutely felt by our forefathers and which has continued as an American tradition through their work without either the aid or the competition of the government."[121] By 1940, the year he sought the presidency, Willkie could argue, in words that became the essence of postwar conservatism, "Today it is not Big Business that we have to fear. It is Big Government." The candidate claimed that the "abuses that corrupted the 1920's have been transferred from Wall Street to Washington."[122] Free enterprisers helped create the world in which "Washington" stands for restrictions on freedom; it is one we still inhabit. The next chapter will explore how they helped invent the modern political landscape in which we associate a particular mixture of conservative temperament and politics with the Republican Party.

5

"The Party of Free Enterprise"

FREE ENTERPRISERS HELPED INVENT modern conservatism and they did so long before the label was widely embraced. They also contributed to the construction of the Republican Party as a self-identified conservative institution. "How is the Republican party to consolidate conservative sentiment and defeat the radical New Deal?" wondered Frank Jenkins, an Oregon newspaper editor, in 1938.[1] Tracing the language of free enterprise helps answer Jenkins's question. In the Depression decade and after, free enterprise served as a language capable of uniting opponents of the New Deal, who initially identified themselves in a variety of ways, but most of whom eventually aligned themselves with both conservatism and the Republican Party. As important, free enterprisers developed a tone of aggrieved victimization that came to embody American conservatism as much as ideology. As Kim Phillips-Fein writes, critics of the New Deal order combined a "utopian certainty" in the free market with a "fierce cultural conservatism."[2]

For much of the twentieth century, intellectuals and politicians celebrated the nonideological nature of the American two-party system. They viewed the major parties as diverse coalitions, each containing members from across the political spectrum. Frustrated by this, some critics called for a parliamentary-style system in which parties were defined by their ideology.[3] But, as Glenn Frank, then the president of the University of Wisconsin, noted in 1933, very early in the New Deal, predictions that the parties would divide neatly into a liberal Democratic Party and a conservative Republican one have "gone repeatedly into the waste basket of forlorn hopes." Frank, however, thought that the political tensions associated with the New Deal might make those forecasts more accurate in the future. Noting the likely alienation of the "conservative South" from what he labeled the "extreme, so-called liberalism" of Franklin Roosevelt's Democratic Party, Frank predicted, "we may be heading into a different situation."[4] The consummation of the realignment Frank presaged was many decades off, but many other observers claimed early in the New Deal that "new political lines are forming in the United States" and that "old party alignments may vanish if the New Deal splits the nation between liberals and conservatives."[5] The idea that, as one observer noted in 1944, the Democratic Party was the home of "New Deal philosophy" and the GOP the base of free enterprise ideas came increasingly to frame elections and other political clashes.[6] The following year, Richard L. Strout of the *Christian Science Monitor* described FDR's ability to keep white southerners and New Deal liberals "in the same boat" as "the feat of the century" and predicted that the wings of the party would eventually "flop off in different directions."[7] The ideological descendants of the anti–New Dealers who embraced free enterprise ultimately did "flop off" to find a home as conservatives in the Republican Party.

This is not to say that free enterprise ideas caused political realignment. Rather, the phrase served as an ideological holding pen for a not-yet-coherent set of political beliefs and attitudes that eventually consolidated as conservatism. Well before opponents of the New Deal and later the welfare state coalesced under this label, they did so as advocates of free enterprise. Advocates of free enterprise helped create a new political type: the citizen who not only objected to the policies that became associated with modern liberalism—state intervention, public spending, regulation—but who took these policies to be a dangerous affront to "common sense," a threat to identity, and a portent of civilizational collapse. These conservatives-in-the-making objected not just to New Deal policies but to what they dismissed as New Deal "emotionalism" or "utopianism," which could easily degenerate into a variant of the totalitarianisms that haunted the world in the twentieth century.[8]

Free enterprise was at its most popular and significant as an ideology in exile during the period from the 1930s to the 1970s, when the ideas it represented shifted from being understood as liberal to conservative. During the era of the New Deal, free enterprise became shorthand for opposition. After the conservative triumph of the late twentieth century, the term remained important but was no longer necessary as a term holding together the coalition of New Deal opponents, although it was available to be deployed whenever a crisis arose.

What a Kansas newspaper referred to in 1950 as "the endless argument these days between the 'free enterprisers' and the 'welfare staters'" began shortly after the election of Franklin D. Roosevelt.[9] This battle shaped the political alignment of the United States for the remainder of the twentieth century, even before it went without saying that liberals identified as Democrats and conservatives as Republicans. The free enterprise vocabulary and temperament became a crucial building block of conservatism. Many of the influential early free enterprisers, such as Albert Ritchie and Samuel Pettengill, politicians who pioneered the use of the phrase in the 1920s and 1930s, were Democrats and others, like most of the GOP presidential candidates from 1936 through 1960, identified as moderate Republicans (and one of those, Wendell Willkie, was a lifelong Democrat until shortly before he took on Roosevelt in 1940). The free enterprise coalition initially included disparate bedfellows—southern Democrats, business lobbyists, pundits, ministers, and the bulk of the Republican Party—who embraced a variety of primary political identities. Over time, the free enterprise worldview helped frame what it meant to be a Republican and a conservative (and made these terms increasingly seem to be synonymous). Free enterprisers called for and helped precipitate an enduring political realignment. Their characteristic binarism, in which one was either for "free enterprise" or for some variant of dangerous statism, left little room for the many self-described moderate supporters of free enterprise to distinguish themselves from conservatives. What one letter writer called "the choice between socialism and a return to the free enterprise, common sense heritage of our founding fathers" eventually became seen as a partisan political one, in which Democrats stood for the former and Republicans for the latter.[10]

During the period from the 1930s to the 1970s, free enterprisers complained that their guiding ideal was ill defined and misunderstood, even by the business leaders and their allies most responsible for propagating it. Indeed, for most of this period, free enterprisers thought they were disastrously losing their battle with the New Deal order. In an address to the thirtieth annual meeting of the National Industrial Conference Board in 1946, shortly after the defeat of global fascism in World War II, the group's president, Virgil Jordan, proclaimed that advocates of free enterprise had been "humiliatingly defeated in the field of ideas and ideals and now stand in greater danger of losing their freedom than they were five years ago."[11] Like many others, Jordan worried that free enterprise had won the war abroad but was in danger of losing the war at home, and in mortifying fashion. Such a view of having lost the battle with the welfare state, and having been not just defeated but humiliated in the process, persisted even during times of triumph. Even in 1980, the year culminating with the election of Ronald Reagan, which many historians view as marking the end of the New Deal order, a worried columnist wrote that "free enterprise no longer exists" in the United States.[12]

Yet even as free enterprisers regularly foretold their imminent defeat, they successfully laid the groundwork for eventual ideological victory. The conservative takeover of free enterprise was, like Hemingway's description of bankruptcy, first gradual, then sudden. During the era of the New Deal, it was a minority discourse. Advocates lost many elections and policy battles and even struggled to explain what the term meant, which led supporters like Jordan to focus on defeat. One free enterprise proponent in 1948 rued that he and his compatriots had "fought the New Deal, but the New Deal won."[13] But in the longer run, free enterprise won the battle of common sense, dramatically shaping political culture, placing limits on reform, and reinforcing the trend of decreasing trust in government. As the liberal consensus crumbled, the framework and worldview of free enterprise, already widely disseminated, quickly became dominant and "suddenly came to seem like common sense."[14]

"The Very Negation of American Liberalism"

Although free enterprise came to be identified with conservatism, when critics first challenged the New Deal, they claimed to be doing so in the name of "liberalism." Free enterprisers argued that Franklin Delano Roosevelt and his colleagues had hijacked and perverted the meaning of liberalism, a term that was rapidly metamorphosing in the 1930s. "The New Deal is not new and is not liberal," said Theodore Roosevelt's son, who emerged as a fierce opponent of his distant cousin Franklin. "It is old and illiberal."[15] Those for whom the word still connoted negative liberty and minimal state interference with the business firm rejected the supposition that a president who promoted aggressive regulation, trade unionism, and a system of provisions provided by the government deserved the label. When FDR pronounced himself a liberal shortly before the presidential election of 1932, he characterized that ideology as the recognition that "the forms [of government] have to catch up with the facts." Platitudes about small government voiced by classical liberals, whom Roosevelt soon labeled conservatives, no longer served the cause of liberty. Comparing governance to gardening, Roosevelt called active pruning rather than the conservative course of ignoring "rot and dead wood" the more responsible and efficacious path.[16]

Many Republicans, including the leading critics of the New Deal, resented Roosevelt's usurpation of the term *liberal* because they viewed him, correctly, as abandoning "historic economic liberalism," as the *Baltimore Sun* called it in 1940.[17] Herbert Hoover embraced the term and he and many other Republicans expressed annoyance that FDR had successfully co-opted the phrase. For example, Alf Landon, the 1936 Republican candidate for the presidency, claimed to stand for "a sane balanced liberalism" rather than "the so-called liberalism in evidence today."[18] Describing the 1940 Republican presidential candidate Wendell Willkie as a "true liberal," South Dakota columnist Stanley Wood wrote that he "represents the revolt of the liberals against dictatorship and regimentation."[19] The previous year, Hoover, identifying a "paradox," observed that the Republicans had "become the conservative party in the sense of preserving true liberalism."[20]

Free enterprise critics thus diagnosed New Deal medicine as poison and decried FDR's attempts to rebrand liberalism. In 1935, Hoover denounced "the perversion and assumption of the term 'Liberalism' by theories of every ilk—whether National Regimentation, Fascism, Socialism, Communism, or what not." Making no distinction among these theories, Hoover claimed, employing the binary framework characteristic of free enterprisers, that they all represented "the very negation of American Liberalism" and thus were equally dangerous.[21] Two years later, Hoover complained that the "term liberal has now become the fashionable clothing of all collectivists, whether they be New Dealers, with creeping collectivism, or frank and open Socialists, or the unconscious Fascists."[22] In this view, the New Deal marked a betrayal of liberal values: "a great program undertaken in the name of liberalism, had become transformed into a program the very opposite of liberalism," said Willkie in 1940. These "militant, self-styled liberals," according to the Republican senator Margaret Chase Smith in 1951, were asking the American people to "trade in their individual freedom for the promised security to be spoon-fed by the government."[23] Although New Dealers sought to distinguish themselves from socialists, communists, fascists, and others, free enterprisers rejected these distinctions since from their point of view, each of these ideologies undermined freedom via statism and the "planned economy" and all of them "have long used big business as their whipping boy."[24] In the view of the critics, New Deal liberalism was merely what the conservative columnist George Sokolsky called "go-slow socialism," and the two were becoming increasingly indistinguishable as liberalism, as one critic said in 1946, "edged closer to centralized totalitarian government."[25] Former liberals and even old-school liberal holdouts like Smith increasingly made *liberalism* a term of opprobrium on par with the socialism that they claimed it promoted. Decrying FDR's rejection of "historic liberalism," which he equated with laissez-faire, an editorialist declared in 1936, "He has been more a Socialist than a liberal."[26]

During the New Deal era, as Roosevelt's conception of liberalism competed with older views, a new term entered the American political lexicon: *neoliberalism*. Those who have traced its early history attribute it to libertarian-leaning economists, such as Friedrich A. Hayek, who helped restore faith in the market economy in the post–World War II years.[27] In the United States, however, critics of the New Deal employed the term first to highlight its dangerous deviations from traditional liberalism.[28] They used the word to tar Rooseveltian liberalism as, in effect, socialism.[29]

This sense of the term *neoliberalism* dated back to the early days of the New Deal. In 1935, for example, a writer for the *Baltimore Sun* contrasted the true liberal, whose "real faith was as much laissez faire as the system could stand without permitting too flagrant abuses," with the neoliberal, who sought to put "the strong arm of the government under the less fortunate members of society" and who favored "restraints and restrictions upon enterprise and liberty."[30] A journalist in 1942 used the term to describe the "motley host of leftists belonging to this New Deal era" who had remade liberalism into socialism.[31]

In 1951, Raymond Moley, the former "Brain Truster," denounced the abuse and degradation of the word *liberalism* by his erstwhile New Deal allies and their descendants.[32] Calling liberalism a "kidnapped mot" that "has been banged around so much and has caught so many virulent infections that it may be impossible to restore it to health," he argued that collectivists like Franklin Roosevelt and his followers had turned liberalism, the traditional American ideology of small government and economic liberty, on its head.[33] Moley too employed "neoliberal" to characterize "the mixture of Socialism, politics, promises and bad economics that afflicts us today." A neoliberal, according to Moley, was a person "who has stolen the good word 'liberal' out of an honored past and is using it as a front for the very sort of political policy against which real liberalism was a great protest." Moley wrote that neoliberalism "consists in the main of support of any and every measure designed to enlarge the power of the government and to restrict the area of individual freedom." Whereas in his preferred version, a liberal was a person who "fought for individualism against the state," neoliberals, according to Moley, had forged an "authoritarian mechanism . . . under the name of a welfare state."[34] No longer, in his estimation, could free enterprise and liberalism be linked, as a result of the New Deal's distortion of the term. Liberalism, in Moley's view, now took its place alongside the "authoritarian" ideologies that Americans should properly oppose in the midst of the Cold War.

Whether neoliberalism meant a revival or a repudiation of liberalism depended on one's understanding of the latter term, which remained contested through the 1950s. Complaining that the term *liberal* had entered a "semantical hall of mirrors," the *Los Angeles Times* worried in 1947 that a word that had traditionally belonged to those who believed "in the greatest possible freedom and consequently the least possible government" had been contaminated by "the authoritarians in the broad belt of territory which is bounded on the left by the Communists and on the right by the orthodox Democrats." Following the linguistic traditions of anti–New Dealism, the newspaper called the latter "neo-liberals."[35] A later generation would treat neoliberalism and free enterprise as close cousins, if not synonyms, but early users of the phrase in the United States took the two to be opposites, as in the columnist John W. Owens's claim in 1945 that Virginia senator Harry Byrd "does not believe in neo-liberalism" but instead "believes in free enterprise."[36]

As liberalism degenerated into what free enterprisers dismissed as extremist neoliberalism, they stopped trying to reclaim it. In 1938, Pennsylvania senator James J. Davis complained, "The so-called liberalism which is flaunted before us today" has "nothing to offer but public spending." This flaunting liberalism, he feared, was "driving the nation to distraction." Those seeking to "put an end to the spirit of free enterprise" were, he believed, "unworthy of the name" liberal. He concluded, as many other formerly liberal critics of the New Deal that, "If this be liberalism than I am a conservative."[37] It has been said that "Donald Trump has no political philosophy beyond pissing off liberals," as if defining political identity in opposition to liberalism was a new thing under the sun in the age of Trump.[38] In an important sense, negating liberalism, as it became understood post-FDR, was the foundational practice of modern conservatism. "In view of the present-day perversion of the meaning of the term 'liberal,'" claimed Ogden Mills, who had served as secretary of the treasury under Hoover, in 1937, foretelling the future of the Republican Party, "I would make this the party of conservatism."[39] The path for the GOP to become the party of conservatism led through free enterprise, understood as anti-liberalism.

One of the first politicians to recognize that the Republicans were becoming a party of antiliberalism was Franklin Roosevelt himself. In his Fireside Chat of June 24, 1938, FDR referred to "two schools of thought, generally classified as liberal and conservative." Roosevelt described his "sane and consistent liberalism" as based upon the recognition that "under modern conditions government has a continuing responsibility to meet continuing problems, and that Government cannot take a holiday of a year, or a month, or even a day just because a few people are tired or frightened by the inescapable pace of this modern world in which we live." Suggesting the binary that soon became widely accepted and was already being embraced by free enterprisers, Roosevelt referred to "the opposing or conservative school of thought" as one that "as a general proposition, does not recognize the need for Government itself to step in and take action to meet these new problems."[40] If many early critics of the New Deal refused the label conservative, eventually many of their descendants employed it as the name for their fear of the overreaching inherent in Roosevelt's redefined modern liberalism.

Many free enterprisers, however, denied having ideological motives, preferring to describe themselves as anti-political purveyors of common sense. Free enterprise discourse formed a building block for modern conservatism, but its proponents often denied that it was political at all. Indeed, sellers of the term described it as natural common sense—the very opposite of an "ism."[41] It was normalized as a tradition, "a basic American principle," as Florida newspaper editor George W. Hopkins wrote in a column that won a prize in 1944 as the best editorial on the idea of American free enterprise. "Free enterprise is not a political term," Hopkins insisted. It was, he continued, in a remarkable comparison involving two historical errors, as "free from politics as the Constitution of the United States itself" and as American as "the Boston Tea Party." Although it had the sanction of American history, according to Hopkins, it preceded the formation of the nation in its embodiment of natural law. Free enterprise represented what he called "American democracy in action," and Hopkins claimed that "we will not surrender Free enterprise to National Socialism; to bureaucracy or dictatorship."[42] Embedded in Hopkins's supposedly nonideological formulation was the binary essence of free enterprise.

Notwithstanding the disclaimers of its promoters, the supposedly apolitical term implied the necessity of a particular kind of politics, understood as the negation of New Deal liberalism. Because its supporters claimed it as a national creed, they described critics as un-American. The either/or language they favored—as in Hopkins's framing, a stark choice between "free enterprise" or "National Socialism"—limited the range of acceptable political discourse, and placed the New Deal in the category of what Earl Bunting, the president of the National Association of Manufacturers, called in 1947 "alien isms."[43] Hopkins's and Bunting's formulation had the effect of casting the New Deal and the burgeoning welfare state as un-American.

This binary vision of free enterprisers also had a profound impact on the nature of those who claimed to be political moderates. An examination of the use of free enterprise ideas by Dwight D. Eisenhower is instructive, since Ike has long been considered the exemplar of moderate Republicanism, the hallmark of which was the acceptance of the New Deal. Throughout his political career, he was an enemy of extremism and an advocate of what he called the "middle way." As president from 1953 to 1961, he also famously maintained and even expanded some New Deal programs and rejected the call to "roll back" the New Deal in domestic policy as he did the call to roll back communism in foreign policy. As reporter Cabell Phillips noted in 1957, President Eisenhower "seemed to never quite put his whole shoulder into rolling back the iniquitous New Deal," a useful formulation since it assumed that he sought to undermine the New Deal but did so cautiously.[44] At the same time, Ike called for the building of a "strong progressive GOP" and said he fought the right wing of his party to try to achieve it.[45]

Eisenhower did not seek to destroy New Deal liberalism, but neither did he embrace it. To demonstrate that he "accepted the New Deal as part of American life," as the historian Garry Wills has asserted, many commentators cite Ike's 1954 claim that "should any political party attempt to abolish social security, unemployment insurance, and eliminate labor laws and farm programs, you would not hear of that party again in our political history."[46] They rarely note, however, that Eisenhower made this claim in a private letter to his conservative brother Edgar.[47] Moreover, the remainder of Ike's letter makes clear that this assertion reflected his pragmatic judgment, not his philosophical agreement. His famous line from that letter about conservatives who wanted to repeal the New Deal has been misinterpreted: "Their number is negligible and they are stupid." A reading of that statement in the context of the letter suggests that he meant that politically they would have no chance of succeeding, not that their critique was incorrect. In a rarely quoted passage in the same letter, Eisenhower also said, "I believe this country is following a dangerous trend when it permits too great a degree of centralization of governmental functions. I oppose this— in some instances the fight is a rather desperate one." Eisenhower's fear of statism put him in the mainstream of free enterprise thinking of his time. The idea that, as one news outlet declared in 2011, "Eisenhower today would be considered a socialist," understates the degree to which he voiced the free enterprise critique of government, even if he accepted the New Deal in practice.[48]

Moreover, Eisenhower's public statements, particularly in the early 1950s, "repeatedly reflect his dislike for, and even fear of, New Deal policies," as one scholar has noted. Furthermore, his administration "was peopled with officials who similarly abhorred the New Deal." While his actions represented a concord with New Dealism, Eisenhower's rhetoric reflected the influence of free enterprise critics of the New Deal. He spoke of "creeping socialism," "inroads on our freedom," the dangers of a "planned economy," and the need for a "complete change" to combat New Deal policies.[49] He also employed free enterprise critiques of "waste" in government spending and of uncaring bureaucrats and claimed, early in his presidency, that a reduction in taxes "is a necessary objective of government."[50] On the campaign trail in 1952, Eisenhower denounced "virtually out of control spending" by the federal government.[51] Shortly after he left office, the leading pundit of the era, Walter Lippmann, observed that Ike remained "deeply suspicious of social security and the welfare state and of aid to education, and above all of the modern conception of the compensatory economy."[52] In 1964, Eisenhower, along with George Romney, came out against a proposal to add to the GOP platform a statement condemning the John Birch Society and extremism. The ultimate moderate Republican supported Barry Goldwater, the candidate of extremism in 1964, even as he condemned "radicalism of any kind, whether it be of the right or the left."[53]

To the extent that Eisenhower acceded to the New Deal order, then, his acceptance was conditional, based on the reality of the New Deal's continuing popularity rather than on any ideological affinity for it. In criticizing a proposal for national health care in 1953, for example, the new president told members of the American Medical Association (AMA) of his dislike for such words as *socialized* and *compulsory*, noting that they would lead the country "to forsake our traditional system of free enterprise."[54] If the pragmatic, politically savvy Eisenhower rejected the (unrealistic) wishes of conservative free enterprisers to roll back the New Deal, at the level of rhetoric he regularly expressed free enterprise sentiments, implying that in the best of all possible worlds—in which Democrats did not control the Congress and in which New Deal sentiments were less popular—he would dramatically reduce the size and scope of government.

Timing was essential. One reason why Eisenhower is considered a moderate and Lewis F. Powell Jr., who was often praised in his lifetime for his moderation, is considered a radical has less to do with the difference in their ideas than in the relative strength of the coalition they opposed. When Eisenhower was president, he faced what Andrew J. Polsky calls a "still-resilient New Deal order."[55] Two decades later, that order was far less resilient and Powell's critique, which for the most part echoed what had been said previously, was converted into action.

"Is the Businessman the Forgotten Man?"

Free enterprise lay at the intersection of many vectors of modern conservatism, not just, or even primarily, economic ones. It was also central in shaping a psychology and temperament that has defined much of the political Right ever since. We normally think about the rise of modern conservatism as the consolidation of distinct strands: libertarians, traditionalists, Cold Warriors, anti–civil rights activists, and even moderates.[56] The ideas of free enterprise, however, appealed to many of the constituencies that opposed the New Deal order long before they allied within the modern Republican Party. Just as historian Darren Dochuk has noted a "remarkable overlap" among religious and business conservatives in the 1930s, the discourse of free enterprise united factions that held different views on any number of issues but shared a set of beliefs and sentiments about the nature of freedom and the role of government.[57] Long before the *National Review* promoted "fusionism" in the 1950s, free enterprisers linked issues of political economy to cultural battles.[58]

Noting that free enterprise offered a shared vocabulary for distinct groups that eventually became part of the New Right is not to suggest that free enterprise itself caused political realignment. Rather, it provided a language of transition for many groups that were shifting their political orientation. By far the leading cause of political realignment in the United States was race; and, as we will see in chapter 7, segregationists spoke not infrequently in the argot of free enterprise. The political emergence of evangelical Protestantism and conservative Catholicism, whose adherents also invoked the phrase, likewise played a large role. Free enterprise was most naturally the organic language of the third group seen as central to the Reagan revolution: economic conservatives. But although business leaders and politicians most prominently developed the language of free enterprise, it was adopted by a wide range of groups that embraced its emotional as much as its economic message.

Free enterprisers also developed a style of inverted populism, spoken on behalf of victimized and desperate elites, that became a staple of conservative rhetoric, drawing the various factions together. They emphasized the fragility of freedom, the ethical (not just economic) rightness of their cause, and warned that what came to be known as liberalism was not just an alien but a dangerous ideology that inevitably tended toward totalitarianism. They suspected even mild reform and maintained a bewildered and aggrieved tone in opposition to it. Their language both elided business and individual freedom and voiced resentments and fears filtered through gendered and racialized lenses. Though they did not invent it, free enterprisers mastered and modernized a genre of elite victimization that has made a lasting imprint on American politics.

One of the means by which free enterprisers expressed their victimization was to claim a label with a long heritage, the "forgotten man." The phrase, most famously used by Franklin D. Roosevelt, had long been associated with the poor and the downtrodden. In his famous 1932 radio address, presidential candidate FDR referred to "the forgotten man at the bottom of the economic pyramid" and spoke of the need to rebuild the economy "from the bottom up and not from the top down."[59]

In the hands of free enterprise advocates, the "forgotten man" quickly became a symbol of a more affluent set of victims. In 1934, Congressman James M. Beck called the taxpayer "the new forgotten man." In 1940, another Republican representative, Bruce Barton, labeled the "middle-class citizen" the "latest reincarnation of the forgotten man." By 1951, Northwestern University political scientist William M. McGovern brought these two images together when he spoke of the "forgotten man of the middle class" who was "rapidly being taxed out of existence." Rather than the "fellow out of work," claimed conservative business columnist Merryle Rukeyser in 1951, the label more properly belonged to "the taxpayer who pays the freight for the adventures of politicians."[60]

The taxpaying, middle-class citizen whose interests trumped that of the poor person who required government assistance formed one image of the anti–New Deal forgotten man. A second trajectory of "forgotten man" discourse was the substitution of the entrepreneur for the worker or, more accurately, the elision of these two categories. "Is the businessman the forgotten man of modern life?" asked an editorialist at the *Newport Daily News* in 1951. The next year, a speaker called the "white collared salaried worker" the "nation's new forgotten man," a suggestion that had first been broached as early as 1937. By 1954, another writer included the "professional man" in this category, and in 1959 a Texas columnist said that those earning more than $10,000 a year (roughly $83,000 in 2018 dollars) are unjustly "characterized as being villainous" when in fact they were part of "a new race of forgotten men, the taxpayers" who "pay the bills." Unconcerned about the woes of those at the bottom of the economic pyramid, conservatives appeared to sympathize with those near the top.[61]

A parallel transformation occurred as the "forgotten man" metamorphosed from Roosevelt's unemployed person to a broader cross-class grouping, like the "farmer, junior executive, union member, corporate head or laborer" whom William Lowndes, the president of the Southern States Industrial Council, placed in that category in 1968.[62] There was increasing anger over the fact that forgotten men, now understood as affluent, were forced to fund what the columnist John Ackelmire called in 1952 "schemes of social ameliorization" aimed at the poor. Two years later, another critic complained that the burden of financially supporting "all the various measures proposed for the betterment of humanity and the salvation of civilization" fell on the "business or professional man." In an editorial report on the "forgotten man" circa 1960, the *Indianapolis Star* praised him for "uncomplainingly paying his taxes." Then the paper, speaking on behalf of the silent taxpayer, launched a complaint of its own, which was that the political class was "too concerned with the interests of minorities, here and abroad, to bother with the interests of 'The Forgotten American,'" who was assumed to be an affluent white man.[63]

The shift from concerns about paying for general "ameliorization" to specific claims about "minorities" marked an important turn in the language of forgotten man rhetoric, which became increasingly a racialized language of backlash against less powerful groups. (This was presaged in the 1959 source quoted above that denominated taxpayers as "a new race of forgotten men.") Over the course of the 1960s, the forgotten man became increasingly resentful and the targets of his resentment became more explicit. Miller Upton, the president of Beloit College, gave a hint of this indignation in 1967 when, in a lecture on "society's forgotten man," he said, "I have just about reached the end of my tolerance for the way our society only seems to have sympathetic concern for the misfit, the pervert, the drug addict, the chronic criminal, the drifter, the loser." His lack of tolerance for the misfits was exacerbated by his view that people like him were being "laughed at" by the very "underachievers" they were subsidizing.[64] Upton's fear of being mocked went hand in hand with a concern that the forgotten man was being not just extorted but humiliated by undeserving people. The forgotten man, in the view of the free enterprisers, was not FDR's poor person at the bottom of the economic pyramid but the successful business owner, corporate shareholder, and taxpayer victimized by the New Deal.

Free enterprise advocates of the forgotten man often used a racialized and gendered language of victimization. Lowndes, for example, complained that the forgotten man, whom he took to be white, was labeled a "bigot" and a "racist" if "he has any personal preference as to the buyer of his dwelling."[65] In his nomination speech for the Republican vice presidential candidate Frank Knox in 1936, Senator Frederick Steiwer contrasted "America [as] a land of free enterprise" with "the 'soft, spineless' paternalism of the regimented state" of the New Deal. The journalist Boake Carter also worried about the death of rugged individualism in the era of the New Deal, and he saw the decline of free enterprise as a crisis of white masculinity. "The men of bygone days had to be rugged men," he asserted, in order to build what he called "white man's industrial civilization." Carter was quite sure that those he described as the "sissy" or the "pussymouth" did not possess the "ruggedness" necessary to preserve free enterprise.[66] The Reverend Harry Hoy told the Lions Club of Paris, Texas, in 1946 that government regimentation "makes weaklings of us."[67] The apostles of free enterprise described free enterprise as a manly endeavor to preserve a threatened civilization. Advocates sought to restore to the forgotten man what the historian Richard Hofstadter once called the "virile prerogatives of enterprise."[68]

"The Republican Party as the Conservative Party"

Toward the end of 1934, less than two years into Franklin D. Roosevelt's presidency, H. C. Kennedy, a longtime Republican judge from Somerset, Kentucky, and an inveterate letter writer, sent a prescient missive to the editor of the *Louisville-Courier Journal*. Even the title of the letter was striking: "The Republican Party as the Conservative Party."[69] This was a (very) premature proclamation of ideological party alignment.

Upon the death of Barry Goldwater in 1998, Haley Barbour, the head of the Republican National Committee, said, "He was the pathfinder in establishing the Republican Party as the conservative party in the United States." But that trail had been blazed earlier. Many critics of the New Deal, like Kennedy, began following that path shortly after Franklin Roosevelt's election in 1932, but the label did not catch on for many years, in part because many opponents of the New Deal were white southerners who remained loyal to the Democratic Party.[70]

Kennedy called for a political realignment. Seeking to accelerate trends that were most visible through the lens of the free enterprise critique of the New Deal, Kennedy called for the purging of squishy Republicans who did not define themselves by their opposition to FDR. "The time has come when Republicans who begin to experience symptoms of Liberalism or Progressivism, so called, should line up with the New Dealers." In parallel fashion, he encouraged disenchanted conservative Democrats to "line up with the Republican Party." Even as many free enterprisers clung to the liberal label, Kennedy predicted that "from now on the lines of cleavage" in the two major political parties would soon break along the tracks of "conservative" and "liberal." Kennedy did not describe the differences between these ideologies in precise detail but he offered that, as a conservative, he was "opposed to all wild-eyed theories of government," most especially "the fight that is being waged against the so-called wealthy." He held that a conservative was "one who believes in safe, sane, government within constitutional limitations." Differentiating the parties according to temperament—"wild-eyed" versus "sane"—and claiming that opposing the wealthy was evidence of irrationality became important means of distinguishing between the parties. It is notable that the beliefs he labeled conservative also fit under the rubric of free enterprise.

As Kennedy presciently suggested, free enterprise language anticipated the future ideological divisions between the two major political parties. The GOP transformed in part by peeling off conservative white Democrats who no longer wished to share political affiliations with New Deal liberals. Free enterprise gestures soon became a litmus test of political affiliations, among them dire predictions about the stresses that Rooseveltian liberalism placed on the "system." "America is in peril!" Kennedy warned as the 1936 election approached, a claim that free enterprisers echoed in almost every subsequent presidential contest, finding the danger in the expansion of the welfare state rather than in Soviet communism. Similarly, his call for a return to "sane business methods" framed the New Deal as not just unfriendly to business—and, by extension, the American people—but irrationally so.[71] Kennedy concluded his 1934 letter by noting, "It will be interesting in the next few years to watch the political changes and new line-ups that take place. Much important history is now in the making." Free enterprisers played a key role in shaping the future of new political "line-ups" that Kennedy foretold, and in envisioning what one editor in 1934 called "a party of common sense—a conservative party which will embrace conservative Democrats and conservative Republicans," foreshadowing a political realignment that became apparent only many decades later.[72]

Others joined Kennedy in predicting what Rodney Dutcher in 1936 called "a more definite cleavage between the New Deal Democratic party as a liberal party and the Republicans as the conservative party."[73] The following year, Senator Arthur Vandenberg said that a political "realignment is inevitable." He believed that free enterprisers would soon unite in the Republican Party and collectivists would constitute what he called the "Roosevelt Party."[74] Although difficulties in defining liberalism and conservatism persisted, an increasing number of people accepted columnist Samuel Grafton's pithy description from 1946 of conservatives as "champions of free enterprise" and liberals as advocates of government intervention.[75] This observation soon closely mapped ideological divisions, even though many free enterprisers remained in the "Roosevelt Party" for decades to come.

Eventually, history did break in the direction that Kennedy, Dutcher, Vandenberg, and Grafton predicted. The change, however, was anything but rapid. Indeed, fifteen years after he penned this letter to the editor, Kennedy published another objecting to the invitation extended to Oregon senator Wayne Morse by the Abraham Lincoln Republican Club of Louisville. Kennedy claimed that Lincoln would "turn over in his grave" if he knew that his party welcomed liberals. Kennedy wrote of Morse: "He calls himself a liberal Republican but a liberal Republican is just a New Deal Democrat."[76] Others expressed similar frustration. "The two parties should represent different governmental policies," wrote Wright A. Patterson in 1949, the same year that Kennedy objected to Morse's visit to Louisville. The GOP, Patterson wrote, "should be reasonably conservative, should definitely stand for our free enterprise economy and for government as a servant of, and supported by, the people."[77] It took several generations for the neat ideological division that Kennedy foretold in 1934 and that remained incomplete in 1949 to come to fruition. Opponents of the New Deal held the key to the transformation of free enterprise.

In 1961, a columnist for an Oregon newspaper complained that the Democratic Party used to be a "firm advocate of free enterprise" but now wanted to make "all people wards of the government." Nearly three decades after the start of the New Deal, he complained that the members of that party had misappropriated the word *liberal*. They want everything, he asserted, "controlled, regulated, restricted, regimented, directed, supervised, guided, ordered, prescribed." But even at this relatively late date, he held out hope that a conservative wing of the party, a free enterprise faction, would prevail in what he called the "internal struggle."[78]

"The Republican Party Must Be the Opposite of the New Deal"

The advocates of anti–New Deal free enterprise paved the way for a political realignment that slowly began to take shape in the 1930s but took many decades to complete. In this remapping, long before conservatives consolidated in the Republican Party, they clustered in an anti–New Deal coalition whose slogan was "free enterprise." Republicans increasingly defined themselves as what one observer in 1947 called "the party of free enterprise," in opposition to the New Deal and what FDR's successor, Harry Truman, would soon label the "Fair Deal."[79] Disaffected Democrats associated with the party of free enterprise as a transitional object on their slow path to changing their party affiliation. As one editorialist predicted in 1946, after the president of the Young Democrats of Wisconsin announced that he was joining the Republican Party, the GOP "will find within its ranks many new faces" if it puts "America back on the road to free enterprise, common-sense spending" and fights against the "stifling clutch of bureaucracy."[80]

Just as important, advocates of this new version of free enterprise catalyzed a cultural and temperamental realignment every bit as significant as the political one that ultimately remade the two political parties as representatives of distinct and clashing ideologies. Other binaries, cultural and psychological, informed these ideological antimonies. Free enterprisers figured political decisions as fundamental ethical choices.

The free enterprise system, according to Ogden Mills in 1935, was more than a "framework of government." It represented a much more comprehensive "American scheme of life." He understood threats to that basic scheme as a life-or-death matter. Although free enterprise had been "tested over a period of a century and a half," Mills feared that in the New Deal, Americans faced an unprecedented and dangerous enemy. Using a trope employed in later years by Ronald Reagan, he claimed that "in all probability this generation will be called upon to decide whether our American scheme of life is to survive," and implored citizens to see elections as civilizational tests. Succeeding generations of free enterprisers would repeat the same charge: a once-stable system was teetering and under threat. The threat for Mills and his successors was the "planned economy," the "antithesis" of the liberty that free enterprise made possible and a reversion to the tyranny that had been "the accepted type before our nation was born."[81]

Thus, to its advocates, free enterprise was not only an economic system but an encompassing protector of fragile liberty.[82] In this system, freedom resulted from a natural "order," not one artificially imposed by planners. Unlike the concept of "free markets," a term that was just migrating from technical economics to popular use in the 1940s, free enterprise, the term more frequently used until the mid-1970s, was not understood by its advocates as purely or even primarily economic in character.[83] "No man in America can be free, spiritually or economically, if permanent governmental bureaucracy ever closes its steel jaws on him," said the automobile executive Homer McKee in 1943. Like many free enterprise advocates, McKee depicted the system's enemies as dangerous; he dismissed and unmanned them as "little conniving, half-pint intellectuals" who "propose that we abandon free enterprise and substitute it for the muddling of bureaucracy."[84] N. D. Alper described free enterprise as "the most natural and the finest economic way of life for the development of man as a free soul." Only it could produce "truly free men."[85] The president of the U.S. Chamber of Commerce, Clem D. Johnson, said that free enterprise was necessary for "a man's spirit as well as his pocketbook."[86] In this view, free enterprise was a spiritual practice.

As the comments of McKee, Alper, and Johnson suggest, free enterprisers both anticipated and catalyzed a political culture in which to be a conservative was not just to support particular policy preferences but to subscribe to a distinct worldview, often described as irreconcilably opposed to the dominant liberal consensus.[87] In the binary framework of free enterprise, compromise and negotiation were not pragmatic but dangerous concessions that would hasten the advance of what Virgil Jordan called "compulsory collectivism."[88]

Free enterprisers took ideas seriously; ideological combat was central to their message and identity. The New Deal, as the 1936 Republican vice presidential candidate Frank Knox said, was "founded on a wrong philosophy." In 1940, presidential candidate Wendell Willkie ranked the New Deal on a continuum with other forms of totalitarianism. They are "different names for the same thing—absolute and arbitrary power in the hands of government."[89] In this view, the New Deal posed a threat not just to free enterprise but to the republic, which free enterprisers took to be one and the same. The New Deal had spawned radical ideas such as profits sharing that were, as Harlow H. Curtice, the president of General Motors, said in 1958, "foreign to the concept of the American free enterprise system."[90] If this were so, it was in large measure because, as we have seen, for free enterprisers the concept came into focus when understood in opposition to the New Deal and the social forces it unleashed.

Free enterprisers sought to reclaim customs abandoned by those they took to be the overzealous bureaucrats of the New Deal. Robert R. Reynolds, disenchanted Democratic senator from North Carolina, expressed hope that in the upcoming election of 1944, "the government of our beloved country will be taken from the New Dealers and returned to the American people."[91] Willkie said that the Democrats had abandoned "the principle of free enterprise" and substituted for it "a huge, centralized government, controlling the enterprises of the people by nonelected commissioners, exactly the doctrine that our forefathers rejected."[92] If Franklin Roosevelt depicted the New Deal as the culmination of American traditions, free enterprisers described it as the destruction of such customs, and called for a restoration.

Advocates described free enterprise as a "system," an "order," or a "philosophy," a comprehensive worldview that represented the only reasonable hope of stemming and then reversing the tide of the New Deal order. It represented less a consistent program, however, than a "fighting slogan" that "Roosevelt haters . . . united upon," as the columnist Sam Tucker wrote in 1943.[93] The "paternalistic, collectivist philosophy," said conservative Nobel laureate Robert Millikan in 1950, "is the antithesis of the American free enterprise philosophy."[94] Unlike the program of the New Dealers, who sought to construct a social welfare state, the main goal of free enterprisers was defensive and negative; it was to halt the New Deal, "with its dangerous economic doctrines and threat to the American way of living," as Vandenberg said at a Lincoln Day Dinner in 1938.[95] As late as 1959, moderate Republican and Eisenhower cabinet member Arthur Larson wrote the book *What We Are For* because he worried that free enterprise advocates, in emphasizing only what they opposed, had yet to offer a positive vision. Yet Larson's warning went largely unheeded because most free enterprisers offered a stance of opposition as the path to political freedom, while his brand of "modern Republicanism" slowly faded.

The free enterprise/New Deal opposition thus preceded and shaped the conservative/liberal binary that eventually emerged. Though not yet "fully reclassified" into liberal versus conservative, the salient division in American politics, columnist Charles P. Stewart noted in 1939, was not between Democrats and Republicans but between "New Dealers and Old Dealers."[96] Free enterprise did more than help create the ideological realignment of the two parties. It also offered a grand vision of politics—and beyond politics—as a fight for the soul of the nation, of two divergent paths that would lead the country in radically different directions. Americans had to choose "between two distinct philosophies of government," said John D. M. Hamilton of the Republican National Committee in 1936, with the New Dealers dangerously and outrageously "holding that the American people are no longer able to govern themselves."[97] Blackburn Hughes, a Memphis Democrat in the cotton business, described "two distinct philosophies of government—the New Deal philosophy and the American philosophy," in 1944. He dismissed the New Deal philosophy, statist to the core, as one that "is trying to run the lives of everyone from Washington." Like free enterprisers before and after, Hughes called the upcoming election a "crucial crossroads," with the choices leading in "opposite directions."[98] Free enterprisers, even Democrats like Hughes, viewed elections as referenda on freedom.

It may seem surprising that a language that sprang from practical-minded businessmen and their allies developed into such a strongly ideological political project built on alarmism and the fear of humiliation. As we have seen, many free enterprisers, for all their celebrations of sober moderation, depicted their efforts as a counterrevolution. "This is a revolution," said Virgil Jordan of the New Deal in 1937. "You cannot compromise with a revolution; you can only co-operate with it or be liquidated by it." In this vision, elections were not simply electoral contests but momentous battles for the future of the nation. "This year cannot be and must not be yet another election year," said the Illinois Republican attorney general George F. Barrett in 1944. The political divisions "are of such tremendous significance to the future of our nation that 1944 must and should go down in our annals as the year in which the American people adopted a new Declaration of Independence for the United States of America," he said, highlighting such a divide in the midst of a global war. According to Barrett, "We must win a rebirth of freedom from the New Deal itself, from New Deal autocracy and from New Deal bureaucratic misrule and mismanagement."[99] Evoking Abraham Lincoln's "new birth of freedom" in another time of war, Barrett identified freedom's enemy not as global fascism but as New Deal bureaucracy.

Free enterprisers thus embraced a politics of negation. Henry F. Schwarz, the toy store president, put the matter bluntly in a letter to the *New York Herald Tribune* in 1938: "The Republican party must be the opposite of the New Deal." Calling this an "elementary political strategy," Schwarz correctly predicted that "the single biggest issue in American politics for at least a generation" would be the legacy of the New Deal. He addressed his comments to "Republicans and anti–New Dealers," recognizing that, for the time being at least, these represented overlapping but distinct categories. "Sooner or later," he maintained, a political party would make opposition to the New Deal an issue on which they could "ride into power."[100] Such a statement minimized the fact that since 1934 at least the Republican Party had been aiming to do precisely this.[101] Schwarz was correct that anti–New Dealism eventually became a winning political formula for the GOP. Free enterprise was the shorthand for this formula. It took far longer than Schwarz probably thought, but eventually the GOP did "ride into power" on the message of free enterprise, understood as the rejection of New Deal liberalism.

Business free enterprisers fought a culture war as vigorously as they did the class war. Felix Morley spelled this out in 1949: "To attack the principles underlying free enterprise is to impugn the traditional morality of the American people."[102] Free enterprisers described their fight as a moral crusade. When Wendell Willkie explained why he was running for president in 1940, he described the New Deal in moral, not political, terms as a "decade of decadence."[103] Free enterprisers understood themselves to be the primary victim of this class and culture war, and so described their fight as a defensive struggle. They fought to resurrect a dying system, thereby saving a nation that was, inexorably, reform by reform, tax by tax, sliding into totalitarianism and immorality.

Racism inflected this process of cultural and ideological consolidation. Many southern white Democrats turned against New Deal liberalism in part because of its perceived embrace (however tentative) of African American civil rights. Some Republicans tried to attract disgruntled southern white Democrats, even as many members of their party retained a commitment to civil rights. In 1950, the leader of the Republican National Committee discussed the possibility of building a "unity ticket" for the next presidential election, consisting of Republicans and white southern Democrats who opposed the civil rights platform that the Democrats had adopted in 1948.[104] Seeking to gain the votes of whites in his state, the chairman of the South Carolina Republican Party claimed in 1958 that "the party as a whole will appeal for the support of the nation's majorities," and further explained that the GOP platform "will become very digestible to the South when contrasted with the extreme liberalism if not the socialism concepts of the Democrats."[105] The linking of whiteness with anti-liberalism became a formula for overturning the solid Democratic South, although the pace was slower than the party leadership might have wished.

Free enterprisers often employed a racialized language to express their victimhood. Sometimes they attributed their victimization to small groups of troublemakers. In 1935, H. W. Prentis, soon to be the president of NAM, condemned "the path of lavish spending and centralized control by selfish minorities which history shows leads eventually to chaos and dictatorship."[106] Prentis did not spell out whom he considered this category of "minorities" to include. Free enterprisers like Prentis frequently allied themselves with a putative majority that had been unfairly treated by the planners and schemers. In a speech to the North Carolina College for Negroes in 1936, Ogden Mills condemned "the frightful fate that has overtaken racial minorities in countries that have abandoned the principles of free enterprise." Speaking to an audience victimized by the Jim Crow system, he complained about policies that "uprooted freedom and tossed it contemptuously aside."[107] Mills did not condemn or even comment on racism or segregation, the enormous impediments to freedom that the African American members of his audience faced. Most white southern free enterprisers endorsed the racial caste system in spite of the centrality of "freedom" to their worldview.

Equally notable is the frequency with which free enterprisers not only invoked the language of slavery but compared themselves with the enslaved. In their language, metaphors of slavery stood in for all manner of abjection faced by businessmen and affluent taxpayers. Yet they rarely wrestled with the legacy of chattel slavery in forging racial and class inequality, focusing instead on their own perceived oppression. In the 1936 campaign, Frank Knox claimed that the evil of slavery of the Civil War era, which "involved 3,000,000" people paled in comparison with the statist regime of Franklin Roosevelt, which "involves the slavery of 140,000,000 of our American citizens."[108] Like many other Republicans during the New Deal era, Knox claimed to be following the path of Abraham Lincoln and the Republican Party in a time of national crisis—the abandonment of free enterprise—that he and many others considered every bit as serious as the one that led the nation to civil war in 1861. "There are many kinds of slavery," stated Representative Joseph Martin, the House Republican leader, at a Lincoln Day dinner in 1940. The most dangerous form in the current world, he averred, was "political slavery, which in these later years has begun creeping like some strange new and insidious malady."[109] Political slavery would be the fate of the American people if they failed to reverse the statist gains of the New Deal. A year later, a speaker claimed that socialized medicine would make "the individual the slave of the state."[110] Enslavement was the condition of those dependent upon government security, but those who belong to an "adventurous race" had no need for a welfare state.[111] Class and whiteness combined in these formulations to create a topsy-turvy conception of "slavery" as the condition of well-to-do whites under the New Deal.

Perhaps the most telling example of free enterprise inversion came in 1947, when Thomas E. Dewey, the once and future Republican nominee for the presidency, addressed a banquet of the "Foremost Fifty," an annual gathering of the nation's top business leaders, hosted by the magazine publisher B. C. Forbes at a fancy New York City hotel. In what *Life* magazine described as "his frankest speech of the year," Dewey identified himself along with the wealthy executives in the audience as "fellow victims of the New Deal." As Democratic congress-

Thomas E. Dewey addresses business leaders, whom he dubbed
"fellow victims of the New Deal," in 1947. (Courtesy of Getty Images.)

man Harold D. Cooley joked afterward, these "victims" earned a total of about
$5.6 million, meaning they could "buy a lot of medicine to ease the pain of
being a victim of the New Deal."[112]

Over time, the business free enterprisers' disparagement of "noisy" and
"selfish" minorities gave way to a claim that they were themselves the minority
group most in need of protection. One of the most dangerous tendencies of the
New Deal was that it "fomented contempt" for business, as *New York Times*
columnist Arthur Krock wrote in 1942. He claimed that, in the New Deal view,
"rich business men were generally undesirable products of free enterprise."[113]
Free enterprisers often celebrated those who refused to "coddle minority or
pressure groups," as Eddie Rickenbacker, the head of Eastern Airlines, said.[114]
Yet they demanded a certain kind of coddling for themselves. During World
War II, Claude Wampler, the president of the Carrier Corporation, complained

that while "paternalistic government coddles" unworthy people, it makes business a "whipping boy."[115] This language appeared to reach its apotheosis in 1962 when Ayn Rand wrote "America's Persecuted Minority: Big Business." In that essay, she complained that "the defense of minority rights" had become a nearly unanimous "moral principle," but that this principle "is applied only to racial and religious minorities" and had not been extended to "that small, exploited, defenseless minority, which consist of businessmen."[116] From the beginning of the New Deal, the idea that "business must be reassured"—which meant no "bureaucratic dictation" alongside the ability to "earn a reasonable profit from its labors"— rested alongside the free enterprise dismissal of security and a celebration of risk for individuals.[117]

Free enterprisers thus conceived of themselves in paradoxical ways: as powerful but ineffectual, as central but peripheral, as confident but insecure, and as risk takers in need of reassurance. While business leaders denigrated the government's security programs for individuals as "coddling" and emphasized the importance of risk, free enterprisers also sought a recognition of their special plight under the New Deal as a "whipping boy." In 1936, Frank Knox called on government to give "business some assurance that there will be no further violent and sudden interferences with the vital implements of industrial enterprise." Knox further specified, in a phrase common among free enterprisers, that this cessation must "not be a breathing spell" but a "moratorium."[118] Vandenberg complained in 1938 that business had been attacked with a "vindictive blunderbuss." It has been "assaulted with punitive taxation," "undermined by government competition," "pursued by swarms of big and little bureaucracies," and had become a "guinea pig upon which irresponsible experimentalists have gaily tried their reckless reforms."[119] Feeling victimized by government policies and competition, free enterprise advocates turned their war against the state into a more general culture war fought in the name of ordinary Americans. The legacy of that battle shaped popular understandings of freedom for generations.

In 1946, the steel magnate Ernest T. Weir prepared a circular for his fellow business leaders advocating that the Republican Party be purged and turned into the "official Conservative Party of America." Evaluating his proposition, the editors of the *Nashville Tennessean* agreed that such a designation made sense since the "Republican Party is and has been the party of conservatism." If the party "chooses to wear its real label, so much the better," concluded the newspaper. Yet it took time for Weir's conception of the GOP as an "open, avowed conservative party" to become a reality.[120] Free enterprise rhetoric played a key role in making Weir's dream come true.

In 1954, G. Mennen Williams, the Democratic governor of Michigan, claimed "as a clear and indisputable fact" that "the Democratic party has been consistently the liberal party and the Republican party has been consistently the conservative party." Such a characterization was problematic in the age of Eisenhower and moderate Republicanism. Williams labeled as "classic conservative doctrine" the belief in the "trickle down theory of economics," which held that the country as a whole benefited when "big business was well taken care of."[121] Not long before the governor made these claims, Republicans like Herbert Hoover would have classified these beliefs (which they would have described more favorably) as classically liberal. As we have seen in this chapter, free enterprise ideas and impulses helped constitute and transform both the Republican Party and conservativism. We will next explore an equally important part of their worldview, "faith in free enterprise."

6

"Faith in Free Enterprise"

"FREE MARKETS REALLY ARE MIRACLES," declared Jonathan Haidt, a social psychologist and professor of ethical leadership at New York University, in a 2014 lecture at the American Enterprise Institute. "You really can turn water into wine, vast quantities of wine, at low, low prices," he said. By proclaiming the miracle of markets, Haidt was paying homage, whether he knew it or not, to a hugely influential parable written in 1958 by Leonard Read.[1] Entitled "I, Pencil," it described the genealogy of an "ordinary wooden pencil" from the pencil's point of view.[2] Claiming that no single person knew how to make a pencil, Read held that the unencumbered market—with its capacity to coordinate thousands of independent human actions undertaken by distant people at different times—miraculously facilitated what no individual or government could accomplish: the unplanned miracle of the pencil.

Read's essay was widely praised well into the twenty-first century. The conservative columnist Jonah Goldberg called "I, Pencil" "one of the most famous essays in the history of libertarianism."[3] Milton Friedman, the most important popularizer of Read's essay, labeled it a "classic" illustration of the "power of the market."[4] Sarah Palin, 2008 Republican vice presidential candidate, called the essay "a timely reminder" of the value of the "invisible hand" at a time when "capitalism seems to need defending these days more than ever."[5] Read's "brilliant story pregnant with economic truth" is frequently retold in conservative media, though not all tellers are familiar with its provenance, some supposing that they invented it themselves or that it came from Adam Smith.[6] It is a sign

Leonard Read, creator of the Foundation for Economic Education.
(Courtesy of the Foundation for Economic Education, Inc. [FEE].)

of its enduring cultural cachet that Read's fable inspired a 2010 TED talk by science writer and British Conservative member of the House of Lords Matt Ridley, who substituted a computer mouse for a pencil.[7]

Read's autobiography of the pencil is deeply connected to the history of free enterprise as it was articulated by opponents of statism. Free enterprisers like Read paradoxically positioned themselves as both hard-headed realists (as distinguished from New Deal dreamers) and faithful adherents of what economic historian Karl Polanyi called "a utopian market economy."[8] Free enterprisers condemned the New Deal as promulgating a false and dangerous promise of "something for nothing." Instead, they promoted a vision of unlimited riches produced by the market's miraculous spontaneous coordination of the human and natural worlds. These professions of faith minimized the power of the business firm as a political and economic force. All of these views were evident in Read's fable.

"The New Deal Has No Faith in This Country"

Free enterprisers believed that the New Deal had precipitated what the young presidential contender Thomas E. Dewey described in 1939 as a nationwide "crisis of faith."[9] Since the start of the New Deal, professions of what Polanyi in 1944 labeled "secular salvation" via free enterprise had become, like expressions of patriotism, standard elements of the rhetoric of business leaders, trade organizations, civic groups, ministers, pundits, and politicians.[10] As had become the custom, a Republican congressman declared in 1944, "I have faith in free enterprise."[11] Upping the ante the next year, conservative oilman J. Howard Pew claimed to have "a strong and fervent faith in the continuing superiority" of the free enterprise system.[12] In 1958, a congressional candidate confessed his "full faith in the free enterprise system."[13] And in 1974, a profile of Alan Greenspan remarked upon his "almost metaphysical faith in free enterprise."[14] Every Republican candidate for the presidency from Alf Landon in 1936 through Mitt Romney in 2012 professed his faith. (I explore the anomalous case of President Donald Trump in this book's epilogue.) In contrast, they accused New Dealers and their descendants of lacking such faith. In a "sweeping indictment," Dewey, who unsuccessfully sought the GOP nomination in 1940, announced, "The New Deal has no faith in this country" and, more specifically, "It has no faith in the system of private enterprise that has made this country great." Dewey's running mate in 1944, the Republican vice presidential candidate, John Bricker, made a very similar comment about the faithlessness of the Roosevelt administration.[15] For free enterprisers, nation and system were one and the same.

The faithful free enterprisers, of whom Read was one, portrayed themselves as hard-headed realists, contrasting their "horse sense" with the naïveté of the New Dealers and welfare statists, whose unrealistic proposals, they claimed, were based on artifice and magic. They believed that misguided New Deal policies resulted from a faulty epistemology that rested on the irrational and the unreal. "For the last 6 years America has been a land of make-believe," claimed Republican Pennsylvania congressman J. William Ditter in a 1939 radio address that articulated an early version of this point of view. Under the New Deal, he claimed, "Magic wands have been waved—stately castles have been built." According to the congressman, the New Deal, an unstable structure built on false foundations, relied on "every exploded economic theory, every wild-goose experiment, every crack-pot notion, and every discredited financial fallacy that the mind of man ever conceived." It was time, Ditter said, to replace the "star-gazing theorists" of the New Deal with down-to-earth "practical men" who would deal with the world as it existed, rather than a fantasy world of "make-believe work, make-believe money, and make-believe security." Ditter hoped America's long national trance would soon come to an end. Demanding "something more than lip service to free enterprise," he called for the restoration of the "rules of simple arithmetic." In this conception, free enterprise represented the reality principle.[16]

Free enterprisers equated faith in an unbounded market and distrust of government with reason, not ideology. In January 1938, for example, Dr. Glenn Frank, the chair of the recently formed Republican Policy Committee, addressed a luncheon of the New York Board of Trade at the Waldorf Astoria. Frank, the former president of the University of Wisconsin and soon to be a candidate for Robert La Follette Jr.'s Senate seat, chose a topic bound to appeal to critics of the New Deal, the importance of faith in free enterprise. As Frank had it, under the Roosevelt administration "faith in magic" had replaced belief in the "intelligent, modernized" system of free enterprise. Unlike the faith in free enterprise that he proudly declaimed, New Dealers displayed an unsound faith of which "we must divest ourselves" if we are to "solve the difficulties of our generation." He explained: "The sooner we learn that there are no rabbits in the hat" and "that artificial devices are a delusion," the "better for us and our children." Faith in "public planning" would only "hamstring the buoyant energies of our national enterprise." Under these conditions, Frank maintained, "maybe the magicians will be the only unemployed." Frank closed his address by calling for a rejection of "irresponsible utopianism" and a return to the "basic American devotion to free enterprise" which, he implied, was a responsible form of utopianism.[17]

Eerily, Frank died in a car accident in 1940 and three years later, Ditter perished in a plane crash. But their claims that the New Deal and the welfare state rested on artificial magic and that the free enterprise system stood, in contrast, on firm reality continued to be articulated long after their deaths. In this view, unrealistic expectations of "omnipotent government" were not just politically dangerous but psychologically naïve.[18] Indeed, some depicted the staying power of the New Deal order as a form of brainwashing. The welfare state flourished, as Chesly Manly wrote in 1954 in his critical analysis of the "the twenty-year revolution" set off by the New Deal, "not only by policy subversion, but by thought subversion on a national scale."[19] Free enterprisers described the political economy they favored as good policy because it was rooted in what Herbert Hoover called "hard commonplace truth," unlike the philosophy of New Dealers, "who ride upon plans of Utopia."[20] Free enterprisers sought the sanction less of ideology than of truth. In so doing, they aimed to naturalize their politics of common sense.

In juxtaposing the magic of the New Deal with the "sound" system of free enterprise, Frank and Ditter invoked an already familiar opposition that would become for many decades the heart of the conservative critique of the New Deal order. As early as 1934, the acerbic conservative H. L. Mencken described the New Deal not as set of policies with which he disagreed but as "a grotesque compound of false diagnoses and quack remedies."[21] That same year, Russell J. Brownback expressed concern that the "average American has an abiding faith in the magic of government to cure ills." Brownback warned his readers in *Barron's* against this misplaced faith in unrealistic economic ideas. FDR's magic rested on a logical fallacy, Brownback claimed, which was that "there is no such thing as something for nothing," a phrase that became central to the free enterprise critique of the welfare state as a Ponzi scheme.[22]

Some free enterprisers understood the New Deal's fetish for security as an assault on human development within the traditional family. They exhibited special scorn for welfare policies that increasingly covered the entire life cycle because these paternalistic policies undermined the hallmarks of a free society: risk taking, autonomy, and the patriarchal family. A 1935 editorial on "the New Deal road to ruin" condemned what it took to be the Rooseveltian principle "that the federal government should govern its citizens like so many incompetent children."[23] Even during World War II, critics denounced the "pure demagoguery" of the "planners" who promised "womb to tomb" security.[24] As Strom Thurmond said in 1949, "Nothing could be more un-American and more devastating to a strong and virile nation than to encourage its citizens to expect government to provide security from cradle to grave."[25] What was appropriate for an infant in the cradle was not a proper basis for policy in a nation of autonomous men. Perhaps this is why Georgia's Senator Herman Talmadge dismissed the New Deal as, among other things, "wet nursin' . . . downright communism, and plain foolishness," a combination that asserted a connection among gender roles, statism, and naïveté.[26] Babies needed security provided by the family, but government provision of insurance smothered adults in an economy built on risk and took away their autonomy.

Free enterprisers suggested that the essential nature of Americans was to be risk takers rather than security seekers and autonomous adults rather than dependent children, "Horatio Algers" rather than "securecrats," in the phrase of Millard G. Fraught, a New York industrialist.[27] Advocates often praised risk as the essence of Americanism, even if it meant demeaning the materialism that free enterprise supposedly made possible. "We must preserve the American tradition of freedom to take a chance—to lose your shirt, if you want to," claimed Eric Johnston of the U.S. Chamber of Commerce in 1943.[28] "Freedom is not for weaklings," said H. W. Prentis said of the National Association of Manufacturers in 1942. It was the "ultra-liberal and socialistic critics" of free enterprise who dangerously "put security first," thereby threatening robust independence.[29] Indeed, "lack of security" and "not the paternalistic spirit" had traditionally been, as Walter Linn pronounced in 1947, "the keynote of America."[30] By 1950, a free enterprise supporter singled out "the freedom to fail" as "our most important freedom."[31]Rejecting the Rooseveltian view that government-promoted security made freedom possible, free enterprisers thus took insecurity to be the hallmark of freedom. One critic of the babying of America went so far as to proclaim that "freedom and security are fundamentally incompatible." It was for this reason, according to O. E. Peterson, the secretary of Kiwanis International, that a "cradle-to-grave welfare policy" was not only undesirable but "not possible within a context of freedom."[32] Barry Goldwater saw the war on the New Deal as a much-needed renunciation of the myth of perpetual childhood. He described his 1964 presidential campaign as "a frontal attack against the false Santa Claus."[33] Reversing the usual gendered language that analogized the welfare state to an overindulgent mother, Goldwater also condemned the "political Daddyism" that manifested itself in "the ever-expanding gift power of the everlastingly growing Federal Government."[34] The anti-union labor relations guru Nathan Shefferman summed this viewpoint up in his book *Labor's Stake in Capitalism*, published by the Constitution and Free Enterprise Foundation in 1954. "Today many grownups have the minds of children," he asserted in the first chapter, "Uncle Sam Is Not Santa Claus." Supporters of the welfare state, he averred, "believe they can get something for nothing—not once a year but every day of the year, from cradle to grave."[35] With government usurping the role of mothers and fathers, it treated all citizens as children, wards of a dangerously powerful state.

Herbert Hoover, who frequently compared Franklin D. Roosevelt to Santa Claus, was only one of many critics of the New Deal to do so.[36] William Mullendore, the president of Southern California Edison, claimed in 1950 that the problem was twofold: "Not only has the common man come to believe in Santa Claus," but the Democratic administration believed the myth too, immorally offering illusions of government-provided riches "without limit."[37] Despite the free enterprisers' own mystical proclivities, the New Deal, from their perspective, amounted to fantasy, not public policy. Comparisons between the topsy-turvy constructs of the New Deal and Alice in Wonderland also abounded. The New Deal was a "wonderland of burocracy," said Ralph E. Church, a Republican candidate for the Illinois Senate in 1940. Church condemned "New Deal dreams of an all-powerful central government and an all-powerful executive," suggesting the lurking totalitarian dangers of a politics based on childish fantasy.[38]

That truth aligned with the free market ideology was not a coincidence but a reflection of the facts of economic nature, which free enterprisers analogized to scientific nature. If free enterprise was both true and natural, free enterprisers described the New Deal as artificial and false. As early as April 1934, little more than a year after Roosevelt took the oath of office in the midst of the Great Depression, Dale Cox, a columnist for the *Cleveland Plain Dealer*, said in a lecture at the Massillon Women's Club that he preferred to wait for the "natural recovery" of the economy, "rather than one attempted through the enactment of emergency legislation," which Cox claimed was unnatural.[39] In an address to the American Society of Civil Engineers on the virtues of "private enterprise" in 1945, John Cyprian Stevens claimed that "natural laws of economics" could not be "repealed like man-made laws." Under "natural laws this country has made the nearest approach to Utopia ever recorded in history," Stevens claimed.[40] Like Cox and Stevens, free enterprisers analogized free enterprise to other natural but finicky systems, such as the human body or the environment.

From the beginning of the New Deal, critics depicted Roosevelt's actions as a rebuke against nature, whose rules governed economics and politics as much as they did science.[41] "Economic laws," announced Herbert Hoover in 1934, "cannot be repealed by official fiat."[42] The state could no more control the economy, in this view, than it could repeal or modify gravity and, in attempting to do so, it "retarded" the "natural recovery" that would have occurred without the "heavy hand" of bureaucracy, according to a member of the Republican National Committee in 1936.[43] Asserting the truth and naturalness of the free enterprise system, 1940 Republican presidential candidate Wendell Willkie said that the unfaithful New Deal "intelligentsia" had "stunted the growth of American enterprise."[44] Many others echoed the view that the New Deal's revocation of "all economic laws" represented a dangerous step toward "the acceptance of totalitarianism in the name of 'managed economy' or the 'welfare state.'"[45]

Free enterprise may have been based on the "sound" principles of the natural order, but in the understanding of its advocates, these were in no sense easy, or even possible, to comprehend. Comparing economists and astronomers, the economics writer Henry Hazlitt claimed that economics was the far more complex discipline, and thus economists could of necessity have less certainty than those who studied faraway planetary bodies, since the "forces they have to deal with are infinitely more numerous, more complicated, more diverse, and more elusive."[46] What was one to do about forces so difficult to understand and impossible to control? To free enterprisers the answer was to avoid the allure of the unnatural solutions promoted by New Dealers. Let natural forces do their miraculous and inexplicable work.

Some critics of the New Deal disliked the promotion of free enterprise faith. "There is a concerted drive to make 'Free Enterprise' into a religion," observed J. Fred Thornton, an editor of the *Montgomery Advertiser*, in 1959. "We are constantly having it dinned in our ears that it is the bounden duty of every patriotic American to adore God, U.S. Steel and General Electric, not necessarily in that order listed." A self-proclaimed conservative, Thornton said that he would "refuse to make a fetish or religion out of free enterprise."[47] But among the growing number of self-proclaimed conservatives, he was in the minority.

In addition to according with truth and nature, lack of planning was, as free enterprisers explained it, the expression of a radically democratic faith in the collective wisdom of discrete individuals who, by their actions in the marketplace, expressed and satisfied their desires and helped others do the same. The sum total of these actions was not just miraculous abundance but also political justice. The anti–New Deal Congress of American Industry in 1935 called for "the abandonment of planned economy" precisely because, it argued, the complexity of the economy made government intervention not just undemocratic but dangerous. Anticipating the central message of Read's "I, Pencil" essay, the group claimed that the economy was at its most efficient and democratic when "directed by an infinite number of individual judgments and decisions, thus utilizing the skill, intelligence and knowledge of the whole people." No small group of experts was "wise enough for such an attempt," the group concluded.[48] Describing the market as a democratic realm of freedom and the state as the domain of undemocratic bureaucratic planners was central to free enterprise critiques of the New Deal.

Other critics of "New Deal psychology" believed that it encouraged unworthy people to take more than their share from the state. In 1934, columnist Mark Sullivan claimed the nascent New Deal was already producing "a nation of money grabbers" who immorally seek "money from Washington."[49] "When it's so easy to get," said one editor in 1938, speaking of government benefits, "who can blame them for taking advantage of it?"[50] Free enterprisers, who celebrated profit seeking in the world of business, sometimes denounced the money-grabbing "takers" as racialized others and class enemies. A 1939 article claimed that a "Sioux Indian" was seen in the "city in the latest style, even wearing a necktie." Questioned about his apparent prosperity, he supposedly replied, "No plow. Big pay." The New Deal encouraged people to "give nothing and expect everything," turning the American work ethic upside down, allowing racialized others to succeed by rewarding their laziness.[51]

The New Deal Order, in this view, fostered a society-wide immaturity, a refusal to face facts, and a rejection of both realism and self-reliance. It manifested a "childlike faith in the ability of government to solve all our problems," as Prentis put it in 1942.[52] Indeed, from the point of view of its enemies, the unfortunate appeal of the New Deal was that it turned the unrealistic whims of children into public policy. To the consternation of its critics, the politics of infantilization seemed to be hypnotizing the American people. Herbert Hoover offered what he called the "Santa Claus interpretation" of the 1934 election results to explain the New Deal's resounding triumph. In the "new school of budgetary magic," according to Hoover, "songs of economic hallucination substitute for the brutal clang of the cash register."[53] This was a variation on the former president's favorite theme: the preference of New Dealers for fantasy over reality represented a clear and present danger to the republic.

The New Deal was, as Senator Robert Taft said in a 1936 speech at the Women's National Republican Club, "foreign to the whole genius of the American people." Yet, through demagoguery on "a gigantic and dangerous scale," the new false ideology was displacing the true traditional one. It was succeeding in "breaking down the faith which the Americans have in the system under which they have grown to manhood." Deviously targeting what Taft called the nation's most "vulnerable point," the New Deal nurtured the childish expectation "that we can get something for nothing."[54] In this view, the New Deal state was not just irresponsible but illegitimate. "We do not have a government," said Senator Josiah Bailey, conservative Democrat from North Carolina, in 1937. Instead, he characterized the Roosevelt regime as an illegitimate "gift enterprise." These presents to the undeserving, he claimed, did not appear by magic but by the state-sanctioned theft of the precious funds of those hardworking Americans who "earn and save."[55] Similarly, Arthur Vandenberg, Republican senator from Michigan, called in 1939 for "a return to sanity; a repudiation of the principle that we can spend our way to prosperity."[56] The New Deal, in his view, was a crime against sanity and its chief victims were the affluent.

The hiving of the country into productive makers and unproductive takers formed the basis of the traditional American belief in "producerism," the idea that people who made and grew things deserved pride of place in the republic.[57] But whereas in the nineteenth century this belief system was associated with the labor movement, in the twentieth century it became the rallying cry of free enterprisers. Rather than the artisan, the maker was now described as a company. The taker was no longer an unscrupulous employer or an enslaver who unfairly took the fruits of labor from the worker but the government, which now did the same through its system of confiscatory taxes and extravagant spending.[58]

Similarly, the images of something for nothing and Santa Claus harked back to a traditional American suspicion of the "unearned increment," as it was called in the nineteenth century. Free enterprisers, however, put a new spin on this idea. In the nineteenth century and into the Progressive Era, radicals used the phrase "something for nothing" to critique the unsavory practices of the new class of business titans. In this producerist vision, the exploitation of labor provided capitalists with unwarranted, and therefore immoral, gain. In 1950, historian Robert Bremner noted the "semantic somersault" that had taken place over the previous decades, as the phrase had become a "missile by the spokesmen of big business and political conservatism to hurl at what they called the 'gimme' attitude of the common folks toward government."[59] Free enterprisers catalyzed this metamorphosis as they turned an image of class warfare on its head.

The affluent declared themselves the victims of the something for nothing policy of the New Deal. As the *Chicago Tribune* editorialized in 1935, "The division is between people who want the government to do things for them and people who, doing for themselves, must pay in the end for whatever the government does."[60] In 1949, C. B. Sweet, the president of the National Retail Lumber Dealers Association, similarly described the New Deal as "taking from the haves and giving to the have-nots," which he described as "pitting the mass against the classes; by giving something for nothing."[61] New Deal magic, in this view, was simply class warfare by other means. Free enterprisers needed to reject "the promised security spoon-fed by the government" that would inevitably require the sacrifice of "individual freedom" by violating natural law and rewarding undeserving people.[62]

This critique of the welfare state as offering handouts, especially to the undeserving poor, continued to be an important component of free enterprise discourse into the twenty-first century. Mitt Romney resuscitated this theory when he said shortly after the 2012 presidential election that Barack Obama won because of the "gifts" he bestowed on poor people and minorities.[63] So too did former Florida governor and 2016 Republican presidential candidate Jeb Bush, who claimed that Democrats appealed to African Americans by offering them "free stuff."[64] In his slim 2012 book *A Nation of Takers: America's Entitlement Epidemic*, conservative intellectual Nicholas Eberstadt used the phrase "something for nothing" four times.[65] Many critics of the welfare state's immoral magic held that the free enterprise system produced and multiplied wealth and that this mysterious process could be distinguished from the "something for nothing" nostrums offered by liberals.[66]

"A Factory Is Like a Tree"

"I, Pencil" concisely and artfully illustrated a strand of already-existing free enterprise thinking, emphasizing its optimistic, faith-based belief in what Read called "the miraculous market" and its generative powers, its "creativities."[67] None of this was original to Read or his essay. In 1944, Senator Fred Norman shared in the *Congressional Record* what he called "one of the best and clearest worded definitions of free enterprise." Norman's favored definition appeared in an advertisement entitled "A Factory Is Like a Tree" for the Harbor Plywood Corporation of Aberdeen, Washington, that had been published in newspapers in Norman's district.[68] Norman claimed that the president of the company,

E. W. Daniels, "and thousands upon thousands of Americans like him have a fiercely burning faith in free enterprise." This faith was, Norman said, a "flame that will continue to grow until it consumes the unbelievers—the Fascists, the Communists, and all their crackpot companions," likening critics of free enterprise to atheistic totalitarians.

Drawing on the theme of elegant complexity, the ad compared a factory to a tree. "Through the chemistry of its complex workings," the copy proclaimed, "it produces fruit in the forms of pay rolls, and pay rolls are manna for the grocer, the baker, the doctor, the preacher, the teacher, and the whole intricate life of a community." Just as a tree, through complex processes invisible to the human eye, converts sunlight and water into fruit, the factory transfigures "labor, materials and risk into the miracle of the American way of life." In its production of manna, free enterprise combined biology and divinity, the natural with the supernatural. This was not the first use of a tree metaphor, which suggested that the complexity of the economy was natural and organic, unlike the artificial complexities of the statists.[69] Those who invoked it also suggested that government intervention would be not only counterproductive but unnatural and dangerous.

Free enterprisers likened industrial economies to natural ecosystems. In October 1943, an illustrated ad for the Chesapeake and Ohio Railway, entitled "The Trunk of the Tree," appeared in a number of major American newspapers.[70] The ad showed an image of a tree, with a railroad track running neatly up the trunk into the branches. Among the branches rested the elements of a typical American town: a church, a factory, a school, a barn and silo, a library, and some houses. "First there was just wilderness," the text began, telling the story of the settling of the town in mythic frontier terms. The move to modern industrial America was rapid; these townsmen appeared to bypass the agricultural stage of development entirely: after clearing away "the trees and the underbrush," they started to build a factory. Given the nature of the company sponsoring the ad, it is not surprising that the second paragraph noted that the settlers "knew they could depend on the railroad's laying a spur line over which they could bring in people and raw materials and ship out their finished product." Commercial and residential development followed, and "an enterprising merchant opened a general store." An array of businesses—drug stores, barbershops, and even a cinema—followed. Eventually, "roads appeared," the ad announces, although it does not say how. The town continued to grow but, according to the copy, "nobody planned it that way." Indeed, the town "grew like a tree—slowly,

The Trunk   of the Tree

First there was just wilderness. Then some men came and cleared away the trees and the underbrush. Pretty soon they started to build a factory—way out to nowhere and gone.

The reason was simple—the land was cheap. Also, they knew they could depend on the railroad's laying a spur line over which they could bring in people and raw materials and ship out to market their finished product.

It wasn't long before a little cluster of houses sprang up for the workers. Roads appeared. An enterprising merchant arrived and opened a general store.

Soon a doctor came and a dentist. A garage went up. Then a drug store, a barber shop, a movie house.

And so the town grew. Nobody planned it that way. American initiative made it that way. The town grew as opportunity grew. It grew like a tree—slowly, steadily, surely. And the trunk of the tree—the trunk through which the lifesap flowed—was the railroad.

Every man who made his living in that town made it from goods that came in by the railroad, or that went out over its bright rails to markets beyond.

* * *

The men who built that town in the wilderness believe with all their hearts in free enterprise. But some of them may not appreciate the extent to which *their* continued economic freedom depends on freedom of the railroads.

The sirens of regimentation may lull us with the theory that it is all very well for private businesses to remain free, but that public carriers should be owned by the government.

But what would this mean in practical terms to every business man in the community we have described? It would mean that his dealings with the railroads would now be on a political instead of a business basis.

And would railroad service be improved? With bureaucrats in charge, and no more competition between lines? You can read the answer in any country in the world where railroads are government-controlled.

* * *

Before you listen to those who would "regiment" our railroads, consider whether our business structure could long remain half slave and half free.

And whether, if the axe is laid at the trunk, the whole tree would not suffer.

CHESAPEAKE AND OHIO RAILWAY
CLEVELAND, OHIO

The free enterprise system is depicted as both natural and machine-like in this 1943 advertisement—which, characteristically, leaves out the role of government in economic development. (Courtesy C&O Historical Society, www.cohs.org.)

steadily, surely." As if the reader needed reminding, the text notes that "the trunk of the tree—the trunk through which the lifesap flowed—was the railroad." Typical of the free enterprise vision, the railroad corporation not only aligned itself with the natural forces of the market but substituted itself for them. The state was notably absent. Indeed, the switch to the passive voice enabled the copywriter to excise government—very likely the builder of the roads that "appeared"— from the parable.

Extracting lessons from the story of the growth of a town in the wilderness, ad writers for the Chesapeake and Ohio explained that those who built it "believe with all their hearts in free enterprise." Yet, according to the copy, "some of them may not appreciate the extent to which their continued economic freedom depends on freedom of the railroads." To convey this appreciation the tone of the ad shifted from heartwarming to stern. Readers, the railroad company warned, needed to be aware that "the sirens of regimentation" might "lull us" into accepting a larger role for government, which would put "bureaucrats in charge." The company, employing the Lincolnian trope much beloved by free enterprisers, questioned "whether our business structure could long remain half slave and half free." Leonard Read built on the lesson that political freedom required business autonomy.

The "I, Pencil" Moment

Leonard Read came of age as an anti–New Deal, pro–free enterprise political actor as the western manager of the U.S. Chamber of Commerce, from which position he called in 1937 for "public spending curtailed and taxation reduced."[71] He changed the popular conversation, however, by packaging these free enterprise beliefs as a timeless fairy tale. In Read's still-influential narrative, abundance is the reward for faith in free enterprise and a distrust of government.

The "suave" Read is celebrated in America's libertarian subculture.[72] His essay—widely available online or in pamphlet form, with an introduction by Milton Friedman—remains popular among libertarians, free market economists, and conservative bloggers. One can purchase an "I, Pencil" coffee mug, T-shirt, bib, or mouse pad. In the late 1980s, Harding University students arranged for a six-foot-tall pencil to visit sixth-grade classrooms to teach the lessons of Read's essay. In 2012, the Competitive Enterprise Institute produced an animated short film, *I, Pencil: The Movie*. Friedman chose to open his own popular 1980 television documentary on the wonders of the market, *Free to Choose*, with an unacknowledged homage to Read. Holding a pencil aloft, he delivered a three-minute riff on its impossibly complex origins and the remarkable way in which markets make pencils appear in spite of the "fact" that no one person can make them.[73] Friedman even deployed one of Read's favorite verbal tics when describing the amazing powers of market forces: "Farfetched? Not at all."[74] A number of economists and teachers, following Friedman's lead, assign the essay in high school and college classes.

Homages to the essay continued well into the twenty-first century. In 2012, the Institute for Faith, Work and Economics produced a video, *I, Smartphone*, modeled on Read's essay. According to the producers, "God has given us the market process as the most powerful tool we have in a fallen world to serve each other by using our gifts."[75] The essay is still referenced as a reason to distrust "planning" in favor of the spontaneous order of the free market. It has been the inspiration for hundreds of newspaper columns, essays, and blog posts on the miracle of cappuccinos, carbonated beverages, iPhones, medical procedures, and all manner of other things.[76] In 2015, the conservative columnist Michelle Malkin, in her essay "I, Toilet Paper," one of dozens of copycat pieces written in the style of Read's classic essay, described that product as the "lofty result of faith in freedom, not the product of a bureaucrat's mandate."[77] A blogger, amazed to find a pair of panties for 88 cents at Wal-Mart, characterized her momentary euphoria as an "'I, Pencil' moment."[78]

Yet among historians, Read, who lived from 1898 to 1983, is not particularly well known. Despite the excellent treatment of Read in the works of Jennifer Burns, Brian Doherty, Bethany Moreton, and Kim Phillips-Fein, among others, when mentioned at all, he is usually cited for his leadership in the conservative world of lobbying and think tanks rather than for his writings.[79] Intellectual historians in particular have shied away from figures like Read, who made no original contribution to economic thought. Yet although even one of his admirers, libertarian writer Doherty, admits, "He was no great intellectual," Read's writings repay study.[80] During the period from the 1940s to the 1980s, when the battle for free enterprise seemed to its participants to be a life-or-death struggle—when, as Doherty writes, "Free enterprise needed an uncompromising fighting force"—Leonard Read, a World War I veteran, served on the front lines of that "intellectual counteroffensive."[81] He did so from his perch as the head of the Foundation for Economic Education (FEE), a think tank based in Irvington, New

York, that he founded in 1946—thanks to many generous corporate donations—
after a decade of working for various branches of the Chamber of Commerce
on the West Coast and a brief stint at the National Industrial Conference Board.[82]

Read saw FEE's role not as a lobby influencing legislation but as a promoter
of free market ideas that—following the double state-empowering whammy of
the New Deal and World War II—he and many of his colleagues feared were
losing in the court of public opinion and even among many business executives
and politicians.[83] Read, according to his friend and mentor Friedrich A. Hayek,
successfully popularized free enterprise through the use of "homely everyday
language."[84] To quote the conservative writer John Chamberlain, Read was a
"publicist," a label Read would likely have proudly claimed.[85] A 1947 profile
noted that Read's "message is always the same": the world was engaged in a
great battle between "collectivism and individualism," the outcome of which
was the key not only to American prosperity but to human freedom.[86] Throughout his long career, Read rarely veered from this script.

Distressed by "the lack of understanding of the significance of individualism,
of the voluntary economy and of economic liberty" among those coming of age
during the New Deal era, Read attributed this ignorance to the fact that, as he
put it in a speech at a town hall meeting in Los Angeles in June 1946, shortly
after he founded his think tank, "a new generation, one which has never experienced economic liberty, is taking over." Read feared that young Americans
coming to adulthood, having experienced only the New Deal's repudiation of
free enterprise values, were losing a sense of what made this system necessary
for the preservation of American liberties. "Only a few know how to make the
case for this philosophy of life," he told the audience, and he numbered himself
among those who could successfully make the free enterprise case. "How many
businessmen, for instance, can, with sound logic and persuasiveness, expose
the fallacies of such managed-economy policies" as Social Security, minimum
wages, and full employment? His answer was "Very few!" Hence the need for
the services of FEE in disseminating the "freedom philosophy."[87]

Making the free enterprise case would require, Read believed, "altering . . .
our present errant ways." It would necessitate, above all, challenging the logic
of the New Deal, which had dangerously become "so thoroughly embedded in
national thinking that one hardly dares challenge the rightness of the principle."
Read worried that younger Americans might "join the parade of those who would
make government the master rather than the servant of the people" and that busi-

ness would become subordinated to the state. His job was to tell people who had known no other system that the "regimentation" that they took for granted was a violation of their liberty. Read spent the rest of his long career seeking to resuscitate what he saw as the older notion of liberty that had been occluded.[88] He sought to create alternative narratives of economic freedom, sowing faith in what he called the "incomprehensible" and "mysterious" free enterprise system so that it would one day become common sense.[89] Read defended free enterprise not just as an economic system that efficiently catalyzed great wealth but also as a spontaneous social order that uniquely and democratically produced justice and peace.

Over the course of his career, Read worked as a Chamber of Commerce officer, Conference Board official, and free market educator and propagandist. Using a commonsense idiom common among free enterprisers, Read sought to expose the unrealistic pretensions of New Deal liberalism, which he saw as every bit as dangerous as socialism. He promoted "sensible and sound" policies in the manner of the businessmen that he represented.[90] At the same time, Read, like a surprising number of free enterprisers, was a spiritual searcher, one who has been labeled a "Christian transcendentalist" and a "rational mystic."[91] Read's Southern California business associates and hard-line free marketeers James Ingebretsen and William Mullendore were, according to Doherty, "obsessed with the worlds of spirit and psychic energy."[92] Often free enterprisers embraced, along with their common sense, miracles and wonderment. One conservative critic of Milton Friedman and Leonard Read complained, "Both of them unintentionally led their readers away from understanding towards mysticism."[93] Similarly, Irving Kristol, noted neoconservative, confessed, "I could not take seriously the seemingly blind faith in 'free enterprise' that was the primal certainty" of many conservatives.[94] For these thinkers, however, mysticism was a central element of free enterprise. Read was a market romantic who presaged the celebrations of what Ronald Reagan later called the "the magic of the marketplace."[95] He hid the steel fist of his anti-statism in the velvet glove of free enterprise celebrations, and he did so largely by depicting capitalism as both a mystical and a moral system.

A "Complex Combination of Miracles"

The conceit of Read's essay is that it is narrated by a pencil, specifically a "Mongol 483" manufactured by the Eberhard Faber Pencil Company, a real company based in Wilkes-Barre, Pennsylvania. Read deliberately selected a familiar and mundane object. He wanted readers to reconsider the status and history of an item that appeared to be quite ordinary. Upon scrutiny, however, the pencil was not simple at all. It was instead a "mystery" that, he told the reader, merits "your wonder and awe," and that was made possible only by a market system that was akin to but even more complex than the natural wonders of the world. Indeed, in 1979 Karl Eller, an advertising executive, called free enterprise "truly the eighth wonder of the world."[96]

In Read's inventive framework, the story of the creation of a pencil, from the Eberhard Faber 483's point of view, turned the quotidian into a symbol of the "complex combination of miracles" that free enterprise uniquely could unleash. By describing a portion of the pencil's incomprehensibly dense genealogy, Read hoped to place the free enterprise system in a new light. He aimed to restore faith in the system that miraculously and without planning or government intervention—and, in his view, only *because* it was without those things—made the pencil and all other everyday commodities plentiful and affordable, and consequently made human flourishing possible. He believed that the market, not the state, best promoted human interconnection and solidarity.

Faith is the key word. It was not possible to understand or explain the complex and far-flung workings of the market—although, remarkably, Read did not employ the word *market* (or, for that matter, *free enterprise*) in the essay. Read preferred to emphasize that the miraculous system "is impossible for me to name," a task "too much to ask of anyone," as the pencil assured the reader. The goal instead was to "become aware of the miraculousness which I symbolize," and therefore to appreciate, if not to comprehend. "Not a single person on the face of the earth can make me," Read's pencil asserted. Moreover, nobody could enumerate all the raw materials, products, and process that made up the pencil's "innumerable antecedents." The biggest mystery of all, the one that Read believed demanded attention, was that the pencil, like all products of the free market, was an unplanned miracle, an expression of what Hayek and others called the "spontaneous order" and what Read, underlining the inability of humans to grasp this miracle, called "incomprehensible order."[97] The product of no "master mind," with nobody "dictating or forcibly directing these countless actions which bring me into being," the humble pencil emerged from an uncountable number of uncoerced individual acts coordinated only by the medium of the market. "We find the invisible hand at work," Read wrote, borrowing a metaphor associated with Adam Smith that served Read's purposes perfectly since it hinted at a divine basis of market operations.[98] The intelligent design that produced the unplanned pencil was an implicit rebuke to the bureaucratic imperative at the root of the New Deal order which, as the *Chicago Tribune* editorialized in 1936, in substituting "government control for free enterprise" forced Americans "to trust the welfare of all to the decisions of a few men."[99] Free enterprisers celebrated the decentralized nature of the market's creation as a metaphor for the democratic political system, in which power was broadly dispersed.[100]

Read's pencil urged the reader to analogize the miracles of the market to the wonders of nature. We agree, Read wrote, that "only God can make a tree" because "we realize that we ourselves could not make one." Moreover, we are able to describe the tree, this singularly complex product of nature, only in "superficial terms" because of its intricate and largely invisible workings. "What mind is there among men that could even record, let alone direct, the constant changes in molecules that transpire in the life span of a tree?" Grasping such processes, to Read, was "utterly unthinkable." Read saw the path of freedom as a radically democratic profession of ignorance rather than an undemocratic and counterproductive reliance on expertise.

Yet the magic of the pencil was even more extraordinary than the miracle of the tree's growth. The making of the pencil required, in addition to raw materials, what Read called the "configuration of creative human energies—millions of tiny know-hows configurating naturally and spontaneously in response to human necessity and desire." No human being could "direct" this complex ballet any more than she or he could "put molecules together to become a tree." Like nature, market forces were the product of an intelligent design that warranted awe rather than understanding. Because these forces coordinated both the labors of far-flung people and the wonders of nature, they were even more miraculous.

And powerful. The centerpiece of a 1944 ad for the Rustless Iron and Steel Corporation entitled "Faith moves mountains" was an image of cranes, tractors, and scaffolds dominating a denuded landscape, what looked like a half-flattened hill. The text of the ad declared that "faith in the American Tradition of Free Enterprise" could help the country achieve "the impossible," which in this particular case amounted to the ability to transform the topography in order to uncover chrome ore concentrates.[101] Unlike the dangerous power of the state, this force, the result of no bureaucratic directorate, was a miraculous good.

In "I, Pencil," in contrast to most of his other writings, Read kept the libertarian lesson implicit. Read's pencil encouraged people to "leave all creative energies uninhibited" and to "organize society in harmony with this lesson." It urged readers to "have faith that free men and women will respond to the invisible hand." The pencil, therefore, embodied the claim by Frank Knox, the 1936 Republican candidate for vice president, that "in our economic system of free enterprise there is an automatic direction of industry."[102] Free enterprise was, in this view, a self-correcting system, which is why planning was not just futile but counterproductive.

In describing the wonders of capitalism, free enterprisers like Read invariably stressed the centrality of individuals—"free men and women," as he called them—and minimized the role of institutions. In doing so, Read built on a key thread in free enterprise discourse. As Frank Branch Riley, a Portland lawyer, told the Rotary Club of Spokane in 1944, "It has been the pioneering business man . . . not the politician-bureaucrat, who has built mills, pumped oil from the earth, generated electric energy for power and light."[103] Absent from these tales were not just federal, state, and local governments but lobbies like the Chamber of Commerce, the Conference Board, NAM, and FEE, for which Read spent most of his life working, or the politicians who did their bidding. Regulation, as free enterprisers understood it, impeded individuals rather than placed limits on powerful corporations—which, of course, were glaringly absent in Read's schematic description of the economy. Read noted that "not a single person" can make a pencil, but he did not mention the entity that generally did produce pencils and almost all other goods: the business firm. His ode to the Eberhard Faber pencil strikingly overlooked the part that the Eberhard Faber Pencil Company played in contributing to its creation.[104]

In cataloguing the nature of the free enterprise system, Read, like most free enterprisers, rendered corporations invisible. Rather than giving the business firm its due as a driver of capitalism, they described a world of individual workers, not unions; consumers, not consumer activists; and entrepreneurs, not corporations. Typical was an ad for the Connecticut Light and Power Company. It was a popular misconception, the copy proclaimed, to assume that the owners of the company "are a small group of portly, pompous Wall Street big shots." Instead, the ad contained images of a "sailor, stenographer, donor, policemen, soldier, housewife, business man, and mechanic," who represented just a few of the nearly twenty thousand stockholders. According to the ad, "This is what people mean what they talk about the 'free enterprise system.'" The company was nothing more than the "working men and women" who constituted it; "that's real public ownership," the ad concluded. Corporations were "business-managed enterprises," owned and operated by discrete individuals, that served the public good. Corporations were simply an accumulation of ordinary folks.[105] A 1948 advertisement for a bank claimed that the message of free enterprise is that "people and businesses run themselves" and "government doesn't run either one," suggesting that there was a natural alliance between people and business which, in this framing, was simply a group of individuals against statism.[106]

This occlusion of the corporation in "I, Pencil," then, was not atypical. A poem by the columnist Benjamin DeCasseres, "I Am Private Enterprise," written and widely republished in the 1940s and 1950s, well before Read's essay appeared, offered a similar conception of the economy as consisting of individuals only, albeit extraordinary ones, whose ability to prosper faced only one menace: the ever-present threat of "government strangulation."[107] Speaking in the voice of free enterprise's soul rather than one of its products, this "spirit" explained how it worked: "I gathered strange people together in friendly concourse" and in so doing "pulled the world together." The businesses it named were generic— "I am the butcher shop and the bank"—or the quintessential small business, the "popcorn stand." It then named names: "I am the Wright Brothers. I am Edison, Ericsson, Goodyear, Gimbel, Westinghouse, Whitney and Morse." Enumerating individuals or small proprietors, the poem did not mention any of the (large) corporations associated, often by name, with these inventors and entrepreneurs. Calling attention to Westinghouse the person rather than the corporation captured the nature of free enterprise discourse, which imagined the state (and sometimes trade unions) as the only powerful force mediating between individuals and the market, and that often depicted the business firm as a person. Thus, DeCasseres continued, it needed "no laws to hobble me" or "government control" since "my checks and balances are the natural ones of the economy." A self-regulating machine and a natural system ("the physical lever of freedom," in the words of the poet), free enterprise operated optimally without interference, which could only hobble it. Significantly, the penultimate verse claimed, "I am the *Old Deal*," explicitly distinguishing this "spirit" from Roosevelt's New Deal.

Read's friend and mentor William Mullendore also spelled out the implicit lesson of "I, Pencil." Speaking as a pencil, Read claimed that business functioned best when left alone. In a 1955 speech before the Rotarians of Los Angeles, Mullendore, the chair of Southern California Edison, described the "danger to the American way of life when the economy is dependent on Big Government and not upon traditional free enterprise." Like Read, the executive described the free enterprise economy as a function of "the initiative and self-reliance of the individual citizen." He was silent about the role of corporations, such as the one he ran. Mullendore explained that the "political-economic powerhouse in Washington D.C." was the locus of a "revolutionary shift in power" under "the new system of statism." Under this system, unlike in democratic free enterprise, a small elite of bureaucrats dictated the lives of the many.[108] If Mullendore saw his company, one of the nation's largest utilities, as a powerful economic entity with political might, he did not mention it.

Like the broader free enterprise discourse from which it drew, Read's parable effaced not only the state but also the corporation in favor of an understanding of the economy as powered by "the creative, risk-taking, profit-seeking, competitive individual," as *Fortune* put it in 1942. The belief that the individual consumer represented the "sovereign throne of the free market" rendered the business firm invisible, important only as a mechanism for satisfying individual wants in the marketplace.[109] Such a vision was regularly proclaimed by executives who depicted the business leader and industrial firm as composed of and representative of the people, standing against the powerful collective forces of the state and trade unions, both of which, in their view, dangerously threatened personal autonomy. The "free enterprise system," Fitzgerald Hall, the president of the Nashville, Chattanooga and St. Louis Railway told his employees in 1943, is "simply democracy at work in the field of business." Hall told his workers that their employer was fundamentally the same as the "corner store" since anyone in America could start a business and eventually become a "merchant prince." Likening the railroad baron to the shopkeeper and depicting both as equally subject to the potentially unjust whims of the state served to minimize the power of corporations such as his own. It also linked the big businessman to the independent proprietor, making them sharers of the same interests and enemies of the same forces. "If those who put nothing into the enterprise," he warned, start to "exercise control"—if, as he put it, in one of the favored metaphors of free enterprisers, "government ceases to be the umpire and becomes the boss"—then, he claimed, "our democracy is gone" along with "the right of those who put up money to profit from good management and honorable and hard work." In this understanding all businesses, regardless of size, faced the same threats by the state: "Destroy the free enterprise system and there will be no corner groceries—all of us will have to buy from a government store," Hall wrote. By conflating his railroad corporation with a "corner grocery," Hall used free enterprise discourse to convey an anti-statist ideology in the name of the liberation of the small capitalist rather than of the corporation—or, rather, to treat the latter as a variant of the former. The lesson was clear: corporations stood for the people—in a sense, corporations *were* people—and the government stood against them. Under free enterprise, people could be their "own boss." But government, an "absolute boss," was inimical to freedom itself.[110]

As with most free enterprise narratives, Read's essay drew attention away from corporate strength, which is absent from his story. He denied the existence of concentrated business power in favor of a story of discrete individuals harmonizing through the miraculous market. In Read's parable, corporations really were, as the Republican presidential candidate Mitt Romney declared on the campaign trail in 2011, people.[111] The promulgation of this view, in which the state is dangerously powerful and the corporation is either invisible or, as in the "I Am Private Enterprise" poem quoted above, anthropomorphized, helps explain not only the denial of the role of government in building the American economy but also the minimizing of corporate power that lies at the root of much of American "common sense" to this day. "Our nation was built by individuals, not government," according to Jerry E. Craft, a resident of Spartanburg, South Carolina, in a letter to the editor of a local newspaper in 2009. Craft, like Read, believed that "all the things we use and enjoy were invented by individuals." As with Read, the step from invention to production was assumed to be frictionless, facilitated by a market that turned wishes to reality by spontaneously coordinating and combining raw materials, processing, and the various stages of labor necessary to make goods. Craft claimed, as free enterprisers had been doing for eighty years, that as excessive government subsumed individualism and freedom, the nation was slowly drifting "into a system of socialism instead of free enterprise."[112] As with Read, who helped develop the free enterprise vision that Craft articulated, corporate power went unmentioned in this conception of the economy.

In his essay, Read celebrated, although he did not name, the market as a mechanism of bottom-up, individual freedom—anarchic yet orderly, powerful but nonhierarchical—and implicitly contrasted it with top-down dictation by government bureaucrats. In so doing, he drew on a strain of free enterprise discourse that treated the market as the apotheosis of individual choice and liberty. "The common denominator of all Welfare States, which vary in degree but not in kind, is that the seat of authority is vested in the State—not in the citizens," claimed conservative commentator Ruth Alexander in 1952.[113] Missing from her description of the economy were the corporations, the business firms, and the politicians, religious leaders, lobbyists, and trade organizations that produced the vast majority of free enterprise proponents. Free enterprisers celebrated individual freedom, not the corporate freedom that their anti-regulatory vision promoted. "In collectivism, by any name, the state and the politicians in power are the boss," as the *Deseret News* editorialized in 1944. "Under free enterprise, the boss is the ultimate consumer, you and I and 130 million other Americans. . . . The people run the economic as well as the political show."[114] For free enterprisers, the choice was binary: the dictating state, which limited freedom, or the individual, who embodied freedom. When corporations were acknowledged at all, free enterprisers described them as the handmaidens of these sovereign consumers who were, in fact, their "bosses." As a manager for the Kimberly-Clark Corporation told a group of high school students in Memphis in 1951, customers "have a rope around the Corporation's neck, like a noose. They are forever yanking for bargains. They want more and more Kleenex, of better and better quality for less money."[115] In this view, corporations were primarily servants of consumers, who dictated what and how they produced.

Free enterprisers denied the power of big business by figuring corporations as small businesses or collections of individuals. By many measures, this effort was successful, as a 1945 Gallup poll revealed. "Iowans definitely do not associate the phrase 'free enterprise' with big business," Gallup noted. Indeed, his survey showed that "only 10% associated it with big business; 46% associated it with any kind of business; 11% associated it with 'little business' and another 16% with 'a business like your own.'"[116] One illustration of this view came in 1962 when Werner P. Gullander became the first full-time general manager of NAM at the generous salary of $100,000 a year (over $800,000 in 2018 dollars). Gullander had spent his career as an executive at some of the nation's biggest corporations, including General Electric, Weyerhaeuser, and General Dynamics. Yet he took pains to assure the public that he was not "an exponent of 'big business.'"[117] When Steve Forbes, publisher and presidential aspirant, claimed in 2015 that "economies are a collection of individuals, working singly or in organizations," it was part of a long tradition of obfuscation.[118]

Sidestepping the role of the corporation (or the business lobby), Read focused on the power of the state, in the form of "planners," to interfere with and undermine market mechanisms. If in "I, Pencil" the government was the specter haunting the miraculous process and threatening to subvert it, the essay barely hinted at the obvious fact that business firms, not individuals, actually produced the vast majority of goods, including pencils. From this perspective, there was, in fact, a "master mind" behind the creation of the pencil: a business owner, corporate board, or manager who made the decision to produce it—most likely at the request of a government entity, such as a school district. Effacing all forces other than government that might alter market relations, Read's story made "planning" the sole province of government.

The moral of Read's fable—that planning leads to chaos and, conversely, that chaos leads to a kind of order—was thus an individualist fantasy. Imagining the world without any institutions save the nefarious state or the trade union makes it easier to understand products of market coordination as magical. In the choice between "a freedom suspected of chaos and a regimentation assured of order," there appeared only one force of regimentation, the state. The free market, in Read's view, was the aggregate of "millions of private decisions," apparently all of equal weight, blessedly free of the heavy, undemocratic, and unnatural hand of the bureaucrat.[119] In the end, Read endorsed the view of Nathan Shefferman that "big government is more dangerous than a big corporation," a view that became the common sense of free enterprisers.[120] But, unlike Shefferman's, Read's endorsement was implicit since the corporation—save as a name embossed on the pencil—didn't exist in his imaginary world, which was made up of heroic inventors, creative entrepreneurs, abundant raw materials, and hardworking craftspeople.

The dominant mood of "I, Pencil," optimism and wonder, was unusual in the free enterprise genre. Fear more typically underlay free enterprise arguments, including many previous claims by Read about the "peril" the American economic system faced at the hands of the "federal government."[121] Following the rules of what I call the businessman's jeremiad, in an aside almost obligatory in free enterprise rhetoric, Read's pencil called on readers to "save the freedom mankind is so unhappily losing." Yet Read's "I, Pencil" focused elsewhere, confident in the alignment of free enterprise with nature. If the market could provide for us so magically, why turn anywhere else? Read's sunny optimism foreshadowed Ronald Reagan's happy conservatism more than Lewis F. Powell's Jr's anxious concern.[122]

Government played no role in Read's story of the creation of a pencil.[123] Nor did government appear in two other essays Read wrote in the same decade about the spontaneous miracles of the market. In these pieces—the unpublished "Golf and Curling" from 1955 and a 1958 essay on cooking—Read highlighted his hobbies to illustrate how the market wove thick, though invisible, relationships across space and time.[124] The piece on golf and curling, Read's two favorite sports, suggested that the perception of the former as an individual activity and the latter as a team sport reflected "nothing but a time-space illusion." Although the individual golfer feels alone, Read urged players to "envision the number of persons who partook in the making of the club one is about to swing," including those who dug the ore, those who "build and make the railroads to haul it," and many "unnamed others." The essay on cooking described how "numberless thousands, perhaps millions, through space and time" had a hand in the making of a "Chinese hash" that he had recently served to great acclaim. He noted that "this remark evoked more in the way of astonishment than did the savoriness in the way of 'ums' and 'ahs.'"

There were hundreds of knockoff essays of "I, Pencil" celebrating the mundane miraculousness of the unfettered economy. As conservative *Boston Globe* columnist Jeff Jacoby wrote in 2003 of the Thanksgiving meal, "No turkey czar sat in a command post somewhere, consulting a master plan and issuing orders." Although Jacoby did not cite Read, his conception of the unimaginable complexity harnessed by the market was reminiscent of Read's. "It is commonplace to speak of seeing God's signature in the intricacy of a spider's web or the animation of a beehive," he wrote. "But they pale in comparison to the kaleidoscopic energy and productivity of the free market. If it is a blessing from Heaven when seeds are transformed into grain, how much more of a blessing it is when our private, voluntary exchanges are transformed—without our ever intending it—into prosperity, innovation and growth?"[125] An observer who noted the similarity of Jacoby's essay to "I, Pencil" concluded: "By becoming aware of the 'miraculousness' of the free market operating without the necessity of government, citizens can help save diminishing freedom by putting government back into its proper place and letting the 'mystery' of the market reign once again."[126]

This faith-based vision positioned government as the enemy of the freedom, comity, and abundance, which were possible only when the state knew its (very limited) place.

Promoting appreciation of the market went hand in hand with propounding skepticism about the state. Read wrote, "I contend that there is no higher cultural pursuit—be it music, art, poetry, drama or whatever—than acquiring an appreciation of the mysteries of the free market." Appreciation was not the same as understanding, since the belief that markets could be comprehended suggested that they could also be regulated in socially productive ways. What he elsewhere described as the "magic of believing" in markets conduced, he believed, to skepticism toward the state.[127]

Magic and faith, then, were important fronts in the war against the mixed economy. If the market performed all the deeds that government promised but usually failed to deliver, what use was government? Moreover, state intervention—planning—counteracted and undermined the market's magic. The ideas that the market was beneficent and mysterious rather than a human creation, that free enterprise was fragile, and that government planning of any sort was undemocratic and inefficient served to advance the view that all the benefits of the market resulted from its independence from the state.

"You Didn't Build That"

Republican senator Marco Rubio denounced President Barack Obama in 2012 because "he doesn't believe in the miracle of free enterprise." Rubio did not claim the president lacked confidence in the system itself—he didn't assert that Obama did not believe in free enterprise—but rather that Obama did not see it as miraculous, which was equally damning because, from Rubio's perspective, to conceive of free enterprise as unmiraculous was tantamount to disclaiming it altogether.[128] Bringing free enterprise down to earth is precisely what Obama did later that year in his notorious "If you've got a business, you didn't build that" campaign speech in Roanoke that infuriated conservatives because he described government as an essential element of "the unbelievable American system that allowed you to thrive."[129] Responses to the speech became the leading theme of the 2012 Republican National Convention, at which delegates carried "We Built That" signs and where repetition of that phrase became almost obligatory for speakers. Obama treated the nation's capitalist economic system as a dynamic but comprehensible partnership between the public and private sectors, and therefore dependent on critical functions provided by the state. Although his critics did not cite Hayek or Read, they preferred to see the market as an "undesigned order," an incomprehensible, unplanned system made possible only with minimal state interference. To comprehend it was to think of it as a social construction that human institutions could shape.

Leonard Read's decentering of the state from the story of wealth creation can be compared not only with Obama's 2012 speech but also with the Massachusetts senator Elizabeth Warren's talk the previous year in which she claimed, "There is nobody in this country who got rich on their own." Business owners "moved your goods to market on roads the rest of us paid for" and benefited from other public investments, Warren stated in a speech that conservatives widely rebuked.[130]

There were points of convergence in the narratives of Read, Obama, and Warren, perhaps surprising in light of the differences in their political views. Read's story of the pencil did not celebrate the lone genius, the heroic inventor, or the creative entrepreneur. Nor was it a glorification of self-sufficiency. Read, as much as Obama and Warren, believed "You didn't build that." Indeed, that could easily have been the title of his essay on the making of the pencil, and it was certainly its chief lesson. Read and those from whom he drew inspiration, as well as those later inspired by him, saw markets as facilitators of human interdependence. He was what we might call a free market communitarian. Libertarian philosopher Jason Brennan is correct that rejection of the notion that the "Randian ideal of the self-made superhero entrepreneur" is not "an especially left-wing point of view."[131] Similarly, Nicole Ciandella of the Competitive Enterprise Institute writes, "Contrary to myth, entrepreneurs are not islands in themselves. Nobody acting in markets is self-sufficient."[132] Jonah Goldberg claims, "The modern market economy is the greatest communal enterprise ever undertaken in the history of humanity."[133] Even the self-proclaimed "capitalist tool" Steve Forbes, publishing executive and two-time presidential aspirant, has marveled at "how markets break down barriers between people."[134] No person is an island in this view because the market links the energies and capabilities of each person to every other person, product, technology, and raw material.

The free enterprise objection, then, was not strictly to Obama's and Warren's claim of interdependence. In "I, Pencil" and the companion essays, Leonard

Read presented a thoroughly linked world in which individual achievement, whether in crafting a pencil or in executing a beautiful golf stroke, is, as he calls it, a "time-space illusion." Read described his mission as "bringing into focus what usually escapes our attention," as he wrote in his essay "Golf and Curling." For Read, this meant becoming aware of the miraculous system that links the labor, raw materials, and previous acts that provide us with goods that we often unthinkingly enjoy or for which, as in the case of golf, we take too much individual credit. Read stressed the human inability to understand the complex workings of the market and sought to foster an appreciation, a willingness to marvel, instead. Read labeled key sections of "I, Pencil" "No One Knows" and "No Master Mind," in which he showed that the ordinary pencil contains the wisdom of multitudes—knowledge that no individual could possibly acquire—and thus embodies an "unintended miracle."[135]

For Obama and Warren, "bringing into focus what usually escapes our attention" meant something different: demystification along the lines of Karl Marx's dictate that "there is nothing mysterious about" fetishized commodities.[136] Their sin, from the point of view of free enterprisers, came in naming the system that Read and others thought ineffable. Like Read, they sought to highlight the hidden, but they did so by shining a light on the often-overlooked role that government played in nurturing entrepreneurs. By emphasizing the role of public goods—the police, public education, fire departments, infrastructure such as roads, bridges, railroads, and the Internet—they, like Read, aimed to show that individual success was a function of unseen, faraway, and determinative forces. Unlike Read, however, they believed these interconnections to be easily explainable, and the state indispensable in facilitating them.

The year before his "You didn't build that" speech, President Obama addressed the issue of the relationship between free enterprise and government even more explicitly. In a speech at George Washington University, the president affirmed his own faith in "free enterprise as the engine of America's wealth and prosperity." Obama acknowledged that Americans were "a self-reliant people with a healthy skepticism of too much government." At the same time, he claimed, "there's always been another thread running through our history—a belief that we're all connected, and that there are some things we can only do together, as a nation." Whereas for Read, this claim of connection would have meant a celebration of the market and a denigration of statism, for Obama one important ligature binding the nation was the government, particularly in those areas that, he said, quoting Lincoln, "we should do together what we cannot do as well for ourselves."[137]

This vision of a symbiosis between government and market contrasts with the view that state "planning" undermines free enterprise. In 1942, for example, Prentis, the NAM leader, claimed, "It is not government that has wrought the miracle that is being accomplished today in the production of war materials. It is the initiative, ingenuity, and organizing genius of private business."[138] Prentis's denial that government demand had catalyzed the astounding levels of production, most of it for military (that is, government) use, during World War II, was in keeping with the free enterprise position.

The debate about "who built that" recalls the New Deal counterpoint to the business discourse of "faith in free enterprise." This discourse, which we can trace from Franklin Roosevelt to Barack Obama, sees the market and the state as mutually interacting, reinforcing, transforming institutions. FDR said that economic laws are not "sacred, inviolable, unchangeable," and Rexford Tugwell, one of his Brain Trusters, offered that "there can be no fixed form of government."[139] This was the flexible, pragmatic spirit of the twentieth-century mixed economy. In 1949, Harry Truman argued that not only was there a symbiosis between the state and the market but that "a completely free enterprise . . . where the government never interferes and never helps" was an unrealistic fantasy.[140] Similarly, in his critique of the totalizing language of free enterprise in 1950, Reinhold Niebuhr said that the nascent welfare state "is not slipping America into totalitarianism. It is the only effective safeguard against totalitarianism."[141] A decade later, John F. Kennedy decried those business leaders and politicians "yearning for a dream world of absolute laissez-faire that never was and never can be."[142] By employing the term "dream world," Kennedy turned the free enterprise critique of liberalism on its head. (Such a view can be contrasted with Ronald Reagan's 1976 statement "I still believe in free enterprise, and the government doesn't have any place in it.")[143] In this account, which we can call the New Deal view, the economy is not magic and/or natural but the creation of people and institutions, including the state. In other words, the market is not the whole of the economy, nor is it independent of the government. It is emphatically not, in this view, an autonomous and mysterious force, a form of divine intelligent design. Having faith in free enterprise, in this conception, is to recognize that markets are not natural but, to use Karl Polanyi's term, "embedded," and they can be harnessed and encouraged by the state for the public good.[144]

Yet prevailing levels of trust in government remained low, and the postwar years saw a growing acceptance of the legitimacy of corporations and, eventually, of markets as independent of and superior to the state. Those who promoted faith in free enterprise succeeded in undermining faith in government by puncturing what Clem Johnson, the head of the U.S. Chamber of Commerce, called in 1954 a "sheeplike trust . . . in the omniscience of government."[145] These proclamations of faith in business and distrust in government remained an enduring thread of American political culture.

At the same time, as we will see in the next chapter, a surprising array of labor leaders, civil rights activists, and progressives challenged conservatives for the right to sole ownership of the phrase *free enterprise*.

7

"Free Enterprise Needs Restatement to Suit Our Modern Needs"

FREE ENTERPRISE IS A KEY TERM in the history of modern American capitalism. But examining only those who defined it in opposition to the New Deal order misses a crucial part of the story, since New Dealers, antitrust activists, trade unionists, and African American freedom fighters also employed the language of free enterprise. In this narrative of contestation, free enterprise temporarily became, as it had been in the nineteenth century, a phrase with multiple champions and subversive meanings. This is significant because the conservative celebrants of free enterprise in the twentieth century argued that even mild modifications to American capitalism as it was practiced at the time would have disastrous and irreversible consequences. By suggesting that reforms were possible, necessary, and consistent not only with social justice but with private business and a market economy, critics from the labor and civil rights movements created a space for the democratic criticism and rethinking of modern capitalism.

In the early 1960s, Milton and Rose Friedman highlighted the importance of understanding "what meaning is to be attributed to 'free' as modifying 'enterprise.'"[1] For business leaders "free enterprise" meant that businesses were at liberty to do as they wished. They believed in free *enterprise*. For opponents of monopoly, like Thurman Arnold, who headed up the Antitrust Division of the Justice Department from 1938 to 1943, the goal was for enterprise to be kept free through the force of regulation. When Arnold said in 1944 that the phrase included his "favorite words," he meant *free* enterprise, the right of government to protect the "crushing" of businesses by more powerful and unregulated firms.[2] For organized labor, free enterprise meant the freedom of workers to bargain collectively and the material freedom made possible by living wages. For civil rights advocates, the essence of free enterprise was the elimination of the Jim Crow system, which would unleash the right to buy, to work, and to engage in politics without discrimination. All of these groups challenged the conservative celebrants of free enterprise who sought sole ownership of the phrase.

Although anti–New Dealers generally succeeded in claiming the term *free enterprise,* in the postwar years other groups with different political views refused to cede that term to conservatives, setting off racialized and class-based contestations over the meaning of free enterprise. The main protagonists of this book, the business free enterprisers, understood it as license for business "to act in its own best judgement," as Republican official Glenn Frank said in 1938.[3] Not all free enterprisers were segregationists, but segregationist business leaders and politicians frequently linked free enterprise with white supremacy. They claimed that "Civil Rights agitation . . . may be getting to the point where free enterprise can become a quaint, even illegal, expression in this land of ours," as the Spokane newspaper declared in the summer of 1958.[4] But from the other end of the spectrum, New Dealers, labor leaders, and civil rights activists also laid claim to free enterprise. Civil rights leaders held that free enterprise, as used by these segregationists, served as code, like "states' rights," to justify discrimination. In demanding economic and political equality they refused to cede the term to racists, claiming free enterprise as a key element in the African American freedom struggle. Labor leaders also embraced free enterprise as part of a just social order, one that promoted trade unionism, limited the power of economic elites, and highlighted the principles of liberty, equality, and security as reinforcing rather than warring underpinnings of a modern democracy. These anti-conservative adaptations of free enterprise were important because the "selling" of free enterprise that began in the 1930s successfully linked the phrase in the minds of many Americans with the nation as a whole. By adapting free enterprise for their own purposes, these groups demonstrated that this linkage could be put to many different political purposes, including progressive ones. While the language of progressive free enterprise did not endure as long or as centrally as the conservative version, its existence in the 1940s and 1950s demonstrated the possibilities of arguing for inclusionary democratic reform within a capitalist regime.

The Slavery of Welfarism

Elite victimization was central to conservative free enterprise rhetoric. Business leaders, as we have seen, typically disavowed their power and depicted themselves as precarious and weak, in the process displacing the claims of workers and African Americans to these subordinate positions. Conservative business proponents of free enterprise rarely acknowledged the realities of racism, although they sometimes employed the language of racial oppression to describe their own plight, even using metaphors of slavery. In this view, free enterprise was imperiled by powerful governmental forces. Businesspeople claimed to be the victimized subjects of those forces, and therefore analogized themselves to victims of white supremacy or totalitarianism. According to conservative journalist Kyle Palmer, for example, California's Proposition 11, the Fair Employment Practices Act of 1946, would lead to a denial of freedom by placing "shackles on human feelings, emotions, sympathies."[5] The word *shackles* evoked unfreedom, and free enterprisers routinely employed this word and its cognates.

Business-oriented libertarian thinkers minimized the significance of racism even as they suffused their language with references to the injustice and even the slavery they faced. Well before Friedrich A. Hayek's *Road to Serfdom* was published in 1944 and popularized in the United States when an excerpt appeared in *Reader's Digest* in April 1945, the notion that the emerging welfare state would lead to enslavement became a commonplace among opponents of the New Deal, and it continued long afterward. Many of them compared not just Soviet communism but European social democracy and even American liberalism to slavery.[6] For F. A. "Baldy" Harper, an economist and staff member of the Foundation for Economic Education, Leonard Read's free enterprise think tank, the connection was not merely metaphorical. As he declared in 1959, "Slavery might be described as just another form of [the] Welfare state."[7] The metaphor of enslavement continued to remain popular into the twenty-first century. One commentator on a website for Hayek fans, noting the dramatic degree to which the "planners" have advanced since the book was published, wrote in 2010, "I cannot distinguish my life from being enslaved."[8]

If free enterprise allowed freedom to flourish, it followed that restrictions on it could infringe American liberty. Asserting that the nation's conception of liberty "started and ended with free enterprise . . . as we Americans have traditionally defined it," conservative Dallas congressman Bruce Alger worried in

1955 about the effects of the welfare state. By acknowledging that others might define the term differently, Alger recognized the instability of free enterprise. But for him, its meaning as an enabler of freedom was clear. Looking back over history, Alger, like many other conservative free enterprise advocates, anachronistically claimed that the Founders had endorsed free enterprise and asserted that, as a result, the United States had "no caste system." At the start of the modern civil rights movement, which sought to overturn precisely that system, Alger defined "caste" in nonracial terms. "Unlike many foreign countries, an American was not forced to stay in the same level that he was born into," he explained, omitting the history of slavery or Jim Crow, which did not accord with this model of castelessness. Free enterprise, by minimizing the constraints imposed by the state, allowed unconstrained individuals to maximize their achievements, Alger believed.[9]

In spite of rejecting the realities of caste for African Americans, some business leaders and politicians described the imposition of limits on business—even those designed to democratize the nation by ending a system of white racial privilege—as an attack on American liberty that they sometimes analogized to slavery. The "ultimate welfare state and slavery are very nearly synonymous," editorialized the *Cleveland Plain Dealer* in 1949. Barry Goldwater predicted that the 1964 Civil Rights Act would "destroy the American way of life, free enterprise, property rights, individual freedom and reduce our dynamic, competitive and cultural life to a single common denominator: Statism."[10] For Goldwater, free enterprise made freedom possible, and white supremacy, which he claimed personally to detest, was a price worth paying to defend this notion of freedom.

Business free enterprisers rarely described such power differentials in explicitly racial terms. Although many business leaders, particularly those representing corporations, spoke in favor of civil rights, others who claimed to stand for free enterprise, usually in the voice of small business proprietors, were silent or complicit in exacerbating racism.[11] Some were not averse to opening their speeches with jokes in black dialect, as H. W. Prentis, Missouri born and a resident of Pennsylvania, did before a regional meeting of the National Association of Manufacturers in 1940.[12] (Much later, in 1967, the minister Stuart McBirnie opened his lecture in Santa Cruz, California, on the dangers of liberalism with a "Southern negro dialect joke.")[13] In 1949, South Carolina governor Strom Thurmond preferred to speak of "a militant socialistic trend in our national government" and the crushing of "local sovereignty" rather than to address outright the white supremacism at the heart of his rejection of federal civil rights advances, as he had the previous year as the presidential candidate of the States' Rights Democratic ("Dixiecrat") Party.[14] In describing the New Deal order as it existed in 1952, Harper said he feared "the demise of all our other hallowed freedoms" that "will follow in the immediate wake of this lost economic freedom." Using the familiar rhetoric of the sovereign consumer-citizen, he noted that the buyer should be "king under the rights of free men" and that "every person must be king over his domain." Harper went so far as to call for top-down civil disobedience to the enslaving welfare state: "What I am confronted with in the present situation in the United States is a matter of choice, then, between moral law and statutory law—a choice which no one of us can escape." Like Alger and Thurmond, Harper depicted an inverted world in which those on top imagined or believed themselves to be subordinate. In this view, business advocates of free enterprise, not the African American victims of Jim Crow, were oppressed and obligated to challenge immoral laws. At the moment when nonviolent resistance was entering the mainstream of the civil rights movement, Harper urged conservatives to borrow the weapons of the weak to defend free enterprise. Using language not dissimilar from Martin Luther King's defense of law breaking in the public interest a decade later, he wrote: "Isn't it a strange paradox that when government, the presumed servant of the people and guardian of their liberty, removes the right of free choice from the citizens, it automatically creates another unavoidable choice—the choice between being immoral and being illegal?"[15] Just as labor and civil rights advocates inverted business's language of free enterprise, so too did some conservatives co-opt the language of social movements. Conservative free enterprisers in the postwar years adopted the populist tone and moral high ground of subordinate groups engaged in social justice campaigns.

Thus conservative free enterprisers often ignored the realities of racial oppression or identified themselves as sufferers of what would later be called reverse discrimination. In his brief on behalf of free enterprise as the force that was winning World War II, John Bricker, the Republican vice presidential nominee in 1944, condemned "racial prejudice," by which he meant not racism but a phenomenon that was already being identified as "reverse racism," or what he called "favoritism to noisy minorities," which had to be resisted if the "shackles of bureaucracy and excessive taxation" were to be destroyed and freedom restored.[16] As early as 1946, J. Howard Pew, oil man and supporter of conservative causes, condemned the "continued unfair and discriminatory legislation granting special privileges for favored minorities at the expense of general welfare." Pew made these comments in a preface to a National Association of Manufacturers pamphlet on the dangerous weakening of free enterprise in the postwar United States.[17] This was a racialized variant of the victimology that had been characteristic of business's free enterprise discourse since the 1920s. Despite free enterprise's supposed centrality to America and the American Way, its proponents in the business lobby described it as fragile and endangered, and its advocates as heroes perpetually under siege. Under the oppressive New Deal regime, according to Pew, business was "molested by the government."[18] By 1949, when Clifton A. Woodrum, the president of the American Plant Council, told the Agricultural Society of South Carolina that "the future of the American system of free enterprise is in great danger," he was echoing familiar language. With his plea that "the businessmen of America must awaken," he was calling for a publicity offensive already at least a decade in the making.[19] Few of those who felt threatened called unambiguously for corporate autonomy, as Glenn Frank had done. Instead, they spoke in a language of inverted populism that highlighted their abjection at the hands of government.

Advocates of free enterprise, as we saw in chapter 2, have voiced such sky-is-falling rhetoric since even before the New Deal. What was notable in the postwar years is the degree to which the fear of government "dictation" was racialized, regionalized, gendered, and premised on a fear of organized labor and civil rights. A parallelism emerged in the language of conservative free enterprise among southern white defenders of Jim Crow, corporate executives, and overburdened taxpayers. All were victimized by the politicians and pundits whom Thurman Sensing, the executive vice president of Southern States Industrial Council in Nashville, denounced as "spenders, South-haters and bureaucracy-worshippers."[20] Sensing, using language that business lobbyists had employed since the 1930s, also referred to the South as the "whipping boy of the nation" and claimed that the political parties, by adopting civil rights platforms in 1960, "have moved the United States closer to the totalitarianism they both profess to abhor."[21] Sensing racialized business free enterprise as he both put business in the position of a subaltern people and depicted civil rights activists as beneficiaries of federal largesse and favoritism.

Vast Governmental Control

Although national business organizations and trade publications largely stayed silent on the question of race—or described themselves as the victims of forms of discrimination that they analogized to racial oppression—for segregationists, free enterprise was, along with the idea of states' rights, an integral part of the vocabulary of white supremacy.[22] As early as 1936, among the provisions on North Carolina senator Josiah Bailey's ten-point program to combat government encroachment were "fiscal restraint, free enterprise, and states' rights."[23] Millard P. Conklin, Dayton Beach lawyer and 1944 candidate for the Florida Senate, championed "the right of free enterprise—free business, big and little, on which civilization alone depends," and "white supremacy" was central to his conception of "civilization," which meant, among other things, preventing the "mingling of the races."[24] Another anti–New Deal candidate for the same seat, Judge J. Ollie Edmunds, called free enterprise "the backbone of American progress and prosperity" and claimed that "white supremacy must be maintained" as an essential part of this free enterprise vision.[25]

As the black freedom movement gained momentum, segregationists increasingly championed free enterprise to oppose civil rights. A group of southern governors at a 1949 conference chaired by recent Dixiecrat presidential candidate Thurmond claimed to "unqualifiedly support the traditional American way of life and our free enterprise system." The group opposed "government regimentation of the individual citizen" (although not the regimentation that Jim Crow enforced on African Americans) and endorsed "freedom of the individual," that is, if that individual happened to be white.[26] "Our organization will carry on its banner the slogan of free enterprise," declared one of the leading segregationist groups made up of southern politicians in 1955.[27] The 1964 Civil Rights Act was "anathema to the free enterprise system," according to the Texas Junior Chamber of Commerce, a position reinforced by segregationist Alabama governor George Wallace, who claimed that he and his compatriots "will have nothing to do with enforcing a law that will destroy our free enterprise system."[28] In the same year, the powerful Georgia senator Richard Russell claimed that the bill of 1964 would authorize "such vast governmental control over free enterprise in this country as to commence the process of socialism."[29] Civil rights opponents deployed freighted keywords of the free enterprise vocabulary—"regimentation," "socialism," "tradition," "states' rights," and "destruction"—in the service of their cause.

What exactly did segregationists in the postwar years mean by free enterprise? Defending the liberty of white business owners, the segregationists posited a producerist understanding of free enterprise, in which the chief victim of civil rights legislation was the white business owner. In contrast, civil rights activists—and eventually the government, defending black citizens—offered a consumerist perspective, in which customer access was the essence of free enterprise.

Segregationists understood the "freedom" in free enterprise to sanction the autonomy of white merchants to employ and to serve whomever they wished. At the extreme, they could argue, as did Lester Maddox, Atlanta restaurant owner and soon to be governor of Georgia, that "we have a divine right to discriminate."[30] An editorial in the Spokane newspaper in 1958 decried any "trend toward dictation on whom a man must hire" that "violated the right of individuals when trying to go into business to choose the people that they will hire," a trend the editors feared "will go on to ridiculous ends."[31] For the conservative writer William F. Buckley, the illegitimate goal of the civil rights movement that he opposed was to "instruct small merchants in the deep South on how they may conduct their business."[32] Such instruction amounted to a violation of their autonomy, Buckley believed. The rights of white property owners, in this view, were absolute. "We can observe in a number of areas how 'racial collectivism' is being used as a crowbar to pry loose rights over private property," wrote the Southern Agrarian Richard M. Weaver in 1957. "There was a time when ownership of property gave the owner the right to say to whom he would and would not sell and rent. But now, with the outlawing of restrictive covenants by the Supreme Court (especially in *Shelley v. Kraemer*), this right has been invaded, if not effectually taken away."[33] Weaver did not appear to ponder the rights of members of the Shelley family in the landmark 1948 Supreme Court decision to which he referred; the Shelleys, unbeknownst to them, purchased a home in the late 1940s with a restrictive covenant preventing people of "the Negro or Mongolian race" from owning the property.[34] Instead, his sympathies lay with the community of white property owners who sought to limit the pool of acceptable buyers.

For these segregationists, free enterprise was synonymous with the absolute rights of white private property owners, which meant, as in the understanding of Maddox, that "every person who is engaged in business has a right to choose the customers of his business." The rights of white sellers and servers, in this view, trumped those of black buyers and citizens. Segregationists deplored the sit-in movement because it "compelled businessmen to serve black customers against their will," observed *Atlanta Constitution* editor Ralph McGill. Characteristic of free enterprise discourse, they invoked the ever-present danger of the slippery slope. "If the federal government can tell me who to have as my customer they could tell me to do anything."[35] The enforcement of civil rights or any other accrual of government power amounted, in the words of Senator Russell, to "vast governmental control." As so often happened in free enterprise discourse, Maddox borrowed the tactics of the insurgent civil rights movement that he opposed. Leading what he called a "march for freedom"—which one newspaper aptly described as "one of the first civil rights marches in reverse"— Maddox connected that liberty to "states' rights, property rights, and free enterprise."[36] An advertisement for Maddox's 1966 gubernatorial campaign called him a "true Champion of Liberty" who supports "Business Enterprise free of the rough hand of Big Government."[37] Segregationists like Maddox took their freedom to discriminate to be freedom writ large and a blow for free enterprise against statism. When George Wallace, the independent candidate for the presidency in 1968, addressed an enormous crowd in New York City's Madison Square Garden, he decried that "our system is under attack," and he specified that he meant "the property system, the free enterprise system."[38]

Sharing this understanding of property rights, Maddox described the Supreme Court decision that enjoined him to serve all paying customers as portending the "death of the American free enterprise system." Referring to the court and also to the social movement that forced the decision, he said, "They have killed my business and have helped to kill the American Free Enterprise system."[39] Ever the publicity generator, Maddox closed his Pickrick's restaurant and reopened it as a souvenir stand/museum, a "shrine to the free enterprise system." (The shrine was also an example of free enterprise at work; Maddox's nostalgic commercial venture reportedly made more than $10,000 in three months.)[40] Even before Maddox's stunt, a hotelier in Jackson, Mississippi, closed his establishment with great fanfare in 1964 rather than "admit Negro guests under our new Civil Rights law." The *Chicago Defender* observed that the hotel was also losing money and that it deserved to close for that reason: "Let free enterprise be free—both ways."[41]

Many white property owners outside of the South also understood free enterprise in these Jim Crow terms. White home owners in Detroit posited that their freedom entitled them to sell to whites only, and to prevent, with violence if necessary, other owners from selling across the color line.[42] Opponents of fair employment and housing laws in California understood property rights, much as southern segregationists did—as, in Mark Brilliant's words, "the right to dispose of property as one saw fit." Edward Howden, the leader of the California Committee for Fair Employment Practices (CCFEP), claimed, in contrast, that the acquisition of property in all its forms "is a vital human right" that "cannot be a right for white folks only, unless we wish to be classed as liars and hypocrites who pay no more than lip service to the principles of free enterprise and equality of opportunity for all."[43] The debate about whether free enterprise favored the rights of sellers to exclude customers or consumers to buy what they wished was reignited by the national publicity attending the 2012 refusal of a Colorado baker, Jack Phillips, to make a wedding cake for a same-sex couple. When some commentators criticized Masterpiece Cakeshop and the state threatened an investigation, Fox News labeled this incident the "death of free enterprise" and a step toward what one reporter called "the slippery slope to the end of constitutional freedoms."[44] In 2018, the Supreme Court sided with Phillips.[45]

In spite of their embrace of producer sovereignty, free enterprisers also used the rhetoric of consumer choice as a tool for employers to fight the civil rights movement. In 1958, for example, Frank J. Mizell, a member of the Alabama State Executive Committee of the Democratic Party, proposed an amendment to "restore choice" to the United States Constitution. Using the language of the "Fifth Freedom" that had developed during World War II, he said, "Freedom of choice means that white employers should be free to employ only people of their race if they so desire."[46] Other white employers also invoked business prerogatives to justify their racism, even describing this as their "civil right."[47] Describing the views of Jim Crow theater operators in 1947, Frank F. Nesbit wrote that free enterprise "includes not only freedom from undue government interference but also freedom to select its own methods of doing business free from picketing, boycotting, or other coercive tactics of a coercive minority."[48] The problem for Nesbit was that "coercive" minorities were impinging on the rights of white property owners who, by virtue of free enterprise, possessed the right not only to self-select their customer base by race but also to disallow any protest that might be a consequence of their decisions. In this view, the enforcement of segregation with the tools of state power was wholly consistent with the free enterprise system, even as proponents generally decried "statism" as the chief obstacle to liberty. Such inferences led to what James J. Kilpatrick, the influential anti–civil rights Richmond editor, called the segregationists' "startled reaction" to the sit-in movement: "This lunch counter was his property. Did he not have a right to control its use?"[49]

Segregationists extended their understanding of business autonomy not only to customers but to employers, assigning to them the analogous right to select their workers. Even if this selection process was racially discriminatory, they insisted on complete autonomy in making such decisions. They described the existence of the Fair Employment Practices Committee (FEPC), created in 1941 to ban discrimination in war-related work, as "a step toward the destruction of free enterprise."[50] The Arkansas Free Enterprise Association called on Southern governors to "map a course of vigorous action against diabolical legislation promoting a permanent FEPC."[51] Such views were not limited to Southerners: Albert W. Hawkes, Republican New Jersey senator and former head of the U.S. Chamber of Commerce, described the authorization of the FEPC as "another nail in the coffin of free enterprise," and the one that might finally finish off the system, since "we have already put many nails in the coffin preparing it for the burial of free enterprise."[52] For similar reasons, proponents of "segregation academies" depicted them as motivated by "free enterprise" and saw those who wished to integrate public schools as its enemies.[53]

There were many ironies in the segregationist embrace of free enterprise. Not only did defenders of Jim Crow use the language of compulsion and servitude to describe their plight, they also celebrated risk over security and bravery over passivity. In short, they celebrated the attributes of those who sought to overturn the system from which they benefited and which, they claimed, fostered these very attributes. Georgia senator Herman Talmadge, for example, said that the rejection of "capitalism and free enterprise" was producing "tame and regulated citizens" rather than "dynamic, ambitious, and unafraid" ones. Although Talmadge and his ilk didn't acknowledge it at the time, these latter characteristics described the participants in the civil rights movement that he opposed.[54] Similarly, the language of incipient serfdom among free enterprisers seemed willfully to ignore the struggles of African Americans seeking full citizenship. "Are we developing our young people into a nation of self-reliant people?" asked Herman W. Steinkraus, president of Bridgeport Brass and a NAM director, in 1949. "Or are we permitting ourselves to be carried down the road to serfdom by encouraging a stronger and more powerful federal government to do for us what we should be doing for ourselves?"[55] Such language did more than ignore racism and the plight of African Americans, even as the serfdom reference evoked a form of "white" slavery. It also denied the legitimacy of the African American quest for citizenship by labeling it as the catalyst of the unfreedom that inevitably accompanied government expansion. As Georgia congressman James C. Davis said, federal intervention in ensuring that African Americans were treated as equal citizens would "usurp the rights of free enterprise and the individual states" and therefore undermine the cause of freedom.[56]

Another irony was that southern segregationists rejected government power when it came to enforced racial equality but demanded it to enforce racial inequality, while also claiming their share of the federal booty that was turning the region into the "sunbelt," a share of what the African American columnist Madeline Murphy later called "a whole new concept of federal welfarism for the rich."[57] Denying any inconsistencies, southern newspaper editor John Temple Graves argued that "being opposed to the federal force bills, which would interfere disastrously in a situation peculiar to the South and capable of being handled by the South alone, is totally different from opposing a federal hand in such integrated national problems as highways and the postal service and land grant colleges, etc."[58] For Graves and other economic modernizers, gaining access to federal funds to improve infrastructure provided an opportunity for the kind of "integration" they endorsed: not racial equality but federally supported links to the national economy. White southern conservative politicians like Thurmond endorsed this understanding of free enterprise, which allowed them to disclaim laissez-faire in demanding federal largesse while resisting the federal government when it came to African American equality and labor rights. One of Thurmond's opponents called him "Santa Claus in South Carolina and Scrooge in Washington" to mock his opportunistic statism; but the hypocrisy was even greater when his views on race are taken into account.[59]

"A Cancer upon the Free Enterprise System"

Business champions of free enterprise, even those who did not publicly defend segregation, often promoted their supposedly universal ideal as if it applied only to white people. Republic Steel's free enterprise advertising campaign of 1943 and 1944 included more than a dozen Norman Rockwellesque images, published in hundreds of magazines and newspapers, of churchgoers, families, children, farmers, restaurant patrons, courting couples, soldiers, and veterans. All of the people depicted in these ads, meant to weave a broad tapestry of the American spirit, looked white. Republic Steel's campaign was not unique; historian Roland Marchand noted the "invisibility" of African Americans in wartime and postwar company publicity meant for general circulation.[60] Walter White, the head of the NAACP, observed in 1947 that the "spokesmen for capitalism" in the Chamber of Commerce and NAM, because of their silence on civil rights issues, "leave entirely the defense of civil and human liberties, which are the base and justification of democracy," to civil rights activists.[61] White and others took silence to be assent.

Black critics saw the exclusion of African Americans from the effort to "sell free enterprise" as a defining feature of free enterprise discourse, not an oversight. Even among black defenders of the emerging conservative version of free enterprise, some believed that racial prejudice undermined its possibilities. In 1944, for example, idiosyncratic black columnist George Schuyler defended "the much-maligned system of free enterprise" while evoking the abolitionist champions of the "free produce" movement to remind his readers that "slave enterprise is the opposite of free enterprise." Black conservatives, more generally, condemned those who, as Schuyler put it during the war, "talk piously" of "freedom, democracy, tolerance, free enterprise and social justice while acting in an opposite manner."[62] In 1942, Schuyler called free enterprise a "right" denied to blacks, just as whites restricted other basic rights, among them education, self-defense, and self-government.[63] For these critics, the biggest threat to free enterprise was not Soviet communism but the subversion of free enterprise by white supremacists in the business community.

For their part, African American freedom fighters condemned the hypocrisy and injustice implicit in the conservative version of free enterprise. Referring to the leading business groups, the Chamber of Commerce and NAM, the head of the NAACP, Walter White, wrote in 1947, "If either of these organizations of free enterprise has ever even passed a resolution recognizing the existence of lynching, disfranchisement, foul housing . . . such pronouncements have escaped my notice." According to the pioneering pan-Africanist and labor activist George McCray, those speaking in the name of free enterprise had poured nonsense "into the ears of the American people" for "so long that they are completely confused by what is really meant by free enterprise." Comparing business leaders with the Congress of Industrial Organizations, the relatively new

All Kinds of People Work for Republic

Nearly 60,000 men and women are working in the 76 plants, mines, warehouses and offices of Republic. They are a true cross section of the people who built America.

21,000 Republic men have left to join the armed services. Republic is going to do everything in its power to place these men in jobs as good or better than the jobs they held before they went to war.

Already nearly 2,000 returned veterans are back on Republic's payrolls . . . producing steel for their buddies still on the fighting fronts . . . looking forward to new opportunities for advancement.

Republic's business is to make steel. But it is also Republic's business to provide jobs and opportunities for all kinds of people . . . now and for the future.

Practically every supervisor or executive at Republic began as a worker and earned his way to his present place. Only in America, land of free opportunity and enterprise, could such an organization take root, grow and flourish.

BUY WAR BONDS AND STAMPS . . . AND *KEEP* THEM

REPUBLIC STEEL

The above text has been condensed from our advertisement appearing in News-Week, June 18th, U. S. News, June 15th, Saturday Evening Post, June 16th, and in newspapers in cities and towns where Republic operates plants and mines.

Free enterprise advocates claimed to speak for ordinary Americans—typically depicted as white—during World War II. (American war posters from the Second World War, BANC PIC 2005.004:0237—D. Courtesy of The Bancroft Library, University of California, Berkeley.)

labor group that worked to "fight against discrimination," revealed to McCray that "business preaches free enterprise with one hand and destroys it with the other." To McCray, the so-called advocates of free enterprise were really its enemies, and because blacks understood the concept in universal terms, "the Negro is about the only citizen of these United States who really believes in the American system of free enterprise."[64] Rarely, if ever, did business free enterprisers contemplate this radical possibility.

A *Defender* editorial in 1949 similarly showed African Americans to be exemplars of a universal ideal of free enterprise. Noting that "throughout the nation, the chamber of commerce and manufacturers' associations have spearheaded the opposition" to fair employment laws, it argued that these groups were not merely ignoring racism but actively opposing civil rights. Even as such businesses "bid sharply for the patronage of Negro customers," they protested "that state FEPC laws which would bar discrimination in employment of these same customers where qualified, would be a blow to the free enterprise system."[65] "The American Negro has never been allowed to taste" the supposedly "American Way of Free Enterprise," said William Kennedy in 1963.[66] African American activists thus posed the question: is free enterprise yet another white-only benefit that defines freedom in racially discriminatory ways?

By rejecting the fight for racial justice, business leaders, according to Walter White, "who have most to conserve, blacken themselves as selfish bigots." Such conservatives did far more damage to free enterprise, White believed, than "all the Communists or fellow travelers in the world."[67] Criticizing those who "hide behind the veil of free enterprise" in a 1952 letter to the editor of the *Pittsburgh Courier*, Frank Pereira noted that these hypocrites condoned "by their actions the very things which aid Russian expansionism: racism, poverty, illiteracy." The bigots who accused them of being "subversive, un-American and the like" were, in Pereira's view, the truly dangerous elements in American society.[68] Gertrude Wilson, a white reporter for the *Amsterdam News*, concurred in 1963: "Communism's best friends are the Southern segregationists and Northern bigots who say that the free enterprise system gives private business catering to the general public license to discriminate because of skin color." Wilson charged that "by their protestations of the sacred privileges of private enterprise to turn away Negroes from hotels, restaurants, swimming pools and other recreational facilities, the South's champions are turning democracy to ashes." Wilson also pointed to the hypocrisy of those who did not recognize the government assistance that they received in the form of "protections afforded by government health laws, fire laws, occupancy laws," and other public goods that, under Jim Crow, were unfairly distributed by race.[69] These advocates of racial equality did not reject free enterprise itself but rather the racially rigged system that was undeservedly given that name by those who benefited from this unfair set of arrangements.

Still, some critics suggested that the ideal itself produced an irredeemable system of racism and oppression that deserved to be discarded rather than re-interpreted. In this view, free enterprise was, like the concept of states' rights, a fig leaf for bigots. In this context, a 1946 editorial in the *Amsterdam News* dismissed "pie in the sky talk about free enterprise (which for the Negro means freedom NOT to be hired, and no F.E.P.C.)."[70] In a satirical piece, *Amsterdam News* columnist Earl Brown described free enterprise as "a great American institution . . . the American way, the only way, the best way." Mocking the hypocrisy of conservatives, Brown then defined it as "the freedom of business, big business, to do as it damn pleases and run to that monster Federal government for help when it gets into trouble."[71] Willard Townsend, president of the United Transport Service Employees of America and the first African American elected to the Congress of Industrial Organizations (CIO) board, criticized the hypocrites "who go about beating their breasts in the name of 'Americanism' and the 'free enterprise system'" while favoring "neither true political democracy nor equality of economic opportunity." Townsend noted that "the slums haven't been eliminated by 'free enterprise,' but the noisy 'enterprise' advocates fight government slum clearance on the ground that it's socialistic."[72] From the perspective of African Americans, free enterprise was, like so many other ideals in Jim Crow America, a concept that spoke in the name of universalism while not only excluding people of color from its benefits but using it as a cudgel to punish them.

Civil rights activists charged that far from promoting freedom, the dominant version of free enterprise sanctioned a system of capitalist racial oppression. White supremacy represented, as the *Amsterdam News* editorialized in 1946, "a cancer upon the free enterprise system."[73] The government should punish those "flying the phony flag of so-called free enterprise," as the *Chicago Defender* advised the new president, Harry Truman, in September 1945.[74] The "system of Jim Crow," Earl Conrad, the *Defender*'s Harlem bureau chief, wrote in 1947, operates "within and as an organic part of the system of free enterprise (sometimes called 'democracy,' 'our way of life,' and 'American ideals,') when actually all that it is is the right to employ people for less than they are worth."[75] One year earlier, Conrad opined that "there is no longer any hope of liberation for the American negro under free enterprise."[76] While business free enterprisers sold the system as essential to averting socialism and as the essence of the Cold War freedom struggle, civil rights activists showed it to be the enemy of freedom for a substantial number of citizens.

One reaction of critics was, as Earl Brown argued, to describe free enterprise as a "masquerade," a high-minded phrase used to justify discrimination.[77] Senator Claude Pepper of Florida, noting the effort to make "free enterprise" and "states' rights" a conservative "battlecry," condemned what he called the "hypocritical and confused abuse of the slogans."[78] A 1947 poem by "Ain't Misbehaving" lyricist Andy Razaf in the *Amsterdam News* included the couplet "The boosters of free enterprise / Will strive to strangle labor."[79] Similarly, the leftist New York congressman Vito Marcantonio wrote, "By free enterprise they meant freedom to charge whatever prices they please, and to pay whatever wages they wanted to pay."[80] Daniel Tobin, the head of the Teamsters Union, wrote that "free enterprise may not last more than five or ten years" unless the "NAM Way" was challenged and changed.[81] Here Tobin, like other critics of mainstream free enterprise discourse, inverted the cause of NAM's fears that free enterprise was on its last legs. A 1948 editorial in the American Federation of Labor (AFL) newspaper also employed the language of crisis: "Today the free enterprise system is on trial."[82] Similarly, the *Pittsburgh Courier* claimed in 1941 that the "Negrophobia of the South" was driving "another nail in the coffin of capitalism and the spirit of free enterprise and free competition for which it stands."[83] Thus, just as business free enterprisers used the metaphor of the death of free enterprise to condemn government, in this case the African American newspaper charged racists who supposedly championed the system with instigating its demise.

Free enterprise, in this view, was a system that favored the rich over the poor and whites over people of color by denying to labor what business took for granted. Free enterprise "is a ghost," according to Solomon Larkin, and it was employed "principally by those who, occupying privileged positions, desire to be left alone to their further profit and advantage."[84] According to the Union for Democratic Socialism, free enterprise "all too often is a euphemism for the right of powerful economic interests to loot the public treasury and the citizen's pocketbook."[85] W. E. B. Du Bois noted in 1943 that the "modern capitalist" was "strangling social security and shrieking for 'free enterprise' for the begging rich." Du Bois concluded, referring to Texas congressman Martin Dies, the head of the House Committee on Un-American Activities, that free enterprisers produce "communists faster than demagogues like Dies can smell them out."[86] Making the same point, civil rights leader Andrew Young in 1967 condemned policies that amounted to "socialism for the rich, free enterprise for the poor."[87] Consumer activist Ralph Nader used the same phrase in 1973, noting that free enterprise "doesn't square with the reality of corporations advocating, and profiting from . . . windfall government policies."[88] For these critics, free enterprise was, in the hands of elites, a purely ideological as well as hypocritical formulation that protected the powerful, notwithstanding their self-understanding as besieged victims.

Despite the conservative uses of free enterprise by segregationists, some civil rights activists and liberals sought to reclaim it. Instead of rejecting it, they called for African Americans to share in the full fruits of the system, arguing that consumer and worker freedom had to be universal for it to be meaningful. "Free enterprise" was a crucial component of the National Resources Planning Board's wartime elaboration of FDR's "freedom from want." In its definition, free enterprise meant freedom from "compulsory labor, irresponsible private power, arbitrary public authority, and unregulated monopoly."[89] In 1947, the *Defender* decried the fact that "some of the great enterprises in the nation continue to operate on the theory that it is good business to practice racial discrimination." These people, it observed, "love neither free enterprise nor civil liberty."[90] As Whitney M. Young Jr., head of the National Urban League, wrote, "Freedom of choice is a cornerstone of American democracy and to deny a man the right to buy a house or rent an apartment because of the color of his skin is to deny his freedom of choice and to make a mockery of free enterprise."[91] Here Young invoked the same phrase segregationists employed to justify the system but for different purposes. Freedom of choice was not solely the prerogative of white businesses or homeowners but a universal right that extended to black home buyers and consumers. If free enterprise was premised on the ability of people to "buy in the open market," claimed Loren Miller, vice president of the National Committee against Discrimination in Houston, in 1957, then African Americans were being excluded from its promises.[92] When black elevator workers were fired and replaced by whites for demanding higher wages (but still less than the whites who had done the job previously received), T. H. Runnels called this an "example of free enterprise in the hands of an unreasonable employer."[93] A system that favored whites and disadvantaged black workers, customers, and businesses did not deserve the name free enterprise, which they refused to define in white supremacist terms.

Most African American critics treated free enterprise as contingent rather than a settled concept. The belief that, as Marjorie McKenzie wrote in 1954, "free enterprise means something relative, not absolute" enabled African Americans to critique conventional understandings and to promote alternatives. McKenzie, for example, opined that "too little planning" would harm the economy.[94] Black columnists and activists contested the notion that free enterprise was monolithic or that it was necessarily incompatible with the welfare state. "There is a role for Government to play in making free enterprise work," said P. L. Prattis, executive editor of the *Pittsburgh Courier*, in 1946, positing a nuance that was not present in NAM pronouncements.[95] That newspaper's publisher, Ira Lewis, claimed during the war, "The American Negro believes in a system of free enterprise giving every citizen the fullest opportunity for education, self-development and rewards."[96] Free enterprise was best understood as a work in progress that "must be made democratic," as the *Amsterdam News* declared in 1944, especially at a time when "Negro soldiers are dying so that 'free enterprise' can survive."[97] The black press used free enterprise rhetoric as a tool to weaken Jim Crow. In a plea during World War II, Frank Bolden, one of the first black war correspondents and a longtime columnist for the *Pittsburgh Courier*, urged Americans to stop catering to Jim Crow's "moronic racial baiters." Bolden said, "This is a land of free enterprise and you can hire just WHOM YOU PLEASE." Bolden acknowledged that "the solid South won't purchase your product if it happens to have any 'local color' in it." But he argued that others could and should use consumer choice to hire freely, giving employment to black workers and undermining racial barriers, and that the "solid South" could be transformed by the fight for racial equality.[98]

During the war, the boisterous enumeration of the wonders of free enterprise opened space for opposition. For example, editor George Peck wrote in a typical encomium to free enterprise in 1945: "Under our American system of Free Enterprise—let us call it THE AMERICAN WAY—we live, move about, . . . wear the kind of clothes we desire, live where we wish, buy what we like and can afford to pay for, follow whatever occupation suits our fancy, choose our political representatives, select our public employees and change or control governments."[99] Yet for those unable to live where they wished (such as in a "white" neighborhood in Detroit) or to buy what they liked (such as a hamburger at a segregated lunch counter) or to choose their occupation (such as in businesses whose management refused to hire black workers) or to select their representatives (because disfranchisement was still the norm in much of the country), this "American Way" of free enterprise hardly seemed the embodiment of liberty. George S. Benson, one of the leading evangelists of postwar white Christian conservatism, said, "Freedom of Enterprise has helped make our land a land of plenty."[100] But critics claimed that free enterprise as it was practiced unfairly distributed that plenty according to race.

In stressing consumption, civil rights activists adapted the rhetoric of the business lobbyists who developed the free enterprise discourse that NAM made familiar beginning in the 1930s. These activists called for merging the business lobby's praise for mass consumption with equal recognition of the rights of consumers themselves. This was a language that described free enterprise as the system that made mass consumption possible, "the reason the American Standard of Living is highest and that luxuries elsewhere are necessities here," as Walter W. Weismann, chairman of Aetna, wrote in 1952.[101] Free enterprise, as Emerson P. Schmidt, director of economics at the U.S. Chamber of Commerce, wrote in the African American newspaper the *Chicago Defender* in 1945, crowned "the consumer the king of production." Schmidt claimed that "there is less force, coercion, and oppression under such a system than any other system yet devised by the mind of man." Indeed, Schmidt titled his 1944 pamphlet for the chamber *Freedom and the Free Market Inseparable*.[102] As we have seen, proponents regularly celebrated choice as the basis of free enterprise; indeed, some publicists sought to rename free enterprise "freedom of choice." As a rural Texas newspaper editor claimed in 1951, "Under free enterprise, the consumer has freedom of choice. He can go into any store, look around and buy or not buy as he pleases."[103] "There is only one freedom," declared an ad for J. Howard Pew's Sun Oil Company: "Freedom of Choice."[104] Civil rights activists insisted that such freedom be extended to African American consumers and that it should supersede the right of Lester Maddox and other white merchants to discriminate.

The fact that free enterprise advocates celebrated choice and liberty along-side the endorsement of Jim Crow led some civil rights leaders to claim that these advocates were actually emboldening challengers to the free enterprise "system" that they saw as sacrosanct. Walter White spoke of "the vacuum of hope created by the failures of the free enterprise system."[105] Noting in 1947 that "even the gifted negro doesn't get a chance today," Du Bois wrote that "our enterprise is not free to act and our initiative is heavily handicapped." Du Bois conceded that "a New England White boy" or a "young, white, Westerner, whether of German, Scandinavian or Irish descent" had such means of upward mobility that most of them "could easily forget or never know" that "vast num-bers of them" at one time were poor.[106] The promise of upward mobility—the heart of free enterprise propaganda—did not exist for African Americans, ac-cording to these critics.

African Americans insisted that all Americans would benefit from a true sys-tem of free enterprise. "We have got to convince our white contemporaries that an exploited, unemployed Negro is one less customer for free enterprise," as Ric Roberts wrote in the *Pittsburgh Courier*.[107] In this view, discrimination was inimical to free enterprise. Whereas Lester Maddox defined it as the essence of freedom, civil rights activists saw it as the opposite. As Arthur Goldberg, John F. Kennedy's secretary of labor, said in 1962, racism "violates the spirit of our democracy and harms our free enterprise system."[108] The Negro "has a chance of realizing his hope for equality under the present social structure called 'free enterprise,'" according to Earl Conrad, but only if racial discrimination was eliminated.[109]

"Free Enterprise Is Variously Understood and Variously Defined"

Labor leaders in the New Deal era also refused to concede the meaning of free enterprise to its business champions. In a talk to members of the AFL in 1944, Robert Gaylord, the head of NAM and president of the Ingersoll Milling Machine Company, observed: "Hardly a speech is made today unless it starts out by extolling free enterprise society."[110] These included speeches by his audience in the AFL leadership as well as by other liberals, antitrusters, and civil rights protesters, all of whom refused to cede the phrase to conservatives. For example, liberal California representative Helen Gahagan Douglas declared in 1946, "Nobody believes in the free enterprise system or its future more than I do," even though Richard Nixon, her opponent in the 1950 California senatorial election, depicted her as "the pink lady," an enemy of "the free enterprise competitive system" whose views placed her far outside of the political mainstream.[111]

While it was largely true, as the labor journalist Oliver Hoyem wrote in an article for the magazine of the U.S. Chamber of Commerce shortly after the war ended, that "organized labor" and "organized capital" were "committed to capitalism, to a system of free enterprise," it was also the case that these groups defined both capitalism and free enterprise in different ways. The mantra of "free enterprise and free labor" promoted by the business lobby suggested a consensus that leaders of the labor movement and the black freedom movement went to great lengths to challenge.[112] Condemning "recalcitrant employers who still cling to the traditional thinking that 'free enterprise' means free exploitation," an editorial in the *Chicago Defender* in 1946 highlighted the "inevitable connection between American race baiting and labor baiting."[113]

Those representing organized labor and civil rights groups highlighted and deconstructed the ideological uses to which free enterprise was put by business leaders. As a writer for the *Machinists' Monthly Journal* advised in 1954, noting the widespread attraction to the term *free enterprise*, "it seems to be the sensible thing to explore what it is."[114] And in the postwar years, labor and civil rights leaders vigorously pursued this process of exploration, an activity that those who sought to naturalize the concept discouraged.

Laborists applied special scrutiny to the binarisms advanced by business advocates of free enterprise, who took any adjustments to what they called "the system of free enterprise" as tantamount to its destruction. Although some business leaders, like shipbuilder Henry J. Kaiser, called for a "definition of free enterprise that would incorporate both social justice and economic progress," most conservatives took their quest for business power to be the essence of social justice. Very few viewed free enterprise as what Kaiser called a "tattered concept"; rather, they saw it as the basis of their war against the New Deal state.[115] "Two roads lie before us," declared George Benson, president of Harding College in Searcy, Arkansas, and a pioneer of business-oriented free enterprise education, in 1943. The choice was clear, according to Benson, who, like other free enterprisers, employed the road metaphor well before Friedrich A. Hayek popularized it in his best seller of the following year, *The Road to Serf-*

dom. Americans must follow the path of "Free Enterprise to standards of living higher even than we have known before" or, Benson opined, they would inevitably "slide down through government ownership and State Socialism to the living standards of the Orient."[116] Here Benson drew on the racist arguments of the anti-Chinese campaigners of the late nineteenth and early twentieth centuries who held that Asia represented the polar opposite of the "American Standard of Living."[117] Benson saw any interference with business prerogatives as a potentially disastrous diversion from free enterprise.

In the postwar years, as conservatives intensified the claim that there was no middle ground between free enterprise and totalitarianism, progressives rejected this defining binary. As a writer for the progressive Catholic journal *Commonweal* observed in 1952, from the viewpoint of conservatives, "there are two and only two possible positions on socio-economic matters. On the one hand there is true one hundred per cent rugged individualism, completely free enterprise and no government intervention." On the other side was "'creeping socialism' which leads inevitably to Communism."[118] Some activists made it their business to show that the welfare state, collective bargaining for organized labor, a regime of regulation and antitrust, and full citizenship for African Americans did not portend the death of free enterprise but rather were necessary for its fulfillment. "Of course I believe in free enterprise," said Senator Harry S. Truman in the spring of 1944, "but in my system of free enterprise the democratic principle is that there never was, never has been and never will be room for the ruthless exploitation of the many for the benefit of the few."[119]

Unlike conservatives who, as we saw in chapter 4, expressed episodic unease about the definitional elusiveness of free enterprise, labor and civil rights groups celebrated its essentially contested nature. "As is the case with many other terms that are widely-used in present-day discussion," observed George Meany, the AFL's secretary-treasurer, in 1944, "free enterprise is variously understood and variously defined." The understanding of free enterprise promoted by the business lobby, he continued, "does not coincide in all particulars with that of wage-earning people." There is, Meany noted, a difference between "a system of free enterprise," which suggested that there could be any number of possible free enterprise systems, and "the system of free enterprise," which he equated with the "feudalistic" view held by some businessmen, who illegitimately attempted to impose a single, self-interested interpretation on an inherently elastic phrase.[120] George Baldanzi, executive vice president of the Textile Workers

Union, made much the same point at a CIO automotive workers meeting in Milwaukee in 1949: "Be for free enterprise if it serves the needs of the people," Baldanzi said. "If it doesn't be for some other system."[121] In one of his last interviews, folksinger and activist Pete Seeger made a similar point. Noting that "no two people attach the same meaning to the same words," he illustrated this observation with the example of the commonly used but ill-understood phrase *free enterprise*.[122] Critics on the left thus challenged business attempts to monopolize the phrase. As Mark Starr, educational director of the International Ladies Garment Workers Union, wrote in 1954, "Free enterprise needs restatement to suit our modern needs," suggesting that the concept could be of use to those on the social democratic end of the labor movement.[123]

Unsurprisingly, labor leaders such as William L. Hutcheson, the notoriously reactionary president of the Carpenters and Joiners Union, George Meany, the business unionist and future AFL president, and the Teamsters' leader Jimmy Hoffa declared, as Hoffa put it, that they were "1000% behind the free enterprise system."[124] But some figures on the more radical spectrum of the labor and civil rights movement did so as well.

The term *free enterprise* appeared almost as often in the labor and African American press as it did in the business periodicals and trade journals. Some New Deal liberals not only claimed the term but called themselves its true champions. Indeed, progressives called out the hypocrisy of the loudest celebrators of free enterprise. "As much as they talk about free enterprise," editorialized the *Pittsburgh Courier* in 1957, racist politicians and businessmen fear "competition from Negroes for jobs, political preferment, legislative advantages, and judicial plums."[125] The problem in this view was not the concept of free enterprise itself but one-sided and self-serving definitions of it. Moreover, the idea that corporations did not want free enterprise, if that phrase was understood as an endorsement of laissez-faire policies—which would include the encouragement of competition and end government support for business—was a commonplace, even in the business press. While "the phrase 'free enterprise' will be on every tongue," observed a skeptical writer for the business periodical *Fortune* in 1946, "it can be confidently asserted that many who make the most to-do over this subject would be the first to cry quits if their words were taken seriously."[126] Even the business press sometimes called out business leaders and their political champions on their hypocrisy.

From a different perspective, antitrusters also sought to separate business propaganda from what they posited as the true meaning of free enterprise: the fostering of competition and the prevention of monopolies, a condition that would require government enforcement and regulation. "All the recent business mergers and consolidations made absurd the old-line talk of free enterprise," claimed Socialist Party leader Norman Thomas in the spirit of the antitrust tradition. Thomas claimed that "the only free enterprise in America today is small boys who shoot marbles for keeps."[127] "The threat to free enterprise in this country is real, just like Republican leaders say," Carroll Kilpatrick wrote in the *New Republic* in 1946. But those who "cry about the threat to free enterprise," he went on, "will go right on fighting against adequate appropriations to the Anti-Trust Division of the Department of Justice."[128] Activists in the consumer movement similarly claimed to be promoting free enterprise and that it was the business community that was destroying this American system through its embrace of monopolies. Critics from Estes Kefauver, Tennessee senator and champion of small business, to consumer advocate Ralph Nader held that the problem with America was precisely its lack of a true free enterprise system, and that business leaders were corrupting the phrase by disseminating a false view of it as corporate power rather than business competition.[129]

Indeed, the Roosevelt administration itself, targeted by conservatives as the staunchest enemy of free enterprise, framed both its New Deal and war efforts as attempts to save free enterprise. The New Deal, Franklin D. Roosevelt claimed in 1938, "is a program whose basic thesis is not that the system of free private enterprise for profit has failed . . . but that it has not yet been tried." The year before he died, FDR said, "I believe in free enterprise—and always have."[130] By 1944, even the American Communist Party, which had briefly disbanded, temporarily becoming a political association rather than a political party, endorsed the free enterprise system in the spirit of wartime unity. This system, the party's leader Earl Browder claimed, was "accepted as one of the political facts of life" by "the democratic progressive majority," and who was he or his organization to challenge this view?[131] The *New York Times* called this "the most amazing episode in the history of American communism," asking, "what is left of Communism?"[132] While this was doubtless an unusual metamorphosis, it showed the degree to which the contours of free enterprise could be stretched, an extension occurring in many other surprising circles both during and after the war. *Life* magazine editorialized in October of that year that the leading New Dealers, "Roosevelt, Harry Hopkins, and Henry Wallace are all expounding the virtues of free enterprise. Earl Browder, too, is for it. Capitalism has too many friends."[133] Throughout the postwar years, opponents of conservatism sought to claim and reframe, rather than reject, the term. Philip Murray, leader of the CIO, for example, argued in 1952 that a guaranteed annual wage would serve the "best interests of the free enterprise system."[134]

As early as 1939, business leaders encouraged "public relations men and women" to do a better job of "telling the story of free enterprise."[135] In the post-war years, NAM and the business lobby launched a free enterprise offensive as part of a drive to roll back the gains of organized labor and to bring business leaders into the good graces of the American people. But even then, NAM did not have a monopoly on free enterprise discourse. During the debates in Congress about the controversial Taft-Hartley labor bill in the spring of 1947, both advocates and opponents regularly invoked the term.[136] Similarly, both segregationists and civil rights activists employed the phrase. Critics of the business lobby rejected its version of "free enterprise" as part of the propaganda of reaction. Labor would "slip back into its former quasi-serfdom," claimed the progressive priest John A. Ryan in 1943, "if the champions of 'free enterprise' are allowed free reign."[137] By putting the term in quotation marks, Ryan, like many other critics, implied that it was not the concept of free enterprise itself that was necessarily the problem but rather the proprietary claims of those business proponents who misused it.

A far greater number of liberals and radicals sought to redefine the term, holding that such an achievement would require democratic input from below and claiming that the free enterprise system was threatened not by workers and civil rights activists but by its purported conservative supporters in business and politics. "Organized labor," as A. J. Hayes, president of the International Association of Machinists, wrote in 1954, "has substantially improved and extended the free enterprise system." Hayes urged the labor movement to commit to a "constant struggle" to force "the free enterprise system to make concessions, to give way and to reform its character."[138] Similarly, United Auto Workers' Union leader Walter Reuther endorsed the effort "to save truly free enterprise from death at the hands of its self-appointed champions."[139] Free enterprise, in this view, was plastic, like capitalism itself, capable of being reformed but only if progressive critics could dislodge the phrase from the sole grip of its conservative champions. A newspaper writer suggested that the labor leader's ideas "are about as close to free enterprise as a Bulgarian's boudoir," but Reuther believed that he was offering an alternative version, not a rejection, of the concept, and one that would salvage and democratize it.[140]

"We Didn't Eat under Free Enterprise"

Like civil rights leaders, labor activists began with vocabulary. They challenged business definitions of free enterprise, sometimes, as we saw in chapter 4, in satirical ways, as when they poked fun at those free enterprisers who declared the lack of a definition to be a national emergency.[141] What business celebrated as such "is obviously not free enterprise," wrote David Siegel of the International Association of Machinists in 1947.[142] Warning of "the fakery that lies in the use of a term or slogan," an editorial in the magazine of the Association of Machinists urged workers to be wary of the "free enterprise" slogan. "Yes, there's a charm and magic in slogans and phrases but charms and magic are dispensed by witches as well as fairy godmothers," it concluded, turning the free enterprise critique of the New Deal on its head by dismissing free enterprisers as living in a fantasy world.[143] Whereas business-oriented free enterprise advocates highlighted the magic and mysteries of the free market and spoke of the free enterprise system in quasi-religious terms, working people mocked what the National Farmers Union head James G. Patton called the "mystic operations of so-called free private enterprise." As Patton concluded, "The so-called system of free enterprise is, from the viewpoint of the working farmer and the city-wage earner, neither a system, nor free, nor very enterprising."[144] George Meany said that he meant by the phrase "something truly free and enterprising" that "is of service to the country and not the monopolistic ambitions of greedy reactionaries."[145] Contrasting his views with those of conservatives, Walter Reuther claimed to be "for free enterprise—minus its defects," which for him were almost all due to corporate malfeasance.[146]

Representatives of working people accused business propagandists of employing free enterprise as a euphemism to obscure their self-serving, destructive politics. NAM, the Chamber of Commerce, and other groups sold free enterprise as a doctrine of populism and classlessness. "It is very noticeable that the Hearst press and the N.A.M. always talk in the language of the little man, the Jeffersonian citizen," media critic Marshall McLuhan observed in the early 1950s in an astute comment that presciently described the rhetorical strategy of Leonard Read's "I, Pencil," which was published a few years later. "They talk as if there were no such thing as economic power as a factor in human freedom."[147] McLuhan put his finger on a glaring omission in the rhetoric of free enterprisers—their denial of corporate power in favor of a view of the business firm as a plucky individual and the state as the only constraint on freedom.

Many labor leaders who believed that business free enterprisers exaggerated union power while minimizing their own called attention to the differences in their political visions. In 1944, Teamsters' leader Daniel Tobin mocked "the kind of Free Enterprise the Republicans are talking about in this campaign." Tobin highlighted the "glaring difference" and "basic conflicts" between the New Deal and free enterprise, summing up, "We ate under the New Deal. We didn't eat under Free Enterprise."[148] Labor leaders sought to redress this imbalance by demanding collective bargaining as a means of improving working-class purchasing power. Inverting the usual charge against New Dealers, Reuther, using a phrase that critics often employed, attacked those groups that "pay lip service to free enterprise." In Reuther's diagnosis, business groups were "afraid of the abundance it implies, and are dedicated to an economy of scarcity."[149] Rather than praising the American Way for its general productivity, labor leaders sought to ensure that the fruits of free enterprise were broadly available, at least for their membership, and equitably distributed. In contrast to the conservatives, the authors of the AFL's 1944 "Recommendations for the Post-war World" understood "free enterprise" to be part of "a progressive economy" that included "ample support for the health, educational, recreational and similar public services so essential to the welfare of the working people in our industrial society" as well as "the free exercise of civil and political liberties."[150] Taking "public services" and free enterprise to be synergistic marked a challenge to the fundamental precepts of the anti–New Dealers.

The labor interpretation of the relationship between free enterprise and consumption differed from the business view, especially in its endorsement of public spending. Both stressed mass consumption and material wealth as proof of the success of the free enterprise system. But labor supporters emphasized, as the Democratic Party platform of 1952 said, that the "free enterprise system flourished under Democratic leadership" because of the expansion of "purchasing power" and that "we are determined that the broad base of our prosperity must be maintained." Maurice Tobin, Harry Truman's secretary of labor, also claimed that by assuring working-class "purchasing power," trade unionism "helps sustain free enterprise."[151] National prosperity required broad-based consumption, which is why the *New York Times* editorialized on Labor Day in 1950 that "if the system of free enterprise is to flourish, it must pay not only owners and stock-holders but also the workers enough to purchase the products of that system."[152] This was Reuther's view as well: "Free enterprise, if it is to survive, must create an ability not only to earn dividends for stockholders but also to give millions of Americans economic security."[153] In connecting free enterprise to security rather than risk, and to workers rather than employers, Reuther challenged the conservative attempt to write working-class security out of the economics of freedom.

It is for this reason that the anti-labor Taft-Hartley Act became such a flashpoint in debates about free enterprise. According to Senator Hubert Humphrey, the bill, which he despised, "strikes at the heart of American industrial democracy and our free enterprise system."[154] AFL president William Green charged that the law removed "the necessary checks and balances needed to assure fair distribution of income and purchasing power."[155] In labor's vision, mass production and mass consumption, aided by a government policy of supporting organized labor, progressive taxation, and business regulation, lay at the heart of a free enterprise system, which is why Green insisted, "To return wage-earners to a share in free-enterprise and other democratic institutions, the whole structure of Taft-Hartley must be wiped out."[156] In labor's view, the right to collective bargaining was as much a key element of free enterprise as the right to consume freely, and the right to security was as important as the "freedom" to go hungry.

Labor leaders claimed that what business leaders called freedom amounted to assurances of security for themselves and the realities of precariousness for everyone else. The view of organized labor and its allies was, much like the arguments of FDR and Truman, that the welfare state, which socialized risk and expanded security to the working and middle classes, was the savior rather than the antithesis of free enterprise. Moreover, they condemned the hypocrisy of free enterprise anti-statism, which did not apply to the forms of government assistance that many business leaders and trade groups demanded. "The opponents of the welfare state want 'welfare,' but for themselves in the form of Government subsidies to business," claimed Humphrey. "The greatest threat to the free enterprise system in America is not social security, minimum wage, aid to education, rural electrical programs and the like, but 'growing monopoly.'"[157]

The continuation of a free enterprise system that married productivity and security, consumption and freedom required a rethinking of the term from a

working-class perspective. Meany noted the plain fact that it was wartime government spending that brought full employment, not free enterprise as it was
usually understood; indeed, the kind of unregulated capitalism free enterprisers
championed, he and other laborists argued, had caused the Great Depression.[158]
As the machinist A. J. Hayes claimed, "Free enterprise would have cracked
without our long history of social reform, government regulations, and essential
controls."[159] Rather than rejecting free enterprise out of hand, however, Hayes
and Meany saw the need to fight for a democratic conception of free enterprise
that accommodated the modern welfare state and trade unionism.

The disparate users of the phrase agreed that free enterprise was a necessary
but flawed system, but they diagnosed these flaws in very different ways. Business leaders viewed theirs as a public relations failure; better narratives and a
system of delivering them, they believed, were all that was necessary. Progressives questioned the conservative assumption of a necessary linkage between
business autonomy and democratic freedom. Labor leaders, in contrast, believed
that collective bargaining and a robust welfare state was consistent with free
enterprise. Civil rights leaders held that racism rendered impossible the realization of the promise of free enterprise.

The post–New Deal progressive appropriations of free enterprise challenged
the conservative position that theirs was the only meaningful version. But if
we recall that the nineteenth-century roots of the term, as we saw in chapter 2,
lay with abolitionists, advocates of free labor, and supporters of government-
sponsored internal improvements, these appropriations can be seen to more
closely align with tradition than did the novel conservative versions that boldly,
but inaccurately, claimed the mantle of custom. It is a tribute to the effectiveness of the business free enterprisers in obscuring the past by their invented
tradition that the civil rights and labor activists who sought to repurpose the
term in the mid-twentieth century rarely highlighted the fact that their preferred
version had more claim to "tradition" than did that of the business leaders who
claimed it as an age-old custom. Even Arthur Schlesinger Jr., who in 1945 wrote
The Age of Jackson, referred to "genuine free enterprise" of the nineteenth century, as if that term meant unregulated capitalism in the antebellum period.[160]

As important as it is to examine the liberals, trade unionists, and civil rights
activists who sought to reclaim free enterprise, it is also necessary to recognize
that their alternative conceptions have been largely forgotten. The perspective
granted by history allows us to see why, at least for the late twentieth and early

twenty-first centuries, the business free enterprise vision largely won out. It did so in part by depicting government as the enemy of freedom rather than a necessary constraint on capitalism and a source of public goods. One of the ways that free enterprisers successfully won the battle of public opinion, as we will see next, was in their denigration of taxation and government spending. But free enterprise is an open political language, and we should not be surprised if future groups reimagine it in a progressive direction, as civil rights and labor activists once did.

8

From Public Spending to "Entitlements"

POLITICAL COMMENTATOR NORMAN ORNSTEIN highlighted in 2014 what he characterized as a new belief among Republicans, "the almost nihilistic attitude that all government is bad—that any attempt to find 'solutions' to problems that in any way involve government is wrong and almost evil, unless it focuses monomaniacally on cutting spending and cutting government."[1] An examination of free enterprise rhetoric reveals that this "nihilism" dates back many decades. In 1986, conservative activist Grover Norquist and his group Americans for Tax Reform had initiated the "Taxpayer Protection Pledge," which called on politicians to resolve to oppose all future tax increases, and which virtually all Republicans signed.[2] Connecting his anti-tax agenda to reduced government spending, Norquist said in 2001 that he wanted to shrink government "to the size where I can drag it into the bathroom and drown it in the bathtub."[3] This was a view of the ideal state not as an unobtrusive "umpire," as free enterprisers had previously described it, but as a menace fit to be murdered, and we can find the roots of this view in the campaign against the New Deal.

Of all their criticisms of the New Deal, free enterprisers repeatedly homed in on excessive public spending, fueled by what a Chamber of Commerce official called in 1938 "the grinding burden of taxes," as the most dangerous of the new liberalism's inequities.[4] Beginning in the 1920s and accelerating after the election of Franklin D. Roosevelt, the condemnation of public spending on selected social programs has remained foundational to free enterprise campaigns against the compensatory state, emerging again in debates over neoliberalism and austerity in the twenty-first century. In this influential view, public expenditures represented an irresponsible "spending spree," as Everett Sanders, chair of the Republican National Committee, described the New Deal in the midst of the Great Depression in 1934.[5] Taxes, according to an ad in the journal of the U.S. Chamber of Commerce in November 1938, support "an army of bureaus" that grind out unnecessary "rules, regulations and edicts which affect not businessmen alone but farmers, wage earners and consumers."[6] The next month, another ad in the same journal, while conceding that "no one resents paying taxes for the necessary functions of government and for relief in times of great emergencies," claimed that too many New Deal expenses supported unnecessary and extravagant "new activities and experiments" that "have a way of becoming permanent burdens."[7] Taxes and welfare spending emerged as the key flashpoints in the free enterprise battle against the New Deal order. In free enterprisers' view, government spending was not merely inefficient; it was unjust and dangerous.[8]

Public spending had vigorous defenders, however, and for a time in the 1950s and 1960s, it appeared to be emerging as a key element of a bipartisan campaign for renewed "national purpose" during the height of the Cold War.[9] Advocates believed that public spending in the postwar years would fulfill the mission of the New Deal. They argued that the government's fiscal actions had rescued the economy during the Great Depression, saved the nation at war, and would enable the country to achieve its mission in its battle against Soviet communism. They agreed with Franklin D. Roosevelt, who said that the New Deal had "saved free enterprise," and in the postwar years, they believed that public spending was the best way to preserve and advance America's interests.[10]

But free enterprise critics of public spending believed otherwise. The road to serfdom in the United States, free enterprisers believed, would likely proceed not via military coup or socialist revolution but from the more mundane but equally dangerous path of taxing and spending. Many critics of public spending believed that the American path to perdition would likely be a gradual descent, following the gradual "footsteps of the British socialist government," rather than Soviet communism. If, as one critic claimed in 1950, "a welfare state is only a way station on the road to socialism," many free enterprisers posited that the path was forged by the tax revenue that funded it.[11] Columnist Louis Bromfield predicted that "excessive public spending" rather than overt socialism would misdirect the country away from "free enterprise and democracy."[12] Others imagined taxation to be the mechanism of the slippery slope. For example, Clem D. Johnson, president of the U.S. Chamber of Commerce, said in 1954, "We are running a great risk of quietly becoming a socialist nation through the back-door medium of confiscatory taxation," a fear that Herbert Hoover had been articulating since the election of Franklin Roosevelt.[13] In this vision, "excessive public spending" was more likely to bolster socialism than democracy and certain to create a "leviathan," a too-powerful state that would constrain individual and business freedom.[14]

One of the geniuses of the conservative free enterprisers, as we have seen, was their ability to craft a convincing commonsense narrative even in seeming defeat. The debate about public spending provides an instructive example of their ability to win ideological victories in hostile times. Although the eminent columnist Walter Lippmann proclaimed "the collapse of effective resistance to public spending" in 1939, that same year the conservative publisher David Lawrence demanded "a reversal of the tide of public spending," a position that had become a central tenet of anti–New Deal free enterprise thinking.[15] Public spending funded by progressive taxation, which remained robust through the early 1980s, proved generally popular throughout the era of the New Deal order, but critics used effective imagery to shape how Americans conceived of spending and provided a ready-made vocabulary for rejecting it when public opinion turned by introducing such phrases as "entitlement spending," "it's your money," taxation as "theft," "throwing money" at problems, and "out-of-control spending," whose rhetorical power endured.[16] The impact of such language was manifest in a 1952 Gallup poll asking which presidential candidate "would do a better job of cutting down unnecessary public spending," a question whose phrasing carried the assumption that at least some forms of government spending were inherently wasteful.[17]

Although they lost many policy battles over spending, free enterprisers also invented the enduring figure of the "tax-and-spend" liberal, a phrase apparently coined by the conservative columnist George Sokolsky in 1956, which suggested that the essence of postwar liberalism was disregard for the value of thrift and disrespect for the taxpayer, whose money the government wantonly wasted.[18] (Sokolsky was mocking the phrasing attributed to Harry Hopkins, one of FDR's advisors, who in the 1930s had reportedly said, "We will tax and tax, and spend and spend, and elect and elect.")[19] Two years later, a supporter of William Knowland, the Republican candidate for governor of California, also parodying Hopkins, condemned the "tax, tax, tax, spend, spend, spend philosophy which is reducing 'free enterprise' to an outdated term."[20]

Campaigns against public spending were highly selective. Many free enterprisers were not averse to seeking government support for their pet projects, and during the Cold War, most of them advocated for what has been called "military Keynesianism."[21] As an editorialist noted in 1950, free enterprise building contractors, who often cried "socialism," did not object "when governmental guarantees give them the opportunity of getting rich."[22] Moreover, the vast majority of the Republican caucus in the House and a majority in the Senate (twenty-seven out of forty-one) voted for the 1956 Federal-Aid Highway Act, which was promoted by a Republican president.[23] Still, the framing of government spending as dangerous shaped views about the limits of the New Deal order. Eventually, as that order weakened, the selective criticism of government spending gained momentum. Such a position was of a piece with the young congressman Newt Gingrich's 1984 dismissal of "pragmatist" Republicans, whom he condemned for having served for half a century as "tax collectors for the welfare state" and abettors of big government.[24]

"Government Extravagance"

Like conservative free enterprise discourse itself, the critique of public spending began before the New Deal. President Calvin Coolidge, for example, viewed "excessive" taxation as "larceny" and condemned in language familiar to us today the "existing system of death taxes."[25] Coolidge was one of the first politicians to refer to the estate tax as the "death tax," which he denounced in 1925 as a step toward socialism "under the guise of a law to collect revenue."[26] In April 1932, almost a full year before Franklin D. Roosevelt took office as president, Robert R. McCormick, owner and publisher of the *Chicago Tribune*, claimed in a speech to the Chicago Association of Commerce, "10 years of excessive taxation have brought the nation on the verge of ruin," a remarkable assertion given that he was referring to a decade of business-friendly Republican presidential leadership.[27] Two months later, the *Tribune* editorialized that the battle between what it called "Socialism or Americanism" was led by "progressives" who "want to destroy private enterprise and replace it with a socialist autocracy" founded on taxation and "bureaucracy."[28]

With the start of the New Deal, the condemnation of public spending as what the editors of the *Corvallis Gazette-Times* called "slavery through taxation" in 1934 gained traction.[29] That year, E. Harold Cluett, a Republican candidate for the Senate in New York, attacked the New Deal's "orgy of spending," which was treating "business as a whipping boy." Such violent imagery redolent of chattel slavery, frequently echoed by free enterprisers, shaped a conception of government bureaucracy as a violator of upstanding citizens.[30] In 1935, Frank Knox, former Bull Mooser and newspaper editor, claimed along these lines that the "whip cracking Simon Legree methods of government" were creating a "militant, tax aroused electorate." Presciently, Knox encouraged the development of what he called "tax consciousness" as a means to combat "government waste."[31] Often that consciousness was extended from individuals to business firms. Free enterprisers believed that government spending supported by taxation both crowded out private spending and sent a signal to business that it was subordinate to government, whereas, as the editors of the *St. Louis Globe Democrat* asserted, "at best, government can assist business only by helping clear away obstacles," not by imposing "hampering restrictions." Since "it is business and business alone that can work out business recovery," government competition was counterproductive.[32] The theory behind public spending, as one columnist wrote in 1960, was that "government is too poor and you are too rich," when the reverse should have been the norm.[33]

Not coincidentally, the New Deal was the first era in which liberalism and conservatism, just coming into formation in their modern senses, as we saw in chapter 5, came to be defined largely by their estimation of the necessity for public expenditures. In 1937, Merwin K. Hart, a New York Republican congressman, described the battle lines in terms that soon became familiar, "with the liberals believing in large public spending and the injection of bureaucracy into everyday life, and the conservatives believing in curbing public spending and keeping private enterprise as free as possible from government interference."[34] Free enterprise versus public spending became convenient shorthand for one of the key ideological struggles of the twentieth century, and this binary shaped the way that both liberalism and conservatism evolved.

Suspicion of government power has deep roots in the United States. Building on this tradition, opponents of the New Deal villainized public spending as a direct threat to the free enterprise system. In August 1936, three weeks after he accepted the nomination as vice president on the Republican ticket, Knox spoke before the United Retail Merchants Association meeting in Hagerstown, Maryland. The heart of the matter, for Knox, as for so many other New Deal critics, was the hubris of an arrogant government that recklessly spent other people's money. Introducing a popular rhetorical device, Knox hinted at the existence of grandiose and wasteful New Deal programs: a federally funded "dog pound in Memphis, Tenn. with marble shower baths," a "$6,000 product in White Plains, NY, to remove 'efflorescence' from some bridges," and the coup de grâce: "I am informed that there are now in Washington three separate and independent commissions working at taxpayers' expense to find out why there are so many unnecessary commissions," said Knox. For Knox, these examples of "government extravagance" revealed the essence of the New Deal, excessive spending on frivolous endeavors funded by coercive mechanisms.[35]

From Knox's point of view, these examples of waste and inefficiency exemplified the New Deal. In his critique of government, Knox did not distinguish between these likely apocryphal examples of government waste and the Social Security Act of the previous year, which he labeled "a dubious social security measure." Indeed, he viewed the Social Security Act as even worse than the frivolous ones because it was permanent and intrusive. It would allow "the Federal government to go into the intimate details of the private lives" of every American. Increased government spending to Knox increased the likelihood of unchecked government power.

Knox viewed public and private spending as a zero-sum competition in which taxation amounted to "a net subtraction from private industry and private consumption." Too many bureaucrats, he believed, support "useless projects" or the hiring of "unnecessary public officials." Even taxes for "useful government projects," a category that Knox defined very narrowly, "subtracted from the living and production of the people," he claimed. Knox attempted to draw broader moral lessons from his view that "the business of the country cannot be run from Washington." This was an expression of the ascending free enterprise view of business over government. Unchecked power to tax and spend, Knox believed, would promote "governmental extravagance." Knox opposed the government's interference with free enterprise because it inevitably undermined the self-correcting system with its ambitious spending program.

Knox anticipated other critics who described and denigrated the operations of government as waste by way of the repetition of hearsay stories. In a later generation, Ronald Reagan became the master of such fables of inexplicable and infuriating federal extravagance. Indeed, Reagan's entrée to the national political stage, his celebrated 1964 speech "A Time for Choosing," given on behalf of Republican presidential candidate Barry Goldwater, included strikingly similar tales of government waste. In that speech, he updated Knox by describing "such spectacles as in Cleveland, Ohio," where "a million-and-a-half-dollar building completed only three years ago must be destroyed to make way for what government officials call a 'more compatible use of the land.'" Highlighting wasteful foreign aid, he noted that "we bought a $2 million yacht for Haile Selassie" as well as "extra wives for Kenyan government officials" and "a thousand TV sets for a place where they have no electricity."[36] Wasteful public spending directed toward unworthy foreign others was of a piece with a discourse that objected to domestic welfare spending on racist grounds. Four years later, making Reagan's subtext explicit, William Lowndes of the Southern States Industrial Council complained that the forgotten man was seeing his tax dollars used to support a "costumed tribal chieftain from some Afro-Asian mini-nation freeloading" at the United Nations.[37] Later in his political career, Reagan personified the welfare state in the person of the "welfare queen" driving a Cadillac and the "strapping young buck" using food stamps to buy fancy cuts of meat.[38] The implication was clear: part of what made the spending state immoral was not just theft from the taxpayer but the way it rewarded undeserving people of color.

"The Disease of the Age"

Using the two most powerful metaphors in the free enterprise vocabulary, free enterprisers described public spending as both tyrannical and enslaving. "Under the New Deal a shift from the free enterprise kind of private spending toward the totalitarian kind of government spending has been steadily in progress," declared a 1947 editorial in the *Milwaukee Sentinel*. "Under free enterprise the citizen wants his OWN money for the kind of living HE WANTS." By contrast, "Under the tyranny of collectivism, the GOVERNMENT confiscates a very great share of the citizen's money through taxation, AND DOES THE SPENDING ITSELF." According to the editorial, "The people must be given back the natural rights of freemen to SPEND THEIR OWN MONEY for their own purposes and as their own judgement dictates."[39] In this widely echoed view, taxes and spending were existential issues, affecting not just policy differences but fundamental questions of liberty. The capitalized words emphasized the dangers that the state posed to the "natural rights" of the individual, whose consumption in the marketplace was an expression of autonomy and hence freedom.

Critics of public spending framed it as a pathology, what the *Los Angeles Times* called in 1948 "the disease of the age," comparing it to "the multiplication of cells in a cancer."[40] Describing public spending as a metastasizing illness undermined the very legitimacy of the fiscal functions of government. "The slogan of the welfare state," explained Herbert Hoover in 1949, was but "a disguise for the totalitarian state by the . . . route of spending."[41] Describing governing (necessarily financed by taxation) as a devious means of undermining freedom has been one of the most enduring and effective elements of free enterprise common sense.[42]

Long before Norquist's anti-tax pledge, some proponents of free enterprise came to see not just government spending but governing itself as a constraint on civic freedom. "A striking commentary on the American attitude toward government is the traditional standard by which statesmanship is measured," wrote Merle Thorpe, the editor of the magazine of the U.S. Chamber of Commerce, in 1931. Too many Americans ranked politicians "based on the laws they have sponsored," he complained. But "rarely, if ever, has a statesman laid claim to public favor on the ground of sponsoring the repeal of a law."[43] (In 2015, the Republican Speaker of the House, John Boehner, made a strikingly similar claim.)[44] This view of legislative governance as in itself potentially dangerous became an enduring component of free enterprise common sense. For many free enterprisers, a putative belief in small government often morphed into a condemnation of governance itself, a conviction that, as the Young Republican National Federation claimed in its "Statement of Belief" in 1964, "business and industry" should "operate unshackled by government regulation and free of burdensome, unfair taxes." This group, reflecting the mythology of free enterprise individualism, believed that people "could make their own way in the world entirely on their initiative and abilities."[45]

Critics treated taxation as a dangerous adjutant of the welfare state, one that could lead to the internal destruction of the republic. Ronald Reagan, actor turned spokesperson for General Electric (but not yet a politician or a Republican), summarized the free enterprise viewpoint well in a 1958 speech to the Chicago Executive Club. At the height of the Cold War, he condemned the New Deal as "the revolution of our times" that had produced "collectivism" and "statism." He identified the increasing danger of "the tendency of all of us to turn to the government for the answer to everything," which was "seriously endangering out private enterprise system." Crucially, he identified taxation as "the machine of that revolution," and his proposed counterrevolution called for reducing taxes as the first step to jam that machine.[46] If free enterprisers relied on a theory of a slippery slope toward totalitarianism, they saw public spending as its most dangerous mechanism.

Well before Proposition 13, a 1978 referendum in California that dramatically cut state property taxes, advocates of free enterprise sought to foment what Thurman Sensing in 1959 described as a "taxpayers revolt." For Sensing this cause was twofold. It was a protest against the confiscation of private wealth by the state, but equally it was a weapon against what he called "the evils of welfare-statism."[47] As early as 1934, a columnist called for a government department "elected by taxpayers only" to "curb, veto or lower appropriations," a set of choices that assumed they would never support increases.[48] In 1940, conservative publisher R. C. Hoiles dismissed New Dealism as nothing more than a search for "government control" based on what he called "public robbery."[49] During this period, "I, Pencil" author Leonard Read gave a lecture on "Americanism" in which he indexed freedom to the level of taxation. "There was a time, about 120 years ago," Read proclaimed, ignoring the plight of the millions of enslaved Americans at that time, "when the average citizen had somewhere between 95 and 98 percent freedom of choice with each of his income dollars."[50] Similarly, the tax revolts of the 1970s were often framed as an attack on wasteful spending in the form of what the advocate of a self-proclaimed "tea party" in 1978 described as misdirected sympathy (toward "freeloaders on welfare rolls") and greedy extravagance ("office redecorating").[51] Many decades later in the wake of a larger "tea party" revolt against the fiscal excesses of the government, Kentucky senator Rand Paul said in 2017, repeating a claim he had made many times previously, "If we tax you at 50%, you are half-slave and half-free."[52] Like Read, Paul believed that people were free to the extent that they were not taxed.

When not invoking images of enslavement, critics of public spending invoked the language of victimization. Indeed, John Krehbiel, chair of the Republican State Central Committee, denounced in 1961 "unnecessary, wasteful Democrat spending" and worried, drawing on a by-then familiar trope, that the California taxpayer had "become the forgotten man."[53] The following year, an editorial in the *Syracuse Post-Standard* condemned "the paternalist liberal do-gooders . . . who club billions out of us in taxes."[54] In this view, the problem was irresponsible, patronizing, and illegitimate government. By labeling government a "power-hungry monopolist," the newspaper explicitly flipped the traditional populist conception of corporations and the state, with the latter now figured as out of control and overly powerful. Such inversions became the essence of the conservative populist defense of free enterprise in the late twentieth century.[55]

Advocates of free enterprise questioned many forms of government spending and labeled the taxpayers who funded it the most victimized class in the country. Arguing that taxation represented an especially nefarious kind of robbery, a 1968 editorial in the *Pampa Daily News* claimed that "taxation is even more morally deplorable than outright theft." While unlawful theft "may or may not involve the use or threat of force," the editor posited that "the use or threat of overt violence are always present in the actions of the tax collectors."[56] In the same year, at a point when the cost of Lyndon B. Johnson's "Great Society" and the Vietnam War were making demands on the taxpayer to support "guns" and "butter," the popular economic columnist Sylvia Porter, also employing violent imagery, titled a column "Taxpayers Bleeding to Death."[57] The free enterprise criticism of public spending/taxation targeted the very legitimacy of government itself. Treating the state as outside the bounds of the private and proper economy, it held that government spending amounted to interference at best and coercion that undermined political and economic liberty at worst.

"It's Your Money"

Throughout the era of the New Deal order, critics of government spending framed taxes as theft. The rallying cry of what we can call "taxpayerism" was the phrase "It's your money."[58] The phrase itself has a history worth recounting. When first introduced in the 1920s, it signified the importance of financial planning ("the safest place to put your money") as well as the dangers of being ripped off in the marketplace, as in Stuart Chase and F. J. Schlink's 1927 best seller, *Your Money's Worth*, which became the bible of the incipient consumer movement.[59] It also took on a new signification as a warning to citizens to see government programs as confiscatory.[60] A 1936 radio play sponsored by the Republican Party, written to "dramatize the cost of the New Deal," used the phrase repeatedly.[61] An early example of this discourse came from the *Saturday Evening Post* which, in an article entitled "It's Your Money, Brother," warned citizens in 1944 that "the administration is considering peacetime spending that will squeeze hard every dollar you or your children earn."[62]

During the height of the public spending debate in the 1960 presidential campaign, Republican candidate Richard M. Nixon condemned Kennedy's call to pay for "more roads, more schools, more hospitals," not so much because of the undesirability of these ends, which, Nixon averred, were worthy, but because "it's not his money he wants to spend, it's yours."[63] By the 1980s, the phrase— reintroduced by Ronald Reagan—suggested that there were very few legitimate nonmilitary expenditures. Reagan stated that people should "keep their money and spend it the way they want to," rather than having the government take it and spend it "the way it wants to."[64] In 1996, when Republican Kansas senator Bob Dole ran for president, he was able to describe this slogan as "time-honored and true" and urged Americans not to "apologize for wanting to keep what you earn."[65] At the end of his unsuccessful campaign the phrase had become a desperate mantra, repeated in doubles and triplets for emphasis, as in his claim one month before Election Day: "Our plan is based on a simple principle. . . . It's your money. It's your money. It's your money."[66]

Republican politicians used this phrase as a way to justify their lack of governing ideas. In 1998, John Rowland of Connecticut said that his governing philosophy was to "give back" the people's money.[67] In 2010, Mark Sanford, outgoing South Carolina governor, described his greatest accomplishment in office as being the "taxpayer's advocate," by which he meant spending as little as possible, even on causes that might benefit the citizenry of the state.[68] George W. Bush frequently invoked the phrase on the presidential campaign trail in 2000 and to justify his tax-cutting agenda once he took office. "Gore views government's role as manipulating people and uses people's own tax money to manipulate their behavior," said Lawrence B. Lindsey, Bush's chief economic advisor, referring to Al Gore, the Democratic candidate. "Bush says it's your money. You keep it. Do what you think is best with it."[69] As Paul Ryan, Speaker of the House, banged the gavel after the House voted for a major tax reform bill in 2017, he said, "Today, we are giving the people of this country their money back."[70] "It's your money" pitted personal autonomy against government manipulation, and delegitimized public goods, which of necessity lessen the right of individuals to spend money as they choose, an act that free enterprisers had long defined as the essence of American freedom.

Critics of public spending also invoked two other phrases with a long history. By the 1920s, they began to use the phrase *other people's money* to condemn government spending. In so doing, they invoked Louis Brandeis's Progressive Era critique of unaccountable private businesses but inverted its meaning. Under the New Deal, according to Herbert Hoover, "Extravagance with other people's money is shifted from a sin to a virtue."[71] One of the common ways to condemn Great Society liberalism was to denounce government officials for "throwing money" at social problems. In 1967, New York politician Carl Spad claimed that Democratic politicians "think that the old 'new deal' philosophy of throwing money at your problems will make them go away." The same year, Los Angeles County district attorney Evelle J. Younger said, "Throwing money at Negro problems will not make them vanish or stop riot threats."[72] The implication of these phrases was that taking other people's money was a form not just of theft but of waste. It was a critique spoken in the name of white taxpayers, whom free enterprisers depicted as the unwilling funders of immoral spenders and unworthy, poor, or nonwhite recipients.

This language of theft has been a central and enduring element of free enterprise discourse. The idea that government took from ordinary Americans in the service of unworthy others has a long history. By substituting grasping government for the rapacious business firm as the villain, free enterprisers provided the grounding for conservative populism. Ronald Reagan explicitly drew on the populist tradition, including William Jennings Bryan's "Cross of Gold" speech, in many of his addresses: "If about 90 per cent of the laws that are passed by Congress and the state legislatures each year were lost on the way to the printer, and if all the people in the bureaus went fishing, I don't think they would be missed for quite a while," he claimed in 1973, when he was governor of California. "But realize your strength, because if you did not go to work, I am sure the country would feel it and grind to a halt in about 24 hours." Here, Reagan invoked Bryan's famous denunciation of cities: "Burn down your cities and leave our farms, and your cities will spring up again as if by magic. But destroy our farms and the grass will grow in the streets of every city in the country."[73] Reagan's reworking put private Americans in the role of farmers and government in the position of urban waste. This inverted populism, which denounced rather than applauded government and celebrated rather than condemned corporate power, became the hallmark of the New Right, but it was rooted in free enterprise discourse.

"Scandalously Starved" Public Institutions

In the 1940s, an important group of historians and economists showed public spending to be a long-standing political tradition. The Committee on Research in Economic History, founded in 1940, aimed for the scholarship it sponsored to have, according to Arthur H. Cole, its chair pro tem, "significant relevance to present-day problems."[74] Its mandate was to provide a useable past for the reforms of the New Deal, in particular its public spending initiatives, and to challenge those voices deeming its innovations illegitimate and un-American. As economic historian and committee member Herbert Heaton wrote in 1941, "It was felt desirable to destroy (if that be possible), the popular notion that until the Fourth of March, 1933, the United States was the land of laissez faire."[75]

Showing that the New Deal era was not the first time that government was centrally involved in economic development, Charles Beard, Louis Hartz, Oscar Handlin, and other scholars made the case that public spending marked the essence of the nation's political economy, especially at the state level. As Handlin wrote of Massachusetts in 1943, "From the very first organization of the Commonwealth in 1780, the state actively and vigorously engaged in all economic affairs of the area, sometimes as participant, sometimes as regulator." These historians demolished the myth of laissez-faire in the early republic and showed that federal, state, and municipal funding were inextricably intertwined with the development of American capitalism.[76]

Drawing from this tradition, proponents of public spending challenged the core assumptions of conservative free enterprisers. Perhaps the strongest case in favor of a robust public spending agenda came from Senator Joseph Clark (D-PA), who in 1959 condemned the "folklore" that "private spending is inherently good and public spending is inherently bad—and therefore public spending should always be minimized and private spending increased to the maximum the gross national product will permit." Noting a pattern already well developed by advocates of free enterprise and that, a generation later, came to characterize the New Right, Clark condemned the rhetorical trick of equating the word *government* with "'other nouns having an evil connotation—such as 'waste,' 'extravagance,' 'socialism,' 'bureaucracy.'" He claimed that "this is a pernicious tendency" because taxation and spending were not "naughty" but merely "the means by which we divide resources between the public and private sectors of the economy."[77] The presidential campaign of 1960 seemed to mark an endorsement of Clark's position, since Democratic candidate John F. Kennedy's mild defense of public spending had seemingly vanquished Nixon's endorsement of the policies he had promoted as Eisenhower's vice president.

For a time, it appeared that the public spending faction had succeeded in making it a part of the nation's political agenda. By 1963, the *New York Times* could report that "the doctrine has now triumphed," and many observers predicted that the "next great debate might very well be on new areas of public spending." During the first years of his presidency, Lyndon Johnson, who had been in correspondence with historian Arthur Schlesinger Jr. about this issue since the late 1950s, embraced the public spending agenda as necessary to achieve what he called the "Great Society." From the mid-1950s through the 1960s, Edwin L. Dale Jr. of the *New York Times* regularly reported on public spending.[78] The issue of public spending eventually faded, brought down by the guns versus butter debate of the Vietnam War, the weakening of the union movement, the perceived fiscal crisis of the 1970s and, more generally, by the relative triumph of long-standing free enterprise arguments against the welfare state. But it is worth revisiting this relatively short-lived debate because it sheds light on one of the primal tensions of modern political culture in the United States.

In the late 1950s and early 1960s, a national discussion about the virtues of public spending became the single most important focus of the ongoing conflict between the free enterprise and New Deal visions. Set off by the general acceptance of Keynesian economics and more specifically by economist Paul Samuelson's important series of articles on the topic, and popularized by John Kenneth Galbraith's best-selling *The Affluent Society*, the syndicated columns of America's most influential pundit, Walter Lippmann, and by Democratic politicians critical of the Eisenhower administration's economic policies and political priorities, the benefits of public consumption became a key issue in political discourse. Public spending emerged as a campaign issue in the 1960 presidential election, which one newspaper described as a choice between the free spending of the Democratic Party (which it denounced as "socialism") versus the "free enterprise" of the Republicans, who, although they had held the presidency for the previous eight years, vowed that they would, if elected, put "brakes on the trend of continually sending more money to Washington."[79]

Support for collective consumption entered general circulation in the late 1950s, as many public intellectuals and Democratic politicians charged that the

Eisenhower administration and the culture at large was repudiating the public-oriented and government-centered spirit of the New Deal and World War II years in favor of both a balanced-budget fetishism and a government-sanctioned private buying spree on useless extravagances, like automobile tailfins.[80] They worried about the spiritual emptiness this would promote but also about the dangers such inwardness posed to a country fighting a Cold War and claiming to lead the "free world." Summarizing this view in 1962, Daniel Bell wrote that "private enterprise cannot produce" the services now "required" by the "American public" in education, health, and recreation.[81]

According to advocates of public spending, American leaders overencouraged private consumption and dangerously discouraged socially beneficial public spending, or what the pro–New Deal economist Alvin Hansen labeled "community consumption."[82] In the 1950s, the government, according to Ike's critics, sanctioned all manner of private consumption but itself did not spend enough in key areas, including defense spending, infrastructure, education, urban renewal, and the environment. Denouncing "the enormous fallacy that the highest purpose of the American social order is to multiply the enjoyment of consumer goods," Lippmann worried in 1957 that "our public institutions . . . have been . . . scandalously starved."[83] Relatedly, according to these critics, politicians preferred tax cuts rather than spending as a mode of stimulating the economy, and the political class often valued balanced budgets over deficit spending during recessionary periods.[84] What Galbraith called the problem of "private opulence and public squalor" suggested that not all forms of consumption were equal, and that public-oriented spending needed to be increased, even if it came at the expense of private consumption. Although these critics described the problem of public spending in the 1950s as unprecedented, it was simply the latest iteration of the ongoing battle between free enterprise conservatives and advocates of the welfare state, a battle that had begun during the Great Depression and was being refought in the era of postwar affluence.

Public spending advocates argued that Eisenhower's policies sanctioned a selfishness that ran counter to the patriotism and public spirit necessary to win the Cold War. Even conservative proponents of free enterprise—who viewed conspicuous consumption as proof of the success of that "system"—condemned the "softness" that, they believed, accompanied postwar affluence. For example, the conservative senator Styles Bridges of New Hampshire wrote, "The time has clearly come to be less concerned with the depth of the pile on the new

broadloom rug or the height of the tail fin on the new car and to be more prepared to shed blood, sweat and tears if this country and the Free World are
to survive."[85] A year before he left office, Eisenhower himself responded de-
fensively to criticism that the nation's priorities had become skewed under
his leadership, denying that the country had turned to "gadgets and shallow
pleasures."[86]

For their part, free enterprisers claimed that private spending was precisely
the best way to win the Cold War and to promote a just society. Eisenhower's
critics on the right denounced him for maintaining rather than rolling back the
New Deal order. Ike himself spoke of being boxed in on this issue and of the
need to repulse his thrifty instincts. In his book on the Eisenhower administration, public spending reporter Edwin Dale claimed that by 1960 many conservative politicians, against their wishes, had become "in effect Keynesians."[87]

But many free enterprisers saw high levels of private consumption, not government spending, as proof of the success of the system. Using language similar to Lippmann's but to very different effect, W. P. Gullander, the president of
NAM, noted in 1963 noted that his countrymen "clog the highways with their
automobiles, and crowd the shopping centers to spend their constantly growing
personal incomes." Unlike the advocates of public spending, Gullander believed this private shopping spree was impressive proof of the genius, rather
than the defining shortcoming, of the free enterprise system. Instead of calling
for a shift from private to public, he implored citizens to defend their right to the
bounty that free enterprise produced. He worried that "far too many" of these
energetic consumers "march to the polls on election day and vote against the
system" of free enterprise by supporting politicians who maintained or expanded
the welfare state.[88]

Critics condemned what one commentator in 1956 labeled Eisenhower's
"allergy to public spending."[89] The nation's most influential columnist, Lippmann, employed Cold War justifications in his diagnosis. Contrasting "public
need" with "private pleasure"—well before Galbraith famously juxtaposed private opulence and public poverty—he devoted a large number of his influential
"Today and Tomorrow" syndicated columns to legitimating public expenditures.
His reasons were not so much economic as political and ethical, driven by the
moral challenge of the Cold War which, he believed, necessitated collective
spending, personal sacrifice, and a reconstituted masculinity. He wished the
president to convey, as he wrote in 1957, "a stern and austere reminder that our

public responsibilities must come ahead of our private pleasures." Enumerating unmet public needs—parks, hospitals, housing, communications, the military— he believed that spending was important, but only if it helped the country to "meet our responsibilities and to do our duty."[90] For Lippmann, individual consumption could not meet the challenges of the Cold War moment, in which civilization hung in the balance.

Other proponents of public spending also challenged the emerging view— preeminent in what historian Lizabeth Cohen has called the "consumers' republic" of postwar America—that shopping for the family enacted patriotism.[91] In "the race between free men and their opponents," liberal economist and political advisor Leon H. Keyserling believed that public economics was crucial. Private and conspicuous wealth was no guarantor of the virtue necessary to successfully fight the Cold War. Indeed, some viewed it as a measure of American weakness vis-à-vis the Spartan Eastern bloc. To Keyserling, the "strengthening of the free world" necessitated not only military expenditures but also what he called "the waging of peace on the economic front."[92] This effort involved not private purchases of the sort later celebrated by Eisenhower's vice president Richard Nixon in his "kitchen debate" with Khrushchev in 1959, but government spending, especially a vigorous anti-poverty program and extensive foreign aid, both of which would, he believed, mitigate the appeals of socialism.[93] In contrast to Nixon, advocates of public spending argued that laying the groundwork for a long-standing and powerful Pax Americana required public as well as private expenditures. For a time, this vision became the heart of "tough minded" midcentury liberalism, promoted by those who denounced both conservatism and "softness."[94]

By far the most popular critique of the midcentury valorization of the private over the public was Galbraith's *Affluent Society*. Late in his life, Galbraith described his 1958 book as a rejoinder to what he called the "revival of the liturgy of free enterprise." The economist observed that "people thought they were defending freedom when they kept down taxes and when they limited government spending." In response, Galbraith said that he "set out deliberately" to "reverse that train of thought" by defending robust government.[95] Less centered on the Cold War than other proponents of public spending, he diagnosed an imbalance between private and public wealth and condemned the view, fast becoming what he called "conventional wisdom," that private wants "are inherently superior to all public desires which must be paid for by taxation and with an inevitable component of compulsion."[96] Galbraith contrasted the private wealth Americans had accumulated in the postwar years with their below-standard public goods. Dismissive of popular culture, the aesthetics of commercial culture, and the "comic books, alcohol, narcotics, and switch-blade knives" that he saw proliferating, Galbraith believed that a privatized consumer culture was immoral and ignoble. Galbraith, however, was no tightwad. He did not condemn spending itself but emphasized the importance of differentiating among different types of spending.

Schlesinger, cofounder with Galbraith of Americans for Democratic Action (ADA), an organization that aimed to revive a tough-minded but public-oriented liberalism, shared this sentiment. He dismissed the Revenue Act of 1954, which transferred some $7 billion (roughly $63 billion in 2018 dollars) from public to private spending, as a shift in priorities "from schools and missiles to gadgets and gimmicks."[97] Whereas many American politicians celebrated the mass consumption of cars, suburban homes, and televisions as proof of American greatness, Schlesinger denounced the complacency and short-sightedness of this privatized vision.

Galbraith's book and the commentary of Lippmann, Schlesinger, and others catalyzed a renewed debate about the purpose of government, but it was one whose terms had already been set by free enterprise critiques of the welfare state. As influential *New York Times* columnist James Reston wrote in 1960, on the eve of a presidential election that he viewed as a referendum on public spending, this debate "raises in acute form that oldest of all American political controversies: whether the power of the Federal Government should be increased to guarantee the security of the American people, or held to a minimum to assure their freedom." Raymond J. Saulnier, chair of the Council of Economic Advisors during Eisenhower's second term, took the mission of the government to be quite straightforward: to assist the private economy to "produce things for consumers." Ike's Democratic opponents, as Reston pointed out, used the exigencies of the Cold War to argue that "the first priority in the allocation of resources must be given to the defense, growth and development of the nation rather than to the private desires of its citizens for more goods and services." Furthermore, these critics feared "materialistic subversion of the American character in this doctrine of the priority of producing things" for private use.[98]

Free enterprisers treated private consumption as a guarantor of liberty, but for a time, public spending proponents refused to cede this ground. Adlai Stevenson, the Democratic candidate for both presidential elections of the 1950s, claimed in 1960, when he was an aspirant for a third consecutive nomination, "Freedom itself has many meanings and has implied different things to different people at different times in our national life." Liberty, he argued, should not be understood only as the capacity to fulfill private wants. Indeed, he claimed, these interests could flourish only within a vibrant public sphere.

Stevenson, like many other midcentury liberals, condemned private mass consumption in the register of a snobbish and masculinist cultural conservatism, dismissing the "mediocre and sometimes intolerable consequences of unchecked private interest" that trumped "the primacy of public good." Similarly, he described the nation's new suburbs as "without shape or grace or any centered form of civic life." The cascade of private and tasteless consumption was fast overwhelming the drive for public purpose. Stevenson, highlighting the growing leverage of free enterprise thought, also lamented: "Never before in my lifetime—not even in the days of Harding and Coolidge—has the mystique of privacy seemed to me so pervasive." The celebration of private spending was dangerous because the fate of the free world depended on a moral seriousness, which Stevenson did not find in the denigration of government and celebration of the private business firm and its products. "The face which we present to the world, especially through our mass circulation media, is the face of the individual or the family as a high consumption unit with minimal social links or responsibilities—father happily drinking his favorite beer, mother dreamily fondling soft garments newly rinsed in a wonderful new detergent, the children gaily calling from the new barbecue pit for a famous sauce for their steak." Presaging Lyndon Johnson's post-materialist message in his "Great Society" speech of 1964, in which Johnson envisioned a world "where men are more concerned with the quality of their goals than the quantity of their goods," Stevenson claimed that "high private consumption is not our ultimate aim of life." That aim, in Stevenson's view, should be the collective wealth that made the country great. A high level of private consumption, he said, "does nothing to end the shame of racial discrimination. It does not counter the exorbitant cost of maintaining good health, nor conserve the nation's precious reserves of land and water and wilderness."[99]

Stevenson ended on a hopeful note, arguing that in the context of the Cold War, advocates of public spending might get the better of free enterprise arguments about the dangers of government and the virtues of private consumption.

Rather than describing public spending and national purpose as a departure from American norms, he called them a venerable tradition. "America and its government as a political instrument for the common weal is being restored once again after all the cheap sarcasm about 'bureaucracy' and 'creeping socialism,'" he said, mentioning two of the buzzwords of free enterprise critics of the New Deal.

Schlesinger shared many of Stevenson's suspicions of private consumption at a time of national crisis. Noting that the country spent $10 billion a year on advertising and less than $3.5 billion on higher education, he called for "freeing as much money as possible for public spending." Moreover, like Stevenson, he was hopeful that patriotic duty would minimize the free enterprise, red-baiting canard, what he called the "delusion—that government is somehow the enemy, and that it is better to watch national defense lag, cities rot, slums multiply, segregation persist, education decay, West Virginia miners starve, pollution spread and the Soviet Union occupy the moon than to give the Government the resources to prevent these scandals or bring them to an end." Seeking to legitimate public spending as an American capitalist ideal, rather than a socialist one, public spending advocates hoped that in post-McCarthyite America government spending would be consensually accepted as patriotic.

"Bigger Government Is the Exact Antithesis of Our Entire System"

Free enterprise logic lay at the root of the critique of the doctrine of public spending. To the extent that the American government's role is to foster consumption, critics believed, it should aim to do so in the private sphere. Public spending involved taking money from citizens better positioned to make judgments about how to spend their money and was therefore a prime example of the statist "dictation" that they abhorred.[100] In 1959, President Eisenhower claimed that the utility of private consumption outweighed that of state spending, when he said at a press conference that "our federal money will never be spent so intelligently and in so useful a fashion for the economy as will the expenditures that would be made by the private taxpayer, if he hadn't had so much of it funneled off into the federal government."[101] In this view, public spending crowded out the more fundamental act of private consumption. Ike's director of the Bureau of the Budget, Maurice H. Stans, posited a similar dichotomy: "We must not be charmed by the notion that government is a wiser manager of our economic fortunes than is private enterprise."[102] In this understanding, public spending replaced the real driver of the economy and marker of freedom, the individual consumer, and it did so with cruel condescension.

Embedded in these arguments was the free enterprise claim that government spending was not just less productive than private consumption but an assault on freedom, a form of theft that more often than not financed undeserving freeloaders and wasteful projects, and a portent of tyrannical state power. Critics of public spending drew from and modified the conservative free enterprise discourse born in reaction to the New Deal. This discourse turned far more on internal subversion than on the Cold War with communism. Socialism was far more likely to emerge from well-meaning but dangerous policies—indeed, they feared, it already was emerging. As the economist Barbara Ward summarized the critique of public spending in 1960, "If we permit government at home to spend more, we shall so increase its encroachments on personal liberty that we will simply become totalitarians by another route. Why fight the Russian dictatorship by means that might create a dictatorship at home?" As Ward noted, critics depicted all forms of public spending as a symbol of "Big Government."[103] Notwithstanding the optimism of Stevenson and Schlesinger that such hysteria would no longer be effective in the era of the Cold War crisis, politicians and intellectuals needed to respond to the fear that public spending was tantamount to unfreedom, whether known as socialism or liberalism.

Such slippery-slope logic had been the essence of free enterprise rhetoric since the 1920s. A hallmark of the modern conservative movement, especially since the 1970s, has been to demonize government as an incompetent, and often corrupt, guardian of the public welfare. This critique of government has extended to federal regulation and legislation, but it has primarily centered on the power of the purse.[104] The attempt to shrink government capacity altogether—to "starve the beast"—has involved a multifaceted dismissal of the state's fiscal policies.[105] Primary among such arguments has been the view that active government is itself anti-American. Edwin Dale wrote in 1960, summarizing the fears, "Bigger and bigger government is the exact antithesis of our entire system, and damaging to our economy as well."[106] Government was, in this view, the enemy rather than the ally of free enterprise.

A Federal Colossus

Employing the binary language typical of free enterprise discourse, critics of public spending described basic functions of governing as inherently dangerous. Eventually, free enterprise common sense, which depicted taxation as larceny, public spending as wasteful, and both as possible mechanisms of totalitarianism, gained an increasing hold on public opinion, especially in the 1970s. Long before the dying days of New Deal liberalism, however, free enterprisers succeeded in framing many forms of government spending as undeserved, unaffordable, and immoral "entitlements."

Edwin Dale, the reporter who narrated the rise of the public spending debate during the Eisenhower and Kennedy administrations, also chronicled its decline. By 1966, he proclaimed the era of public spending to be over.[107] In the early 1970s, his economics beat shifted from a focus on debates about the virtues of government spending to the necessity of cutbacks. In an article written toward the end of his tenure with the *Times* in 1974, Dale quoted Gerald Ford's treasury secretary William E. Simon, who described the budget as an out-of-control "juggernaut." Dale highlighted the bipartisan consensus about the need to get a "handle on entitlement programs."[108] The latter phrase was novel: only in the recent past had earned benefits begun to be referred to as "entitlements."[109] (In 1975, Daniel Bell, who had defended public spending in the early 1960s, diagnosed a "revolution of rising entitlements" that was making even liberals "suspicious of government and planning" and leading to increasing confidence in the "market mechanism.")[110] After leaving the *Times*, Dale became the spokesperson for David A. Stockman, director of the Office of Management and Budget in the first Reagan administration, and thus went from explaining the salience of public spending in the 1950s and 1960s to justifying reductions in "programs of entitlement" (what his boss, Ronald Reagan, called "extravagant spending") in the 1980s.[111] This marked the beginning of the denigration of collective goods as "entitlements" that became central to neoliberalism (in this signification, not pro–New Deal, but pro–liberated markets and public austerity) in the following decades. In this period, Pete Peterson and other business executives were lionized in bipartisan fashion for their fight against deficit spending and "entitlement spending." From the 1980s through the early 2000s, Peterson's alarmist books about "entitlement spending," "crushing debt," and the "coming social security crisis" framed the stark political choice: austerity or national self-destruction.[112]

Although contemporary critics targeted the Eisenhower administration for its privileging of private over public, in the twenty-first century commentators celebrated the 1950s as the high point of American faith in public spending projects.[113] Public spending advocates of that decade would likely be surprised that Ike was later held up as an exemplar of public-oriented spending, given how they pummeled him at the time. They criticized what the free enterprisers celebrated: high levels of private consumption and an insufficiently robust program of public spending.

The period from the Eisenhower through the Johnson administrations turned out also to be the last era of the twentieth century in which nonmilitary government spending proved politically popular. Notwithstanding his supposed "allergy" to public spending, Dwight Eisenhower defended his administration's record on this front in his final inaugural address when he boasted of having "increased public expenditures to keep abreast of the needs of a growing population and its attendant new problems, as well as our added international responsibilities."[114] There were fewer countervailing pressures during the period that historian Sean Wilentz has called "the age of Reagan," when most forms of nonmilitary or noncarceral public spending were deemed antithetical to the American spirit.[115] Between 1983 and 2008, the imbalance between private and public spending, according to one analyst, "entered a new and even extreme phase." Galbraith's paradox of private wealth and public squalor had not only intensified but become an "absurdity."[116]

In the second decade of the twenty-first century, popular support for investment in infrastructure and other public goods emerged again.[117] A popular consensus held that the nation's highways, airports, energy grid, and mass transit were in desperate need of modernization, that policies should be implemented to combat global warming and other environmental crises, and that the United States lagged behind other countries in green technology.[118] Although as candidates, Democratic politicians such as Bill Clinton and Barack Obama and the Republican Donald J. Trump all emphasized the value of government spending—with Clinton describing an $80 billion infrastructure plan as his "first priority," Obama promising "the largest public works construction program since the inception of the interstate highway system a half century ago," and Trump vowing on election night in 2016 to "rebuild our highways, bridges, tunnels, airports, schools, and hospitals"—as presidents none of them made it a top priority.[119] Obama emphasized the importance of strategic investments and promoted a large stimulus to combat a dangerous recession. But he also spoke of the need for government "belt tightening" and in 2010 created the National Commission on Fiscal Responsibility and Reform (called Simpson-Bowles after its co-chairs Alan Simpson and Erskine Bowles), whose focus was spending cuts, to solve what many believed to be a looming fiscal crisis.[120] Despite the booming economy that followed the tax increases on the wealthy enacted during the Clinton and Obama administrations, faith in tax cuts as an engine of economic growth remained popular among the political class, at least until the unpopular Republican tax cuts of 2017, which favored corporations and the wealthy.[121]

The rejection of government spending was, it must be noted, more rhetorical than real, as actual spending did not decrease. The vast majority of federal increases, however, consisted of maintaining safety net programs and massive increases in defense, policing, and prisons, not expanding social welfare or modernizing infrastructure. Commentators have frequently noted the hypocrisy of the celebration of minimal government alongside the tremendous demands on government made by the American people and largely supported by politicians.

Alongside a challenge to the regulatory state came a rejection of the idea that collective consumption goods were a category that government should care about at all. Despite periodic claims that the United States had entered into what Obama said in his 2011 State of the Union address was "our generation's Sputnik Moment," in which, for the national good, a robust public spending plan was necessary, no signature plan on the order of the Eisenhower/Kennedy era space program emerged.[122] Bill Clinton's call for an "information superhighway" did not inspire a public spending renaissance. Indeed, his view that "the era of big government is over" made such inspiring programs seem anachronistic. As columnist Walter Shapiro wrote in 2001, Clinton "almost never directly challenged the Reaganites' view that the government that governs best governs least."[123]

In the long run, taxpayerism proved to be a more potent political force than public spending, even when its benefits were skewed toward the wealthy minority of the population. Whereas FDR called tax avoidance "unethical and contrary to the spirit of law," those who condemned "wasteful spending" by government saw it as an obligation.[124] By the twenty-first century, it became almost de rigueur for Republican candidates to equate their personal desire to pay as little in taxes as possible with political virtue. "I pay all the taxes that are legally required and not a dollar more," said Mitt Romney in January 2012, shortly before he captured the Republican presidential nomination. "I don't think you want someone as the candidate for president who pays more taxes than he owes."[125] In January 2016, Donald Trump, soon to be the Republican nominee, boasted: "I pay as little as possible. I use every single thing in the book."[126] Both Romney and Trump not only highlighted their efforts to minimize their tax payments but equated personal tax avoidance with patriotism.

The free enterprise case against government spending thus proved a formidable challenge for those seeking to justify the public sphere.[127] Republicans described the Obama administration as undermining free enterprise by, as governor of Virginia Bob McDonnell said in his 2010 response to the president's State of the Union address, "over-regulating," "overtaxing," and engaging in "massive new spending."[128] In 2012, Republican residential candidate Romney accused Obama of putting "free enterprise on trial," largely on the basis of the expansion of social provisions under the Affordable Care Act.[129]

The cumulative impact of the attack on spending was to denigrate public goods as a form of theft that led to the loss of personal freedom.[130] As an alternative, free enterprisers celebrated business autonomy, private consumption, low rates of taxation, and unregulated markets, all of which they associated with freedom. By the late twentieth century, this set of beliefs, sometimes called "neoliberalism," had become common sense, embraced in largely bipartisan fashion until the economic crash of the early twenty-first century briefly forced even conservative business leaders to question free enterprise verities.[131]

Epilogue

IN 1978, MIDWAY THROUGH THE FIFTH and final Democratic presidency of the "New Deal order," Patrick J. Buchanan, conservative columnist and former Nixon speechwriter, claimed that for the first time since FDR's election, "the locus of intellectual ferment, the action in national politics, is within the Republican Party." Buchanan attributed this state of affairs to the "intellectual exhaustion of liberalism." The only example of the newly energized Republican attack on "conventional wisdom" that Buchanan mentioned, however, was a series of proposals for tax cuts, long a staple of the free enterprise opposition to the New Deal.[1] The ferment could be attributed less to new ideas than to a sense not just among Republicans but among many Democrats that the New Deal order was on its last legs. New Deal ideals were succumbing to those of free enterprisers.

One year earlier, the argument of a letter writer to the *Chicago Tribune* gave texture to Buchanan's observations by putting them in historical perspective. "After 45 years of liberalism, what have we got?" asked George W. Fyler, an electrical engineer in his sixties who published many letters to the editor in the 1970s and 1980s. His assessment was damning. In Fyler's view, New Deal liberalism, now well past its sell-by date, punished rather than supported business leaders and productive citizens, not only the groups most responsible for economic growth but the most authentic Americans. "The businesses which have built America and provided jobs and the overburdened taxpayer have been victimized by Democratic liberalism," he wrote. In contrast, this liberalism had emboldened three undeserving types—"union monopolists, welfare freeloaders, and political jobholders"—to whom the government unjustly redistributed wealth and power by taxing the productive fruits of businesses and taxpayers. Summing up this liberalism, which had reigned since the start of the New Deal, Fyler wrote: "Democratic Party liberalism is against capitalism, business, profits and free enterprise, and for tax-and-spend, inflation, welfare waste, and governmental bureaucracy and controls, permissiveness, unbalanced budgets, and escalating debts—all leading inevitably to social and economic collapse." This was an expansive list. In Fyler's view, "liberalism" was not merely a suboptimal set of policies—it was a system inimical to American values.[2]

Fyler pitted the virtues of free enterprise against threats to that system and, following a long tradition that this book has traced, named those dangers "liberalism." These threats, the poison fruits of an unjust long-term New Deal regime, were dangerous not just economically (excessive spending, inflation, debt) and politically (bureaucrats and controls) but morally and ethically (promoting "permissiveness") as well. Moreover, they pointed the way toward civilizational "collapse," one that had been predicted by free enterprise critics since the first days of the New Deal. By the time Fyler set pen to paper, free enterprise had long been a favored expression because it had come to stand for the multifaceted battle against liberalism in the simultaneous registers of economics, politics, and morality. Fyler, as his list suggests, distinguished between free enterprise and capitalism; although he did not spell out the nature of the differences between the two, for many advocates, the free enterprise "system" was the more encompassing idea because it provided both the economic and the cultural wherewithal to combat a misbegotten liberalism.

Fyler's letter came toward the end of a multidecade battle against the New Deal fought in the name of free enterprise. His binary perspective was not new. Like many other critics before him, he understood economic policies with which he disagreed as having catastrophic social and political consequences. His cast included good guys who stood for American traditions (business leaders, taxpayers) and bad guys who undermined them (trade unionists, welfare recipients, and bureaucrats). The former, the living heartbeat of the nation, stood arrayed against the state; the latter, beneficiaries of a powerful but perverse state, aligned in sync with it. Fyler was voicing the perspective, expressed by a letter writer to the *Burlington Free Press* in 1972, that the "average American is fed up with Liberalism, Socialism, Welfarism," and that these three *isms* were interchangeable.[3] This was an old image. As early as 1936, commentators described opponents of the New Deal as "fed up on liberalism." The Republican slogan during the campaign season of 1946, "Had enough?" had a similar connotation, the suggestion being that New Deal liberalism had gone too far and that a backlash was in effect.[4]

By August 1977, when Fyler felt compelled to post his letter, the reign of what he called the "liberal Democrats" was coming to an end. Jimmy Carter, the Democrat who had become president earlier that year, rejected the label, which had already become something of an epithet.[5] (The denigration of liberalism reached its apogee in the following decade, when George H. W. Bush, Republican candidate for the presidency in 1988, labeled opponent Michael Dukakis as a liberal "out of step with the political mainstream," as if this label, which Dukakis disclaimed throughout most of the campaign, were reason enough to disqualify a candidate for political office.)[6] There were many reasons for the collapse of what historians have come to call the age of the "liberal consensus," or the "New Deal order."[7] One important reason was the rhetorical power of the idea of the "free enterprise system," which promised a comforting return to American traditions and a rejection of the dangerous forces that Fyler enumerated and called products of liberalism.

The phrase at the heart of anti–New Deal liberalism efforts, *free enterprise*, is disarming: uncomplicated, easy to take for granted, and a symbol, for its proponents, of a liberated, even utopian, society. In taking the meaning of "free enterprise" for granted, we have misunderstood its import, flattened its history, and underestimated its breadth.

The history of free enterprise as a constant foil for the New Deal order challenges the commonly held view that, as one scholar has recently put it, "the Roosevelt vision of a powerful federal government—one that intervened aggressively in the economy to insure a measure of basic opportunity and security for all—reigned unchallenged" until the election of Ronald Reagan.[8] A counter-history of the New Deal, with free enterprise at the center, suggests that it was far from hegemonic, even at its peak. If Gary Gerstle is correct in claiming that the "power of a political order" can be measured by "its ability to shape the thinking of its opponents," then the New Deal order must be viewed as partial and incomplete, even when it "was riding high."[9] Free enterprise was a critical, slowly gestating building block of what became known as the conservative revolution of the late twentieth century. At the same time, the conservative turn that began with the election of Ronald Reagan for the presidency in 1980 remained far from an era of unalloyed free enterprise triumph. Despite the undoubted ex-

pansion of "neoliberal" ideas—and this version of neoliberalism, unlike the earlier iteration, implied not an expansion of the welfare state but its demolition—
much of the architecture of the New Deal order survived under Reagan and the
Bushes and even expanded under Clinton and Obama. Yet free enterprise discourse "won" in many ways, especially in supplying the dominant language of
politics that even Democrats felt the need to wrestle with (and sometimes even
employ) when they maintained the majority in Congress.

In the wake of the 2016 Republican electoral victory, at a moment that could be
seen as the apex of conservative triumph, the language of free enterprise appeared, by some measures, to be on the wane. In that election, the GOP captured the presidency, the House, and the Senate, a level of power it had achieved
only twice before since the start of the New Deal, in 1953–54 and 2003–6. That
the century-long era of free enterprise appeared to be ebbing may have had
more to do with a shift in the position of its putative advocates rather than of its
critics.

Given how the term has evolved, it may not be surprising that Bernie Sanders, the self-described democratic socialist senator from Vermont, said, "I personally happen not to be a great believer in the free-enterprise system for many
reasons." The fact that the conservative magazine *Forbes* called the push led
by Sanders and many Democrats for single-payer health care "the most radical
departure from 230 years of Adam Smith–inspired free enterprise capitalism in
American history" represents continuity with the conservative tradition of free
enterprise that became dominant in the twentieth century. So too did President
Barack Obama's largely ineffectual efforts to reclaim the term from conservatives.[10] Democratic presidents, civil rights activists, and some labor leaders since
Franklin D. Roosevelt had similarly tried and largely failed.

What was noteworthy, starting with the so-called Tea Party rebellion in 2010
and accelerating with Donald Trump's campaign for the presidency beginning
in 2015, was the seeming abandonment of the term by many figures on the right.
In spite of its continued use by the likes of the American Enterprise Institute's
Arthur Brooks and Paul Ryan, the Speaker of the House from 2015 to 2019, the
so-called populist turn in the GOP seemingly left little room for the celebration
of free enterprise as that term had been defined for much of the previous century.[11] Indeed, the phrase *free enterprise* was less central to Donald Trump's
campaign and administration than to those of any Republican president or pres-

idential candidate since the nineteenth century. Trump rarely used the phrase, in striking contrast to every major Republican politician and most conservative thought leaders since the New Deal.[12] Unlike Ronald Reagan or Leonard Read, Trump did not celebrate the "magic" of the free market or preach the need for "faith" in the free enterprise system.

Beyond Trump himself, leaders of the broader "populist" antiestablishment turn in conservatism rarely invoked "free enterprise" in worshipful tones either. Although the phrase appeared twice in the 2016 Republican platform, the references were less frequent and less central than in any previous GOP statements of principle since 1932. The 2012 GOP platform, by contrast, invoked the "proven values of the American free enterprise system" on its opening page, the first of seven celebratory mentions.[13] While Senator Marco Rubio never said of Trump, as he did of President Obama, that he "doesn't believe in free enterprise," he and other Republican candidates who sought the Republican nomination in 2016 tried to position themselves as more vigorously in favor of "reversing all that damage" caused by "big government" Obamaism.[14] Donald Trump made it his mission to undo President Obama's achievements, to be sure. Yet the man who won the presidency in 2016, and many of his followers, treated the government less as an "umpire" and the market less as an abstract arena for the performance of miracles than as a mode to reward friends and undermine enemies. He and his allies willingly used state authority to help their favored groups and to punish those they opposed, whether refugees, undocumented immigrants, residents of Democratic-leaning states, or organized labor. When politicians employed state power in 2014 to help defeat a union vote at the Volkswagen plant in Tennessee, one commentator claimed, "The Republican interference in a private business is sheer hypocrisy when they claim to be champions of free enterprise and oppose government interference with business."[15]

Trump's conservative critics took note of his seeming lack of faith in free enterprise. When Republican Arizona senator Jeff Flake denounced President Trump on the Senate floor in October 2017, he claimed that Trumpism marked a retreat from the free enterprise agenda. "It is clear at this moment that a traditional conservative who believes in limited government and free markets, who is devoted to free trade, and who is pro-immigration, has a narrower and narrower path to nomination in the Republican party—the party that for so long has defined itself by belief in those things. It is also clear to me for the moment we have given in or given up on those core principles in favor of the more viscerally satisfying anger and resentment."[16] William Kristol criticized Trump on similar grounds in late 2017, claiming that the president had "done little to advance key principles such as free markets." Kristol noted, "It looks more like he's doing favors for his buddies in the business world than doing something driven by conservative principles."[17]

Shortly after Election Day in 2016, the *Economic Policy Journal* ran an article titled "Does Donald Trump Believe in Free Enterprise?" For those on the right, it had not been necessary to ask this question about any previous Republican candidate in the last century. Author Michael S. Rozeff asked, "Has Trump ever given the slightest indication that he supports free enterprise in labor markets?" The question was rhetorical and his answer was clear: "Far from it." In the immediate aftermath of the election, another conservative columnist, Josh Hammer, condemned Trump for "his gallingly cronyist strong-arming of Carrier," a reference to the air-conditioner manufacturer that Trump urged to avoid laying off American workers, and for "planning an infrastructure splurge so massive it might make FDR blush."[18] The fear expressed by conservatives was not that Trump exhibited poor salesmanship but the more fundamental concern that he lacked faith in free enterprise.

From the onset of his campaign, Trump blatantly used his political efforts to enrich his business, and his relatives and cronies unapologetically did the same. Shortly after he took office, he ordered a senior staffer to advertise his daughter Ivanka's apparel in a news segment on national television. The managers of the family real estate business of Jared Kushner, Ivanka's husband, continued to try to ink lucrative deals with China. Trump's sons bragged about how the presidency had boosted the footprint of the Trump Corporation. Columnists highlighted his "contempt for the free market" and have decreed that Trumpism is leaving "free enterprise . . . in peril."[19]

This is not a new criticism of the developer-turned-reality-star-turned-politician. From the beginning of his career, Donald Trump unashamedly used government and underworld connections to build his real estate empire. As Al Rodbell, one neighbor, complained during Trump's reconstruction of the Plaza Hotel in the 1990s, "If he hits a market slump and the apartments don't sell, taxpayers ante up, and he still actually makes a profit; if he catches a boom, then it's goodbye taxpayers and hooray for 'free enterprise.'"[20] Although Christopher Lehmann-Haupt, reviewing Trump's ghostwritten 1987 best seller *The Art of the Deal*, wrote that Trump "is proud to be at play in the fields of American free enterprise," the second part of his sentence seemed to invalidate the claim: Trump looks "for every loophole in the law and edge on his competitors he can get."[21] Trump's economic worldview was not of the anonymous, miraculous, communal market celebrated in Read's "I, Pencil," which downplayed the power not just of the business firm but of business leaders. Nor was it Lewis Powell's free enterprise vision of corporate citizenship and pluralism. For Trump, heroism inhered not in the frictionless market but in the connections and power that enabled him and other like-minded businessmen (and in Trump's masculinist vision, they were almost always men) to impose their will on others.

Guardian columnist George Monbiot argued in 2016 that Trump's election marked the culmination of a "neoliberal" historical moment that began in the late twentieth century with Thatcherism in the United Kingdom and Reaganism in the United States. It was a situation, as he describes it, in which "the market would discover a natural hierarchy of winners and losers, creating a more efficient system than could ever be devised through planning or by design."[22] What Monbiot calls neoliberalism and traces to Hayek can also be called free enterprise and followed, as this book has done, back to the 1920s. Yet Trump rarely stressed the efficiency or the wonders of markets. He was also unafraid to highlight the power of the state (albeit often by praising its punitive functions) in a way that conservatives had routinely done, but not celebrated at the level of rhetoric.[23] As the stock market declined precipitously toward the end of 2018, Trump blamed the Federal Reserve Board for the downturn and criticized that body for lacking a necessary "feel for the market," which he connected not to the natural workings of the price mechanism but to government policies like "trade wars," a strong dollar, and a border wall.[24]

Free enterprise ideology, however, was never limited to the worship of unencumbered free markets. Indeed, the "anger and resentment" that Flake identified as a recent divergence from the party's economic vision cannot easily be separated from the broader free enterprise message. In the spring of 1943, Frank Birch, a Milwaukee advertising executive, addressed a joint luncheon meeting of the Lions and Optimists Club. The tone of his lecture, "What Makes America Great," was hardly bullish, in spite of his putatively hopeful audience. Birch laced what a newspaper described as his "absorbing talk on free enterprise" with nostalgia and fear. "We must not forget that there are people who would change, tear down, and destroy these principles, and we must fight to preserve what we have," he warned in the climax of his talk, after a brief summation of the economic miracles at one time produced by the free enterprise system. Although the nation was at war against global fascism, Birch, like other free enterprisers, identified the enemy as internal. There were "men in state capitals [and] Washington who are trying to take free enterprise away from us," he cautioned. Notwithstanding the desires of the bureaucrats, Birch held, "There must be no ceiling on rewards for private business."[25] Birch measured American greatness in proportion to free enterprise's strength. He feared that enemies in the nation's midst—in prominent positions in federal and state government, empowered by the war—were bent on weakening that system.

Birch's speech, down to its title, presaged Trumpism, and it did so in the language of free enterprise. This suggests that even though Trump eschewed the phrase, he imbibed much of its belligerent tone and message of grievance. Trumpism can be seen as an amplification of the broader cultural and psychological elements that have been central to free enterprise discourse since the term was reformulated in the 1920s. "This is not simply another four-year election," proclaimed Trump on the eve of the 2016 presidential election. "This is a crossroads in the history of civilization that will determine whether we the people reclaim control over government." This was a pitch-perfect invocation of the apocalyptic stand of free enterprise discourse. It was also a specimen of elite victimization made pungent by the fact that he gave this speech shortly after the release of a videotape showing him bragging about sexually assaulting women.[26] Moreover, the nostalgia at the core of Trumpism paralleled not just Birch's speech but the broader free enterprise discourse by referring back to a mythical time when America "was great" and demanding a counterrevolution of sorts to restore past glories. New York congressman John J. Faso followed this pattern of employing the phrase as a weapon in the culture wars when in 2018 he claimed that his Democratic opponent Antonio Delgado had "denigrated our free enterprise system" in a rap recording he had made many years before.[27]

It could be argued, therefore, that Donald Trump disregarded the economic scaffolding of free enterprise discourse while amplifying its characteristic temperament of elite victimization. Trump eschewed the Reaganesque celebration of the "miracle" of the free enterprise system, but he viewed wealth as a measure of human worth and not only maintained but extended the rhetoric of cataclysm, internal enemies, and danger. In his inaugural address in 2017, Trump did not mention "free enterprise" or its sister concept of the "American Way" but, in the free enterprise tradition of highlighting the injury done to ordinary taxpayers, he did empathize with "the forgotten men and women of our country" who were, he claimed, subject to "American Carnage."[28] Yet the signature accomplishment of the first years of Trump's presidency was a tax cut for the wealthy, revealing once again that a rhetoric of grievance was not inconsistent with conservative economic policy.[29]

The death of free enterprise has been predicted many times in the past—always, it turns out, prematurely. But the political era of Donald Trump may leave an opening for versions of free enterprise that have been crowded out by the ill-defined but hegemonic version celebrated by DeWitt Emery and his cohort. One possible response to Trumpism might be a revival of a left-leaning free enterprise discourse. This version can be traced back to the anti-monopoly and the antitrust tradition, to people like Robert Jackson, Estes Kefauver, and Ralph Nader but also, as we have seen, to labor leaders like Walter Reuther and civil rights heroes like Martin Luther King Jr. With the conservative version in eclipse due to the weakening of the opposition that it has always depended upon and the rise of a new Republican/populist coalition, perhaps this alternative version will become a new political common sense.[30]

It is more likely, however, that a post-Trump conservatism will return to the free enterprisers' language that worked effectively in opposition to the New Deal order and as a symbol of their governing strategy once in power. We should not rule out the possibility of a conservative free enterprise revival, one marked, as it has been in the past, by the highlighting of this vague, enduring, and talismanic symbol of a "system" in which corporate freedom is celebrated as people power, and in which governance is looked upon with deep suspicion.

The language of free enterprise that emerged in opposition to the New Deal has been a political success story. Even in defeat, it fundamentally shaped American political culture.[31] The free enterprisers' success, however, has come at a cost. By turning debates about policy into condemnations of government itself, free enterprise advocates contributed to a narrowing of the range of economic debates in the United States. For several generations advocates of free enterprise worked to preempt that discussion with their either/or worldview, their "sky is falling" rhetoric, and their pervasive mislabeling of progressive reform as nascent totalitarianism. As economic historian Karl Polanyi observed in 1944 in *The Great Transformation*, the book he wrote while in the United States during the previous two years when these issues were at play not only in a global military conflict but also, as we have seen, in the fear that the wartime government in the United States was dangerously amassing power, such a world-view narrowed conceptions of freedom. Polanyi noted near the close of his book that government planning and regulation are "attacked as a denial of freedom" and, as a consequence, "freedom thus degenerates into a mere advocacy of free enterprise."[32]

The free enterprise vision depicted a large number of economic matters—shaped by the interests of elites, corporations, and the governments that they have often controlled—as "natural" and therefore off-limits to "artificial" political solutions. Adherents have viewed capitalism as the embodiment of a system—the "free enterprise system"—whose existence is endangered by the recognition that it is constructed, not natural. Any effort to regulate it means recognizing at a fundamental level that "the economy" is a political project. To accept that capitalism's worst excesses can and should be redressed is to acknowledge that economic and political flourishing requires government intervention—the use of the power of the state to shield workers, consumers, and their environment from the storm gusts of the market. It is to highlight the hypocrisy of business conservatives who have condemned government in the abstract while endorsing many of the most potent forms of modern state power, such as mass incarceration and military spending, that have shaped modern capitalism far more than the free market they celebrate. It is also to challenge the view that political freedom is best embodied by unrestrained capitalism, and to insist that democracy requires a state strong enough to regulate and sometimes displace capitalists. In short, it is to question the view that freedom, justice, and prosperity are best achieved through faith in free enterprise alone.

NOTES

Introduction

1. "Worshipping Two Gods; or, The Free Enterprise System," *Des Moines Register*, Feb 28, 1940, 6.
2. "Mills Fears for Country," *Los Angeles Times*, Jun 3, 1936, 6.
3. "Worshipping Two Gods," *Des Moines Register,* Feb 29, 1940, 8.
4. Samuel B. Pettengill, *Smoke Screen* (New York: Southern, 1940), 94. The second quotation is from an ad for Pettengill's book that appeared in the *New York Herald Tribune*, Sep 29, 1940, H11.
5. Oscar Handlin, "Laissez-Faire Thought in Massachusetts, 1790–1880," in "The Tasks of Economic History," Supplement, *Journal of Economic History* 3 (Dec 1943): 55. In the same issue see Louis Hartz, "Laissez-Faire Thought in Pennsylvania, 1776–1860," 66–77. Samuel Eliot Morison made much the same point in "What Free Enterprise?" *Boston Globe*, Jul 10, 1965, 4. Lawrence Fertig, "Johnny Learns in College Economics of Fusfield's Idea of Free Enterprise Myth," *Amarillo Globe-Times*, Jan 3, 1964, 3. In the same year, historian Rowland Berthoff noted that "there is very little historical evidence" for the American tradition of free enterprise. "When the U.S. Had Free Enterprise: Talk of a Return to a 'Golden Age' Is Unrealistic, History Professor Says," *St. Louis Post-Dispatch*, Oct 20, 1964, 26. For an expression of the myth that I seek to debunk, itself written as if it were challenging falsehoods, see Arthur Brooks, "Five Myths about Free Enterprise," *Washington Post*, Jul 13, 2012, B2.
6. Roy Kidwell, "Ignore Big Oil's Free Enterprise Myth," *Hartford Courant*, Sep 19, 1979, 20.
7. James Marlow, "Free Enterprise Myth?" *Abilene Reporter-News*, Sep 3, 1965, 28. He also wrote, "Free enterprise has been an American myth since the first Congress in 1789 passed the first tariff act to protect businessmen and farmers from the competition of foreign goods." "Free Enterprise Myth Is Being Revived Again," *Great Bend Tribune*, Feb 24, 1958, 4. See also Carl Rowan, "When Will We Drop the 'Free Enterprise Myth'?" *Rochester Democrat and Chronicle*, Aug 8, 1977, 8.

8. Henry Hazlitt, "The Ideological War," *Newsweek*, Jun 20, 1949, in *Business Tides: The Newsweek Era of Henry Hazlitt* (Auburn, AL: Ludwig von Mises Institute, 2011), 130–31.

9. Ad for First National Bank, *Baltimore Sun*, Nov 7, 1944, 24.

10. "Rotary Hears Address of Labor," *Hattiesburg American*, Sep 4, 1945, 9.

11. "G.O.P. Urged to Right New Deal: Ogden Mills Seeks Platform Based on 'Free Men, Free Enterprise,'" *Indianapolis News*, May 9, 1935, 7.

12. Harry H. Rosen, "Footnote on Free Enterprise," *Rotarian* (Jul 1944): 2. George Charles Roche, the president of Hillsdale College, wrote, that "America has prospered when it followed its faith in free enterprise." "The Real American Revolution," *Freeman*, Jul 1, 1973, http://fee.org/freeman/detail/the-real-american-revolution.

13. "Senator Willis Upholds Faith in Americanism," *Steuben Republican*, May 19, 1943, 2.

14. Ronald Reagan, "What Ever Happened to Free Enterprise?" Nov 10, 1977, http://www.americanrhetoric.com/speeches/ronaldreaganhillsdalecollege.htm.

15. "Sharpe Will Fight Legislature Again," *Sioux Falls Argus-Leader*, May 22, 1946, 14.

16. Russell Varney, the head of public relations for Standard Brands, Inc., quoted in "Re-elected Head of Baker's Group," *Baltimore Sun*, Jan 22, 1941, 12.

17. Steve Fraser and Gary Gerstle, eds., *The Rise and Fall of the New Deal Order, 1930–1980* (Princeton: Princeton University Press, 1989).

18. Samuel B. Pettengill, "Wake-Up America," *Pampa Daily News*, Apr 27, 1944, 10.

19. Robert Shogan, *Backlash: The Killing of the New Deal* (Chicago: Ivan R. Dee, 2006). Eric Rauchway, "The New Deal Was on the Ballot in 1932," *Modern American History* (2019): 1–13.

20. Bliven is quoted in *Wake Up America*, 2nd ser., program 26, *What Is Free Enterprise?* part 1 (New York: Radio-Recording Division, National Broadcasting Company, 1943). The recording is available at the Marr Sound Archives, Nichols Library, University of Missouri, Kansas City. Quinn Slobodian argues that early European "neoliberals" did not seek a free market but rather institutions to "encase" markets from democratic control. *Globalists: The End of Empire and the Birth of Neoliberalism* (Cambridge, MA: Harvard University Press, 2018), 2.

21. Andrew Jackson, "President's Message," *Adams Sentinel*, Dec 11, 1832, 4.

22. James J. Curry, "Letters to the Editor," *Pittsburgh Press*, Jul 9, 1946, 10.

23. R. C. Hoiles, "Economist Writes N.A.M. President on Meaning of Free Enterprise," *Pampa Daily News*, Feb 26, 1947, 6.

24. "Local Businessmen," *Klamath Falls Herald and News*, Jul 7, 1958, 10.

25. "Dr. Glenn Frank's First Try," *St. Louis Star and Times*, Jan 14, 1938, 16.

26. "Fredonia Memorial Services Held in Forest Hill Cemetery," *Dunkirk Evening Observer*, May 31, 1940, 17.

27. "Bankers Report Free Enterprise Is Disappearing," *Canandaigua Daily Messenger*, Dec 12, 1940, 1.

28. "Willkie Would Revamp Taxes: Tells Grand Rapids Audience New Deal Is Killing Free Enterprise," *York Gazette and Daily*, Oct 2, 1940, 14.

29. "Grade Labeling Called Danger to All Industry: Maxon Says Canned-Goods Plan Is Step in Killing Free Enterprise in U.S.," *New York Herald Tribune*, Nov 24, 1943, 23.

30. "Sen. Davis Hits Lack of Foreign Policy; Declares FDR Killing Free Enterprise," *Franklin News-Herald*, Oct 27, 1944, 2.

31. "Speakers Meet at Wood River: Toastmasters Discuss Free Enterprise," *Alton Evening Telegraph*, Nov 17, 1949, 11.

32. James Marlow, "Marlow Explains Background of American Free Enterprise," *Sheboygan Press*, Nov 26, 1948, 3.

33. Donald I. Rogers, "There Goes Free Enterprise: Socialism Is Hovering over Our Shoulders," *Vital Speeches of the Day*, Dec 15, 1962, 131.

34. "Crusade Is Urged for Enterprise," *New York Times*, Dec 14, 1940, 10.

35. "Are You Willing to Be Shackled?" *American Builder*, Oct 1, 1954, 26.

36. Frank R. Kent, "The Real Dictatorship Threat," *Louisville Courier-Journal*, Oct 28, 1936, 6. On the internal threat, see Kevin M. Kruse, *One Nation under God: How Corporate America Invented Christian America* (New York: Basic Books, 2015), 22.

37. Ruth Alexander, "What Price the Welfare State? Government—the Guardian or Master?" *Vital Speeches of the Day*, Jan 15, 1952, 199.

38. E. F. Scoutten, "The American Free Enterprise System: The Welfare State," *Vital Speeches of the Day*, Feb 15, 1964, 269–73.

39. "'Political Miracle Man,'" *Danville Advocate-Messenger*, Jun 30, 1940, 4.

40. James R. Dickenson, "Reagan Running against the Clock," *Santa Rosa Press Democrat*, Nov 1, 1978, 29.

41. Alexander, "What Price the Welfare State?" 199.

42. "Private Sector Needs Fund to Defend Itself," *Reading Eagle*, Dec 6, 1976, 29.

43. Walter Trohan, "Two Powerful Appeals for Guarding Our Liberty," *Chicago Tribune*, Oct 5, 1952, B2.

44. Daniel Bell, "America's Un-Marxist Revolution: Mr. Truman Embarks on a Politically Managed Economy," *Commentary*, Mar 1, 1949, 213.

45. "The Challenge to Free Enterprise," address by W. P. Gullander, President, NAM, before the 16th Annual Conference of the Public Relations Society of America, Inc., on Monday, Nov 18, 1963, San Francisco, CA, series 1, box 67, Free Enterprise File, "Free Enterprise, General, 1951–63," Manuscripts and Archives Department, Hagley Museum and Library, Wilmington, DE. See also "Sell Free Enterprise, PR Conference Told," *Pasadena Independent*, Nov 19, 1963, 23.

46. "Vandenberg for Two-Price Crop Systems," *Washington Post*, Oct 12, 1938, 2.

47. "Taft Says Some Proposed Bills Reflect Socialist Feeling," *Dayton Journal Herald*, Oct 14, 1949, 17; Frank W. Klineberg, "Free Enterprise: A Historical View," *Los Angeles Times*, Jan 8, 1956, B5.

48. Lewis F. Powell Jr., "Attack on American Free Enterprise System," Aug 23, 1971. http://law2.wlu.edu/powellarchives/page.asp?pageid=1251.

49. Ronald Reagan, "First Conservative Political Action Conference," Jan 25, 1974, in *The Last Best Hope: The Greatest Speeches of Ronald Reagan* (West Palm Beach: Humanix Books, 2016), 26.

50. Sean Wilentz, *The Age of Reagan: A History, 1974–2008* (New York: Harper Collins, 2008).

51. Sophia Rosenfeld, "Beware of Republicans Bearing *Common Sense*," *Washington Post*,

Apr 4, 2011, B1, 4. See also her important book *Common Sense: A Political History* (Cambridge, MA: Harvard University Press, 2011).

52. William Brock, "Letter from the Publisher," *Common Sense: A Republican Journal of Thought and Opinion* (Summer 1978): iii–iv.

53. David Treadwell, "It's Altering Economic, Political Thinking," *Los Angeles Times*, Aug 24, 1984, B4.

54. Daniel Patrick Moynihan, "Of 'Sons' and Their 'Grandsons,'" *New York Times*, Jul 7, 1980, A15; "Democrats May Face Battle over Chairman's Post," *San Bernardino Sun*, Nov 12, 1980, 3. Even at the time, several critics noted that the ideas were not new. Mark Green, "Those 'New Republican Ideas' Sound Just a Bit Familiar," *Washington Post*, Nov 23, 1980, C1; John L. Hess, "Still No New Ideas," *Baltimore Sun*, Dec 24, 1981, A11.

55. Ornstein is quoted in Treadwell, "It's Altering Economic, Political Thinking."

56. Clifford Geertz, "Common Sense as a Cultural System," in *Local Knowledge: Further Essays in Interpretive Anthropology* (New York: Basic Books, 1983), 75. See also Wendy Brown, *Undoing the Demos: Neoliberalism's Stealth Revolution* (Boston: Zone Books, 2015), 35; Bethany Moreton, *To Serve God and Wal-Mart: The Making of Christian Free Enterprise* (Cambridge, MA: Harvard University Press, 2009), 126–27; Daniel T. Rodgers, *Age of Fracture* (Cambridge, MA: Harvard University Press, 2011), 2, 5, 10, 12. As Rodgers points out, many elements of common sense were remade after World War II. He claims that "free enterprise" was one such concept that was replaced by the idea of "the 'market' that came into vogue in the 1970s" (42). I would argue instead that the "free enterprise system" assimilated the idea of the free market rather than being subsumed by it.

57. As John Maynard Keynes wrote, "A definition can often be vague within fairly wide limits and capable of several interpretations differing slightly from one another, and still be perfectly serviceable." Quoted in John Coates, *The Claims of Common Sense: Moore, Wittgenstein, Keynes and the Social Sciences* (New York: Cambridge University Press, 1996), 86.

58. "He Urges System Based on Free Enterprise," *Washington Post*, Aug 20, 1936, X11.

59. Arthur Sears Henning, "U.S. Split Wide Open over 'Red' Issue at Polls," *Chicago Tribune*, Oct 13, 1936, 11.

60. "Landon Attacks Sham Liberalism," *Lawrence Daily Journal-World*, Oct 12, 1936, 1.

61. Clarence Page, "Talk Like Newt with the Gingrich Diatribe Dictionary," *Chicago Tribune*, Sep 19 1990.

62. "Public Service Ads Are Urged by NAM," *New York Times*, Nov 5, 1949, 24.

63. "Common Sense at the Capital," *Chicago Tribune*, Mar 18, 1933, 12. This was the "editorial of the day"; it originally appeared in the *Boone News-Republican*.

64. "Road Sign for America: Turn Right!" *Nation's Business,* Oct 1940, 34.

65. "Dr. Peale Finds That the New Deal Lacks Common Sense," *Hanover Evening Sun*, Feb 15, 1936, 5.

66. "Broken Glass Democrats," *Wall Street Journal*, Feb 19, 2004.

67. "Bricker Is Impressive," *Milwaukee Sentinel*, Mar 16, 1944, 17; "Business Men Asked to Join Move for Preservation of Free Enterprise," *Spokane Daily Chronicle*, May 24, 1940, 27.

68. Ima Slammer, "Free Enterprise," *York Gazette and Daily*, Aug 21, 1944, 13; Freda Stolper, "Graves Finds City Kin; Says Demo Party Split," *McAllen Monitor*, Sep 26, 1946, 1; "United Nations 'Chief Force' Keeping the World at Peace," *Abilene Reporter-News*, Aug 22, 1948, 10; Wesley Smith, "March of Finance," *Los Angeles Times*, Dec 29, 1943, A8. A similar formulation about "NAM's version of free enterprise" can be found in Alexander H. Uhl, "'Boom and Bust' Policies or Real American Interests?" *York Gazette and Daily*, Aug 29, 1945, 15.

69. "Economic Reform Up to Business," *Danville Bee*, Feb 18, 1939, 10.

70. David Levering Lewis, *The Improbable Wendell Willkie: The Businessman Who Saved the Republican Party and His Country, and Conceived a New World Order* (New York: Liveright, 2018), 98; Arthur Larson, *What We Are For* (New York: Harper and Brothers, 1959), 69.

71. "Resist Communism, Hoover Demands," *New York Times*, Aug 12, 1945, 1, 34.

72. "The Middle of the Road," *New York Herald Tribune*, Sep 7, 1949, 28.

73. Henry Hazlitt, "Economics and Finance: Free Enterprise or Government Planning?" *New York Times*, Dec 17, 1945, 24.

74. "Legal Gambling Asked by Youth," *Kalispell Daily Inter Lake*, Aug 20, 1950, 1.

75. Elizabeth Anderson, *Private Government: How Employers Run Our Lives (and Why We Don't Talk about It)* (Princeton: Princeton University Press, 2017).

76. James J. Kilpatrick, "Kilpatrick Answers Jack Anderson," *Chamber of Commerce of the United States Washington Report*, Oct 23, 1972, 1–2, Powell Archives, Washington University School of Law, http://law2.wlu.edu/deptimages/Powell%20Archives/PowellSCSF ChamberofCommerce.pdf.

77. "Dr. Glen Frank Points Way to Abundant Life," *Minneapolis Star Tribune*, Dec 10, 1937, 18. Frank's first name is misspelled in this headline.

78. See, for example, Jennifer Burns, *Goddess of the Market: Ayn Rand and the American Right* (New York: Oxford University Press, 2009); Angus Burgin, *The Great Persuasion: Reinventing Free Markets since the Great Depression* (Cambridge, MA: Harvard University Press, 2012); Tula A. Connell, *Conservative Counterrevolution: Challenging Liberalism in 1950s Milwaukee* (Urbana: University of Illinois Press, 2016); N. D. B. Connolly, *A World More Concrete: Real Estate and the Making of Jim Crow Florida* (Chicago: University of Chicago Press, 2014); Joseph Crespino, *Strom Thurmond's America* (New York: Hill and Wang, 2012); Darren Dochuk, *From Bible Belt to Sunbelt: Plain-Folk Religion, Grassroots Politics, and the Rise of Evangelical Conservatism* (New York: Norton, 2011); Elizabeth Fones-Wolf, *Selling Free Enterprise: The Business Assault on Labor and Liberalism, 1945–1960* (Urbana: University of Illinois Press, 1994); Darren E. Grem, *The Blessings of Business: How Corporations Shaped Conservative Christianity* (New York: Oxford University Press, 2016); Howell John Harris, *The Right to Manage: Industrial Relations Policies of American Business in the 1940s* (Madison: University of Wisconsin Press, 1982); Katherine Rye Jewell, *Dollars for Dixie: Business and the Transformation of Conservatism in the Twentieth Century* (New York: Cambridge University Press, 2017); Kevin M. Kruse, *White Flight: Atlanta and the Making of Modern Conservatism* (Princeton: Princeton University Press, 2005); Kruse, *One Nation under God*; Moreton, *To Serve God and Wal-Mart*; Kathryn S. Olmstead, *Right out of Califor-*

nia: The 1930s and the Big Business Roots of Modern Conservatism (New York: New Press, 2015); Kim Phillips-Fein, *Invisible Hands: The Businessmen's Crusade against the New Deal* (New York: Norton, 2009); Elizabeth Tandy Shermer, *Sunbelt Capitalism: Phoenix and the Transformation of American Politics* (Philadelphia: University of Pennsylvania Press, 2013); Wendy L. Wall, *Inventing the "American Way": The Politics of Consensus from the New Deal to the Civil Rights Movement* (New York: Oxford University Press, 2008); Benjamin C. Waterhouse, *Lobbying America: The Politics of Business from Nixon to NAFTA* (Princeton: Princeton University Press, 2014). See also Kim Phillips-Fein and Julian Zelizer, eds., *What's Good for Business: Business and American Politics since World War II* (New York: Oxford University Press, 2012).

79. Lloyd A. Free and Hadley Cantril, *The Political Beliefs of Americans: A Study of Public Opinion* (New Brunswick: Rutgers University Press, 1967), 52.

80. Matthew D. Lassiter, "Political History beyond the Red-Blue Divide," *Journal of American History* 98 (Dec 2011): 764.

81. "Businessmen Should Speak Out," *Council Bluffs Nonpareil*, Oct 7, 1946, 4.

82. Rodgers, *Age of Fracture*, 98.

83. "New Group Acclaims Free Enterprise Ideal," *Harvard Crimson*, Jan 13, 1947, 1; "Charters Given to New Groups," *Daily Princetonian*, Dec 10, 1948, 1.

84. "The most vocal champions of free enterprise," as Michael O'Shaughnessy observed, "are the managerial class and their spokesmen of the press and radio." *Economic Democracy and Private Enterprise: A Study of the Relation of Economic Groups to the Federal Government* (New York: Harper and Brothers, 1945), 92.

85. The first use of the phrase I have found is "Selling Free Enterprise Is Full-Time Work," *Saturday Evening Post*, Dec 11, 1948, 168. See also "Apostle of Free Enterprise and Critic of Government," *Des Moines Tribune*, Aug 7, 1953, 4.

86. Dochuk uses the helpful phrase "network of free enterprise organizations." *From Bible Belt to Sunbelt*, 187.

87. Note the frequent references to "free enterprise" in Sacvan Bercovitch, *The American Jeremiad* (Madison: University of Wisconsin Press, 1979). See also Richard L. Johannesen, "Ronald Reagan's Economic Jeremiad," *Central States Speech Journal* 37 (Summer 1986): 79–89. He notes (86) that "lamentation and optimism" were essential components.

88. Walter Lippmann, *An Inquiry into the Principles of the Good Society* (Boston: Little Brown, 1937). For an excellent analysis of the book's argument and impact, see Burgin, *Great Persuasion*, 55–67.

89. Seeking to find the roots of "extreme hostility to social insurance" in the United States, philosopher Elizabeth Anderson writes that its roots "can be traced to Austrian economist Friedrich Hayek [who] warned that the emerging social democratic regimes of Europe were stepping onto a slippery slope to totalitarianism." According to Anderson, Hayek's book "fueled American opposition for decades," and Ronald Reagan was "probably inspired by Hayek" when he opposed Medicare. "Common Property: How Social Insurance Became Confused with Socialism," *Boston Review*, Jul 25, 2016, http://bostonreview .net/editors-picks-us-books-ideas/elizabeth-anderson-common-property.

90. Hayek is quoted in Nancy Maclean, *Democracy in Chains: The Deep History of the Radical Right's Stealth Plan for America* (New York: Viking, 2017), 83. On Hayek's

affinity for business lobbies as free enterprise messengers, see Jewell, *Dollars for Dixie*, 245–46.

91. "DeWitt Emery, Salesman for Free Enterprise: Biggest Small Business Man Visits Here," *Council Bluffs Nonpareil*, Nov 13, 1949, 1.

92. Isaiah Berlin, *The Hedgehog and the Fox: An Essay on Tolstoy's View of History* (1953; repr. New York: Simon and Schuster, 1966).

93. For a critique of those who see conservatives as an "unchanging monolith," see Geoffrey Kabaservice, "Liberals Don't Know Much about Conservative History," *Politico*, Sep 9, 2018, https://www.politico.com/magazine/story/2018/09/09/liberals-dont-know-much -about-conservative-history-219742.

94. George F. Will, foreword to *Conscience of a Conservative*, by Barry M. Goldwater (Princeton: Princeton University Press, 2007; 1960), x.

95. Raymond Williams, *Keywords: A Vocabulary of Culture and Society*, rev. ed. (Oxford: Oxford University Press, 1983), xxiii–xxix.

96. Gerald L. Houseman, *Economics in a Changed Universe: Joseph E. Stiglitz, Globalization, and the Death of "Free Enterprise"* (Lanham, MD: Lexington Books, 2008), 3.

97. Robert Darnton, *The Great Cat Massacre and Other Episodes in French Cultural History* (New York: Basic Books, 1984), 5.

Chapter 1. "A Memo That Changed the Course of History"

1. Memorandum from Lewis F. Powell, Jr. to Messrs. Buckley, Jeffries, and Owens, Nov 12, 1973, Powell Archives, Washington and Lee University, School of Law, Lexington, VA, http://law2.wlu.edu/powellarchives/. Buckley et al. were Powell's 1973–74 Supreme Court law clerks.

2. Lewis F. Powell Jr. to Eugene B. Sydnor Jr., Chairman, Education Committee, U.S. Chamber of Commerce, "Confidential Memorandum: Attack on American Free Enterprise System," Aug 23, 1971, Powell Archives, http://law.wlu.edu/deptimages/Powell%20 Archives/PowellMemorandumTypescript.pdf. All quotations are from this version of the memo.

3. Indeed, the title of Powell's document is sometimes mislabeled as "Attack of American Free Enterprise System." See, for example, the PBS website http://www.pbs.org/wnet /supremecourt/personality/print/sources_document13.html.

4. Powell wrote to the conservative journalist Jeffrey St. John, "Now that I am on the Court, I no longer feel free even to advise or consult old friends as to issues which may be deemed controversial." St. John had published an article on the need for business to "fight back" that Powell referenced in his memo. St. John wrote to Justice Powell after the memo had been made public, seeking his counsel about "how to wage an effective campaign on behalf of business civilization." Even so, Powell noted that he had read the lecture on promoting free enterprise that St. John had enclosed "with interest" and would be forwarding it to Sydnor. Powell to St. John, Nov 20, 1972. See also St. John to Powell, Nov 14, 1972, Powell Archives, http://law.wlu.edu/deptimages/Powell%20Archives/St John_SCGC.pdf. As late as 1974, Powell wrote to a correspondent, "Following Jack Anderson's 'disclosure,' I have had a number of requests to attend meetings, comment on

criticisms, or otherwise indicate a viewpoint with respect to the memorandum. I have always declined." Powell to Charles H. Zeanah, Apr 3, 1974, Powell Archives, http://law .wlu.edu/deptimages/Powell%20Archives/PowellSCSFChamberofCommerce.pdf.

5. Jack Anderson, "Powell's Lesson to Business Aired," *Washington Post*, Sep 28, 1972, F7; "FBI Missed Blueprint by Powell," *Washington Post*, Sep 29, 1972, C27; "Chief Justice Lobbies against Bill," *Washington Post*, Oct 5, 1972, H7.

6. Norman W. Worthington, "Confidential Document," *Washington Post*, Nov 9, 1972, A19.

7. Eugene B. Sydnor Jr., "The Powell Memo," *Richmond Times-Dispatch*, Oct 4, 1972, 7.

8. "Transcript of Radio Editorial Broadcast over WARM, Aired Jan 16/17, 1973," Powell Archives.

9. Henry J. Cappello to Phillip L. Geyelin, editor of the *Washington Post* editorial page, Sep 29, 1972, Powell Archives.

10. Sydnor, "Powell Memo," 7.

11. *The Best of H. T. Webster: A Memorial Collection* (New York: Simon and Schuster, 1953); H. T. Webster, *The Timid Soul* (New York: Simon and Schuster, 1931).

12. Harry F. Byrd Jr., "The Lewis Powell Memorandum," *Congressional Record*, Oct 10, 1972, 34456–662; Sydnor, "Powell Memo," reprinted on 34462.

13. William H. Jones, "Powell Advises Businesses on Politics," *Washington Post*, Nov 12, 1973, D12. Powell also provided two paragraphs of brief background in a letter to his friend Ross Malone. In this letter, he acknowledges meeting with Arch Booth of the chamber, a fact that he did not mention to his clerks. Powell to Malone, Sep 13, 1971, Powell Archives. Powell "never returned" Jack Anderson's phone calls asking for comment. Jack Anderson, "Powell Gave Big Business a Pep Talk, Secret Pre–Supreme Court Memo Shows," *Pittsburgh Press*, Sep 28, 1972, 21.

14. Powell to Buckley, Jeffries, and Owens, Nov 12, 1973.

15. Powell may have held a "small investment" in Xerox, but he owned more than thirty other stocks and maintained a portfolio worth more than $1 million, making him one of the richest Supreme Court nominees in history. "Financial Holdings of Court Nominees Lists: Powell's Assets More Than $1 Million, Rehnquist's $77,050, Statements Show," *Los Angeles Times*, Oct 30, 1971, 15.

16. In a letter written several months before requesting the memo, Sydnor attached two articles "emphasizing the very points you and I discussed recently and which we plan to discuss with Archie Davis and Arch Booth." Sydnor to Powell, May 21, 1971, Powell Archives, These clippings can be found at the Powell Archives, 14–68, http://law.wlu .edu/deptimages/Powell%20Archives/PowellSpeechResearchAOFESMemo.pdf.

17. Powell to Malone, Sep 13, 1971.

18. Powell to K. A. Randall, Sep 16, 1971, Powell Archives.

19. Sydnor to Powell, Oct 22, 1971, Powell Archives, http://law.wlu.edu/deptimages/Powell %20Archives/PowellSpeechResearchAOFESMemo.pdf.

20. Arch Booth, "Our Free Market Is Threatened," *Boca Raton News*, Oct 12, 1971, 5. Nixon nominated Powell and William Rehnquist on Oct 21.

21. Bernard G. Segal to Powell, Nov 15, 1972, Powell Archives.

22. Lewis F. Powell, "America Is Not a Repressive Society," *New York Times*, Nov 3, 1971, 47.

23. "What Justice Powell Says Is Wrong with America," *U.S. News and World Report*, Aug 23, 1972, 41–42.

24. Sydnor to Powell, Nov 22, 1972, Powell Archives; Powell to Buckley, Jeffries, and Owens, Nov 12, 1973.

25. Among the few mentions in the 1970s are Holmes Alexander, "Slim Cats' Lobby," *New Castle News*, Feb 25, 1974, 4; and Louis Kohlmeier, "Justice Powell: For Business, a Friend in Court," *New York Times*, Mar 14, 1976, F5. The next reference to the memo in the *Times* came more than twenty years later: Robert D. Hershey Jr., "President of U.S. Chamber Will Resign After 21 Years," *New York Times*, Feb 25, 1997, D2. The Chamber of Commerce celebrated the memo periodically: "Lewis F. Powell, Jr.: His Warning Brought a New Era of Business Activism," *Nation's Business*, Aug 1987, 66; "The Powell Memorandum: As Valid on Its 20th Anniversary as It Will Be on Its 100th," *Nation's Business*, Nov 1991, 87.

26. See, for example, Douglas Martin, "Jack Anderson, Investigative Journalist Who Angered the Powerful, Dies at 83," *New York Times*, Dec 18, 2005.

27. John C. Jeffries, *Justice Lewis F. Powell, Jr.* (New York: Charles Scribner's Sons, 1994). Jeffries, the former dean of the University of Virginia Law School, has acknowledged that leaving the memo out of the biography was a "mistake." Jeffries, email to author, Sep 18, 2014. Nor was the memo mentioned in Powell's obituaries in 1998. See Linda Greenhouse, "Lewis Powell, Centrist Justice, Dies at 90," *New York Times*, Aug 26, 1998, A1; Joan Biskupic and Fred Barbash, "Retired Justice Lewis Powell Dies at 90," *Washington Post*, Aug 26, 1998, A1. David Vogel's definitive 1989 account of business influence barely mentioned it as well. See *Fluctuating Fortunes: The Political Power of Business in America* (New York: Basic Books, 1989), 59.

28. One of the few conservative commentators to highlight the importance of the memo in recent years, Lyman Johnson, has called it "a playbook for combating leftist critiques of capitalism." "Justice Powell and Free Enterprise," *Richmond Times-Dispatch*, Aug 24, 2011, http://www.richmond.com/news/article_81f16d98–369f-502a-b84c-55835324d612 .html. Historian and journalist John B. Judis was among the first to discuss the Powell memo as an important historical document in *The Paradox of American Democracy: Elites, Special Interests, and the Betrayal of Public Trust* (New York: Pantheon, 2000), 116–19. See also Alliance for Justice, *Justice for Sale: Shortchanging the Public Interest for Private Gain* (Washington, DC: Alliance for Justice, 1993), 10–11.

29. The "master plan" quotation is from Representative Hank Johnson (D-GA), "The Republican Agenda," *Congressional Record*, Dec 20, 2011, http://www.gpo.gov/fdsys/pkg /CREC-2011–12–20/html/CREC-2011–12–20-pt1-PgH10009.htm. See also David Harvey, *A Brief History of Neoliberalism* (New York: Oxford University Press, 2007), 43–44.

30. According to one columnist, Powell represented a rarity in history: "one person as [a] force of change." "While We Were Sleeping: The Powell Memorandum," *Seattle Star*, Mar 23, 2014, http://www.seattlestar.net/2014/03/while-we-were-sleeping-the-powell -memorandum/.

31. The phrase "lifelong Democrat" can be found in Biskupic and Barbash, "Retired Justice Lewis Powell Dies at 90," A1.

32. David L. Chappell, "The End of the Boom," *Journal of the Historical Society* 11:3 (Sep 2011); Hedrick Smith, *Who Stole the American Dream?* (New York: Random House, 2012), xiii, 3; *Heist: Who Stole the American Dream?* www.heist-themovie.com; *Thom Hartman Show*, https://www.youtube.com/watch?v=7313St3UoyM; Steven Higgs, "A Call to Arms for the Class War, from the Top Down," https://www.counterpunch.org /2012/05/11/a-call-to-arms-for-class-war-from-the-top-down/; "The Lewis Powell Memo: The Intellectual Genesis of the American Corporatocracy," *Daily Kos*, Dec 10, 2011; Robert Kuttner, "Still Nader After All These Years," *American Prospect*, Aug 29, 2014; Bill Moyers, "How Wall Street Occupied America," *Nation*, Nov 20, 2011, 12; Katrina Vanden Heuvel, "The Brothers Koch," *Monterey County Weekly*, Apr 26, 2012, 15; Jeffrey D. Clements, *Corporations Are Not People* (San Francisco: Berrett-Koehler, 2012), 26; Egberto Willies, "Meet the Man Who Told the GOP How to Destroy America's Middle Class," Dec 26, 2013, www.addictinginfo.org/2013/12/26/powell-memo-gop-blue print/; Barb Vogds, "GOP Thwarts Obama," *Fond Du Lac Commonwealth Reporter*, Sep 4, 2016, B4. See also Adam Winkler, *We the Corporations: How American Businesses Won Their Civil Rights* ((New York: Liveright, 2018), 281.

33. Sean Wilentz, *The Age of Reagan: A History, 1974–2008* (New York: Harper, 2008). An excerpt from the Powell memo is reproduced in Ronald Story and Bruce Laurie, eds., *The Rise of Conservatism in America, 1945–2000: A Brief History with Documents* (Boston: Bedford, 2008), 84–89.

34. "Connally Says Nixon No 'Shoe-In,'" *Boston Globe*, Aug 22, 1972, 13.

35. Alexander, "Slim Cats' Lobby."

36. "The Alliance of Ideas," *Chicago Tribune*, May 19, 1968, 28.

37. Seymour Martin Lipset and Earl Raab, "The Message of Proposition 13," *Commentary* 66 (Sep 1978): 42–46.

38. "Chambers Start Move to Defend Free Enterprise," *Christian Science Monitor*, Jul 18, 1938, 13.

39. Hutton is quoted in Allan J. Lichtman, *White Protestant Nation: The Rise of the American Conservative Movement* (New York: Atlantic Monthly, 2008), 168.

40. *Free Enterprise: What Is It, What Has It Accomplished, What Is Its Future?* (Milwaukee: Kearney and Trecker, 1945), introduction.

41. Goldwater, quoted in S. Oliver Goodman, "Free Economy Is a Challenge, Retailers Told," *Washington Post*, Apr 22, 1953, 20; "Goldwater Scores Retailers for Attitude on Politics," *Women's Wear Daily*, Apr 22, 1953, 2.

42. "Threat to Capital Held U.S. Menace: Jackson, Head of U.S. Chamber, Says 'Murrays, Reuthers' Are Attacking System," *New York Times*, Jan 14, 1947, 8.

43. Nathan W. Shefferman, *Labor's Stake in Capitalism* (New York: Constitution and Free Enterprise Foundation, 1954), 50. In 1943, an editorial proclaimed an "attack on free enterprise." "To the Foregoing *Railway Age* Replies," *Railway Age*, Feb 6, 1943, 320.

44. Jeff Engelhardt, "Rauner Tells Local Business Leaders He'll Fight for Them," *Northwest Herald*, Sep 19, 2014, http://www.nwherald.com/2014/09/19/rauner-tells-local-business -leaders-hell-fight-for-them/atlr40s/.

45. "Threat to Capital Held U.S. Menace."

46. Powell here quoted the economist Milton Friedman, agreeing with his claim that ordinary Americans were "unwittingly serving ends they would never intentionally promote."

47. Alfred P. Haake, "Preserving the Free Enterprise System," in *The What, Why, and How of American Free Enterprise*, ed. C. W. McKee (New Wilmington, PA: American Economic and Business Foundation, 1941), 15.

48. "Transcript of Radio Editorial Broadcast over WARM," 39.

49. See, for example, Lemuel R. Boulware, "Politics . . . the Businessman's Biggest Job in 1958" (lecture to Phoenix Chamber of Commerce, May 21, 1958), quoted in Elizabeth Tandy Shermer, *Sunbelt Capitalism: Phoenix and the Transformation of American Politics* (Philadelphia: University of Pennsylvania Press, 2013), 283.

50. Jennifer Harper, "U.S. Chamber of Commerce President Lauds American Free Enterprise as 'Economic Populism,'" *Washington Times*, Jan 14, 2015, http://www.washington times.com/news/2015/jan/14/us-chamber-commerce-president-lauds-american-free-/.

51. William Graham Sumner, *The Forgotten Man, and Other Essays* (New Haven: Yale University Press, 1918), 466. Jefferson Cowie and Nick Salvatore also discuss the use of the phrase by Sumner and Roosevelt in "The Long Exception: Rethinking the Place of the New Deal in American History," *International Labor and Working-Class History* 74 (2008): 1–32.

52. H. W. Prentis Jr., *The Catalyzers of Liberty: An Address at the 44th Congress of American Industry, Dec 8, 1939* (New York: NAM, 1939).

53. "Business Told to Sell Nation Free Enterprise," *Washington Post*, Dec 5, 1963, F9.

54. Richard Hofstadter, "The Paranoid Style in American Politics," *Harper's*, Nov 1964, 77–86, http://harpers.org/archive/1964/11/the-paranoid-style-in-american-politics/.

55. Robert Lund to J. Howard Pew, Jan 27, 1950, quoted in Lichtman, *White Protestant Nation*, 168; Phelps Adams, "What Is Free Enterprise?" *New York Sun-Herald*, Jan 5, 1948, 19, 33, 103; John A. Davenport, "Free Enterprise's Forgotten Virtues," *Wall Street Journal*, Jul 27, 1973, 8; Lee Holloway, "Anderson off the Mark," *Washington Post*, Oct 12, 1972, A19.

56. Frank Chodorov, "Stand Up and Fight," *Human Events*, Jun 21, 1950, 1–4.

57. James M. Brewbaker, "Men to Match My Mountains: A Blueprint for Business Political Action," *Human Events*, Apr 7, 1958, 1–4.

58. Stephen H. Fifeld, "Tell the Story of Free Enterprise," *Bankers Magazine*, Oct 1939, 358.

59. "Business Boswell's: National Association of Public Relations Men Projected during N.A.M. Meeting to Lift Activity to Professional Plane," *Business Week*, Dec 19, 1942, 23, 26.

60. Norman Vincent Peale, "Your Future Is What You Make It: Correct Muddled Thinking and Erroneous Ideas," *Vital Speeches of the Day*, Dec 15, 1948, 146; Norman Vincent Peale, *The Power of Positive Thinking* (New York: Prentice-Hall, 1952).

61. Bell is quoted in Howard Brick, *Transcending Capitalism: Visions of a New Society in Modern American Thought* (Ithaca: Cornell University Press, 2006), 198.

62. Quoted in Mark Schmitt, "Legend of the Powell Memo," *American Prospect*, Apr 27, 2005, http://prospect.org/article/legend-powell-memo.

63. "'NAM Attacks Welfare State at Convention," *Los Angeles Times*, Dec 8, 1949, 25.

64. The quotation is from Chris Hedges, *Death of the Liberal Class* (New York: Nation Books, 2011), 176.

65. Brewbaker, "Men to Match My Mountains," 1.

66. H. W. Prentis Jr., *The Mobilization for Understanding of Private Enterprise: One of the Indispensable Supports of Individual Freedom* (New York: National Association of Manufacturers, 1940), 8.

67. Elizabeth Fones-Wolf, *Selling Free Enterprise: The Business Assault on Labor and Liberalism, 1945–1960* (Urbana: University of Illinois Press, 1994).

68. See, for example, *Make Mine Freedom* (Searcy, AR: Harding College, 1948).

69. Benjamin C. Waterhouse, *Lobbying America: The Politics of Business from Nixon to NAFTA* (Princeton: Princeton University Press, 2014), 59. The journalist Mark Schmitt was the first to challenge what he called the "legend of the Powell memo." Laura Kalman writes that "some in the twenty-first century 'routinely'—and wrongly" credit the document with providing a "blueprint" for the ascending conservative infrastructure: *Right Star Rising, A New Politics, 1974–1980* (New York: Norton, 2010), 198. See also Kim Phillips-Fein, *Invisible Hands: The Businessmen's Crusade against the New Deal* (New York: Norton, 2009), 158–63; Gary Robertson, "Power, Politics, and Powell," *Richmond Magazine*, Jul 14, 2014, http://richmondmagazine.com/news/features/lewis-powell-jr -manifesto/.

70. "Talbott Urges Political Role," *Washington Post*, Oct 25, 1958, C14.

71. Lorene Frederick, "Free Enterprise Forged Its Own Shackle Chains," *Times Daily*, Mar 9, 1966, 1, 2; "Business Finding a Voice," *Fort Scott Tribune*, Mar 3, 1966, 2.

72. Progressive radio host Sam Seder presented this view of the pre–Powell memo chamber as "old fashioned" in his *The Majority Report with Sam Seder* on Aug 25, 2011. "The Birth of Everything Corporate and Conservative," https://www.youtube.com/watch?v =ITkWZCKllsA. The word *lackluster* is from Waterhouse, *Lobbying America*, 61. The word *asleep* is from Alyssa Katz, *The Influence Machine: The U.S. Chamber of Commerce and the Corporate Capture of American Life* (New York: Spiegel and Grau, 2015), 38. See also Phillips-Fein, *Invisible Hands*, 157–58. On the chamber's refutation of this view before the Powell memo, see "Refutes Chamber's Stodgy Image," *Fort Scott Tribune*, Mar 12, 1970, 2; John Cuniff, "Chamber Deemed Tool of Change," *Tuscaloosa News*, Mar 13, 1970, 13.

73. Jeffrey St. John, "Memo to GM: Why Not Fight Back?" *Wall Street Journal*, May 21, 1971; "Analyzing Youth," *Richmond Times-Dispatch*, Jul 7, 1971, http://law.wlu.edu /deptimages/Powell%20Archives/PowellSpeechResearchAOFESMemo.pdf.

74. "GM's Roche Says Attacks on Big Business Undermine Free Enterprise, Slander U.S.," *Wall Street Journal*, Mar 26, 1971, 4.

75. In his article "The End of the New Deal Order: It Won't Win the Future," *Weekly Standard*, Sep 5, 2011, conservative writer Matthew Continetti characterizes it as the period when "the idea that the good life could be had for free, that the government 'owed' people certain material goods, became widespread."

76. Chodorov, "Stand Up and Fight," 3.

77. James L. Wick, "Can the GOP Win in 1960?" *Human Events*, Nov 3, 1958, 3.

78. Mark Tushnet, "Justice Lewis F. Powell and the Jurisprudence of Centrism," *Michigan*

Law Review 93:6 (1995): 1854–84; interview with Allen C. Goolsby, Jul 2016. Goolsby joined Hunton and Williams in the late 1960s and worked closely with Powell.

79. According to Linda Greenhouse, Powell "was a person of a particular time and place, a patrician son of the Old South." "Black Robes Don't Make the Justice, but the Rest of the Closet Just Might," *New York Times*, Dec 4, 2002, A27. See also Charles H. Ford and Jeffrey L. Littlejohn, "Reconstructing the Old Dominion," *Virginia Magazine of History and Biography* 121:2 (Apr 2013): 146–72, which shows that convention cut both ways. Powell mildly challenged the dogma of "massive resistance" and was a leader of the moderate campaign against "right-wing reactionaries" in Virginia.

80. After his visit to the Soviet Union, Darnton noted, he "inspired" a course in the Richmond public schools on life under communism—"one of the first in American public schools anywhere"—which suggests that, like other free enterprisers, he was not averse to using the state to shape society. John Darnton, "Lewis Franklin Powell, Jr." *New York Times*, Oct 22, 1971, 25.

81. Jack Eisen, "New Chamber Head Assails Extremists," *Washington Post*, May 7, 1964, A36.

82. James J. Kilpatrick, "Citizen Powell Handed Down a Good Opinion," *Washington Star*, Oct 8, 1972, entered into the record by Senator Byrd in the *Congressional Record*, 34461.

83. Anders Walker, "Diversity's Strange Career: Recovering the Racial Pluralism of Lewis F. Powell, Jr.," 50 *Santa Clara Law Review* (2010): 667.

84. Jeffries, *Justice Lewis F. Powell, Jr.*, 232–36; "Rehnquist Called 'Right-Wing Zealot' as Labor Joins Attack: AFL-CIO and UAW Spokesmen Urge Senate Committee to Reject Nominee's Confirmation for Supreme Court," *Los Angeles Times*, Nov 10, 1971, 2; Glen Elasser, "Powell Hearings End: Senators Laud Nominee," *Chicago Tribune*, Nov 9, 1971, 5.

85. "What Justice Powell Says Is Wrong with America."

86. Jeffries, email to author, Sep 18, 2014.

87. Quoted in Lichtman, *White Protestant Nation*, 63.

88. "Business Is Still in Trouble," *Fortune*, May 1949, 69.

89. Prentis, *Mobilization for Understanding of Private Enterprise*, 5.

90. "Board Dinner Told Buyers' Market Due: Saving of American Private Enterprise Urged by Daley," *Florence Times*, Apr 4, 1947, 1, 9.

91. Quoted in Lichtman, *White Protestant Nation*, 126–27.

92. "Advertising Men in Convention Lay Stress on Free Enterprise," *Christian Science Monitor*, Jun 22, 1938, 6.

93. Sacvan Bercovitch has called attention to the "mutuality (not conflict) between free enterprise and the common good" in American rhetoric. *The American Jeremiad* (Madison: University of Wisconsin Press, 1979), 137.

94. "Board Dinner Told Buyers' Market Due," 1.

95. Prentis, *Mobilization for Understanding of Private Enterprise*, 4.

96. "Business Is Still in Trouble," 67.

97. "G. E. Board Chairman Warns against Attacks on Free Enterprise: P. D. Reed Says U.S. Will Lose Ground until Government Is Friendly to Business," *Wall Street Journal*, Oct 16, 1940, 7.

98. "Attack on Free Enterprise Hit by Steel Man," *Los Angeles Times*, Oct 31, 1958, B3.

99. F. A. Hayek, *The Road to Serfdom* (Chicago: University of Chicago Press, 1944).

100. Shepard's 1971 lecture was published in revised form as Melvin J. Grayson and Thomas R. Shepard Jr., *The Disaster Lobby: Prophets of Ecological Doom and Other Absurdities* (Chicago: Follett, 1973), 189–91.

101. St. John, "Memo to GM."

102. "Exchange Urges 'Sale' of Free Enterprise," *Los Angeles Times*, Dec 7, 1949, 26.

103. Prentis, *Mobilization for Understanding of Private Enterprise*, 3, 5.

104. "Stop Nursing That Guilty Feeling," *Saturday Evening Post*, Jul 11, 1942, 84.

105. Harold B. Dorsey, "Economic View: Benefits of Free Enterprise Left Unsung," *Washington Post*, May 1, 1961, A20.

106. "Businessmen Told to Sell Nation Free Enterprise."

107. "Strengths of the Free Enterprise System," *Intellect*, Jan 1976, 281–82.

108. John A. Davenport, "Free Enterprise's Forgotten Virtues," *Wall Street Journal*, Jul 27, 1973, 8.

109. The speech, delivered on Dec 30, 1937, was published under a different title: Robert H. Jackson, "The Philosophy of Big Business: Rebellion against Reforms," *Vital Speeches of the Day*, Jan 15, 1938, 208–11. See also "Jackson Sees Big Business 'Strike' Plot," *Washington Post*, Dec 30, 1937, 1, 12.

110. Leon Davis, "Yes, You Can 'Do Something about It'!" *Nation's Business*, Oct 1938, 33.

111. "Advertising's Big Job: Selling Business to U.S.," *Christian Science Monitor*, Jun 26, 1940, 3.

112. James P. Selvage, "Selling the Private Enterprise System: Business Needs to Study Public Relations," *Vital Speeches of the Day*, Dec 15, 1942, 145.

113. Haake, "Preserving the Free Enterprise System," 16.

114. "The Challenge to Businessmen," *Los Angeles Times*, May 17, 1946, A4.

115. "Board Dinner Told Buyers' Market Due," 9.

116. Edward C. Bursk, "Selling the Idea of Free Enterprise," *Harvard Business Review* 26:3 (May 1948): 372–84.

117. Peter Wehner, "Conservatives in Name Only," *New York Times*, Jan 15, 2015, A29. For a more long-term history focusing on religious discourse, see Matthew Avery Sutton, *American Apocalypse: A History of Modern Evangelicalism* (Cambridge, MA: Harvard University Press, 2014).

118. "Industry Hears Call to Defend Free Enterprise," *New York Times*, Dec 6, 1941, 1, 10.

119. Allen Arthur Stockdale, "Contributions of Free Enterprise to America," in *The What, Why, and How of American Free Enterprise*, 7.

120. *Ronald Reagan Speaks out against Socialized Medicine* (Chicago: American Medical Association, 1961).

121. Such extremism, Jonathan Chait writes, is "the very thing that propelled conservatism to power in the first place." Chait understates the degree to which what he calls the "old moderate establishment," peopled by Powell, among others, used such language as well. "It Would Be Nice If True Conservatives Were Empiricists but Let's Face It," *New York*, Jan 16, 2015, http://nymag.com/daily/intelligencer/2015/01/itd-be-nice-if-conservatives-were-empiricists.html.

122. Quoted in Dana Milbank, "Free Enterprise Still Exists. Do Free Lunches?" *Washington Post*, Jan 15, 2015, A2.

123. Doyle McManus, "Mitt Stays Put," *Los Angeles Times*, Apr 29, 2012, A24.

124. Paul Ryan, "Real Solutions Will Take Leadership and Courage," *Real Clear Politics*, Aug 11, 2012, http://www.realclearpolitics.com/articles/2012/08/11/full_text_of_paul _ryans_speech_115074.html.

125. *The Eleventh Hour for American Enterprise* (New York: NAM, 1946). The first section of this pamphlet is titled "An Hour of Crisis for Our Enterprise System."

126. Bill Clinton, "Remarks at the World Trade Organization in Geneva, Switzerland, May 18, 1998," in *Public Papers of the Presidents of the United States, Will. J. Clinton, 1998* (Washington, DC: Government Printing Office, 2000), 809.

127. Powell, "America Is Not a Repressive Society."

Chapter 2. From "Free Labor" to "Free Enterprise"

1. The article was reprinted thirteen years later in the leading abolitionist newspaper: Penn., "Propositions on Slavery," *Liberator*, Apr 6, 1833, 2. Presumably the author was Elihu Embree, the publisher of this newspaper, which was sold the next year to Benjamin Lundy, who renamed it the *Genius of Universal Emancipation*. This phrase regularly appeared in the leading abolitionist newspaper afterward. See, for example, "Foreign Items," *Liberator*, Jan 18, 1834, 4; "New England Anti-slavery Convention: Address to the People of the United States," *Liberator*, Sep 6, 1834, 1–3. The second quotation is from B. B. Davis, "Slave Labor Products—No. 4," *Anti-Slavery Bugle*, Sep 3, 1847, 2.

2. "The Georgia Result," *New York Daily Tribune*, Oct 14, 1851, 4.

3. "What the South Needs," *Paxton Record,* May 22, 1880, 6; "Vicksburg and Richmond," *New York Times*, May 16, 1863, 4.

4. Benjamin M. Anderson, "Dangerous Class Legislation," *Springfield Leader*, Mar 21, 1924, 7. Anderson was criticizing the proposed McNary Haugen Farm Adjustment Act.

5. "Smoothing Down Platform Planks," *San Francisco Chronicle*, Aug 7, 1912, 3.

6. As C. C. Schiller wrote in 1946, free labor was now "treading in the footsteps of the enterprise system." "For Nationalization," *St. Petersburg Times*, Nov 28, 1946, 4.

7. For thoughts on how "our thinking is muddled because we describe actions as things," see David Brooks, "The 2016 Sidney Awards, Part I," *New York Times*, Dec 27, 2016.

8. The influential term was coined in Steve Fraser and Gary Gerstle, eds., *The Rise and Fall of the New Deal Order, 1930–1980* (Princeton: Princeton University Press, 1989).

9. "Bawl St. Journal Made $9,000 Profit," *New York Times*, Jun 22, 1927, 39.

10. "Why Free Enterprise Matters," http://freeenterprisealliance.org/front/

11. Eric Foner, *Free Soil, Free Labor, Free Men: The Ideology of the Republican Party Before the Civil War* (New York: Oxford University Press, 1994), xxiv, xxxvi, 11, 15, 25.

12. "Cause of the Growth and Prosperity of Cities," *Louisville Examiner*, Mar 18, 1848, 2.

13. "Oshkosh True Democrat," *Louisville Examiner*, May 19, 1849, 2.

14. "The Assembly Nominations," *Brooklyn Daily Eagle*, Sep 16, 1856, 2.

15. The Detroit petition is quoted in *Public Ledger*, Dec 5, 1843, 2. Andrew Jackson, "President's Message," *Adams Sentinel*, Dec 11, 1832, 4; J. Willard Hurst, *Law and the Con-*

ditions of Freedom in the Nineteenth-Century United States (Madison: University of Wisconsin Press, 1956), 6.

16. "Splendid Operation," *Kansas Free State*, Oct 1, 1855, 2.

17. Richard White, *The Republic for Which It Stands: The United States during Reconstruction and the Gilded Age, 1865–1896* (New York: Oxford University Press, 2017), 220.

18. "Whig State Convention, *Vermont Phoenix*, Jul 11, 1845, 2.

19. "The Theory of the Tariff," *New York Evening Post*, Jan 10, 1845, 2.

20. "The Reward of Labor," *New York Tribune*, Mar 27, 1845, 2.

21. "How They Talk in Canada," *Detroit Free Press*, Jul 6, 1854, 2.

22. "Educational," *Woodstock Sentinel*, Nov 25, 1880, 8. In 1897, a columnist described the "free enterprise and untamed energy" of Portland and Los Angeles. "The Western Growth," *San Francisco Call*, May 2, 1897, 22.

23. See the website of the American Presidency Project for a complete set of major party platforms: http://www.presidency.ucsb.edu/platforms.php.

24. Ida M. Tarbell, *The History of the Standard Oil Company* (New York: P. Smith, 1904); Richard L. McCormick, "The Discovery That Business Corrupts Politics: A Reappraisal of the Origins of Progressivism," *American Historical* Review 86 (Apr 1981): 247–74; Robert H. Wiebe, *Businessmen and Reform: A Study of the Progressive Movement* (Chicago: Ivan Dee, 1989, 1962); Arthur S. Link, "What Happened to the Progressive Movement in the 1920s?" *American Historical Review,* 64 (Jul 1959), 833–51.

25. "Wilson Finds Tariff the Root of All Evil," *New York Times*, May 24, 1912, 6. This is a central theme of Otis Graham, *An Encore for Reform: The Old Progressives and the New Deal* (New York: Oxford University Press, 1967) and is also developed in Wiebe, *Business and Reform*, chapter 9, "Business and the Progressive Movement." As Wiebe writes, "In the late progressive years, big businessmen had started cooperating with erstwhile enemies such as the NAM, U.S. Chamber of Commerce and the American Bankers' Association, which they had disdained before" (222).

26. On the history of this idea, see Michael Kammen, *A Machine That Would Go of Itself: The Constitution in American Culture* (New York: Knopf, 1986), 19–20.

27. As Martin J. Sklar wrote, "Wilson's position was not that of a representative of the 'little man,' or the 'middle class,' *against* 'big business'; but that of one who, affirming the large corporate industrial capitalist system, was concerned with establishing the legal and institutional environment most conducive to the system's growth, while at the same time preserving some place within the system for the 'little man.'" Quoted in John B. Judis, "Meet the Sarah Palin Enthusiast Who May Have Been the Best American Historian of His Generation," *New Republic*, Jun 17, 2014, https://newrepublic.com/article/118187/martin-j-sklar-and-search-usable-past.

28. "Will Woodrow Get After Money Trust?" *Chicago Day Book*, Dec 27, 1912, 12.

29. "Full Text of Woodrow Wilson's Acceptance of Democratic Nomination," *Chicago Daily Tribune*, Aug 8, 1912, 4.

30. "Truce at Jackson's Dinner: Wilson Assails Business Control—Clark Seeks Insurgent Aid," *New York Times*, Jan 9, 1912, 2.

31. "Wilson Dissects Roosevelt," *Los Angeles Times*, Apr 9, 1913, 6.

32. Quoted in Charles Postel, *The Populist Vision* (New York: Oxford University Press, 2007), 139–40.

33. McCormick, "The Discovery That Business Corrupts Politics."

34. "Just Like a Business: That Is How the Mayor Wants the City Run," *Baltimore Sun*, Sep 28, 1904, 12.

35. Daniel T. Rodgers, "In Search of Progressivism," *Reviews in American History* 10 (Dec 1982): 113–32.

36. "Galveston—The City of the New Idea," *New York Times*, June 2, 1907, SM10.

37. "Running a City Like a Business," *Hartford Courant*, Jul 31, 1909, 15.

38. "President Taft's Opportunity," *Wall Street Journal*, Mar 31, 1909, 1. Some critics fought against this idea, but they were in the minority. See, for example, "Can't Run a City Like a Business, Says Mullaney," *Chicago Tribune*, Feb 23, 1910, 2.

39. "Run Government Like a Business Lowden Keynote," *Dixon Evening Telegraph*, Apr 5, 1920, 5.

40. "Four Ballots, No Nomination, Wood Leads," *New York Times*, Jun 12, 1920, 2. Addison Del Mastro, "A Day at the DMV; or, Why Conservatives Hate Government," *American Conservative*, Jan 10, 2018, https://www.theamericanconservative.com/articles/a-day-at -the-dmv-or-why-conservatives-hate-government/.

41. Arthur Sears Henning, "Uncle Sam Can Run Government Like a Business: Gen. Dawes Proves It in One-Year Course," *Chicago Tribune*, Jun 29, 1922, 14.

42. "Blames Politics for Depression," *Boston Globe*, May 2, 1931, 1; Otto H. Kahn, "Care for Idle, Kahn Advises," *Des Moines Register*, Aug 30, 1931, 21.

43. "Dedicated to Freedom," *Monroe Morning World*, Nov 17, 1957, 4.

44. G. R. Davis, "Our March toward Liberty," *New York Times*, Oct 28, 1934, E5.

45. "Lumber Men Meet Here," *New York Times*, Sep 18, 1936, 42.

46. "Platform Drafted by Manufacturers," *New York Times*, May 16, 1923, 4.

47. "Simplify Federal Taxes," *Scranton Republican*, Aug 25, 1920, 8.

48. Anderson, "Dangerous Class Legislation."

49. Scrutator, "Man Losing His Liberty, Warning on Lincoln Day," *Chicago Tribune*, Feb 12, 1925, 23; "Galls Rail Rate Another Statistics Orgy," *Chicago Tribune*, Sep 25, 1925, 25. On the veneration of the "price mechanism," see Angus Burgin, *The Great Persuasion: Reinventing Free Markets since the Depression* (Cambridge, MA: Harvard University Press, 2012).

50. "Prying into Private Business Attacked," *Lancaster Eagle*, Feb 15, 1927, 4. On the Pro- gressive concern with domination, see K. Sabeel Rahman, *Democracy against Domina- tion* (New York: Oxford University Press, 2016).

51. R. C. Hoiles, "Does the Administration Want Free Enterprise to Survive?" *Santa Ana Register*, Oct 31, 1942, 14.

52. James Truslow Adams, *Our Business Civilization: Some Aspects of American Culture* (New York: A. and C. Boni, 1929), 16.

53. Coolidge made his famous remark in an address to the Society of American Newspaper Editors on Jan 17, 1925, in Washington, DC: https://www.presidency.ucsb.edu/documents /address-the-american-society-newspaper-editors-washington-dc.

54. Paul W. Glad, "Progressives and the Business Culture of the 1920s," *Journal of American History* 53 (Jun 1966): 79.

55. Harper Leech, "Babbitt Pays for Babbitt-Baiting," *Nation's Business*, Jul 1925, 13–15.

56. Leech, "Babbitt Pays for Babbitt-Baiting," 13.

57. Harper Leech, "This Word War on the Capitalist," *Nation's Business*, Jan 1926, 25–27.

58. Harper Leech, "Does Nations' Mark Trend of Business World?" *Chicago Tribune*, Oct 26, 1925, 28.

59. Herbert Hoover quoted in John Gerring, *Party Ideologies in America, 1828–1998* (New York: Cambridge University Press), 137.

60. Luther K. Bell, "The New Trade Association: New Ideals, New Aims, a New Type of Leadership Must Be among the Tools Which Organized Business Uses to Solve the Problems of the Future," *Nation's Business*, Jan 1938, 33, 34, 90.

61. "The Wisconsin Planks," *Ironwood Daily Globe*, Jun 16, 1924, 4.

62. "Colby Condemns New Deal Policies: He Asserts Wilson Believed Government Should Be an Umpire, Never a Master," *New York Times*, Apr 14, 1935, 6.

63. "Business Men Asked to Join in Move for Preservation of Free Enterprise," *Spokane Daily Chronicle*, May 24, 1940, 27.

64. "Labor Warned by Col. Knox," *Marion Star*, Sep 1, 1936, 8.

65. "Edward A. Hayes out for Illinois Governor's Post," *Freeport Journal-Standard*, Aug 1, 1939, 1.

66. Robert Quillen, "Plain Talk," *Bridgewater Courier News*, Dec 4, 1940, 10.

67. John Corbin, "What Hoover Is Aiming At: Team Play between Government and Business, with Fairness and Real Brain Work on Both Sides," *New York Times*, May 29, 1921, 7:1, 4.

68. "Harding Outlines Policies He Favors: Declares for Less Government in Business and More Business in Government," *New York Times*, Nov 5, 1920, 7; "Harding Declares for Less Government in Business: American Enterprise Must Be Left Free to Develop, He Says for Government Economies," *Wall Street Journal*, Nov 12, 1920, 12. See also "Harding Asserts Honest Commerce Is Nation's Need," *New York Times,* May 19, 1922, 1.

69. "Triumphant" capitalism, from a Chamber of Commerce writer in 1925, is quoted in Howard Brick, *Transcending Capitalism: Visions of a New Society in Modern American Thought* (Ithaca: Cornell University Press, 2006), 33.

70. William Trufant Foster and Waddill Catchings, "Profits: A Man Who Isn't in Business to Make Money Isn't in Business at All," *Nation's Business*, Mar 1925, 26–28.

71. Milton Friedman, "A Friedman Doctrine: The Social Responsibility of Business Is to Increase Its Profits," *New York Times*, Sep 13, 1970, SM33–36.

72. Leech, "Babbitt Pays for Babbitt-Baiting," 15.

73. "More Business in Government, Ritchie's Topic," *Wilmington News Journal*, May 12, 1926, 1, 3. See also Albert C. Ritchie, "Makes Plea for Business: Too Much Regulation, Says Governor Ritchie of Maryland," *Emporia Gazette*, Feb 15, 1927, 1.

74. "Rules and Results," *Chicago Tribune*, Dec 2, 1931, 12.

75. Quoted in Graham, *An Encore for Reform*, 45.

76. Glenn Frank, "Pettengill on Big Government," *Los Angeles Times*, Feb 21, 1939, 24.

77. "Commonwealth Unable to Curb Power of Trade Buccaneers," *San Francisco Call*, Mar 7, 1907, 5.

78. "The Die Is Cast," *Akron Beacon Journal*, Jun 25, 1923, 4.

79. John Temple Graves, "Let the Buyer Beware," *Asheville Times*, Jan 16, 1945, 4.

80. Norman Beasley, *Frank Knox, American: A Short Biography* (Garden City, NY: Doubleday, Doran, 1936), 165, 153, 155.

81. "Dewey Declares New Deal Makes 'a House Divided,'" *New York Times*, Feb 13, 1940, 1.

82. Fred DeArmond, "The Creed of a Conservative," *Freeman,* Sep 1956, https://fee.org/articles/the-creed-of-a-conservative/.

83. Merle Thorpe, "Our Vanishing Economic Freedom: Government Inflated," *Saturday Evening Post*, Oct 3, 1931, 21, 73–76; Merle Thorpe, "Our Vanishing Economic Freedom: Paternalism at High Tide," *Saturday Evening Post*, Oct 17, 1931, 25, 118–19, 122, 124. This series was cited for its invocation of "over-centralization and paternalism" in "Bureaucracy under Fire," *Hartford Courant*, Dec 28, 1931, 8.

84. Thorpe, "Our Vanishing Economic Freedom," Oct 3, 1931, 73.

85. See, for example, Amity Shlaes, *The Forgotten Man: A New History of the Great Depression* (New York: Harper Collins, 2007). The Pence quotation is from Jonathan Chait, "Wasting Away in Hooverville," *New Republic*, Mar 18, 2009, https://newrepublic.com/article/63351/wasting-away-hooverville.

86. James M. Beck and Merle Thorpe, *Neither Purse nor Sword* (New York: Macmillan, 1936), 126, 135, 187–88.

87. Political scientist McGee Young has shown that many anti–New Deal groups modeled their discourse on the 1920s, when "NAM and Chamber of Commerce lurched rightward, with NAM's James Emery and his counterparts at the Chamber launching attacks on organized labor and any hint of government intervention in the economy." "The Political Roots of Small Business Identity," *Polity* 40:4 (Oct 2008): 436–63.

Chapter 3. Free Enterprise versus the New Deal Order

1. Ben Mathis-Lilley, "Washington Man Wearing Anti-Government T-Shirt Thanks Firefighters for Saving His Home," *Slate*, Aug 24, 2015, http://www.slate.com/blogs/the_slatest/2015/08/24/less_government_more_freedom_t_shirt_firefighters_thanked_washington_state.html.

2. "Stevenson Named at Mock Convention," *St. Louis Post-Dispatch*, Apr 21, 1956, 3.

3. Snell is paraphrased in "Snell Pits Past against New Deal," *New York Times*, Aug 26, 1935, 1, 10. J. Melbourne Shortliffe said in 1941, "Until the latter part of the nineteenth century, the American economic way was that of free private enterprise." "The Greatest Test in Our History," *Vital Speeches of the Day*, Oct 1, 1941, 755.

4. W. Kee Maxwell, "Two Genuine Liberals," *Los Angeles Times*, Feb 18, 1940, 2:4.

5. "Wells Fargo—Revival of the Pioneer Spirits," *Congressional Record Appendix*, Feb 3, 1938, 430–31.

6. On the rapid spread of the term in the 1930s, see Wendy L. Wall, *Inventing the "American Way": The Politics of Consensus from the New Deal to the Civil Rights Movement* (New York: Oxford University Press, 2008), 48–49.

7. "Text of Hoover Speech Urging Party Rally: Coalition of Anti–New Dealers Approved and New Declaration of Aims Called For," *Los Angeles Times*, Oct 27, 1937, 6. See also

"Democrats Seek Coalition to End New Deal in '36," *Washington Post*, May 31, 1935, 1, 4; "Vandenberg Calls for Anti–New Deal Coalition: Senator Outlines Plan for Successful Opposition to the 'The Roosevelt Party,'" *Los Angeles Times*, Sep 19, 1937, 7; Mark Sullivan, "Attitude of Indiana Republicans toward Black-Listed Van Nuys Holds Important Signal for Anti–New Deal Coalition," *Washington Post*, Jun 28, 1938, X7. The first mention of "New Deal coalition" I have found is Jay Franklin, "Mr. Wallace's Predicament," *Boston Globe*, May 3, 1939, 16, which refers to the "farm wing of the New Deal coalition."

8. Leon Davis, "Yes, You Can 'Do Something about It'!" *Nation's Business*, Oct 1938, 36.

9. "Elect Mr. Willkie," *Baltimore Sun*, Aug 19, 1940, 10.

10. Robert Taft, "Something for Nothing," *Congressional Record—Senate*, Feb 26, 1936, 2808.

11. "Steiwer's Address of Notification," *New York Times*, Jul 31, 1936, 8.

12. "Dr. Frank Declares New Deal 'Fascist,'" *New York Times*, Jan 30, 1938, 1.

13. "The Case for Private Medicine: Give the Doctors a Hand!" *Nation's Business,* May 1940, 55.

14. W.S.R., "Did You Know?" *Lawrence Daily Journal-World*, Jul 22, 1941, 2.

15. "The Final Chance," *Chicago Tribune*, May 6, 1944, 10.

16. "Dr. Palyi, a New Citizen, Assails New Deal Rule," *Chicago Tribune*, Jun 15, 1939, 30.

17. "Rep. Nixon to Run for Senate Seat," *Philadelphia Inquirer,* Nov 4, 1949, 2. "New Deal Is Road to Chaos, Hoover Tells G.O.P.," *St. Petersburg Times*, Jun 11, 1936, 14; "Dewey Speaks Tonight on Road to Dictatorship," *Chicago Tribune*, Oct 16, 1940, 5; Thomas E. Dewey, *The Case against the New Deal* (New York: Harper and Brothers, 1940), 15. Byrnes is quoted in "The Road to Statism," *San Francisco Examiner*, Jun 28, 1948, 16. H. E. Humphreys, "A Father's Message to the New President," *Deseret News*, Oct 27, 1952, 12.

18. "Economic System to Be Open Forum," *Indianapolis News*, Jan 9, 1943, 8.

19. "Pettengill Favors Free Enterprise," *Philadelphia Inquirer*, Nov 12, 1936, 30.

20. Frank Gannett used the phrase: "Gannett Consents to Run with Borah," *Boston Globe*, Feb 27, 1936, 6.

21. "Free Enterprise on Death Bed, Admen Told," *Milwaukee Sentinel*, Jun 23, 1961, 5.

22. Daniel T. Rodgers, "Republicanism: The Career of a Concept," *Journal of American History* 79 (Jun 1992): 11–38.

23. *Facts: The New Deal versus the American System* (Chicago: Republican National Committee, 1936).

24. The American Presidency Project contains links to all of the major party platforms: http://www.presidency.ucsb.edu/platforms.php.

25. "Text of Willkie's Address in Milwaukee," *Minneapolis Morning Tribune*, Oct 22, 1940, 6; Wendell L. Willkie, *Free Enterprise: The Philosophy of Wendell L. Willkie as Found in His Speeches, Messages, and Other Papers* (Washington, DC: National Home Library Foundation, 1940).

26. Dewey, *Case against the New Deal*, vii, x.

27. Roscoe Drummond, "Goldwater Becomes His Own Kingmaker," *Lawton Constitution*, Jul 15, 1964, 22; "Anyhow, This Is Our Theory about It," *Des Moines Tribune*, Oct 24, 1946, 26.

28. Glenn Frank, "The Fear of Size," *Ithaca Journal*, Aug 15, 1935, 6; "Willkie Quotes Churchill's 1937 Warning of World Effects from Roosevelt's War on Business," *Burlington Free Press*, Sep 23, 1940, 10.

29. Arthur Sears Henning, "U.S. Split Wide Open over 'Red' Issue at Polls: Not since '60 Have Voters Been So Aroused," *Chicago Tribune*, Oct 13, 1936, 11.

30. "The Logic of Free Enterprise," *Prescott Evening Courier*, Dec 8, 1947, 2:2. For a very similar sentiment, see David Baxter, "Eleanor Again," *Odessa American*, Sep 17, 1950, 26.

31. Albert O. Hirschman, *The Rhetoric of Reaction* (Cambridge, MA: Harvard University Press, 1991).

32. Russell W. Davenport, "The Greatest Opportunity on Earth," *Fortune,* Oct 1949, 65.

33. "Creed Approved by 'Grass Root' Republicans," *Washington Post*, Jun 12, 1935, 4.

34. Felix Bruner, "Industrial Conference Denounces Trend to Dictatorship," *Washington Post*, Dec 6, 1935, 1, 2.

35. "Implications of 'Planning,'" *Wall Street Journal*, Jun 26, 1942, 4.

36. "Centralized Planning Opposed: Business Men Fight for Free Enterprise; Fear Post-war Regimentation If They Neglect Safeguards," *Pittsburgh Post-Gazette*, Dec 8, 1941, 18.

37. "Wolf in Sheep's Clothing," *Moline Dispatch*, Sep 11, 1936, 1.

38. "Reawakening of Citizens Is Goal of 'Manifesto,'" *NAM News*, Dec 22, 1951, 12–13, National Association of Manufacturers Collection, series 1, box 2, Manuscripts and Archives Department, Hagley Museum and Library, Wilmington, DE; Si Steinhauser, "Ad Club Selects Courageous Bob Montgomery as Speaker," *Pittsburgh Press*, May 24, 1953, 5, 10.

39. Ralph Becker, "Youth Must Choose between Individualism and the Welfare State," Extension of Remarks, Hon. J. Caleb Boggs (DE), *Congressional Record*, May 27, 1949, A3333.

40. Willard Edwards, "Stevenson Held Front for Plot to Socialize U.S.: La Varre Reveals Plans for Super-State," *Chicago Tribune*, Sep 16, 1952, 5.

41. "Free Private Enterprise in the Americas," address by Honorable Spruille Braden at News, Knowledge and Freedom of the Americas Meeting, Oct 12, 1955, series 1, box 67, Free Enterprise File, "Free Enterprise, General, 1951–63," Manuscripts and Archives Department, Hagley Museum and Library.

42. Henry Hazlitt, "The Road to Totalitarianism," in *On Freedom and Free Enterprise: Essays in Honor of Ludwig von Mises*, ed. Mary Sennholz (Princeton: D. Van Nostrand, 1956), 83.

43. "Taft Attacks Truman Policy," *Baltimore Sun*, Apr 1, 1950, 5.

44. Bruner, "Industrial Conference Denounces Trend to Dictatorship."

45. Lemuel R. Boulware, "Where Do We Go from Here? The Need for Economic Education," *Vital Speeches of the Day,* Sep 15, 1952, 728, 725.

46. Lorene Frederick, "Free Enterprise Forged Its Own Shackle Chains," *Florence Times,* Mar 9, 1966, 1, 2.

47. Blair Moody, "Truman Aims at Vast Program of Expansion," *Boston Globe*, Oct 2, 1949, C6.

48. Friedman is quoted in Angus Burgin, *The Great Persuasion: Reinventing Free Markets since the Depression* (Cambridge, MA: Harvard University Press, 2012), 223, 211.

49. Lloyd A. Free and Hadley Cantril, *The Political Beliefs of Americans: A Study of Public Opinion* (New Brunswick: Rutgers University Press, 1967), 32, 33, 36.
50. "Landon Attacks Sham Liberalism," *Lawrence Daily Journal-World*, Oct 12, 1936, 1.
51. Harold J. Laski, *The American Democracy: A Commentary and Interpretation* (New York: Viking, 1948), 167.
52. Burton W. Folsom, *New Deal or Raw Deal? How FDR's Economic Legacy Has Damaged America* (New York: Threshold Editions, Simon and Schuster, 2009), 43.
53. "'War on Poverty' Has Become a War on Business," *Human Events*, Aug 27, 1966, 7.
54. "Utahns in Limelight on Hearings for International Women's Year," *Salt Lake Tribune*, Sep 15, 1977, B1.
55. William Feather, "Build America!" *Nation's Business*, Jun 1940, 45.
56. Alpheus Thomas Mason, "Welfare Capitalism: Opportunity or Delusion?" *Virginia Quarterly Review* (Autumn 1950): 530.
57. "'Hybrid' Economy a Recent Thing," *Washington Post*, Jan 28, 1951, B8.
58. "The Coming Conflict," *Bankers Magazine,* July 1939, 1.
59. "Lumber Men Met Here," *New York Times*, Sep 18, 1936, 42.
60. "Topics of the Times: Half and Half," *New York Times*, Oct 23, 1936, 22. On invocations of Lincoln in the 1930s, see Nina Silber, *This War Ain't Over: Fighting the Civil War in New Deal America* (Chapel Hill: University of North Carolina Press, 2018).
61. "Text of President's Address," *Boston Globe*, Jun 28, 1936, A16.
62. "Fight for American Traditions to Unite Republicans, Mills Says," *New York Herald Tribune*, Apr 22, 1937, 10.
63. "New Deal Failure, Gannett Asserts," *New York Times*, Feb 4, 1940, 2.
64. "Implications of 'Planning.'"
65. "Socialism Marches On," *Fort Lauderdale News*, Feb 15, 1947, 4; "Urge Extending Jobless Pay to 7 Million More: Workers' Tax Proposed by Senate Group," *Chicago Tribune*, Jan 2, 1949, 14.
66. "'Recapture the Citadels of Liberty,' Hoover Exhorts G.O.P.," *Chicago Tribune*, Jun 11, 1936, 6.
67. "Resolutions Adopted at Meeting of National Association of Manufacturers," *New York Times*, Dec 8, 1944, 16.
68. "What Kind of Regulation?" *Los Angeles Times*, Jan 2, 1949, 2:4.
69. C. B. Alexander, "The President's Column," *American Builder*, Sep 1, 1949, 110.
70. "Clean Cut Alternative to New Deal: Free Govt, Free Men, Free Enterprise Asks Mills," *Nashua Telegraph*, May 9, 1935, 8.
71. "Knox Acceptance Attacks Regimentation, Pledges Freedom of Enterprise," *Boston Globe*, Jul 31, 1936, 2.
72. Arthur Herman, *Freedom's Forge: How American Business Produced Victory in World War II* (New York: Random House, 2012). "The '40s were among the worst times in history for the ideals of freedom and free markets," as libertarian writer Donald Boudreaux wrote. "At the time, government control of the economy was all the rage." Donald Boudreaux, "Remembering an Unsung Defender of Freedom," *Investor's Business Daily*, Sep 24, 1998, A28.

73. Fifield letter of May 10, 1944, quoted in Brian Doherty, *Radicals for Capitalism: A Free-wheeling History of the Modern American Libertarian Movement* (New York: Public Affairs, 2007), 222.

74. Mark R. Wilson, "Spinning Mars: Democracy in Britain and the United States," in *In War's Wake: International Conflict and the Fate of Liberal Democracy*, ed. Elizabeth Kier and Ronald R. Krebs (New York: Cambridge University Press, 2010), 175. See also Mark R. Wilson, *Destructive Creation: American Business and the Winning of World War II* (Philadelphia: University of Pennsylvania Press, 2016); Nancy Bernhard, *U.S. Television News and Cold War Propaganda, 1947–1960* (Cambridge: Cambridge University Press, 2003), 21.

75. "Centralized Planning Opposed."

76. "For Free Enterprise: Manufacturers Head Offers Solution of Post-war Crisis," *Lawrence Daily Journal-World*, Nov 4, 1941, 3.

77. "Federal Financing of Defense Program Stifling Private Initiative, Says Connely," *New York Times*, Sep 26, 1940, 39.

78. "Warns That Fascism May Be Forced on Us," *New York Times*, Nov 30, 1938, 17.

79. "Free Enterprise Fights the War," *Prescott Evening Courier*, Aug 17, 1942, 4.

80. Milton V. Burgess, "War Being Won by Free Enterprise, Says Bricker," *Milwaukee Sentinel*, Sep 20, 1944, 4.

81. "Socialism Growth in U.S. Traced to New Deal Era," *Los Angeles Times*, Dec 2, 1949, 12.

82. "Harold E. Stassen, Youthful Governor of Minnesota, Sounds Keynote for Republican National Convention," *Chicago Tribune*, Jun 25, 1940, 4.

83. H. W. Prentis, "Competitive Enterprise versus Planned Economy," *Vital Speeches of the Day*, April 15 1945, 413.

84. Alf Landon, "Will We Keep Faith?" speech in Knoxville, Feb 11, 1944, *Congressional Record Appendix*, Feb 15, 1944, A719.

85. Carleton Putnam, *Our Two Front War in Domestic Aviation: The Challenge to Free Enterprise in the Air* (Memphis, 1944); Lee Morris, "Free Speeches," *St. Petersburg Evening Independent*, Aug 12, 1943, 10.

86. John Costello, "Planning for Free Enterprise," *Congressional Record Appendix*, Mar 8, 1943, A1084.

87. "Without It the Freedoms Are Just Talk," *Deseret News*, Feb 19, 1944, 3.

88. Frederick C. Crawford, "Free Speech for a Free Future," *New London Day*, Jul 28, 1943, 6.

89. Burgess, "War Being Won by Free Enterprise, Says Bricker"; Wilson, *Destructive Creation*, 96–97; Katherine Rye Jewell, *Dollars for Dixie: Business and the Transformation of Conservatism in the Twentieth Century* (New York: Cambridge University Press, 2017), 167.

90. Drucker is quoted in Bruce Crawford, "When the Soldiers Come Back," *Virginia Quarterly Review* 19:1 (Winter 1943): 73.

91. "Hickenlooper Declares Bureaucracy Is Threat," *Lawrence Daily Journal-World*, Dec 8, 1943, 2.

92. "Super-State Peril Seen by Johnston," *New York Times*, Mar 25, 1943, 8.

93. "Postwar Plan Is Demanded: Head of Inland Firm Calls for 'Clearing for Free Enterprise,'" *Reading Eagle*, Jun 28, 1943, 7.

94. "Kiwanis Head Lists 'Cannots' for Democracy," *Columbus Herald*, Nov 15, 1944, 2.

95. "Bureaucracy After the War," *Nation's Business*, Feb 1944, 79; Lawrence Sullivan, *Bureaucracy Runs Amuck* (Indianapolis: Bobbs-Merrill, 1944).

96. Sen. Albert W. Hawkes, "A Practical Postwar Program," *Nation's Business*, Aug 1943, 42.

97. E. E. Cox, "We Could Lose This War," *Nation's Business*, Mar 1942, 60, 69.

98. "NAM Head Hits Reform," *Milwaukee Journal*, Dec 2, 1942, 10.

99. Merle Thorpe, "The Promise of Free Enterprise," *Nation's Business*, Aug 1942, 15.

100. George is quoted in Ralph Hendershot, "United for Victory!" *Nation's Business*, Jun 1943, 26.

101. "One of These Days I'll Turn in My Jeep for a Job!" *Wall Street Journal*, Oct 20, 1943, 6.

102. "Orator Defends Free Enterprise: Bureaucrats Flayed by Portland Lawyer," *Spokane Spokesman-Review*, Oct 27, 1944, 6.

103. Charles G. Bolte, "When Joe Is out of Uniform: Soldier into Civilian," *New York Times*, Jul 1, 1945, 11, 19.

104. Crawford, "When The Soldiers Come Back," 72.

105. "What about Opportunities for Future Americans?" *Lawrence Daily Journal-World*, Jan 11, 1944, 8.

106. Thorpe, "Promise of Free Enterprise."

107. This is similar to Mitt Romney's decision to start Bain Capital only if there "was no professional or financial risk." Ezra Klein, "Romney's Risk-Free Deal with Bain," *Washington Post*, Jul 17, 2012, https://www.washingtonpost.com/blogs/ezra-klein/wp/2012/07/17/romneys-risk-free-deal-with-bain/.

108. Arthur Evans, "G.O.P. in Indiana Adopts a 'Win War' Platform: Warns Voters Burocracy Must Be Curbed," *Chicago Tribune*, Jun 19, 1942, 15.

109. "Postwar Plan Is Demanded: Head of Inland Firm Calls for 'Clearing for Free Enterprise,'" *Reading Eagle*, Jun 28, 1943, 7.

110. Crawford, "Free Speech for a Free Future."

111. "Martin Defends Free Enterprise: Republican Candidate Assails Bureaucrats," *Reading Eagle*, Oct 9, 1946, 2.

112. Mark Wilson writes, "Although this interpretation fit poorly with the realities of the industrial mobilization, it was nonetheless surprisingly successful in influencing American public discourse." "Spinning Mars," 175–76.

113. "Free Enterprise Return Is Urged When War Ends," *Berkeley Daily Gazette*, Feb 12, 1944, 6.

114. "1944 Issues," *Washington Post*, Dec 11, 1943, 8.

115. "Hawkes Condemns Bureaucrats' Rule," *New York Times*, Jan 30, 1944, 32.

116. "Freedom in Peril, Bricker Asserts," *New York Times*, June 10, 1944, 28.

117. "Hoover, Gibson Discuss Hard Job in 'Problems of Lasting Peace,'" *Pittsburgh Press*, Jun 28, 1942, 37.

118. Cox, "We Could Lose This War," 69; "Cox Hits 'Confusion' Made by Bureaucrats: Rep-

resentative Says There Is Too Much Testing of Theories," *New York Times*, Feb 23, 1943, 29.

119. "Lyons Assails New Deal over 'Win War' Cry," *Chicago Tribune*, Sep 1, 1944, 6.

120. Harvey J. Kaye, *The Fight for the Four Freedoms: What Made FDR and the Greatest Generation Truly Great* (New York: Simon and Schuster, 2014).

121. "Free Enterprise Is Described as 'Fifth Freedom," *St. Petersburg Evening Independent*, Sep 28, 1942, 11. Kaye, *Fight for the Four Freedoms*, 118–20; Wilson, *Destructive Creation*, 213; Roland Marchand, *Creating the Corporate Soul: The Rise of Public Relations and Corporate Imagery in American Big Business* (Berkeley: University of California Press, 1998), 321–24.

122. "The 5th Freedom," *Blair Press*, Nov 4, 1943, 6.

123. "A Day to Give Thanks for Free Enterprise," *Chicago Tribune*, Nov 25, 1943, 40.

124. "Boys, I'll Tell You What Free Enterprise Really Is," *Saturday Evening Post*, Apr 23, 1944. For a parody of this ad, see William A. Caldwell, "Simeon Stylites," *Bergen Evening Record*, Mar 29, 1944, 24.

125. "Let's Keep for Them the Human Values of Free Enterprise," *Ellensburg Daily Record*, Aug 31, 1943, 3.

126. "We Are Thankful for 'The Fifth Freedom,'" *Toledo Blade*, Nov 22, 1943, 16. The Thanksgiving ad mentions the Four Freedoms.

127. "Blow at Freedom: McClure Describes Efforts to Undermine Free Enterprise," *Lawrence Daily Journal-World*, Jun 28, 1943, 1.

128. "Realty President Says Free Press Vital to Freedom," *St. Petersburg Evening Independent*, Jan 18, 1943, 5.

129. "'Fifth Freedom' Waged by Butler," *Miami News*, Sep 6, 1943, 11.

130. "A Fifth Freedom," *Milwaukee Sentinel*, Aug 23, 1943, 8.

131. "A 'Fifth Freedom' Proposed," *Los Angeles Times*, Aug 4, 1943, A4.

132. S. S. Humphreys, "The Letter Box," *Newmarket News*, Sep 15, 1944, 13. For a similar formulation, see "The New Deal Trend," *Rapid City Journal*, Dec 16, 1942, 9.

133. "Capt. Rickenbacker Believes 'America Needs a Man,'" *Burlington Free Press*, May 31, 1944, 14.

134. "Without It The Freedoms Are Just Talk."

135. "Resist Communism, Hoover Demands," *New York Times*, Aug 12, 1945, 1, 34.

136. "Free Enterprise Faces New Test in America: Next Two Decades May Decide Future of U.S.," *Reading Eagle*, Oct 17, 1946, 11.

137. Charles A. Plumley, "Socialism Unadulterated," *Congressional Record Appendix*, Oct 19, 1949, A6667.

138. "'Fifth Freedom Flight' Will Be Launched Oct. 1," *Victoria Advocate*, Sep 28, 1947, 2.

139. John T. Flynn, *The Road Ahead: America's Creeping Revolution* (New York: Devin-Adair, 1949), 90.

140. Ethel Lyman Stannard, "Let Us Explore the Full Extent of Freedom," *Hartford Courant*, Feb 10, 1953, 12.

141. Mario Einaudi, *The Roosevelt Revolution* (New York: Harcourt, Brace, 1959), 104, 83. While he noted that FDR "would not sit idly by and in the name of free enterprise allow

the free enterprisers to destroy freedom," he made it clear that the New Deal sought to strengthen both free enterprise and freedom in a mixed economy. For a very early use of the phrase, see Ernest K. Lindley, *The Roosevelt Revolution: First Phase* (New York: Viking, 1933).

142. Jennifer Mittelstadt, "Reimagining the Welfare State," *Jacobin*, Jul 23, 2015, https://www.jacobinmag.com/2015/07/fdr-social-security-gi-bill/.

143. "After Two Years," *Cincinnati Enquirer*, Mar 5 1935, 4. For a historical assessment of the New Deal as a "patchwork of limited reforms," see Howard Brick, *Transcending Capitalism: Visions of a New Society in Modern American Thought* (Ithaca: Cornell University Press, 2006), 250.

144. "Control of Industry," *Chicago Tribune*, May 21, 1933, 14.

145. "Defense of the Middle Class," *Chicago Tribune*, May 27, 1934, 16.

146. Samuel Crowther, "Free Enterprise in U.S. Seen Giving Way to Social Revolution of Controlled Economy," *Outlook*, Aug 10, 1941, S7.

147. "Free Enterprise or Dictatorship Seen as Choice," *Los Angeles Times*, Mar 19, 1947, 6.

148. Chesly Manly, who quoted this approvingly, spoke of the "creeping revolution" begun by FDR and continued by Truman. *The Twenty-Year Revolution from Roosevelt to Eisenhower* (Chicago: Henry Regnery, 1954).

149. "The Ethics of Free Enterprise," *Christian Science Monitor*, reprinted in *Montreal Gazette,* Nov 1, 1946, 8.

150. "Free Enterprise Offensive Asked," *Los Angeles Times*, Jul 9, 1946, 2.

151. Larry Kudlow, "Would Adam Smith Approve?" *National Review*, May 26, 2006, http://www.nationalreview.com/article/217751/would-adam-smith-approve-larry-kudlow.

152. Hume is quoted in Chris Lehman, "Let Them Eat Dogma," *Baffler* 18 (2009), http://thebaffler.com/salvos/let-them-eat-dogma.

153. Merle Thorpe, "The Liquidation of Enterprise," *Nation's Business*, Mar 1939, 15.

154. Rexford G. Tugwell, *Roosevelt's Revolution: The First Year—A Personal Perspective* (New York: Macmillan, 1977), 42.

155. Richard V. Gilbert, George H. Hildebrand Jr., Arthur W. Stuart, Maxine Yaple Sweezy, Paul M. Sweezy, Lorie Tarshis, and John D. Wilson, *An Economic Progress for American Democracy* (New York: Vanguard, 1938), 88, 47–48.

156. "Ogden Mills Says New Deal Kills Liberty," *Southeast Missourian*, Aug 17, 1935, 1.

157. "Implications of 'Planning.'"

158. "Ogden Mills Says New Deal Kills Liberty."

159. Henry Steele Commager, "Appraisal of the Welfare State," *New York Times*, May 15, 1949, SM30.

160. Alfred Jay Nock, *Journal of Forgotten Days: 1934–1935* (Chicago: Regnery, 1948), 75 (Nov 25, 1934). "Of course the New Deal is here to stay: the only real competition of political parties will be for the privilege and emoluments of administering it. Probably there will be superficial changes, but none essential." Peter Berkowitz used language very similar to Nock's in "Moderation Is No Vice," *Weekly Standard,* Jul 27, 2009, 28–32. Berkowitz wrote, "Like it or not, the New Deal is here to stay. It has been incorporated into constitutional law and woven into the fabric of the American sensibility

and American society." Garet Garrett, *The Revolution Was* (Caldwell, ID: Caxton, 1944), https://mises.org/library/revolution-was.

161. Matthew Continetti, "The End of the New Deal Order," *Weekly Standard*, Sep 5, 2011. Conservative columnist Ross Douthat wrote, "Ronald Reagan also accepted the New Deal settlement." "What's the Matter with Republicans?" *New York Times*, Oct 18, 2017.

162. David Edwards, "Forcing Walmart to Pay Living Wage Could be 'the Death of Free Enterprise,'" *Raw Story*, Jul 12, 2013; John Amato, "To Elisabeth Hasselbeck, Gay Rights Are Death to Free Enterprise," *Crooks and Liars*, Dec 11, 2013, http://crooksand liars.com/2013/12/elisabeth-hasselbeck-gay-rights-are-death.

163. Norbert Michel, "We Haven't Had a True Free Enterprise System for Decades," *Daily Signal*, Mar 1, 2015, https://www.dailysignal.com/2015/03/01/we-havent-had-a-true -free-enterprise-system-for-decades/.

164. Andrew Hartman, "The New Historiographic Consensus on the 1970s," *USIH Blog*, Apr 21, 2011, https://s-usih.org/2011/04/new-historiographic-consensus-on-1970s/.

165. "Defeat Muddled Thinkers, Ex–New Dealer Tells G.O.P.," *Chicago Tribune*, Apr 25, 1936, 4.

166. Gary Gerstle and Steve Fraser, introduction to *The Rise and Fall of the New Deal Order, 1930–1980*, ed. Fraser and Gerstle (Princeton: Princeton University Press, 1989), ix. With the election of Ronald Reagan, they note, "an epoch in the nation's political history came to an end." In my view, it is better understood in terms of rises and falls. Jefferson Cowie and Nick Salvatore call the New Deal "a historical aberration." Jefferson Cowie and Nick Salvatore, "The Long Exception: Rethinking the Place of the New Deal in American History," *International Labor and Working-Class History* 74 (2008): 4–5. See also Jefferson Cowie, *The Great Exception: The New Deal and the Limits of American Politics* (Princeton: Princeton University Press, 2016).

167. Arthur Evans, "NRA Spell Over, Sloan Tells His Hope of Revival: Industry to Advance on Old Lines," *Chicago Tribune*, Dec 12, 1934, 1, 6; Clifford Kennedy Berryman, "The Death of the New Deal Has Been Greatly Exaggerated," editorial cartoon in *Washington Star*, Sep 24, 1944, at Library of Congress, http://www.loc.gov/pictures/item /2016679383/.

Chapter 4. A "Beautiful but Much-Abused Phrase"

1. John Chamberlain, "We Are Ruled by Phrases," *Tucson Daily Citizen*, Aug 24, 1964, 12.

2. Felix Morley, *The Power in the People* (New York: D. Van Nostrand, 1949), 207.

3. DeWitt Emery, "What Is It?" *Mexica Daily News*, Oct 12, 1948, 4, reprinted in many newspapers as "Wanted: One Reference Book to Define Free Enterprise."

4. "Emery Says Free Enterprise Is Definitely a Way of Life," *San Marino Tribune*, Feb 17, 1949, 10.

5. John S. Piper, "Wanted—A Good Definition for 'Free Enterprise'! Small Business Group Head Fails to Uncover One," *San Francisco News*, Nov 15, 1948, 21. The definition in its entirety was "the doctrine or practice of a minimum amount of Government control

of private business and industry." John S. Piper, "Two Readers Find Dictionary Definition of Free Enterprise," *San Francisco News*, Nov 26, 1948, 19.

6. Malcolm W. Bingay, "Free What?" *Detroit Free Press*, Dec 31, 1948, 4.

7. Pat Frayne, "Have You a Definition for Free Enterprise?" *American Flint* 38 (Jan 1949):
34.

8. "For Free Enterprise," *Washington Post*, Dec 18, 1939, 8.

9. Ima Slammer, "Free Enterprise," *York Gazette and Daily*, Aug 21, 1944, 13.

10. "What Do You Mean 'Free Private Enterprise'?" *Business Week*, Feb 2, 1946, 108.

11. "Little Business Man from Ohio Is in Town to Enlist Recruits," *New York Herald Tribune*, Feb 13, 1938, 26.

12. "Drum Beaters' Warning," *Akron Beacon Journal*, May 3, 1947, 6.

13. "Introducing DeWitt Emery," *Casa Grande Dispatch*, Feb 9, 1945, 8.

14. DeWitt Emery, "Planned Economy: The American Way," *Pampa Daily News*, Apr 15,
1945, 4.

15. Harry Flood Byrd, "The Menace of the Budget," *National Review*, May 11, 1957,
445–46.

16. Susan Thayer, "The Business of Living: What Does 'Free Enterprise' Mean?" *Springville
Herald*, Jan 20, 1944, 10.

17. A. D. H. Kaplan, "The Role of Small Business and Free Enterprise," *Proceedings of the
Academy of Political Science* 22 (May 1947): 269.

18. Michael O'Shaughnessy, *Economic Democracy and Private Enterprise: A Study of the
Relation of Economic Groups to the Federal Government* (New York: Harper and Brothers, 1945), 92.

19. Elisha P. Douglass, *The Coming of Age of American Business: Three Centuries of Enterprise, 1600–1900* (Chapel Hill: University of North Carolina Press, 1971), 75, 6, 5.

20. Creston Wolfe, "Letters," *St. Louis Star and Times*, Aug 11, 1945, 10.

21. O'Shaughnessy, *Economic Democracy and Private Enterprise*, 91.

22. "Portrait of 'Free Enterprise,'" *Eugene Guard*, May 26, 1944, 4.

23. "Questions for Republicans," *Pittsburgh Press*, Feb 18, 1940, 18.

24. Henry Meritt Wriston, "Real Meaning of Free Enterprise," *Vital Speeches of the Day*, Jan
15, 1944, 197.

25. George Gallup, "Gallup Poll: Only Three in Every Ten Are Able to Give Correct Defini-
tion of 'Free Enterprise,'" *Washington Post*, Nov 6, 1943, 7. See also George Gallup,
"Business Has Teaching Job, Survey Shows: Free Enterprise Meaning Known by Only
Three in Ten Asked," *Pittsburgh Press*, Nov 6, 1943, 16; George Gallup, "Poll Shows
Only Three in Every 10 Had Right Definition of Free Enterprise," *Tampa Bay Times*,
Nov 6, 1943, 4. Information on the survey, which was conducted between Oct 8 and 13,
1943, can be found in George H. Gallup, *The Gallup Poll: Public Opinion, 1935–1971*,
vol. 1, *1935–1948* (New York: Random House, 1972), 416.

26. H. R. Baukhage, "U.S. Businessmen Try to Define Free Enterprise," *Louisville Leader*,
Apr 20, 1944, 2.

27. Bliven took on Ruth Alexander in the debate, which was moderated by Fred G. Clark.
Wake Up America, 2nd ser., program 26, *What Is Free Enterprise?* part 1 (New York:
Radio-Recording Division, National Broadcasting Company, 1943). The recording is

available at the Marr Sound Archives, Nichols Library, University of Missouri, Kansas City.

28. "Free Enterprise," *Salisbury Times*, Nov 13, 1943, 4.

29. "What's Free Enterprise?" *Advertising Age*, Nov 15, 1943, 12.

30. H. W. Prentis Jr., "Competitive Enterprise versus Planned Economy" (NAM, August 1945), series 1, box 67, Free Enterprise File, "Free Enterprise, General," Manuscripts and Archives Department, Hagley Museum and Library, Wilmington, DE.

31. Leonard Dreyfuss, "Just What Is Free Enterprise?" *Printers' Ink*, Mar 24, 1944, 85.

32. "Here, Mr. Dreyfuss, Are Some Definitions of Free Enterprise," *Printers' Ink*, Apr 7, 1944, 85.

33. H. A. Wolff, "Free Enterprise Definition in Verse," *Printers' Ink*, Sep 1, 1944, 96. Wolff was the editorial and research director of Kelly-Read and Co., Inc.

34. "Here, Mr. Dreyfuss, Are Some Definitions of Free Enterprise."

35. Jim Donnelly to Wilbur J. Brons, Feb 8, 1944, National Association of Manufacturers Collection, series 3, box 844, folder: Inadequacy [?] of the Term Free Enterprise, Manuscripts and Archives Department, Hagley Museum and Library.

36. *Free Enterprise: It's Past and Future: Some Basic Facts about Our American System of Competitive Enterprise* (NAM, 1945), 3, Hagley Library Imprints Collection, Manuscripts and Archives Department, Hagley Museum and Library.

37. Lifford Murragh, "Is Defending Free Enterprise Tilting at a Windmill?" *Printers' Ink*, Sep 1, 1944, 100–104.

38. "Free Enterprise," *Annapolis Capitol*, Oct 17, 1944, 4.

39. "Letters to the Editor," *Printers' Ink*, May 19, 1944, 90.

40. John Orr Young, "Stop Shouting 'Free Enterprise' Unless You Give the Term Meaning," *Printers' Ink*, May 5, 1944, 17–18, 88–92.

41. Erwin H. Klaus, "Free Enterprise Definitions Make a Soldier Anxious, So He Enters His Own," *Printers' Ink*, May 5, 1944, 18.

42. "You Haven't Given Mr. Dreyfuss What He Asked For!" *Printers' Ink*, June 9, 1944, 24.

43. Eric A. Johnston, "Free Enterprise Now Faces Crisis and Opportunity," *Printers' Ink*, Apr 14, 1944, 19–20, 94. It should be noted that Johnston's positive spin seemed quite different from the opinion of most of his colleagues: "There has been a most significant change in the viewpoints and attitudes of people in regard to free enterprise. A few years ago, it took a great deal of courage to speak for and to defend free enterprise. In fact, many of the valiant souls who did so, spoke in low and guarded tones, and only a few were willing to be quoted. But things have changed! Now, you have to look very far indeed to find anyone who is not for free enterprise. Yet that phenomenon should not occasion too much surprise. You know the answer—so does everyone else. It's because we've made free enterprise work!"

44. "What Do You Mean 'Free Private Enterprise'?"

45. "Securing the Ideals for Which We Fought," address by Paul H. Griffith, National Commander of the American Legion, Congress of American Industry, Dec 6, 1946, series 1, box 67, Free Enterprise File, "Free Enterprise, General," Manuscripts and Archives Department, Hagley Museum and Library.

46. "American Survey: Free Enterprise," *Economist*, Mar 31, 1945, 413–14.

47. Herbert Hoover, *The Challenge to Liberty* (New York: Charles Scribner's Sons, 1934), 51.

48. Margaret D. Armstrong, "Second Negative," "Permanent Economic Controls," Syracuse University versus Middlebury College, in *University Debaters' Annual*, 1944–45, ed. Edith M. Phelps (New York: H. W. Wilson, 1945), 229.

49. Warren B. Francis, "Dewey Outlines Broad Program of Jobs for All," *Los Angeles Times*, Sep 22, 1944, 1, 6.

50. John Chamberlain, "On the Free Society," *American Mercury* 70 (Feb 1950): 240.

51. Henry Merritt Wriston, *Challenge to Freedom* (New York: Harper and Brothers, 1943). 75.

52. "Hoover Speech at Lincoln Dinner," *New York Times*, Feb 13, 1946, 9.

53. Willard Edwards, "Stevenson Held Front for Plot to Socialize U.S.: La Varre Reveals Plans for Super-State," *Chicago Tribune*, Sep 16, 1952, 5.

54. "Restoring Freedom," *Fortune,* Dec 1942, 9.

55. Charles P. Taft, "A Landon Liberal," *Forum and Century* 96 (Nov 1936): 195.

56. H. W. Prentis Jr., *The Mobilization for Understanding of Private Enterprise: One of the Indispensable Supports of Individual Freedom* (New York: National Association of Manufacturers, 1940), 3.

57. J. Strom Thurmond, "'O'er the Ramparts We Watched!' Local Sovereignty Is Being Whittled Away," *Vital Speeches of the Day* (Oct 15, 1949), 30.

58. Robert Liebenow, "Let's Keep Free Enterprise Free" 10, address in Spokane to the Pacific Northwest Advisory Board, Sep 18, 1959, series 1, box 67, Free Enterprise File, "Free Enterprise, General, 1951–63," Manuscripts and Archives Department, Hagley Museum and Library.

59. Alan S. Boyd, "Free Enterprise Threatened? Economy & Politics," *Vital Speeches of the Day*, Nov 15, 1974, 75–77.

60. Robert A. Taft, "How Much Government Can Free Enterprise Stand?" *Colliers,* Oct 22, 1949, 16.

61. Harold D. Koontz, "Government Control: The Road to Serfdom?" *Education,* Jan 1951, 312.

62. Richard L. Lesher, "Can Capitalism Survive? The Unbelievable Growth of Government Power and Spending," *Vital Speeches of the Day*, Sep 15, 1975, 732.

63. "'Hybrid' Economy a Recent Thing," *Washington Post*, Jan 28, 1951, B8.

64. "Spread It on Thick, Brother," *Lincoln Star*, Aug 24, 1936, 6; Poncho, "Working Man's Friend," *St. Louis Post-Dispatch*, Nov 1, 1948, 2B.

65. Proquest Newspapers Online (assessed Jan 6, 2018). As Wendy L. Wall has written, "The rapidity with which the word[s] 'free enterprise' entered general usage in the late 1930s is stunning even by the standards of political speech." *Inventing the "American Way": The Politics of Consensus from the New Deal to the Civil Rights Movement* (New York: Oxford University Press, 2008), 49.

66. Ernest L. Meyer, "The Old Hokum Is Back Again," *St. Louis Post-Dispatch*, Dec 17, 1939, 20.

67. John Algeo, ed., *Fifty Years among the New Words: A Dictionary of Neologisms, 1941–1991* (New York: Cambridge University Press, 1991), 112, 122. The reference work also contains a 1958 entry for "free enterpriser," 150.

68. Nathan Robertson, "What Do You Mean, Free Enterprise?" *Harper's Weekly*, Nov 1948,

70–75. The radical journalist George Seldes claimed that the term was "coined" and "originated" by NAM. George Seldes and Helen Seldes, *Facts and Fascism* (New York: In Fact, 1943), 119, 196.

69. Adolph Reed Jr. quoted in Thomas Frank, "We Are All Right-Wingers Now: How Fox News, Ineffective Liberals, Corporate Dems and GOP Money Captured Everything," *Salon*, Mar 9, 2014, http://www.salon.com/2014/03/09/we_are_all_right_wingers_now _how_fox_news_ineffective_liberals_corporate_dems_and_gop_money_captured_every thing/; Glen Yeadon and John Hawkins, *The Nazi Hydra in America: Suppressed History of a Century* (Palm Desert, CA: Progressive, 2008), http://home.roadrunner.com/~mark wrede/NonFic/NaziHydra.pdf.

70. Milton Friedman and Rose Friedman, *Free to Choose: A Personal Statement* (New York: Harcourt Brace Jovanovich, 1980), 133; Arthur C. Brooks, *The Battle: How the Fight between Free Enterprise and Big Government Will Shape the Future* (New York: Basic Books, 2011), 3.

71. "Fascist Trend in Government," *Arizona Republic*, May 10, 1941, 22.

72. Florence Fisher Perry, "I Dare Say," *Pittsburgh Press*, Nov 21, 1941, 2.

73. "Everybody Liberal," *Kane Republican*, Sep 25, 1944, 4.

74. "Letter to the Editor," *East Liverpool Evening Review*, Apr 10, 1959, 4.

75. Frank Getlein, "The Unfree Nonenterprisers," *Christian Century*, April 14, 1971, 461–65.

76. Lewis H. Brown, "Freedom or Planned Economy: There Is no Middle Road," *Reference Shelf*, May 26, 1946, 133–43.

77. "Free Enterprise to Be Issue in Next Election, N.A.M. Told," *Washington Post*, Jun 22, 1943, 13.

78. "Leadership for Peacetimes," speech by Ira Mosher, President NAM, 25th Annual Meeting of the Associated Industries of Maine, Dec 14, 1945, series 1, box 67, Free Enterprise File, "Free Enterprise, General," Manuscripts and Archives Department, Hagley Museum and Library.

79. Alan Greenspan, "Strengthening Freedom through Free Enterprise," in *An Economic Philosophy for a Free People*, ed. Paul C. Goelz (San Antonio: St. Mary's University Press, 1979). See also, in the same volume, William E. Simon, "The Philosophical Foundations of the Interlocking Relationships between Economic Liberty and Political Liberty." Simon wrote: "And so today, here in the United States, the last great bastion of Free Enterprise, we have a government rolling out of control and careening crazily down the road to socialism" (148).

80. DeWitt Emery, "Who Killed Horatio Alger?" *Waterloo Press*, Aug 26, 1948, 4.

81. As Orson Welles said in 1944 of the GOP, "By free enterprise they want exclusive right to freedom." Quoted in Stanley Weintraub, *Final Victory: FDR's Remarkable World War II Presidential Campaign* (Cambridge, MA: Da Capo, 2012), 259.

82. Gilcrafter, "Free Enterprise," *Fredericksburg Standard*, Oct 4, 1944, 4.

83. "J. C. Penney," *Kingston Daily Freeman*, Jul 2, 1947, 1, 10.

84. Free Enterprise Defined," *Jefferson Bee*, Aug 4, 1964, 6.

85. "What Is 'Free Enterprise'?" *Bismarck Tribune*, May 3, 1944, 4.

86. Economic Principles Commission of the N.A.M., *The American Individual Enterprise System: Its Nature, Evolution, and Future* (New York: McGraw Hill, 1946), 1:2–4.

87. "The Right to Be a Bum," *Pittsburgh Post-Gazette*, May 27, 1944, 6.

88. "We're Ready to Scrap 'Free Enterprise,'" *Deseret News*, Aug 2, 1945, 3.

89. Henry R. Johnston, "Don't Overlook America's Internal Affairs," *American Druggist*, Jul 23, 1945, 68–69; "Freedom of Choice," *Council Bluffs Nonpareil*, Jul 23, 1945, 4.

90. Nathan W. Shefferman, *Labor's Stake in Capitalism* (New York: Constitution and Free Enterprise Foundation, 1954), 50–51.

91. Leonard Read, foreword to *Do We Want Free Enterprise?* by Vernon Oral Watts (Los Angeles: Los Angeles Chamber of Commerce, 1944).

92. "'Free Enterprise' Is Defined," *Prescott Evening Courier*, Feb 6, 1957, 3.

93. Larson, quoted in Robert J. Graf Jr., "A New Weapon for the War of Ideologies," *Chicago Tribune*, Feb 8, 1959, 4:3. David L. Stebenne discusses Larson's notes on a cabinet meeting of May 16, 1958, in which the phrase "enterprise democracy" was discussed in *Modern Republican: Arthur Larson and the Eisenhower Years* (Bloomington: Indiana University Press, 2006), 340n17.

94. N. D. Alper, "Free Enterprise," *Miami News*, Apr 4, 1943, 25.

95. "Free Enterprise Can Mean Different Things," *Tuscaloosa News*, Feb 21, 1944, 3.

96. "American Survey: Free Enterprise," *Economist*, Mar 31, 1945, 413–14.

97. Ray Tucker, "Strauss: Fight One of Socialism vs. Free Enterprise," and Thurman Sensing, "Intellectuals Ignorant about Free Enterprise," *Beckley Post-Herald*, May 19, 1959, 4.

98. "A Rose by Any Other Name Is Just as Sweet," *Central New Jersey Home News*, Dec 3, 1947, 20.

99. Ad for Rockland Light and Power Co., *White Plains Journal News*, Mar 14, 1952, 9. The same text was later used for the Warner and Swasey Precision Machinery Company of Cleveland and other companies in 1952 to 1954 (e.g., *New Philadelphia Daily Times*, Nov 18, 1952, 2; *Coshocton Tribune*, Jun 28, 1953, 12) and was reused in 1963 by the Idaho Power Company (*Idaho State Journal*, Oct 27, 1963, 26). This was labeled a "Reddytorial," a trademark of Reddy Communications, Inc., of Greenwich, CT.

100. Thomas Bayard McCabe, *The Committee for Economic Development: Its Past, Present and Future* (New York: CED, 1949), 5.

101. "Traditional Economy Urged by Mullendore," *Los Angeles Times*, Mar 26, 1955, 8.

102. "That's a Lie," *Cincinnati Enquirer*, Nov 6, 1938, 40.

103. Merle Thorpe, "A Stranger in Its Own Home," *Muncie Evening Press*, Nov 3, 1937, 6. For a similar sentiment, see Walter Locke, "Trends of the Times," *Miami News*, Aug 10, 1944, 10.

104. "What Is Capitalism?" *Wall Street Journal*, May 17, 1948, 4.

105. "Filibusterers, Keep Out of the Way," *New York Herald Tribune*, Aug 2, 1962, 18.

106. "Road Sign for America: Turn Right!" *Nation's Business*, Oct 1940, 34.

107. Wall, *Inventing the "American Way."*

108. "Emery Says Free Enterprise Is Definitely a Way of Life," *San Marino Tribune*, Feb 17, 1949, 10.

109. Prentis is quoted in "Crusade Is Urged for Enterprise," *New York Times*, Dec 14, 1940, 10.

110. "Text of Senator Taft's Talk Opening G.O.P. Campaign in Ohio," *New York Times*, Sep 18, 1952, 25.

111. "Gannett Sees 1776 Tyranny Copied by FDR," *Rochester Democrat and Chronicle*, Apr 30, 1940, 1.

112. "Free Enterprise," *Altoona Tribune*, Apr 5, 1940, 6.

113. "U.S. Public More Concerned with Jobs Than World Peace," *Washington Post*, Apr 1, 1945, B5. The top five issues were jobs, inflation, world peace, labor union troubles, and rehabilitating wounded veterans, all challenges that arguably required enhanced government powers.

114. "Wane of 'Control' Seen by Industry: Leaders Report Trend Back to 'Free' System," *New York Times*, Dec 8, 1938, 1.

115. Malvina Reynolds, "Free Enterprise," in *Sing Out!* 1:12 (New York: Peoples Artists of New York, 1951), 11.

116. George Peck, "Management Has Duties," *Casa Grande Dispatch*, May 19, 1944, 6.

117. Millard C. Faught, "It's Your Story—You Tell It," *Nation's Business,* Mar 1947, 47–49, 75.

118. "U.S. Business Gives Its Post-war Views," *New York Times*, May 30, 1944, 26.

119. "What Free Enterprise Means to Us," *Indian Journal*, Jan 11, 1945, 2.

120. Malcolm W. Bingay, "Read This Pamphlet," *Detroit Free Press*, Nov 26, 1944, 4.

121. Wendell L. Willkie, "Government vs. Industry, Industrial Achievement," in *Free Enterprise: The Philosophy of Wendell L. Willkie as Found in His Speeches, Messages, and Other Papers* (Washington, DC: National Home Library Foundation, 1940), 50. This was originally an address to the Economic Club of Detroit given on Feb 28, 1933.

122. Wendell L. Willkie, "Freedom: Love and Reform vs. Hate and Punishment," in *Free Enterprise*, 12. This was originally an address to the Toledo Civic Forum, Rotary Club given on Mar 4, 1940.

Chapter 5. "The Party of Free Enterprise"

1. Frank Jenkins, "Editorials on the Day's News," *Klamath Falls Evening Herald*, Feb 15, 1938, 1, 4.

2. Kim Phillips-Fein, "Our Political Narratives," *Modern American History* 1 (Mar 2018): 83.

3. Sam Rosenfeld, *The Polarizers: Postwar Architects of Our Partisan Era* (Chicago: University of Chicago Press, 2018).

4. Glenn Frank, "Sharp Political Lineups," *Arizona Republic*, Oct 19, 1933, 16.

5. "New Political Alignments," *Burlington Free Press*, Jul 12, 1934, 6; Lyle C. Wilson, "Recent Political Maneuvers May Lead to Third Party by Time Roosevelt Leaves Office," *Stevens Point Journal*, Aug 25, 1934, 1.

6. "What People Talk About: Southerner on New Deal," *Boston Globe*, Nov 3, 1944, 20.

7. "Toward Democratic Split," *Greenville News*, Feb 4, 1945, 4. The first quotations are from Strout and the last from the editorialist. See also Katherine Rye Jewell, *Dollars for Dixie: Business and the Transformation of Conservatism in the Twentieth Century* (New York: Cambridge University Press, 2017), 164–66.

8. See Darren Dochuk, *From Bible Belt to Sunbelt: Plain-Folk Religion, Grassroots Politics, and the Rise of Evangelical Conservatism* (New York: Norton, 2011), 114–15. The

phrase "New Deal emotionalism" is from Hamilton Butler, "The World Should Be Its Own Banker," *Detroit Free Press*, Mar 7, 1947, 6. "New Deal utopianism" is from "What Price 'Social Security'?" *Uniontown Morning Herald*, Oct 29, 1935, 6.

9. "A Study in Grays," *Hutchinson News*, Mar 9, 1950, 26.

10. Ronald Libby, "System Is Off Course," *Ukiah Daily Journal*, Oct 19, 1992, 4.

11. Virgil Jordan, *One Year After,* American Affairs Pamphlets 3 (New York: National Industrial Conference Board, 1946), 4.

12. Ben Borsook, "'Free' Enterprise No Longer Exists in U.S.," *Los Angeles Times*, Mar 15, 1980, 2:4.

13. "Free Enterprise Two-Way Street," *Eau Claire Leader*, Dec 2, 1948, 6.

14. Phillips-Fein, "Our Political Narratives," 3.

15. "Col. Roosevelt Lashes 'Tyranny,'" *Des Moines Register*, Sep 18, 1934, 1, 4.

16. Anne O'Hare McCormick, "Roosevelt's View of the Big Job," *New York Times*, Sep 11, 1932, SM2. On the significance of FDR's embrace of the term, see Kathryn S. Olmstead, *Right out of California: The 1930s and the Big Business Roots of Modern Conservatism* (New York: New Press, 2015), 28.

17. "Elect Mr. Willkie," *Baltimore Sun*, Aug 19, 1940, 10.

18. "'Sane, Balanced Liberalism' Encouragement of Business Needed, Landon Tells Akron," *New London Day*, Oct 13, 1936, 8.

19. Stanley Wood, "Scouting Around: Why Wendell Willkie?" *Lead Daily Call*, Oct 28, 1940, 2.

20. "Text of Lincoln Day Speech by Hoover," *Hartford Courant*, Feb 14, 1939, 7.

21. Herbert Hoover, *The Challenge to Liberty* (New York: Charles Scribner's Sons, 1934), 7–8.

22. "Text of Hoover Speech Urging Party Rally: Coalition of Anti–New Dealers Approved and New Declaration of Aims Called For," *Los Angeles Times*, Oct 27, 1937, 6.

23. Margaret Chase Smith, "Washington and You: So-Called 'Liberals' Undermined Own Ideals," *Lewiston Daily Sun*, Mar 2, 1951, 4.

24. "What about Big Business?" *Beckley Post-Herald*, May 5, 1951, 4.

25. Sokolsky, quoted in Steven M. Gillon, *Politics and Vision: The ADA and American Liberalism, 1947–1985* (New York: Oxford University Press, 1987), 90; Kent Hunter, "New Deal Communism Is Repudiated by Voters," *Milwaukee Sentinel*, Nov 6, 1946, 3.

26. "What's in a Party Name?" *Ottawa Journal*, Sep 16, 1936, 6. A similar point was made in "Liberal or Socialist?" *Washington Post*, Sep 7, 1938, 6.

27. Angus Burgin, *The Great Persuasion: Reinventing Free Markets since the Great Depression* (Cambridge, MA: Harvard University Press, 2012).

28. On the changing usage of *liberalism* and *neoliberalism*, see Lawrence Glickman, "Everyone Was a Liberal," *Aeon*, Jul 5, 2016, https://aeon.co/essays/everyone-was-a-liberal-now-no-one-wants-to-be.

29. Towner Phelan, "Reactionary Liberals," *American Affairs* 9:1 (1947): 54–55.

30. "Assorted Liberals," *Baltimore Sun*, Oct 3, 1935, 10.

31. Albert Lee, "Charter of Principles," *New York Herald Tribune*, Dec 4, 1942, 28.

32. Raymond Moley, "Befuddled Liberals," *Newsweek*, Feb 12, 1951, 84.

33. Raymond Moley, "'Liberal,' a Brave Name, Dishonored by Socialists," *Los Angeles Times*, Jan 12, 1950, 2:5.
34. Raymond Moley, "Example of Neoliberalism: Brannan's Road to Serfdom," *Los Angeles Times*, Jan 17, 1950, 2:5; Raymond Moley, "Willkie's Son Improves His Father's Role," *Los Angeles Times*, Jan 4, 1950, 2:5.
35. "What's in a Name?," *Los Angeles Times*, Sep 2, 1947, 2:4.
36. John W. Owens, "Byrd and Wallace," *Baltimore Sun*, Jan 31, 1945, 8.
37. "Senator Davis in York Raps at New Deal Methods: Says Reformers Attempt Change in Every Thing; Strikes Public Spending," *Harrisburg Telegraph*, Mar 31, 1938, 3.
38. Alex Shephard, "Minutes," *New Republic*, Jun 1, 2017, https://newrepublic.com/minutes /143059/donald-trump-no-political-philosophy-beyond-pissing-off-liberals.
39. "Ogden Mills' View of Future of G.O.P.," *St. Louis Post-Dispatch*, Apr 22, 1937, 40.
40. https://www.presidency.ucsb.edu/documents/fireside-chat-14.
41. "There is no ism in the world that has given its people as much as free enterprise has given the United States." "DeWitt Emery, Salesman for Free Enterprise: Biggest Small Business Man Visits Here," *Council Bluffs Nonpareil*, Nov 13, 1949, 1.
42. "Salesman for Free Enterprise"; "Free Enterprise in American Democracy," *Altoona Tribune*, Sep, 9, 1944, 3.
43. "NAM Set to Fight Alien 'Isms' Here: Bunting Calls on Advertising Men to Help Industry to 'Sell' Our System," *New York Times*, Oct 9, 1947, 22.
44. Peter Viereck, "Will America Prove Marx Right?" *Antioch Review*, Sep 1952, 333; Cabell Phillips, "Eisenhower's 'New Deal' Disturbs Some in GOP," *New York Times*, Feb 17, 1957, E10.
45. Stephen E. Ambrose, *Eisenhower*, vol. 2, *The President* (New York: Simon and Schuster, 1984), 220.
46. Dwight D. Eisenhower to his brother Edgar, Nov 8, 1954, http://teachingamericanhistory .org/library/document/letter-to-edgar-newton-eisenhower/.
47. For example, Garry Wills, whose claim about Ike's acceptance of the New Deal is quoted above, writes that Eisenhower "said" this. "The Triumph of the Hard Right," *New York Review of Books*, Feb 11, 2016, 4.
48. "Eisenhower Today Would be Considered a Socialist by the Modern Radical GOP," *Buzzflash*, Jul 24, 2011, http://www.truth-out.org/buzzflash/commentary/eisenhower-today -would-be-considered-a-socialist-by-the-modern-radical-gop.
49. Douglas B. Harris, "Dwight Eisenhower and the New Deal: The Politics of Preemption," *Presidential Studies Quarterly* 27:2 (Spring 1997): 335, 337.
50. "Eisenhower Charges Waste by Democrats: Says, in St. Louis Address, Administration Has Made Spending a 'Way of Life,'" *New York Herald Tribune*, Sep 21, 1952, 1, 36; "First Press Conference Held by Pres. Dwight Eisenhower," *Arizona Daily Star*, Feb 18, 1953, 12.
51. Clay Gowran, "Gen. Eisenhower Assails Waste as a 'Way of Life,'" *Chicago Tribune*, Sep 21, 1952, 3.
52. Walter Lippmann, "Today and Tomorrow," *San Mateo Times*, Feb 20, 1962, 22.
53. "Goldwater Backers Vote Down Scranton's Anti-Bircher Plank and His Rights and A-Bomb Plans," *New York Times*, Jul 16, 1964, 1. Thanks to Sam Rosenfeld for sharing this article.

54. Paul P. Kennedy, "Eisenhower Tells Physicians He Bars Socialized Medicine," *New York Times*, Mar 15, 1953, 1, 46.

55. Andrew J. Polsky, "Shifting Currents: Dwight Eisenhower and the Dynamic of Presidential Opportunity Structure," in *The Eisenhower Presidency: Lessons for the Twenty-First Century*, ed. Polsky (Lanham, MD: Lexington Books, 2015), 233.

56. Kim Phillips-Fein, "Conservatism: A State of the Field," *Journal of American History* 98:3 (Dec 2011): 723–43.

57. Dochuk, *From Bible Belt to Sunbelt*, 121–22. See also Darren E. Grem, *The Blessings of Business: How Corporations Shaped Conservative Christianity* (New York: Oxford University Press, 2016), 5.

58. Burgin, *Great Persuasion*, 148. This suggests that we need to revise the view that "the most striking and lasting victories of the right have come in the realm of political economy rather than that of culture." Kim Phillips-Fein, *Invisible Hands: The Businessman's Crusade against the New Deal* (New York: Norton, 2009), xii.

59. Franklin D. Roosevelt, "The Forgotten Man," Apr 7, 1932, http://teachingamericanhistory .org/library/document/the-forgotten-man/.

60. Arthur Evans, "Cong. J. M. Beck Warns of a New Forgotten Man: Predicts an Awakening of the Taxpayer," *Chicago Tribune*, May 4, 1934, 7. Barton is quoted in "Remembering the Forgotten Man," *Montana Standard*, Mar 3, 1940, 4. McGovern is quoted in "Socialism-Capitalism Debate Here Provides Brain-Tingling Session," *Woodstock Daily Sentinel*, Apr 17, 1950, 5. "Rukeyser Analyzes Republican Platform as an Appeal to Workers and Taxpayers, with Promise to Lighten Their Burden," *Cincinnati Inquirer*, Jul 11, 1952, 7.

61. "The Business Man," *Newport Daily News*, Nov 28, 1951, 14; "White Collared Salaried Worker Called Nation's New Forgotten Man," *Washington C.H. Record Herald*, Sep 26, 1952, 3; "What of These: Unorganized White Collar Man May Soon Be the New Forgotten Man of Industry," *Austin American*, May 30, 1937, 28. "Professional man" is quoted in John Franklin Carter, "Forgotten Man Is Key to Economy," *San Bernardino County Sun*, May 21, 1954, 48. "The 'Forgotten Man,'" *Odessa American*, Jun 5, 1959, 18, http:// law2.wlu.edu/deptimages/Powell%20Archives/PowellMemorandumPrinted.pdf.

62. "Who Is the Forgotten Man?" *Longview News-Journal*, Sep 18, 1968, 4.

63. John Ackelmire, "The Forgotten Man? He May be You, Sir," *Indianapolis Star*, Nov 2, 1952, 27; Carter, "Forgotten Man Is Key to Economy"; "The 'Forgotten Man'—'60," *Indianapolis Star*, Jan 10, 1960, 24.

64. "Society's Forgotten Man," *Ithaca Journal*, Aug 25, 1967, 6.

65. "Who Is the Forgotten Man?"

66. "'Keep America Free' Is Knox's Goal for G.O.P.," *Chicago Tribune*, Jul 31, 1936, 1, 8; Boake Carter, "Frisco Contrasts Rugged Country Lessons Unheeded," *Boston Globe*, Dec 17, 1938, 4.

67. "Free Enterprise Most Threatened Freedom, Hoy Says," *Paris News*, Mar 7, 1946, 12.

68. Richard Hofstadter, "What Happened to the Antitrust Movement?" in *The Paranoid Style in American Politics and Other Essays* (New York: Vintage, 1967), 215.

69. H. C. Kennedy, "The Republican Party as the Conservative Party," *Louisville Courier-Journal*, Dec 19, 1934, 6.

70. A 1938 Gallup Poll described the GOP as having liberal and conservative factions, but suggested that the former faction was stronger. Dr. George Gallup, "Rank and File Republicans Favor More Liberal Party," *Honolulu Star-Bulletin*, Nov 1, 1938, 11.

71. H. C. Kennedy, "Senator Logan and the New Deal," *Louisville Courier-Journal*, Oct 28, 1936, 6.

72. "No New Leadership," *Corvallis Gazette-Times*, Nov 15, 1934, 2.

73. Rodney Dutcher, "New Deal Platform Widens Liberal-Conservative Split, Says Dutcher; Roosevelt's Boldness and Timidity Are Both Reflected," *Elmira Star-Gazette*, Jun 27, 1936, 1.

74. "Vandenberg Calls for Anti–New Deal Coalition: Senator Outlines Plan for Successful Opposition to the 'The Roosevelt Party,'" *Los Angeles Times*, Sep 19, 1937, 7.

75. "New Definitions," *Eau Claire Leader*, Oct 27, 1946, 12.

76. H. C. Kennedy, "Objects to Senator Morse," *Louisville Courier-Journal*, Jan 25, 1949, 4. See also H. C. Kennedy, "A Staunch Republican Proposes His Party Disband, Reorganize," *Louisville Courier-Journal*, Feb 13, 1949, 3:2.

77. Wright A. Patterson, "No Real Choice," *Boise City News*, Jan 13, 1949, 9.

78. Charles V. Stanton, "Collision Impending," *Roseburg New Review*, Nov 16, 1961, 4.

79. "The Republican Party's Revolution," *Miami News*, Dec 15, 1947, 14.

80. "Wisconsin Bolter," *Berkshire Eagle*, Apr 25, 1946, 14.

81. "'Bureaucracy Gone Mad' Seen by Mills as Threat to Liberty," *New York Herald Tribune*, Oct 17, 1935, 12.

82. John A. Davenport, "Free Enterprise's Forgotten Virtues," *Wall Street Journal*, Jul 27, 1973, 8.

83. A Google Books Ngram shows that "free market" overtook "free enterprise" in 1975, after having lagged behind it from the late 1930s: https://books.google.com/ngrams/graph?content=free+market%2C+free+enterprise&year_start=1800&year_end=2000&corpus=15&smoothing=3&share=&direct_url=t1%3B%2Cfree%20market%3B%2Cc0%3B.t1%3B%2Cfree%20enterprise%3B%2Cc0.

84. "Free Enterprise Guaranties Urged," *Indianapolis News*, Sep 27, 1943, 13.

85. N. D. Alper, "Free Enterprise," *Miami News*, Apr 4, 1943, 25.

86. "Chamber Head Sees Golden Age from Free Enterprise," *Newport News Daily Press*, Dec 11, 1954, 9.

87. Roger W. Babson, "Free Enterprise and Common Sense, with Returning Service Men in Charge, Babson's Hope: Crack-Pot New Dealism Ought to Be Pushed out of Picture in Post War Planning," *Franklin News-Herald*, Jun 4, 1943, 9.

88. Jordan, *One Year After*, 18.

89. "Text of Willkie's Address in Milwaukee," *New York Times*, Oct 20, 1940, 16.

90. "Auto Big 3 Assail UAW Profit Plan," *Baltimore Sun*, Jan 14, 1958, 1.

91. Reynolds's piece for the *National Record* in Nov 1943 was widely reprinted. "Bob Reynolds Does Not Fancy the New Deal," *Selma Johnstonian-Sun*, Dec 2, 1943, 4.

92. "Willkie Warns New Deal Brings Poorhouse Near," *Chicago Tribune*, May 12, 1940, 19.

93. Sam Tucker, "As I View the Thing," *Decatur Herald*, Dec 10, 1943, 8.

94. "Dr. Millikan Opposes Federal Education Aid," *Los Angeles Times*, Apr 5, 1950, 2:2.

95. Jenkins, "Editorials on the Day's News."

96. Charles P. Stewart, "Presidential Elections May Line Up Liberals against Conservatives," *Middlesboro Daily News*, Jul 22, 1939, 1.

97. "Relief-Political Link Is Charged," *Roseburg News-Review*, Aug 6, 1936, 4.

98. B., "What People Talk About: Southerner on New Deal," *Boston Globe*, Nov 3, 1944, 20.

99. George Tagge, "Halt New Deal Slavery in '44, Barrett Urges," *Chicago Tribune*, Apr 7, 1944, 3.

100. Henry F. Schwarz, "No Sham Battle! Republicans Urged to Fight New Deal Corruption," *New York Herald Tribune*, Jul 25, 1938, 10.

101. For example, in 1936, a letter writer claimed, "The man who runs for President on the Republican ticket, to be successful must be against the New Deal and all its followers." Burdette Parry, "Are the People Fed Up on Isms, Including Liberalism?" *Pittsburgh Post-Gazette*, Jan 22, 1936, 8.

102. Felix Morley, *The Power in the People* (New York: D. Van Nostrand, 1949), 30.

103. "Willkie Warns New Deal Brings Poorhouse Near."

104. Eric Schickler, *Racial Realignment: The Transformation of American Liberalism, 1932–1965* (Princeton: Princeton University Press, 2016), 248. A good explanation of why realignment was such a slow process can be found in Devin Caughey, *The Unsolid South: Mass Politics and National Representation in a One Party Enclave* (Princeton: Princeton University Press, 2018).

105. "Southern Support for Republicans Will Be in Single Digits," *Florence Morning News*, Sep 18, 1958, 4.

106. "U.S. Business Declares War on New Deal," *Baltimore Sun*, Dec 6, 1935, 11.

107. "Mills Fears for Country," *Los Angeles Times*, Jun 3, 1936, 6.

108. "Save Free Enterprise, Knox Urges," *Alton Evening Telegraph*, Jul 31, 1936, 1.

109. "New Deal Condemned in Speeches Made by Lincoln Day Orators," *Pittsburgh Post-Gazette*, Feb 13, 1940, 2.

110. "Free Enterprise Medicine," *Murphysboro Daily Independent*, Jan 11, 1941, 2.

111. Charles A. Merrill, "We Know Who We Are on the Way," *Boston Globe*, Jan 16, 1949, A20.

112. "The Foremost Fifty: Nation's Top Businessmen Assemble for a Banquet and Hear Dewey Make His Frankest Speech of the Year," *Life*, Nov 17, 1947, 42. Cooley is quoted in Zoe Kincaid Brockman, "Unguarded Moments," *Gastonia Gazette*, Dec 11, 1947, 5.

113. Arthur Krock, "In the Nation: If the People Should Talk Back a Little," *New York Times*, Jan 30, 1942, 18.

114. "Marshall Type for President, Rickenbacker Tells Ad Club," *Boston Globe*, Mar 4, 1944, 15.

115. "Says Nation Must Be Free of Coddling," *Schenectady Gazette*, Apr 16, 1943, 5; Mark R. Wilson, *Destructive Creation: American Business and the Winning of World War II* (Philadelphia: University of Pennsylvania Press, 2016), 93.

116. Ayn Rand, "America's Persecuted Minority: Big Business," *Pampa Daily News*, Aug 13, 1962, 5.

117. "Stop the Recession," *Desert Sun*, Jan 7, 1938, 2.

118. "The Text of Col Knox's Address to Business Group in Hagerstown," *Boston Globe*, Aug 20, 1936, 15.

119. "Vandenberg in Bold Blast at New Dealers," *Woodstock Daily Sentinel*, Oct 12, 1938, 1.

120. The newspaper is quoted in "Mr. Kelland's Lesson," *St. Louis Star and Times*, Feb 26, 1946, 14; "Republicans Waste Time Longing for Those 'Good Old Days,'" *Brooklyn Daily Eagle*, Feb 2, 1946, 4.

121. "G.O.P. Hit by Williams," *Lansing State Journal*, Mar 8, 1954, 2.

Chapter 6. "Faith in Free Enterprise"

1. According to Brian Doherty, Read used similar language when speaking to audiences about his think tank. He would tell audiences "how the miracle of the free market waters your lawn while you sleep and makes your car while you practice music." *Radicals for Capitalism: A Freewheeling History of the Modern American Libertarian Movement* (New York: Public Affairs, 2007), 161.

2. The essay was originally published as Leonard E. Read, "I Pencil: My Family Tree as Told to Leonard E. Read," *Freeman*, Dec 1958, 32–37.

3. Jonah Goldberg, "I, Pencil in the iPhone Age," *Tulsa World*, Sep 12, 2010; also published as "I, Market Economy," *Townhall*, Sep 8, 2010.

4. Milton Friedman, introduction to "I, Pencil" (FEE, 1999), http://www.econlib.org/library/Essays/rdPncl0.html.

5. Sarah Palin, *America by Heart: Reflections on Family, Faith, and Flag* (New York: Harper Collins, 2013), 89.

6. Jay W. Richards, 'I, Pencil' to 'I, Smartphone': Working Together for Good," *Investor's Business Daily*, Aug 14, 2012, A13.

7. Matt Ridley, "When Ideas Have Sex," Ted Talk, 2010. In Readian terms, Ridley claimed that the mouse "was made for me by millions of people" and that "nobody knows how to make a computer mouse." https://www.ted.com/talks/matt_ridley_when_ideas_have_sex. Ann Elizabeth Moore has called "I, Pencil," "the progenitor of TED Talks." "Milton Friedman's Pencil," *New Inquiry*, Dec 17, 2012, http://thenewinquiry.com/essays/milton-friedmans-pencil/.

8. Karl Polanyi, *The Great Transformation: The Political and Economic Origins of Our Time* (Boston: Beacon, 1944), 107.

9. "Defeatism Blamed on New Deal," *Arizona Republic*, Dec 7, 1939, 1.

10. Polanyi, *Great Transformation*, 141. On the continuing hold of "free-market faith," see Darren E. Grem, *The Blessings of Business: How Corporations Shaped Conservative Christianity* (New York: Oxford University Press, 2016), 192–225.

11. The speaker was the Republican representative Frederick C. Smith of Ohio. *Congressional Record–House*, Feb 15, 1944, 1709.

12. Pew, quoted in *National Petroleum News*, May 2, 1945, cited in Mary Sennholz, *Faith and Freedom: The Journal of a Great American, J. Howard Pew* (Grove City, PA: Grove City College Press, 1975), 86–87.

13. The Republican candidate, Homer P. Hargrave Jr., is quoted in "G.O.P. Hopeful Urges Summit Parley Here," *Chicago Tribune*, Mar 16, 1958, 3:4.

14. TRB, "The Story of a Disastrous Administration," *Los Angeles Times*, Aug 8, 1974, II:5.

15. "Dewey Lashes Out at New Deal Here," *Milwaukee Journal*, Mar 30, 1940, 3; "Bricker Is Impressive," *Milwaukee Sentinel*, Mar 16, 1944, 12.

16. J. William Ditter, "The Land of Make-Believe," *Congressional Record Appendix*, May 31, 1939, 2323–24; WCAU Radio, Philadelphia, address of May 27, 1939.

17. "Frank Urges Faith in Free Enterprise: Republican Policy Head Calls for 'Intelligent' Revival of Competitive System," *New York Times*, Jan 13, 1938, 1, 9.

18. Virgil Jordan, *One Year After*, American Affairs Pamphlets 3 (New York: National Industrial Conference Board, 1946), 8.

19. Chesly Manly, *The Twenty-Year Revolution from Roosevelt to Eisenhower* (Chicago: Regnery, 1954), 2.

20. Herbert Hoover, *The Challenge to Liberty* (New York: Charles Scribner's Sons, 1934), 27.

21. H. L. Mencken, "Notes on the New Deal," *San Francisco Examiner*, Aug 22, 1934, 12.

22. Russell J. Brownback, "A Guinea Pig Looks at the New Deal," *Barron's*, Jul 9, 1934, 6.

23. "Choice in 1936," *Hammond Times*, Jul 30 1935, 4.

24. "Without It the Freedoms Are Just Talk," *Deseret News*, Feb 19, 1944, 3.

25. J. Strom Thurmond, "'O'er the Ramparts We Watched!' Local Sovereignty Is Being Whittled Away," *Vital Speeches of the Day*, Oct 15, 1949, 30.

26. Talmadge is quoted in Dewey W. Grantham, *The South in Modern America: A Region at Odds* (Fayetteville: University of Arkansas Press, 2001), 127.

27. "'Securecrat' Peril Related at Forum," *Los Angeles Times*, Jul 14, 1949, 2:6.

28. "What Others Say," *Muncie Evening Press*, Sep 7, 1943, 4.

29. H. W. Prentis, "The Way to Freedom," Dec 4, 1942, 10–11, Manuscripts and Archives Department, Hagley Museum and Library, Wilmington, DE. This was presented as a radio address on WEAF. "Radio Programs," *Baltimore Sun*, Dec 4, 1942, 40.

30. Walter Linn, "Dangers to Our American Way of Life: Social Security, the Root of All Political Evil," *Vital Speeches of the Day*, Mar 15, 1947, 343.

31. Arthur H. Motley, "Our Most Important Freedom: The Freedom to Fail," *Vital Speeches of the Day*, Nov 15, 1950, 74–77.

32. Peterson's article with this phrase was entered into the record by Congressman Howard W. Robison "Economic Illiteracy," *Congressional Record Appendix*, Jun 13, 1963, A3823.

33. William Fulton, "Democrats' Santa Role Hit by Goldwater: Senator Would Make Reliefers Work," *Chicago Tribune*, Jan 16, 1964, 17.

34. "Text of Senator Goldwater's Address at Madison Sq. Garden in Only Campaign Appearance in City," *New York Times*, Oct 27, 1964, 30.

35. Nathan W. Shefferman, *Labor's Stake in Capitalism* (New York: Constitution and Free Enterprise Foundation, 1954), 1.

36. "Text of Hoover's Address on the 'Economic Consequences of the New Deal,'" *New York Times*, Nov 6, 1938, 46.

37. "Truman Thinks He's Santa, Executive Tells Credit Men," *Los Angeles Times*, May 18, 1950, 2:3.

38. "Church Pictures Wonderland of Alice Burocracy," *Chicago Tribune*, Mar 28, 1940, 3. The unconventional spelling was "routinely" used by the *Tribune*; see Joanna L Grisinger,

The Unwieldy American State: Administrative Politics since the New Deal (New York: Cambridge University Press, 2012), 159.

39. "Demand Natural Recovery in U.S.," *Massillon Evening Independent*, Apr 20, 1934, 8.

40. John Cyprian Stevens, "Private Enterprise," *Civil Engineering*, Aug 1945, 1.

41. "Full Text of Knox Address," *Lewiston Daily Sun*, Jul 30, 1936, 10.

42. Hoover, *Challenge to Liberty*, 27.

43. "Plight of Nation Laid to Tinkering under the New Deal: Everett Sanders Blames Repudiated Pledges," *Chicago Tribune*, Apr 26, 1936, 8.

44. "Nation's Women Must Teach You to Respect American Ideal, Says Willkie," *Spokane Daily Chronicle*, Oct 1, 1940, 7.

45. "Economic Illiteracy," *Chicago Tribune*, Nov 30, 1948, 20.

46. Hazlitt, quoted in "America's Economic Experiments Perilous, Editor Finds," *Washington Post*, Apr 15, 1934, B2.

47. J. Fred Thornton, "Saxons and Vandals: Free Enterprise," *Montgomery Advertiser*, Apr 26, 1959, 11.

48. "Industrialists Reject All New Deal Policies," *Chicago Tribune*, Dec 6, 1935, 39.

49. Mark Sullivan, "Sullivan Declares New Deal Psychology Is Breeding Nation of Money Grabbers," *Hartford Courant*, Oct 21, 1934, 5: 1, 7.

50. "Head Lights," *Belvidere Daily Republican*, Jan 15, 1938, 4.

51. "No Plow, Big Pay," *Wilmington Morning News*, Jun 28, 1939, 6.

52. Prentis, "The Way to Freedom."

53. "Text of Hoover Speech at Lincoln Dinner: Former President Declares New Deal Policies Peril to Nation's Liberty," *Los Angeles Times*, Feb 14, 1939, 8.

54. Robert Taft, "Something for Nothing," *Congressional Record—Senate*, Feb 26, 1936, 2808.

55. Bailey to Sen Peter G. Gerry (RI), Oct 19, 1937, quoted in John Robert Moore, "Senator Josiah W. Bailey and the 'Conservative Manifesto' of 1937," *Journal of Southern History* 31 (Feb 1965): 26.

56. "Vandenberg Cites Way to Recovery: Return to Free Enterprise and 'American System' Urged at Syracuse Commencement," *New York Times*, Jun 6, 1939, 20.

57. Bruce Laurie, *Artisan into Worker: Labor in Nineteenth-Century America* (New York: Hill and Wang, 1989).

58. "Paternal Government," *Washington Post*, Aug 24, 1948, 10.

59. Robert Bremner, "Turnabout on Something for Nothing," in *The Welfare State*, ed. Herbert L. Marx (New York: H. W. Wilson, 1950), 84–89.

60. "Your Stake in the National Decision," *Chicago Tribune*, Nov 17, 1935, 16.

61. C. B. Sweet, "The President's Column," *American Builder*, Sep 1, 1949, 110, 111.

62. Margaret Chase Smith, "Washington and You: So-Called 'Liberals' Undermined Own Ideals," *Lewiston Daily Sun*, Mar 2, 1951, 4. The same phrase was used in "Promise and Reality," *Lafayette Journal and Courier*, Jun 29, 1949, 4.

63. Jonathan Cohn, "Stuff White People Like," *New Republic*, Nov 12, 2012, http://www.newrepublic.com/article/110041/republicans-say-obama-won-promising-free-stuff-who-was-real-panderer-election.

64. Charles M. Blow, "Jeb Bush, 'Free Stuff,' and Black Folks," *New York Times*, Sep 28, 2015.

65. Nicholas Eberstadt, *A Nation of Takers: America's Entitlement Epidemic* (West Consho-
hocken, PA: Templeton, 2012), 76, 78, 108, 131.

66. Bremner, "Turnabout on Something for Nothing."

67. A chapter of *The Free Market and Its Enemy* was entitled "the miraculous market." See
The Free Market and Its Enemy (Irvington-on-Hudson, NY: Foundation for Economic
Education, 1965), 13, 15.

68. Fred Norman, "A Factory Is Like a Tree," Extension of Remarks, *Congressional Record*,
Apr 26, 1944, A1988–89. The ad was also reprinted in "Portrait of 'Free Enterprise,'"
Eugene Guard, May 26, 1944, 4.

69. Nor was it the last. See the editorial cartoon "The Tree That Bears the Fruits of Free
Enterprise," *Hendersonville Times-News*, Apr 17, 1952, 2, which contains branches la-
beled "Good Things for Everyone," "Jobs," Dividends," and "Plant Expansion to Provide
More Jobs."

70. "The Trunk of the Tree" appeared in many newspapers, including the *Boston Globe*,
Baltimore Sun, *Philadelphia Inquirer, Wall Street Journal* (Oct 18), and *New York Times*
(Oct 26).

71. "Public Spending Declared Menace," *Salem Statesman Journal*, Oct 10, 1937, 1.

72. Doherty, *Radicals for Capitalism*, 164. The word *suave* is from Drew Pearson, "Foundation for Economic Education Has Big Lobby," *Sayre Evening Times*, Mar 24, 1949, 4.

73. On the six-foot pencil, see Bethany Moreton, *To Serve God and Wal-Mart: The Making of
Christian Free Enterprise* (Cambridge, MA: Harvard University Press, 2009), 193–97.
For a challenge to Friedman's claim, see Moore, "Milton Friedman's Pencil"

74. "The Power of the Market," episode 1 of *Free To Choose*, https://www.youtube.com
/watch?v=R5Gppi-O3a8. See also Milton Friedman and Rose Friedman, *Free to Choose:
A Personal Statement* (New York: Harcourt Brace Jovanovich, 1980), 11–13, in which
they credit Read with a "delightful story" that "dramatizes vividly how voluntary exchange enables millions of people to cooperate with one another."

75. *I, Smartphone*, 2012, http://www.youtube.com/watch?v=V1Ze_wpS_o0.

76. Kevin D. Williamson, "iPencil: Nobody Knows How to Make a Pencil or a Health Care
System," *National Review*, May 20, 2013, 29–31. On cappuccino, see Tim Harford, "It's
a Mug's Game," *FT.com*, Dec 7, 2007. For an essay on surgery offered "in the spirit of
Leonard Read," see Leonard A. Metildi, "Cholecystectomy, How Is It Made?" *Freeman*,
Jul 1995, 419–21.

77. Michelle Malkin, "I, Toilet Paper," in *Who Built That: Awe-Inspiring Stories of American
Tinkerpreneurs* (New York: Simon and Schuster, 2015), 114. Part 2 of the book is called
"The Miracle of the Mundane."

78. Tyler Cowen, "Blogs as Self-Revelation," *Marginal Revolution*, Feb 4, 2007, http://mar
ginalrevolution.com/marginalrevolution/2007/02/blogs_as_selfre.html.

79. Jennifer Burns, *Goddess of the Market: Ayn Rand and the American Right* (New York:
Oxford University Press, 2009); Doherty, *Radicals for Capitalism*; Moreton, *To Serve
God and Wal-Mart*; Kim Phillips-Fein, *Invisible Hands: The Businessmen's Crusade
against the New Deal* (New York: Norton, 2009).

80. Doherty, *Radicals for Capitalism*, 164.

81. Doherty, *Radicals for Capitalism*, 156. The latter phrase is from Mary Sennholz, "Leonard Read, the Founder and Builder," *Freeman*, May 1, 1996.

82. Howell John Harris calls FEE "the most generously funded and broadly based of all the conservative business pressure groups." *The Right to Manage: Industrial Relations Policies of American Business in the 1940s* (Madison: University of Wisconsin Press, 1982), 196. John Chamberlain called Read "the creator of the first important conservative foundation to come into being in the aftermath of World War II." "Read Was a Great Man," *Park City Daily News*, May 23, 1983, 3.

83. As Donald Boudreaux writes, "The '40s were among the worst times in history for the ideals of freedom and free markets. At the time, government control of the economy was all the rage. Intellectuals snickered at individual liberty and private property rights as quaint, outmoded notions. Almost everyone assumed that prosperity required extensive central planning. Most friends of liberty assumed their cause was lost. But not Read." Donald Boudreaux, "Remembering an Unsung Defender of Freedom," *Investor's Business Daily*, Sep 24, 1998, A28.

84. Friedrich V. Hayek, "Bruno Leoni (1913–1967) and Leonard Read (1898–1983)," in *The Collected Works of F. A. Hayek*, vol. 4, *The Fortunes of Liberalism*, ed. Peter G. Klein (Chicago: University of Chicago Press, 1991), 262.

85. John Chamberlain, "Triumph of a Willful Man," *Sumter Daily Item*, Apr 30, 1963, 6A.

86. "Economic Education: A Clearing House for Information Tries to Educate U.S. Citizens in How Free Enterprise Works," *Tide: The Newsmagazine of Advertising, Marketing and Public Relations*, Sep 19, 1947, 72.

87. Leonard E. Read, speech at town hall meeting, LA, Jun 17, 1946, published as "Dealing with Collectivism," *Vital Speeches of the Day*, Jul 15, 1946, 602–6. Perhaps few people "took Hayek seriously in the 1950s and 1960s," as Gary Gerstle writes, but free enterprise ideas circulated widely in this period from many other sources. "The Rise and Fall (?) of America's Neoliberal Order," *Transactions of the Royal Historical Society* 28 (2018): 249.

88. "Dealing with Collectivism."

89. Leonard Read, "Incomprehensible Order," in *The Free Market and Its Enemy*, 59.

90. Irene Powers, "Illinois Clubwomen Told of Waste in Government," *Chicago Tribune*, May 10, 1961, 3:10.

91. Irving Kristol, "Human Freedom and Our Economic System," in *An Economic Philosophy for a Free People*, ed. Paul C. Goelz (San Antonio: St. Mary's University Press, 1979), 52; Max Borders, "Rational Mysticism for a Young Movement," *Freeman*, Jan 2013, 6–9.

92. Doherty, *Radicals for Capitalism*, 151.

93. Gavin Kennedy, "A Classic Spoiled by Mysticism," *Adam Smith's Lost Legacy*, Jan 19, 2009, http://adamsmithslostlegacy.blogspot.com/2009/01/classic-spoiled-by-mysticism .html.

94. Irving Kristol, "American Conservatism, 1945–1995," *Public Interest* (Fall 1995): 82.

95. "Magic of the Market Place," *Ocala Star-Banner*, Oct 5, 1981, 15A.

96. Karl Eller, "Miracle in a Glass: The Free Enterprise System," *Vital Speeches of the Day*, Feb 1, 1979, 229–33. Eller was president of the Combined Communications Corporation.

97. Louis Hunt and Peter McNamara, eds., *Liberalism, Conservatism, and Hayek's Idea of Spontaneous Order* (New York: Palgrave Macmillan, 2007).

98. Emma Rothschild notes that Smith rarely used the phrase and meant something different by it than Read and many other later readers assumed. See *Economic Sentiments: Adam Smith, Condorcet, and the Enlightenment* (Cambridge, MA: Harvard University Press, 2001), chapter 5, "The Bloody and Invisible Hand."

99. "The New versus the Old World," *Chicago Tribune*, Jul 5, 1936, 8.

100. Wendy L. Wall, *Inventing the "American Way": The Politics of Consensus from the New Deal to the Civil Rights Movement* (New York: Oxford University Press, 2008).

101. "Faith Moves Mountains," *Wall Street Journal*, Mar 21, 1944, 4.

102. "He Urges System Based upon Free Enterprise," *Washington Post*, Aug 20 1936, X11.

103. "Orator Defends Free Enterprise: Bureaucrats Flayed by Portland Lawyer," *Spokane Spokesman-Review*, Oct 27, 1944, 6.

104. An interesting take on the concept that turned the pencil factory itself rather than the market into the miracle, came in a photo essay: Christopher Payne and Sam Anderson, "Inside One of America's Last Pencil Factories," *New York Times*, Jan 12, 2018, https://www.nytimes.com/2018/01/12/magazine/inside-one-of-americas-last-pencil-factories.html. Anderson wrote, "Radical simplicity is surprisingly hard to produce."

105. "This Is the Power Trust," *Naugatuck Daily News*, Nov 8, 1944, 3.

106. "What Does It Mean?" *White Plains News*, Nov 3, 1948, 2.

107. For the original poem, apparently written in 1943 and published in the *New York Journal-American*, see Benjamin DeCasseres, *I Am Private Enterprise* (New York: National Industrial Information Committee, n.d.), http://www.benjamindecasseres.com/pamphlets/i-am-private-enterprise/. Many newspapers called it "I Am the Spirit of Free Enterprise." The *Amarillo-Globe Times*, Dec 30, 1966, 14, attributed this poem to "Robert Morris, President, University of Plano."

108. "Traditional Economy Urged by Mullendore," *Los Angeles Times*, Mar 26, 1955, 8.

109. "Restoring Freedom," *Fortune*, Dec 1942, 9.

110. "A Railroad President Talks to His Men about Free Enterprise," *Dixon Evening Telegraph*, Aug 11, 1943, 10.

111. Phillip Rucker, "Romney Loses GOP Front-Runner Status," *Washington Post*, Aug 25, 2011, A2.

112. Jerry E. Craft, "Signs of Dictatorship," *Spartanburg Herald-Journal*, Apr 3, 2009.

113. Ruth Alexander, "What Price the Welfare State? Government—the Guardian or Master?" *Vital Speeches of the Day*, Jan 15, 1952, 199.

114. "Without It the Freedoms Are Just Talk."

115. "Our Free Enterprise System," address by C. G. Eubank, Mill Manager, Kimberly-Clark Corporation, Memphis, TN, for Delivery to Junior and Senior Students of Memphis High Schools, March 1951, series 1, box 67, "Free Enterprise, General, 1951–63," Manuscripts and Archives Department, Hagley Museum and Library.

116. "Meaning of Free Enterprise," *Des Moines Register*, Apr 27, 1945, 4.

117. "Business Spokesman: Werner Paul Gullander," *New York Times*, Dec 6, 1962, 29.

118. Steve Forbes, "Why Economic Policymakers Make Big Mistakes: They Think Economies Are Machines," *Forbes*, Oct 19, 2015, https://www.forbes.com/sites/steveforbes

/2015/09/29/why-economic-policymakers-make-big-mistakes-they-think-economies
-are-machines/#4f76e362430c.

119. Read, "Incomprehensible Order," 52.

120. Shefferman, *Labor's Stake in Capitalism*, 10.

121. "America's Peril Told," *Los Angeles Times*, Jun 2, 1936, A1.

122. Steven M. Gillon has written that Reagan's "greatest achievement was in transforming conservatism" with "a sunny smile." But Read's branch of free enterprise evangelicalism marked another root of political optimism. "A Historian Argues That the Reagan Revolution Started in 1966, not 1980," *Chicago Tribune*, Oct 29, 2000, 14:5.

123. For three excellent critiques of Read's essay, see Dani Rodrik, "Milton Friedman's Magical Thinking," *Project Syndicate*, Oct 11, 2011, http://www.project-syndicate.org/commentary/milton-friedman-s-magical-thinking; John Quiggin, "'I Pencil': A Product of the Mixed Economy," *Crooked Timber*, Apr 16, 2011, http://crookedtimber.org/2011/04/16/i-pencil-a-product-of-the-mixed-economy/; Moore, "Milton Friedman's Pencil."

124. Leonard Read, "Golf and Curling," Feb 13, 1955, http://fee.org/files/doclib/Golf-and-Curling-By-Leonard-E.-Read.pdf; "Recipe for a Good Meal," *Freeman*, May 1958, 46–50, reprinted as Leonard Read, "Recipe for a Good Meal," *American Mercury*, Jan 1959, 65–68.

125. Jeff Jacoby, "Giving Thanks for Capitalism," *Boston Globe*, Nov 27, 2003, A23.

126. Bob Adelmann, "Thanksgiving Redux: Of Turkeys and Pencils," *Light from the Right*, Nov 28, 2011, http://lightfromtheright.com/2011/11/28/thanksgiving-redux-turkeys
-pencils/.

127. Quoted in Sennholz, "Leonard Read, the Founder and the Builder."

128. "Rubio: 'Obama Denies Miracle of Free Enterprise,'" *Palm Beach Post*, Aug 3, 2012, 4A.

129. Quoted in "Obama Campaign in Full Swing in Virginia," *San Francisco Chronicle*, Jul 13, 2012.

130. Elizabeth Warren, "There Is Nobody in This Country Who Got Rich on His Own," *CBS News*, Sep 22, 2011, http://www.cbsnews.com/news/elizabeth-warren-there-is-nobody
-in-this-country-who-got-rich-on-his-own/. For a similar analysis of Obama and Warren, see Patrick Iber and Mike Konczal, "Karl Polanyi for President," *Dissent*, May 23, 2016, https://www.dissentmagazine.org/online_articles/karl-polanyi-explainer-great
-transformation-bernie-sanders.

131. Jason Brennan, "You Didn't Build That Pencil," *Bleeding Hearts Libertarians*, Aug 8, 2012, http://bleedingheartlibertarians.com/2012/08/you-didnt-build-that-pencil/.

132. Nicole Ciandella, "The Enduring Lesson of 'I, Pencil,'" *Freeman*, Nov 16, 2012, https://fee.org/articles/the-enduring-lesson-of-i-pencil/.

133. Goldberg, "'I, Pencil' in the iPhone Age."

134. Steve Forbes, *Freedom Manifesto: Why Free Markets Are Moral and Big Government Isn't* (New York: Crown, 2012), 182–83.

135. Bruce Caldwell, "Ten (Mostly) Hayekian Insights for Trying Economic Times," Heritage Foundation, Feb 1, 2011, http://www.heritage.org/research/reports/2011/02/ten-mostly
-hayekian-insights-for-trying-economic-times.

136. Karl Marx, *Capital*, vol. 1, section 4, "The Fetishism of Commodities and the Secret

Thereof," in *The Marx-Engels Reader*, 2nd ed., ed. Robert C. Tucker (New York: Norton, 1978), 319.

137. Barack Obama, "Remarks by the President on Fiscal Policy," George Washington University, Apr 13, 2011, https://obamawhitehouse.archives.gov/the-press-office/2011/04/13/remarks-president-fiscal-policy.

138. Prentis, "The Way to Freedom."

139. FDR is quoted in Gordon Lloyd and David Davenport, eds., *The New Deal and Modern American Conservatism: A Defining Rivalry* (Stanford, CA: Hoover Institution Press, 2013), 6; Rexford G. Tugwell, "The Ideas behind the New Deal," *New York Times*, Jul 16, 1933, SM1. See also Rexford G. Tugwell, *Roosevelt's Revolution: The First Year—A Personal Perspective* (New York: Macmillan, 1977), 47.

140. James Marlow, "Truman Speeches Show His Faith in Free Enterprise," *St. Petersburg Evening Independent*, Nov 8, 1949, 2.

141. Reinhold Niebuhr, "Halfway to What?" *Nation*, Jan 14, 1950, 28.

142. "President and Business," *Washington Post*, Sep 28, 1962, A18.

143. Quoted in Rick Perlstein, *The Invisible Bridge: The Fall of Nixon and the Rise of Reagan* (New York: Simon and Schuster, 2013), 691.

144. Polanyi, *Great Transformation*.

145. "Chamber Head Sees Golden Age from Free Enterprise," *Newport News Daily Press*, Dec 11, 1954, 9. See also Richard Hofstadter, "What Happened to the Antitrust Movement?" in *The Paranoid Style in American Politics and Other Essays* (New York: Vintage, 1967), 212, 213, 223.

Chapter 7. "Free Enterprise Needs Restatement to Suit Our Modern Needs"

1. Milton Friedman, *Capitalism and Freedom* (Chicago: University of Chicago Press, 1962), 26. See also Milton Friedman, "Free Enterprise in the United States," *University of Chicago Roundtable,* Jun 1, 1952, 12, Milton Friedman Papers, Hoover Institution, Stanford University, Stanford, CA.

2. "Address of Honorable Thurman Arnold, Associate Justice, United States Court of Appeals, at the Dinner to Miss Freda Kirchway on the Occasion of the 25th Anniversary of Her Association with the Nation," 1, Hotel Commodore, NY, Feb 27, 1944, Lowell Mellett, Official Correspondence, 1938–1944, Fed Works Agency (Cont.) National Housing Agency, Personal Files: A, box 8, FDR Library, Hyde Park, NY. Thanks to Richard John for sharing this address with me.

3. "Frank Urges Faith in Free Enterprise: Republican Policy Head Calls for 'Intelligent' Revival of Competitive System," *New York Times*, Jan 13, 1938, 1, 9.

4. J. A. Smith, "Unionism Hits Free Enterprise," *Spokane Spokesman-Review*, Aug 26, 1958, 3; "Business Has Less Freedom in Hiring," *Spokane Spokesman-Review*, Jul 16, 1958, 3.

5. Anthony Chen, *The Fifth Freedom: Jobs, Politics, and Civil Rights in the United States, 1941–1972* (Princeton: Princeton University Press, 2009), 129.

6. Daniel Hayes Murphy, *Our Precious Legacy: The Free Enterprise System and Its Preservation* (New York: Newcomen Society in North America, 1961), 16, Hagley Library

Imprints Collection, Manuscripts and Archives Department, Hagley Museum and Library, Wilmington, DE.

7. R. C. Hoiles, "Better Jobs: The Welfare State Idea," *Harlingen Valley Morning Star*, Jan 22, 1959, 4.

8. See "Taking Hayek Seriously," http://hayekcenter.org/? p=682.

9. Bruce Alger, "Free Enterprise versus the Something-for-Nothing Philosophy," speech before SMU's Businessmen's Day, Dallas, Texas, Apr 26, 1955, box 2, Bruce Alger Papers, Dallas Public Library.

10. The *Plain Dealer* editorial is quoted in "Slavery and the Welfare State," *Shreveport Times*, Dec 9, 1949, 14. Goldwater is quoted in Geoffrey Kabaservice, *Rule and Ruin: The Downfall of Moderation and the Destruction of the Republican Party, from Eisenhower to the Tea Party* (New York: Oxford University Press, 2012), 102.

11. Kabaservice, *Rule and Ruin*, 104.

12. H. W. Prentis Jr., *The Mobilization for Understanding of Private Enterprise: One of the Indispensable Supports of Individual Freedom* (New York: National Association of Manufacturers, 1940), 3. Prentis told a dialect joke about a "negro preacher" speaking at a "Georgia turpentine camp."

13. Wally Traber, "Conservative Speaker Says Liberalism Is a Form of Socialism at SCHS," *Santa Cruz Sentinel*, Jan 25, 1967, 27.

14. J. Strom Thurmond, "'O'er the Ramparts We Watched!' Local Sovereignty Is Being Whittled Away," *Vital Speeches of the Day*, Oct 15, 1949, 29–32.

15. F. A. Harper, 'What to Do about Preserving the Free Market," *Vital Speeches of the Day*, Jan 15, 1952, 203–7. For Harper's continuing impact on conservative thought, see Timothy Noah, "Charles Koch, Listen to Your Guru!" *Politico*, Nov 30, 2015. See also Cockburn, "Oh No: Charles Koch's Favourite Economist Is a Huge Racist," *Spectator USA*, Oct 13, 2018, https://spectator.us/charles-koch-fa-harper/.

16. Milton V. Burgess, "War Being Won by Free Enterprise, Says Bricker," *Milwaukee Sentinel*, Sep 20, 1944, 4. For a claim of "the reverse racism developing among Negroes today," see Ludlow W. Werner, "Across the Desk," *New York Age*, Jul 8, 1944, 6.

17. *The Eleventh Hour for American Enterprise* (New York: National Association of Manufacturers 1946), foreword by J. Howard Pew, Chairman, National Industrial Information Committee, Hagley Library Imprints Collection, Manuscripts and Archives Department, Hagley Museum and Library.

18. "Pew Sees Dangers in Oil Regulation," *New York Times*, Nov 18, 1938, 31.

19. "Woodrum Cautions against Threat to Free Enterprise," *Charleston News and Courier*, Jan 13, 1949, 1.

20. Thurman Sensing, "Coalition Is Bad News for 'Liberals,'" *Rome News-Tribune*, Jan 26, 1959, 3. Sensing was referring especially to Senator Paul Douglass.

21. Thurman Sensing, "Conservative Coalition Needs South's Support," *Jackson Sun*, Aug 7, 1960, 4.

22. A 1944 editorial in a Florida newspaper observed, "'Free Enterprise' and 'States Rights'— two slogans which the conservatives, both north and south, are attempting to make a battlecry." "What Is 'Free Enterprise'? A Florida Senator's Answer," *St. Petersburg Times*, Feb 16, 1944, 4. Free enterprise, as historian Doug Rossinow observes, was "posed by

segregationist politicians as the opposite of integration." *The Politics of Authenticity: Liberalism, Christianity, and the New Left in America* (New York: Columbia University Press, 1998), 133.

23. Jason Morgan Ward, *Defending White Democracy: The Making of a Segregationist Movement and the Remaking of Racial Politics, 1936–1965* (Chapel Hill: University of North Carolina Press, 2011), 25.

24. "Opponent Says Race Issue Will Defeat Pepper," *Chicago Defender*, Apr 15, 1944, 11.

25. "Make This Your Creed Too," *Tallahassee Democrat*, Mar 28, 1944, 5.

26. "Governors Skirt Segregation Issue at Regional Meet," *Pittsburgh Courier*, Dec 10, 1949, 2.

27. Anthony Lewis, "Segregation Group Confers in Secret," *New York Times*, Dec 30, 1955, 1, 12.

28. Texas Junior Chamber, quoted in Patrick L. Cox, *Ralph L. Yarborough, the People's Senator* (Austin: University of Texas Press, 2009), 187. George Wallace, "The Civil Rights Movement Fraud, Sham and Hoax," Jul 4, 1964, http://www.let.rug.nl/usa/documents/1951-/speech-by-george-c-wallace-the-civil-rights-movement-fraud-sham-and-hoax-1964-.php.

29. Quoted in Ward, *Defending White Democracy*, 173.

30. Quoted in Kevin M. Kruse, *White Flight: Atlanta and the Making of Modern Conservatism* (Princeton: Princeton University Press, 2005), 214.

31. "Business Has Less Freedom in Hiring."

32. William F. Buckley, "The Big March on Washington," *Los Angeles Times*, Aug 19, 1963, 2:5. For a similar claim, see N. D. B. Connolly, *A World More Concrete: Real Estate and the Making of Jim Crow Florida* (Chicago: University of Chicago Press, 2014), 210.

33. Richard M. Weaver, "Integration Is Communization," *National Review*, Jul 13, 1957, 67.

34. Jeffrey D. Gonda, *Unjust Deeds: The Restrictive Covenant Cases and the Making of the Civil Rights Movement* (Chapel Hill: University of North Carolina Press, 2015).

35. Kruse, *White Flight*, 210.

36. "Lester Maddox Leads Segregation Marchers," *Hendersonville Times-News*, Apr 26, 1965, 7.

37. "Georgians Love Liberty," *Rome News-Tribune*, Sep 27, 1966, 8.

38. George C. Wallace, speech at Madison Square Garden, Oct 24, 1968, http://www-personal.umd.umich.edu/~ppennock/doc-Wallace.htm.

39. "Atlanta Restaurant Closes, but Owner Continues to Fight," *Tuscaloosa News*, Aug 14, 1964, 2.

40. "Maddox Denies Barring Negroes in Restaurant," *Washington Post*, Feb 3, 1965, A3.

41. "Free Enterprise," *Amsterdam News*, Jul 11, 1964, 18.

42. Thomas J. Sugrue, *The Origins of the Urban Crisis: Race and Inequality in Postwar Detroit* (Princeton: Princeton University Press, 1996).

43. Mark Brilliant, *The Color of America Has Changed: How Racial Diversity Shaped Civil Rights Reform in California, 1941–1978* (New York: Oxford University Press, 2010), 199. See also David Freund, *Colored Property: State Policy and White Racial Politics in Suburban America* (Chicago: University of Chicago Press, 2007), 155; Thomas J. Sugrue, *Sweet Land of Liberty: The Forgotten Struggle for Civil Rights in the North* (New York: Random House, 2008), 153.

44. Rebecca Leber, "Fox News: It's the 'Death of Free Enterprise' if Baker Can't Discriminate against Gay Couples," *Think Progress*, Dec 10, 2013.

45. Lawrence B. Glickman, "Don't Let Them Eat Cake," *Boston Review*, Jun 7, 2018, http://bostonreview.net/law-justice/lawrence-glickman-masterpiece-cakeshop.

46. Clyde Bolton, "Mizell Proposes Changes in U.S. Constitution," *Gadsden Times*, Nov 14, 1958, 1.

47. David Lawrence, "Who Protects Civil Rights of Employers?" *Ocala Star-Banner*, May 15, 1964, 4.

48. Frank F. Nesbit, "Jim Crow Theater," *Washington Post*, May 1, 1947, 6.

49. James J. Kilpatrick, *The Southern Case for School Segregation* (New York: Crowell-Collier, 1962), 30.

50. Marquis Childs, "Washington Calling: Seeds of the Southern Revolt," *Washington Post*, May 29, 1948, 7.

51. "Urge Dixie to Fight FEPC," *New York Amsterdam News*, Jan 17, 1948, 14.

52. Hawkes is quoted in Timothy N. Thurber, *Republicans and Race: The GOP's Frayed Relationship with African Americans, 1945–1974* (Lawrence: University of Kansas Press, 2013), 15.

53. John J. Synon, "Why Not Free Enterprise Schools?" *Citizen*, Oct 1965, 18.

54. "U.S. Slipping, Talmadge Says in Talk," *Washington Post*, Jan 2, 1950, B7.

55. Herman W. Steinkraus, "We Need a Fifth Freedom," *American Magazine*, Sep 1949, 24–25, 124–26.

56. Quoted in Ralph McGill, "States Rights and Suffering," *Toledo Blade*, Apr 10, 1961, 12.

57. Madeline Murphy, "States Rights Again?" *Baltimore Afro-American*, Jan 30, 1982, 4; Bruce J. Schulman, *From Cotton Belt to Sunbelt: Federal Policy, Economic Development, and the Transformation of the South, 1938–1980* (New York: Oxford University Press, 1991).

58. John Temple Graves, "This Morning," *Avondale Sun*, Feb 27, 1950, 3.

59. The quotation about Thurmond is from Jack Bass and Marilyn W. Thompson, *Ol' Strom: An Unauthorized Biography of Strom Thurmond* (Columbia: University of South Carolina Press, 2002), 264.

60. Roland Marchand, *Creating the Corporate Soul: The Rise of Public Relations and Corporate Imagery in American Big Business* (Berkeley: University of California Press, 1998), 435n63.

61. Walter White, "Chamber Music on Communism," *Washington Post*, Jan 19, 1947, B5. This was a commentary on Whitaker Chambers's pamphlet *Communist Infiltration in the United States: Its Nature and How to Combat It*, which ignored the problem of racism.

62. George S. Schuyler, "View and Reviews," *Pittsburgh Courier*, Mar 11, 1944, 7.

63. George S. Schuyler, "Views and Reviews," *Pittsburgh Courier*, Jan 24, 1942, 6.

64. Walter White, "Incomplete Story," *Akron Beacon Journal,* Jan 4, 1947, 6; George Mc-Cray, "Labor Front: Negro and Free Enterprise," *Chicago Defender*, Dec 11, 1943, 6.

65. "State FEPC Laws on the Increase," *Chicago Defender*, Apr 9, 1949, 1.

66. William Kennedy, "Up Front . . . This Week: The Negro Surplus Down South," *Pittsburgh Courier*, May 4, 1963, 10.

67. White, "Chamber Music on Communism."

68. Frank Pereira, "We Must Study, Take Pride in Africa's Past," *Pittsburgh Courier*, Jun 21, 1952, 29.
69. Gertrude Wilson, "Communism's Best Friends," *Amsterdam News*, Jun 29, 1963, 11.
70. "A Broken-Down Buggy," *Amsterdam News*, Mar 2, 1946, 10.
71. Earl Brown, "Timely Topics: Mr. Ask and Mr. Tell," *Amsterdam News*, Mar 11, 1944, A8.
72. Willard Townsend, "Fancy Slogans, Poor Substitute for Action against Nation's Intolerance," *Chicago Defender*, Jun 3, 1950, 7.
73. "Light on the Housing Problem," *Amsterdam News*, Jan 5, 1946, 8.
74. "It's Your Ball, Mr. Truman," *Chicago Defender*, Sep 8, 1945, 12.
75. Earl Conrad, "Yesterday and Today: What Jim Crow Means," *Chicago Defender*, May 10, 1947, 15.
76. Earl Conrad, "Yesterday and Today: Crumbs of Democracy," *Chicago Defender*, Jul 20, 1946, 15.
77. Earl Brown, "Timely Topics," *Amsterdam News*, Dec 13, 1947, 10.
78. "What Is 'Free Enterprise'?"
79. Andy Razaf, "All Ears," *Amsterdam News*, Jan 18, 1947, 8.
80. Speech of Apr 15, 1947, in *I Vote My Conscience: Debates, Speeches, and Writings of Vito Marcantonio*, ed. Annette Rubinstein (New York: Vito Marcantonio Memorial, 1956), 226.
81. Daniel Tobin, "The NAM Way: Profiteering, Depression, Fascism," *American Federationist* 54 (May 1947): 8–9.
82. "Midsummer Meeting of the Executive Council," *American Federationist* 55 (Feb 1948): 4–6.
83. "Capital Swap," *Pittsburgh Courier*, Nov 22, 1941, 6.
84. Solomon Larkin, "Big Business Must Answer to the American People," in "How Free Is 'Free Enterprise'?" *Proceedings of the 49th Annual League for Industrial Democracy Conference* (New York: League for Industrial Democracy, 1954), 18.
85. *Creeping Socialism* (New York: Union for Democratic Socialism, 1951), 3–4.
86. W. E. B. Du Bois, "As the Crow Flies," *Amsterdam News*, Oct 16, 1943, 12A.
87. "Socialism for the Rich, Free Enterprise for the Poor," Southern Christian Leadership Conference news release, Feb 1, 1967.
88. Nader, quoted in Morton Mintz, "Businessmen Challenged to Resist Monopoly Trend," *Washington Post*, Jun 4, 1973, D7.
89. Quoted in Gunner Myrdal, *An American Dilemma: The Negro Problem and American Democracy* (New York: Harper and Row, 1944), 210.
90. "The Metropolitan Story," *Chicago Defender*, Nov 15, 1947, 14.
91. Whitney M. Young, Jr. "To Be Equal: The 1966 Civil Rights Bill," *Chicago Defender*, Sep 17, 1966, 11.
92. "Loren Miller Says: 'Negroes Buy Homes under Worst Terms,'" *Pittsburgh Courier*, Jan 5, 1957, 2:1.
93. T. H. Runnels, "Negro Elevator Operators Fired," *Chicago Defender*, Nov 25, 1944, 10.
94. Marjorie McKenzie, "Democracy in Action: Free Enterprise Is Relative," *Pittsburgh Courier*, Oct 23, 1954, 20.
95. P. L. Prattis, "Labor Everywhere," *Pittsburgh Courier*, Jun 8, 1946, 16.

96. "'Negro Has Earned Status as a Citizen': Lewis: Courier Head Says Race Merits Postwar Consideration," *Pittsburgh Courier*, May 22, 1943, 24.

97. "This Is Not Democracy," *Amsterdam News*, Jul 22, 1944, A10.

98. Frank F. Bolden, "Orchestra Whirl: A Letter to a Friend in America," *Pittsburgh Courier*, Mar 21, 1942, 20.

99. George Peck, "Voluntary Cooperation," *Casa Grande Dispatch*, Jul 6, 1945, 6.

100. George S. Benson, "Looking Ahead: An Enterprise Story," *Journal-Advance*, Apr 7, 1949, 2.

101. Walter W. Weismann, "Promoting Free Enterprise: Industry Urged to Relate Defense of System to Peace and Jobs," *New York Times*, Jun 10, 1952, 26.

102. Emerson P. Schmidt, "Negro's Best Chance for Equality Seen in Private Enterprise," *Chicago Defender*, Apr 14, 1945, 1; Emerson P. Schmidt, *Freedom and the Free Market Inseparable* (Washington, DC: U.S. Chamber of Commerce, 1944). The use of "free market" was relatively rare in 1944, and it is notable that in a mainstream newspaper Schmidt spoke of "private enterprise" instead.

103. "Freedom of Choice," *Aspermont Star*, Nov 29, 1951, 4.

104. Full-page ad of the Sun Oil Company, *New York Sun*, Jan 5, 1948, quoted in Marshall McLuhan, *The Mechanical Bride: Folklore of Industrial Man* (Berkeley: Gingko, 1951), 115.

105. White, "Chamber Music on Communism."

106. W. E. B. DuBois, "The Winds of Time: Planning," *Chicago Defender*, Oct 12, 1946, 15, reprinted Aug 23, 1947, 15.

107. Ric Roberts, "A New Challenge," *Pittsburgh Courier*, Jan 7, 1961, 13.

108. "President Kennedy Meets NACW Delegates in D.C.," *Amsterdam News*, Aug 11, 1962, 13.

109. Earl Conrad, "Clare Luce Takes Her Stand," *Chicago Defender*, Dec 5, 1945, 11. It is unclear if Conrad is quoting or paraphrasing Luce.

110. Robert Gaylord, "Free Enterprise in the Postwar Period, Business Must Respect Rights of Others," speech delivered to the Postwar Forum of the American Federation of Labor, New York City, Apr 13, 1944, *Vital Speeches of the Day*, May 15, 1944, 457.

111. Helen Gahagan Douglas, "My Democratic Credo" (speech delivered to the U.S. House of Representatives, Mar 29, 1946). See the biography by Sally Denton: *The Pink Lady: The Many Lives of Helen Gahagan Douglas* (New York: Bloomsbury, 2009), 108–9, which explains that she gave the speech because Mississippi congressman John Rankin, a reactionary racist, had referred to her as a "communist." See also Greg Mitchell, *Tricky Dick and the Pink Lady: Richard Nixon vs. Helen Gahagan Douglas—Sexual Politics and the Red Scare, 1950* (New York: Random House, 1998), 98, which quotes a solicitation letter drafted by Nixon's finance committee chair that calls him "a firm believer in the American Way of Life and the free enterprise competitive system." On the other hand, Douglas, according to Nixon, was "seeking to substitute Socialism for our American freedoms."

112. Oliver Hoyem, "As Good Fellows Get Together," *Nation's Business*, Oct 1945, 44, 46, 48, 50, 58. Business advertisements during the war routinely treated "free enterprise" and "free labor" as a linked pair.

113. "United We Stand," *Chicago Defender*, Aug 3, 1946, 14.

114. A. J. Hayes, "Labor's Effect on Free Enterprise," *Machinists' Monthly Journal*, May 1954, 130.

115. "Kaiser Discusses 'Free Enterprise,'" *New York Times*, Jan 28, 1945, 16.

116. George S. Benson, "Looking Ahead," *Benton County Journal-Advance*, Jul 8, 1943, 4. On Benson's use of the crossroads metaphor, see Bethany Moreton, *To Serve God and Wal-Mart: The Making of Christian Free Enterprise* (Cambridge, MA: Harvard University Press, 2009), 165.

117. Lawrence Glickman, "Inventing the 'American Standard of Living': Gender, Race and Working-Class Identity, 1880–1925," *Labor History* 34 (1993): 221–35.

118. "Creeping Socialism," *Commonweal*, Jul 18, 1952, 355–56.

119. Harry S. Truman, address to the Missouri State Democratic Party Convention, Jefferson City, May 8, 1944, quoted in *Congressional Record Appendix*, May 9, 1944, 2255.

120. George Meany, "Free Enterprise: What It Means to Labor," *American Federationist* 51 (Jun 1944): 3–4.

121. "Baldanzi Asks UAW to Jump into Saddle," *Atlanta Constitution*, Jan 24, 1949, 5.

122. "I mean freedom to one person means free to use the free enterprise system, to make as much money as I can. And freedom to somebody else means free to enjoy the world without having to breathe in poison that some factory left behind." Pete Seeger, interview with David Hajdu, 1999; see *New Republic*, Jan 28, 2014, http://www.newrepublic.com/article/116385/previously-unpublished-interview-pete-seeger.

123. Mark Starr, "The Impact of Business on Free Enterprise: Business Subsidies and Social Planning," in "How Free Is 'Free Enterprise'?" *Proceedings of the 49th Annual League for Industrial Democracy Conference*, 14. See also Joseph Crespino, *Strom Thurmond's America* (New York: Hill and Wang, 2012), 82; Wendy L. Wall, *Inventing the "American Way": The Politics of Consensus from the New Deal to the Civil Rights Movement* (New York: Oxford University Press, 2008), 49.

124. Hoffa is quoted in "Lawmakers Set to Debate Labor-Management Role," *Rome News-Tribune*, May 2, 1963, 1.

125. "Southern Senators' Red Herring," *Pittsburgh Courier*, Jul 20, 1957, A5.

126. "What Do They Mean, Enterprise?" *Fortune*, Sep 1946, 2.

127. Thomas, quoted in "People," *Time*, May 21, 1956.

128. Carroll Kilpatrick, "Real Threat to Free Enterprise," *New Republic*, Nov 18, 1946, 650–51.

129. See, for example, Daniel Scroop, "The Anti–Chain Store Movement and the Politics of Consumption," *American Quarterly* 60 (Dec 2008): 925–49.

130. Franklin D. Roosevelt, "Message to Congress on the Concentration of Economic Power," Apr 29, 1938, http://www.informationclearinghouse.info/article12058.htm; "60 Million Jobs in Postwar Era Is Roosevelt Goal," *Atlanta Constitution*, Oct 29, 1944, 1A.

131. "Unity for Victory, for the Elections and for Post-war Security by Earl Browder," *Communist*, Jun 1944, 485–500. Browder said, "Marxists will not help the reactionaries by opposing the slogan 'free enterprise' with any form of counter slogan. If anyone wishes to describe the existing system of capitalism in the United States as 'free enterprise' that's all right with us." Quoted in Maurice Isserman, *Which Side Were You On? The*

Communist Party during the Second World War (1982; repr. Urbana: University of Illinois Press, 1993), 189.

132. "Communism, 1944 Model," *New York Times*, Jan 11, 1944, 18. According to Westbrook Pegler, Communists were now "preaching free enterprise, according to instructions." "Fair Enough," *Atlanta Constitution*, Jan 13, 1944, 6.

133. "The Election, III: Why Dewey Deserves the Independent Vote," *Life*, Oct 16, 1944, 34.

134. "Murray Proposes Guaranteed Wage," *Southeast Missourian*, Feb 1, 1952, 1.

135. Stephen H. Fifield, "'Tell the Story of Free Enterprise,'" *Banker's Magazine,* Oct 1939, 358.

136. George Pullom Scharf, "The Topic of Free Enterprise in the Senate Debates on the Taft-Hartley Labor Bill, April 23–June 23, 1947" (MA thesis, University of Illinois, 1950), 30. According to Scharf, supporters used the phrase forty times in legislative debates and opponents invoked it twenty-seven times.

137. "Warns of Labor Losses After War if the Free Enterprisers Win Control," *Observer*, Jan 3, 1943, 3.

138. Hayes, "Labor's Effect on Free Enterprise," 130, 132.

139. Carroll Thompson, "Labor's Problem: Real Wages, Walter Reuther," *Current History*, May 1950, 290.

140. Sid Feder, "Reuther Shines Rather Dimly as Advocate of Free Enterprise," *Victoria Advocate*, Jan 16, 1958, 5.

141. *Machinists' Monthly Journal*, Mar 1948, 80–81.

142. David Siegel, "Can This Be Free Enterprise?" *Machinists' Monthly Journal*, Aug 1947, 280–81.

143. *Machinists' Monthly Journal*, Mar 1948, 81. Garry Wills described "the American cult of free enterprise" in *Nixon Agonistes: The Crisis of the Self-Made Man* (New York: Signet, 1970), 504.

144. James G. Patton, "Farmer and Worker," *American Federationist* 51 (Mar 1944): 27–30.

145. Meany, quoted in "Historic Meeting," *American Federationist* 51 (May 1944): 3.

146. Herman Benson, "What Is Walter Reuther? A Report on the Auto Workers' Convention," *New International* 13 (Dec 1947): 259–64.

147. McLuhan, *Mechanical Bride*, 133.

148. Daniel J. Tobin, "We Ate under the New Deal—We Didn't Eat under Republican Free Enterprise," *International Teamster*, Nov 1944, 17–18. See also the letter to the editor by Frank Lafavre, "Free Enterprise," *Miami News*, Mar 13, 1943, 6, in which he calls critics of the New Deal "modern Rip Van Winkles" and condemns corrupt business leaders as "shining examples of free enterprise."

149. "Reuther Warns Wallace," *New York Times*, Feb 28, 1948, 2.

150. "Text of American Federation of Labor Committee's Recommendation for the Post-war World," *New York Times*, Apr 12, 1944, 26.

151. Maurice Tobin, "America Was Built on Free Labor," *American Federationist* 57 (Nov 1950): 6–7, 32–33.

152. "Labor Day, 1950," *New York Times*, Sep 4, 1950, 10.

153. "General Motors Walks out on Fact-Finding Hearing," *Atlanta Constitution*, Dec 29, 1945, 2.

154. Hubert H. Humphrey, "What They Say," *American Federationist* 66 (May 1949): 32.

155. William Green, "T-H Law: Scabs' Friend," *American Federationist* 55 (Nov 1948): 22–23.

156. William Green, "Mandate for Repeal," *American Federationist* 56 (Feb 1949): 22.

157. Lucy Freeman, "Bias Laid to Foes of Welfare State: They Want Their Benefits, but Would Deny Them to Others, Senator Humphrey Says," *New York Times*, Apr 25, 1950, 19.

158. Meany, "Free Enterprise: What it Means to Labor."

159. A. J. Hayes, "Your Job and Mine—Target for Tomorrow?" *Machinists' Monthly Journal*, Oct 1951, 229.

160. Arthur M. Schlesinger Jr., *The Age of Jackson*, abridged ed. (New York: New American Library, 1960, 1945), 82, 106, 119. Yet Schlesinger's characterization of "that enduring struggle between the business community and the rest of society which is the guarantee of freedom in a liberal capitalist state" well described the motives of the alternative free enterprisers in his own time. In a talk at the Harvard Free Enterprise Society, Schlesinger "questioned the meaning of the term 'Free Enterprise.' He said it either meant freedom from government intervention or freedom from monopolies and cartelization." "Schlesinger and Cherington Argue Merits of 'Fair Deal,'" *Harvard Crimson*, May 4, 1949.

Chapter 8. From Public Spending to "Entitlements"

1. Norm Ornstein, "The New Nihilism Is Stifling the Republican Party," *Atlantic*, Jun 11, 2014, https://www.theatlantic.com/politics/archive/2014/06/the-new-nihilism-is-stifling-the-republican-party/372626/.

2. See the website of Americans for Tax Reform, the organization Norquist founded: https://www.atr.org/about-the-pledge.

3. Mara Liasson, "Conservative Advocate," *National Public Radio*, May 25, 2001, http://www.npr.org/templates/story/story.php?storyId=1123439.

4. Leon Davis, "Yes, You Can 'Do Something about It'!" *Nation's Business*, Oct 1938, 35. For an excellent overview, see Molly C. Michelmore, *Tax and Spend: The Welfare State, Tax Politics, and the Limits of American Liberalism* (Philadelphia: University of Pennsylvania Press, 2012).

5. "Everett Sanders Rakes 'New Deal' Spending Spree," *St. Louis Post-Dispatch*, Feb 18, 1934, 1.

6. "You've Got Me Wrong—You Pay Them!," *Nation's Business*, Nov 1938, 76.

7. "Tick! Tock! $120,000 a Minute. For What? For Government," *Nation's Business*, Dec 1938, 76.

8. Darrell Peacock, "Foreman-Rutherford Race Grows Hotter as Election Nears," *Odessa American*, Oct 28, 1962, 37.

9. John K. Jessup et al., *The National Purpose* (New York: Holt Rinehart and Winston, 1960).

10. "Roosevelt Takes Credit for Saving Free Enterprise," *Poughkeepsie Eagle-News*, Oct 15, 1936, 1, 13.

11. "Where the Road Leads," *Galveston Daily News*, Mar 5, 1950, 4.

12. Louis Bromfield, "Increasing Costs Crush U.S. Way of Life," *Cincinnati Enquirer*, Sep 15, 1946, 6.

13. "Chamber Head Sees Golden Age from Free Enterprise," *Newport News Daily Press*, Dec 11, 1954, 9; "On 'Last Mile to Collectivism,' Hoover, at 75, Warns Country," *Washington Post*, Aug 11, 1949, 1, 14.

14. M. S. Rukeyser, "Pulling Truman's Chestnuts out of the Fire," *San Francisco Examiner*, Jul 21, 1948, 14; Milton Friedman, "Can We Halt Leviathan?" *Newsweek*, Nov 6, 1972, 98.

15. Walter Lippmann, "The New Spending Policy," *Hartford Courant*, Jun 3, 1939, 2; "David Lawrence," *Nebraska State Journal*, Mar 25, 1939, 10.

16. "Knox Assails 'Tax Monster,'" *Rochester Democrat and Chronicle*, Dec 28, 1935, 3.

17. George Gallup, "Public Gives Taft Nod over Ike as More Likely to Cut Public Spending," *Munster Times*, Feb 20, 1952, 14. One critic in 1949 mocked the Republican Party's "wholesale condemnation of federal activity." Claude L. Stinneford, "GOP Policy," *Muncie Star Press*, Nov 30, 1949, 6.

18. George E. Sokolsky, "Growing Population and Its Problems," *Staunton News Leader*, Aug 7, 1956, 4. Molly C. Michelmore argues that this image is "largely a fiction." *Tax and Spend*, 155.

19. Hopkins, who denied saying this, was quoted in Arthur Krock, "Win Back 10 States," *New York Times*, Nov 9, 1938, 4.

20. John E. Upston Jr., "Lest We Forget about Knowland," *San Rafael Daily Independent*, Oct 25, 1958, 4.

21. James M. Cypher, "The Origins and Evolution of Military Keynesianism in the United States," *Journal of Post-Keynesian Economics* 38 (2015): 449–76.

22. "Both Sides Give Their Arguments on Proposed Low-Cost Housing Project for Miami," *Miami News*, Jun 25, 1950, 34; N. D. B. Connolly, *A World More Concrete: Real Estate and the Making of Jim Crow Florida* (Chicago: University of Chicago Press, 2014), 189.

23. HR 10660, Highway Construction Act, Apr 11, 1956, https://www.govtrack.us/congress /votes/84–1956/h95.

24. Peter J. Boyer, "'Guerilla of the Right' Is Celebrity; Gingrich 'Teaching' Delegates," *Los Angeles Times*, Aug 23, 1984, 1:5; "G.O.P. Women Hear Taxes Condemned," *Philadelphia Inquirer*, May 19, 1936, 34. For an early use of the phrase that Gingrich made famous, see "Sales Tax Talk Brings Protests," *Minneapolis Star Tribune*, Mar 11, 1958, 4. See also Richard A. Viguerie, "The Tax Collector for the Welfare State," *Newton Record*, Dec 12, 1984, 4.

25. "Excessive Taxation Is Larceny," *Philadelphia Inquirer*, Mar 7, 1925, 12.

26. "Stop the Death Tax: Coolidge," *Chillicothe Gazette*, Feb 19, 1925, 1.

27. "Tax Parasites Ruin U. S., Warns Col. McCormick: Rallies Business Leaders to Combat Peril," *Chicago Tribune*, Apr 7, 1932, 6.

28. "Socialism or Americanism," *Chicago Tribune*, Jun 30, 1932, 12. Eventually, the *Tribune* began to spell the term "burocracy." On the change, see "Tribune Adds 18 Words to Saner Spelling List," *Chicago Tribune*, Feb 11, 1934, 1, 10.

29. "Newspaper Comment," *Corvallis Gazette-Times*, Dec 15, 1934, 2.

30. "Cluett, at Buffalo, Hits 'Spending Orgy': Republican Candidate Sees New Deal Leading Voters to the 'Poor House,'" *New York Times*, Oct 26, 1934, 10.

31. "Knox Assails Tax Monster," *Rochester Democrat and Chronicle*, Dec 28, 1935, 3.

32. The *Globe Democrat* editorial was quoted in "The New Peril," *Detroit Free Press*, May 19, 1934, 6.

33. John Ackelmire, "Growthmanship: A Rigged Game of the New Radicals," *Indianapolis News*, Jul 16, 1960, 6.

34. "Leader Bids Republicans Ban Liberalism, Stay Conservative to Fight Democrats," *New York Times*, Jan 17, 1937, 1. For a characterization of liberalism as "public altruism" and conservatism as "social selfishness" traced back to the 1930s, see Hevie Haufler, "Rekindling the Good Spirit behind the 'L' Word," *New York Times*, Dec 4, 1988, CN42.

35. "Knox Tells Retails Merchants Evils of Regimenting Economic System," *Los Angeles Times*, Aug 20, 1936, 4.

36. Ronald Reagan, "Address on Behalf of Senator Barry Goldwater: 'A Time for Choosing,'" Oct 27, 1964, http://www.presidency.ucsb.edu/ws/index.php?pid=76121.

37. "Who Is the Forgotten Man?" *Longview News-Journal*, Sep 17, 1968, 4.

38. Paul Krugman, "Innocent Mistakes," *New York Times*, Nov 10, 2007, https://krugman.blogs.nytimes.com/2007/11/10/innocent-mistakes/.

39. "Your Money and Your Freedom," *Milwaukee Sentinel*, Nov 17, 1947, 12.

40. "The Disease of Big Government," *Los Angeles Times*, Oct 6, 1948, 2:4.

41. Hoover is quoted in Arthur M. Schlesinger Jr., "The Welfare State," *Reporter*, Oct 11, 1949, 28.

42. "Free Enterprise," *Kingsport Times*, Jan 1, 1960, 4.

43. Merle Thorpe, "Our Vanishing Economic Freedom," *Saturday Evening Post*, Oct 3, 1931.

44. "We should not be judged on how many new laws we create," he told Bob Schieffer, the host of *Meet the Press*. "We ought to be judged on how many laws we repeal." Steve Benen, "The Legacy Speaker Boehner Leaves Behind," Sep 25, 2015, http://www.msnbc.com/rachel-maddow-show/the-legacy-speaker-boehner-leaves-behind. See also "In the House, a Refusal to Govern," *New York Times*, Jul 12, 2013, A20. In 2015, Republican Tea Party congressman Raul Labrador dismissed the very idea of governing because it "means bringing more government," suggesting that governing itself was an inappropriate function for Congress. Quoted in Ryan Lizza, "A House Divided," *New Yorker*, Dec 14, 2015, 32.

45. Even before 1964, these phrases were frequently repeated verbatim by Republican politicians. See, for example, the statement of defeated congressional candidate Robert G. Bartlett in "Scott Predicts Bright Future in Politics for Bob Bartlett," *Pocono Record*, Sep 11, 1963, 3. Watt E. Smith, who was attempting to form a Young Republicans club in South Carolina, used the same language. See Paul Jones, "Young Republicans Set Organizational Aims," *Orangeburg Times and Democrat*, Jan 21, 1964, 10.

46. "Actor Ronald Reagan Blasts Discriminatory Use of Government Income Tax Practices," *Executive Club's News*, May 9, 1958, 6, 7, ILR Kheel Documentation Center, collection number 5583/1, box 52, folder 8, "Executives Club of Chicago—Communications," Catherwood Library, Cornell University, Ithaca, NY.

47. Thurman Sensing, "Welfare-State Evils Feed upon Themselves," *Jackson Sun*, Apr 19, 1959, 4. In a letter to the editor, J.W. suggested the formation of a "Taxpayers' Party." "Tax Revolt Urged," *Los Angeles Times*, Oct 15, 1951, 40.

48. Edward F. Bullard, "For a Taxpayer's Ticket," *New York Herald Tribune*, Nov 14, 1934, 14.

49. R. C. Hoiles, "Why Discuss Wage Scale?" *Pampa Daily News*, Mar 4, 1940, 4.

50. Leonard Read, "The Essence of Americanism," https://fee.org/articles/the-essence-of -americanism/. First delivered in 1961, this speech became Read's "traditional opening address at dozens of FEE seminars." See also "Economic Foundation Head Will Give Address Here," *Moline Dispatch*, Sep 11, 1958, 30. In a tweet on Nov 22, 2017, Grover Norquist wrote: "The best tax rate? one clue. In 1774 the average American in the 13 colonies paid between one and two percent of their income in taxes. 1–2%. Seems reasonable. One rate. One time. No double taxation. Good target."

51. Tea Party '78, "Writer Discusses Tax Revolt," *Indianapolis Star*, Jun 20, 1978, 12.

52. Will Wilkinson, "The Tax Bill Shows the G.O.P.'s Contempt for Democracy," *New York Times*, Dec 20, 2017.

53. "GOP Chief Mentions Several for Governor," *Los Angeles Times*, Feb 1, 1961, 8.

54. "Tax Revolt Urged," *Syracuse Post-Standard*, May 2, 1962, 4.

55. For more on this transformation, see Michael Kazin, *The Populist Persuasion: An American History*, 2nd ed. (Ithaca: Cornell University Press, 2017).

56. "Taxation and Theft," *Pampa Daily News*, Dec 29, 1968, 18.

57. "Taxpayers Bleeding to Death," *Salem Statesman Journal*, Jul 24, 1968, 6.

58. Lawrence B. Glickman, *Buying Power: A History of Consumer Activism in America* (Chicago: University of Chicago Press, 2009), 294.

59. See, for example, O'Brien Atkinson, "It's Your Money," *Scribner's Magazine*, Dec 1935, 353–55; Guy Emery Shipler Jr., "It's Your Money," *McCall's*, Mar 1957, 157–58; Stuart Chase and F. J. Schlink, *Your Money's Worth: A Study in the Waste of the Consumer's Dollar* (New York: Macmillan, 1927).

60. See, for example, Barnet Hodes, *It's Your Money: A Plain-Talk Revelation about Government Costs to You and a Program of Tax Reduction Ahead* (Chicago: Reily and Lee, 1935).

61. "Republicans Put Show on Radio to Dramatize Cost of New Deal: 'Liberty at the Crossroads,'" *New York Herald Tribune*, Jan 15, 1936, 1, 10.

62. John H. Chider, "It's Your Money, Brother," *Saturday Evening Post*, Feb 26, 1944, 20–21, 57, 59–60.

63. Theodore H. White, *The Making of the President, 1960* (New York: Athenaeum, 1961), 277, 303.

64. "Excerpts from President's Talk," *New York Times*, Jun 12, 1981, D4.

65. "Dole's Speech Accepting the G.O.P. Nomination for President," *New York Times*, Aug 16, 1996, A26.

66. "In His Own Words," *New York Times*, Oct 8, 1996, A21. See also G. Robert Hellman, "Dole's 'Consumers' Guide' Attacks President's Trustworthiness," *Dallas Morning News*, Oct 2, 1996, 11A. In that speech Dole said: "It's your money. It's not my money. It's not his money. It's your money."

67. Mike Allen, "A New Rowland Preaches Flexible, 'Fun' Republicanism," *New York Times*, Oct 31, 1998, B8.

68. "Work Will 'Bear Fruit,'" *State*, Dec 12, 2010, A14. "Just as Democratic Gov. Dick Riley is known for his focus on education and the late Republican Gov. Carroll Campbell is

known for his focus on jobs . . . Sanford says he should be known as the governor who always was the taxpayer's advocate." Mark Sanford, "Today's Forgotten Man Is the Taxpayer," *Greenwood Index-Journal*, Apr 29, 2009, 7.

69. Alison Mitchell, "Gore and Bush Agree on Basics, but Differ Sharply on the Details," *New York Times*, July 4, 2000, A1.

70. "House Republicans Push through $1.5 Trillion Tax Bill," *Week*, Dec 19, 2017, https://theweek.com/speedreads/744284/house-republicans-push-through-15-trillion-tax-bill.

71. "Text of Hoover Speech at Lincoln Dinner: Former President Declares New Deal Policies Peril to Nation's Liberty," *Los Angeles Times*, Feb 14, 1939, 8.

72. "Carl Spad Urges Unity in Rensselaer GOP Talk," *Troy Times Record*, Feb 20, 1967, 18; Evelle J. Younger, "Money Won't End Race Riot Threat," *San Mateo Times*, Aug 3, 1967, 3.

73. Ronald Reagan, "Free Enterprise: Economics," *Vital Speeches of the Day*, Jan 15, 1973, 196–201. The text of Bryan's Jul 9, 1896, address at the Democratic National Convention in Chicago can be found at http://historymatters.gmu.edu/d/5354/.

74. Three important pieces arguing that public spending and government intervention were long-standing traditions are Charles Beard, "The Myth of Rugged American Individualism," *Harper's Magazine*, Dec 1931, 13–22; Charles A. Beard, "The Idea of Let Us Alone," *Virginia Quarterly Review* 14:4 (Autumn 1939): 500–514; Reinhold Niebuhr, "Halfway to What?" *Nation*, Jan 14, 1950, 26–28. The first major publication of the Committee on Research in Economic History was "The Tasks of Economic History," Supplement, *Journal of Economic History* 3 (Dec 1943). See also Arthur H. Cole, "Committee on Research in Economic History: A Description of Its Purposes, Activities, and Organization," *JEH* 13 (Winter 1953): 79–87; Arthur H. Cole, "The Committee on Research in Economic History: An Historical Sketch," *Journal of Economic History* 30:4 (Dec 1970): 723–41.

75. Herbert Heaton, "General Memorandum of State Studies in the Role of Government in American Economic Development, July 14, 1941." This memorandum is quoted as an appendix in the revised edition of Oscar Handlin and Mary Flug Handlin, *Commonwealth: A Study of the Role of Government in the American Economy; Massachusetts, 1774–1861* (Cambridge, MA: Harvard University Press, 1987), 270.

76. Oscar Handlin, "Laissez-Faire Thought in Massachusetts, 1790–1880," Louis Hartz, "Laissez Faire Thought in Pennsylvania, 1776–1880," and Milton Heath, "Laissez Faire in Georgia, 1732–1860," all in "The Tasks of Economic History." See also Louis Hartz, *Economic Policy and Democratic Thought: Pennsylvania, 1776–1860* (Cambridge, MA: Harvard University Press, 1948); Handlin and Handlin, *Commonwealth*; E. A. J. Johnson. *The Foundations of American Economic Freedom: Government and Enterprise in the Age of Washington* (Minneapolis: University of Minnesota Press, 1973).

77. "Private vs. Public Spending" *Atlantic*, Mar 1959, 16, 19; Senator Joseph S. Clark, "Five Fallacies of Public Finance," *Washington Post*, Dec 10, 1958, A18.

78. Vice President Lyndon Johnson claimed that "public spending is strengthening, not weakening, the nation's free-enterprise economy." "Johnson Sees Good in Public Spending," *New York Times*, Mar 3, 1962, 31. For Lyndon Johnson's full-throated defense of public spending at the height of the Great Society, see "The Nation," *New York Times*, Nov 14, 1965, E2. Before signing a pioneering higher education bill, Johnson said, "Too many

people, for too long argued that education and human welfare were not the government's concern. Even as they spoke, our schools fell behind, our sick went unattended and our poor fell deeper into despair. Now, at last, in 1965, we have quit talking and started acting." Tevi Troy, *Intellectuals and the American Presidency: Philosophers, Jesters, or Technicians?* (Lanham, MD: Rowman and Littlefield, 2002), 45. George Schwartz, "The Keynes Formula Sweeps On," *New York Times*, Sep 8, 1963, SM32, 128–30; "Great Debate Looms on Public Spending," *Bloomington Pantagraph*, Dec 21, 1963, 4; Edwin L. Dale Jr., "Are We Americans Going Soft?" *New York Times*, Dec 1, 1957, SM21, 120, 122, 124–25; Edwin L. Dale Jr., "Public Spending Reported on Rise: Economists Say This Will Be Only 'Upward Thrust' in the Economy for '58," *New York Times*, Jan 29, 1958, 24; Edwin L. Dale Jr., "'Great Debate' in Capital: Is U.S. Misusing Wealth?" *New York Times*, Feb 7, 1960, 1; Edwin L. Dale Jr, "Big Debate: Public vs. Private Spending," *New York Times*, Mar 13, 1960, E5; Barbara Ward, "The Great Silence in the Great Debate," *New York Times*, May 8, 1960, SM 26; Irvin Molotsky, "Edwin Dale Jr., 75, Reporter and an Expert in Economics," *New York Times*, May 11, 1999, 10.

79. "The Republican Challenge," *Lafayette Journal and Courier*, Jul 22, 1960, 6. See also "Public Spending," *Wichita Catholic Advance*, Aug 12, 1960, 4.

80. Vance Packard, *The Waste Makers* (New York: David McKay, 1960), 70–71, 85–87; Ralph Nader, *Unsafe at Any Speed: The Designed-in Dangers of the American Automobile* (New York: Grossman, 1965), 181.

81. Bell is quoted in Howard Brick, *Transcending Capitalism: Visions of a New Society in Modern American Thought* (Ithaca: Cornell University Press, 2006), 195.

82. Hansen is quoted in Brick, *Transcending Capitalism*, 167.

83. Quoted in Dale, "Are We Americans Going Soft?" SM21.

84. Calling for "government intervention on a major scale to halt the downward slide of economic activity," the *Times* editorialized with disappointment that the Eisenhower administration would propose tax cuts rather than a "new large public works program." "Tax Cuts vs. Spending," *New York Times*, Mar 13, 1958, 28.

85. Quoted in Dale, "Are We Americans Going Soft?" SM21.

86. "Text of Departure Talk by Eisenhower," *New York Times*, Dec 4, 1959, 10.

87. Edwin L. Dale Jr., *Conservatives in Power: A Study in Frustration* (New York: Doubleday, 1960), 138.

88. "The Challenge to Free Enterprise," address by W. P. Gullander, President, NAM, before the 16th Annual Conference of the Public Relations Society of America, Inc, on Monday, Nov 18, 1963, San Francisco, CA, series 1, box 67, Free Enterprise File, "Free Enterprise, General, 1951–63," Manuscripts and Archives Department, Hagley Museum and Library, Wilmington, DE.

89. H. M. Groves et al., "The Economics of Eisenhower: A Symposium," *Review of Economics and Statistics* 38: 4 (Nov 1956): 378.

90. Walter Lippmann, "Public Need and Private Pleasure," Sep 5, 1957, quoted in *The Essential Lippmann: A Political Philosophy for Liberal Democracy* (Cambridge, MA: Harvard University Press, 1982), 361, 362.

91. Lizabeth Cohen, *A Consumers' Republic: The Politics of Mass Consumption in Postwar America* (New York: Knopf, 2003).

92. Leon H. Keyserling, "For a National Prosperity Budget," *New York Times*, Mar 25, 1956, SM7; Edmund F. Wehrle, "Guns, Butter, Leon Keyserling, the AFL-CIO and the Fate of Full-Employment Economics," *Historian* 66:4 (Dec 2004): 730–48.

93. In contradistinction to Galbraith, Keyserling believed that all forms of consumption were essential, and he denigrated "anti-consumptionists" who "say that schools are needed more than tailfins, and so they are." Nevertheless, he thought that increased public spending should not lead to decreased private consumption. "Less for Private Spending?" *New Republic*, May 23, 1960, 15–16.

94. Christopher Lasch, *The New Radicalism in America, 1889–1963* (New York: Vintage, 1967), 308.

95. James Ronald Stanfield and Jacqueline Bloom Stanfield, eds., *Interviews with John Kenneth Galbraith* (Oxford: University Press of Mississippi, 2004), 49.

96. John Kenneth Galbraith, *The Affluent Society* (New York: Houghton Mifflin, 1958), 208–9.

97. Arthur Schlesinger Jr., "A Democratic View of the Republicans," *New York Times*, Jul 17, 1960, 165.

98. Saulnier is quoted in James Reston, "The Underlying Issue of the Campaign," *New York Times*, Mar 13, 1960, E8. Questioned by the Scripps Howard news service about whether the government should shift toward more public spending, both Nixon and Kennedy, for different reasons, answered no. "Both Candidates Oppose Increase in Public Spending," *Pittsburgh Press*, Oct 1, 1960, 5.

99. Adlai E. Stevenson, "National Purpose: Stevenson's View," *New York Times*, May 26, 1960, 30; Lyndon Johnson, "Remarks at the University of Michigan," May 22, 1964, https://millercenter.org/the-presidency/presidential-speeches/may-22-1964-remarks -university-michigan. On "post-materialism," see Jeffrey M. Berry, *The New Liberalism: The Rising Power of Citizen Groups* (Washington, DC: Brookings Institution Press, 1999).

100. Herbert J. Marx Jr. "Should We Reject the Welfare State?" *Senior Scholastic*, Oct 4, 1950, 11.

101. "Transcript of President Eisenhower's News Conference at the National Press Club," *New York Times*, Jan 15, 1959, 18. Reagan said virtually the same thing early in his presidency. "Excerpts from President's Talk," *New York Times*, Jun 12, 1981, D4.

102. Stans is quoted in Richard E. Mooney, "Business Warned on Tax Practices," *New York Times*, May 4, 1960, 27.

103. Ward, "Great Silence in the Great Debate," 89.

104. Paul Krugman, "America Goes Dark," *New York Times*, Aug 8, 2010.

105. The first use of the term "starving the beast" I have found is in Maureen Dowd, "The Crisco Kids," *New York Times*, Oct 12, 1995, A23. See also Richard W. Stevenson, "The High-Stakes Politics of Spending the Surplus," *New York Times*, Jan 7, 2001, WK3; Paul Krugman, "The Tax-Cut Con," *New York Times*, Sep 14, 2003, SM54.

106. Dale, "Big Debate."

107. Edwin L. Dale Jr. "What Went Wrong? Another Look at the New Economics," *New York Times*, Sep 18, 1966, SM50, 102–10.

108. Edwin L. Dale Jr., "Must the Budget Be Uncontrollable? Big Snag Is Growth of Entitlement Programs," *New York Times*, Sep 22, 1974, F2.

109. As late as 1980, newspapers used quotation marks to refer to "'entitlement' programs." Edward Cowan, "Tax Cut Proponents Challenge Carter Stand," *Tampa Tribune*, Feb 3, 1980, 13.

110. Daniel Bell, "The Revolution of Rising Entitlements," *Fortune*, Apr 1975, 178–85.

111. Molotsky, "Edwin Dale, Jr., 75"; "A Cure for Deficits," *Pittsburgh Post-Gazette*, Sep 17, 1981, 6.

112. See Peter G. Peterson's works: *On Borrowed Time: How the Growth in Entitlement Spending Threatens America's Future* (San Francisco: ICS, 1988); *Facing Up: How to Rescue the Economy from Crushing Debt and Restore the American Dream* (New York: Simon and Schuster, 1993); *Will America Grow Up Before It Grows Old? How the Coming Social Security Crisis Threatens You, Your Family and Your Country* (New York: Random House, 1996); *Running on Empty: How the Democratic and Republican Parties Are Bankrupting Our Future and What Americans Can Do about It* (New York: Picador 2005).

113. E. J. Dionne Jr., "Public Spending Is an Investment: But the GOP's Big Tax Cuts Are Not a Long-Term Growth Strategy," *Pittsburgh Post-Gazette*, Dec 11, 2001, 19.

114. State of the Union address, Jan 12, 1961, http://www.infoplease.com/t/hist/state-of-the -union/173.html.

115. Sean Wilentz, *The Age of Reagan: A History, 1974–2008* (New York: Harper, 2008).

116. Martin Walker, "The New Normal," *Wilson Quarterly* 33:3 (Summer 2009): 63–66. Walker writes, "For several decades after World War II, private consumption measured as a share of gross domestic product had remained within a range of 61 to 63 percent. But in 1983 consumption began a steady rise, peaking at 70 percent in 2007."

117. Rebecca Savransky, "Poll: Majority Supports Increased Infrastructure Spending, Opposes Border Wall Funding," *Hill*, Mar 8, 2017, http://thehill.com/homenews/adminis tration/322975-poll-majority-supports-increased-spending-on-infrastructure-opposes.

118. http://www.infrastructurereportcard.org/.

119. Bill Clinton, "America Is Buckling and Leaking," *New York Times*, Jun 24, 1988, A31; "Priorities, Priorities," *New York Times*, Nov 11, 1992, A24; Peter Baker and John M. Broder, "Obama Pledges Public Works on a Vast Scale," *New York Times*, Dec 6, 2008; Trump's 2016 election night speech can be found at http://abcnews.go.com/Politics /full-text-donald-trumps-2016-election-night-victory/story?id=43388317.

120. Paul Krugman, "The Hijacked Commission," *New York Times*, Nov 12, 2010, A31; Jack Lew, "Tightening Our Belts," Nov 29, 2010, https://obamawhitehouse.archives.gov/ blog/2010/11/29/tightening-our-belts.

121. The gospel of tax cuts has periodically been called into question. See, for example, Adam Nagourney, "Tax Cuts from '70s Confront Brown Again in California," *New York Times*, Jan 9, 2011, 21.

122. Bruce J. Holmes, "Sputnik Moments," *Atlantic*, Jan 31, 2011, http://www.theatlantic .com/national/archive/2011/01/sputnik-moments/70493/.

123. Walter Shapiro, "It's Your Money! And Government Is Free, Right?" *USA Today*, Jun 8, 2001, 11A.

124. David Lawrence, "Avoidance and Evasion Differ," *Des Moines Tribune*, Jun 2, 1937, 8.

125. Philip Rucker, Jia Lynn Yang, and Steven Mufson, "Romney Tax Rate 14.1% in 2011," *Washington Post*, Sep 22, 2012 A6.

126. Colin Campbell, "Donald Trump Says He Uses 'Every Single Thing in the Book' to Avoid Paying Taxes," *Business Insider*, Jan 24, 2016, http://www.businessinsider.com /donald-trump-tax-rate-mitt-romney-2016–1.

127. "Rep. Eric Cantor Makes Remarks on Insurance Regulation at White House Health Summit," *Washington Post*, Feb 25, 2010, http://www.washingtonpost.com/wp-dyn/content /article/2010/02/25/AR2010022503128.html.

128. "Republican Party Response to President Obama's "Address before a Joint Session of the Congress on the State of the Union," Jan 27, 2010, http://www.presidency.ucsb.edu /ws/index.php?pid=109253.

129. Robert Reich, "Free Enterprise on Trial," *Business Insider*, Jan 16, 2012, http://www .businessinsider.com/free-enterprise-on-trial-2012–3.

130. Ackelmire, "Growthmanship."

131. See, for example, Randall Rothenberg, *The Neoliberals: Creating the New American Politics* (New York: Simon and Schuster, 1984); Adam Tooze, *Crashed: How a Decade of Financial Crises Changed the World* (New York: Viking, 2018), 173.

Epilogue

1. Patrick J. Buchanan, "GOP Becomes the Activist Party," *Chicago Tribune*, Aug 1, 1978, B3.

2. George W. Fyler, "Democratic 'Chaos,'" *Chicago Tribune*, Aug 9, 1977, B2.

3. Mrs. Merrill Corley, "George Wallace Could Win," *Burlington Free Press*, Apr 24, 1972, 14.

4. Burdette Parry, "Are the People Fed Up on Isms, Including Liberalism?" *Pittsburgh Post-Gazette*, Jan 22, 1936, 8; Chris Suellentrop, "Campaign Like It's 1946," *New York Times*, Mar 29, 2006, https://opinionator.blogs.nytimes.com/2006/03/29/campaign-like -its-1946/.

5. Marianne Means, "Label Them with Care," *Lansing State Journal*, Mar 28, 1976, 14.

6. "Bentsen Ticket Pleases Delegates," *Sioux City Journal*, Jul 13, 1988, 3.

7. See Godfrey Hodgson's influential chapter "The Ideology of Liberal Consensus" in *America in Our Time* (1976; repr. Princeton: Princeton University Press, 2005).

8. Brian Leiter, "Roosevelt, Reagan and the Sanders Moment," *Huffington Post*, Jan 31, 2016, https://www.huffingtonpost.com/brian-leiter/roosevelt-reagan-and-the-_b_9120586 .html.

9. Gary Gerstle, "The Rise and Fall (?) of America's Neoliberal Order," *Transactions of the Royal Historical Society* 28 (2018), 243, 249.

10. John Hart, "Republicans Shouldn't Underestimate Sanders' Push for Single-Payer," *Forbes*, Sep 15, 2017, https://www.forbes.com/sites/johnhart/2017/09/15/republicans -shouldnt-underestimate-sanders-push-for-single-payer/#129cb590324f; Brian Rogers, "Different Clinton and a Changed Democratic Party," *Philadelphia Inquirer*, Jul 27, 2016, A13.

11. https://www.aei.org/publication/trumps-rise-was-predictable-heres-what-conservatives -need-to-do-next/; http://www.hughhewitt.com/house-speaker-paul-ryan-ahca/.

12. Other than a 2015 promise that he would "unleash the incredible spirit of free enterprise in this country—to get America moving again," and a mention in a 2016 debate, I have found no references to Trump using the phrase. "Trump Starts Online Fundraising Drive," *Hill*, Aug 8, 2015.

13. https://www.gop.com/the-2016-republican-party-platform/; http://www.presidency.ucsb.edu/papers_pdf/101961.pdf.

14. "Marco Rubio: 'Obama Doesn't Believe in Free Enterprise,'" *Sunshine State News*, Aug 2, 2012, http://sunshinestatenews.com/blog/marco-rubio-obama-doesnt-believe-free-enterprise.

15. R. Muse, "GOP Hypocrites Interfere with Private Business to Keep Union out of Tennessee VW Plant," *Politicsusa*, Feb 13, 2014, https://www.politicususa.com/2014/02/13/republican-hypocrites-interfere-private-business-union-tennessee-vw-plant.html.

16. Quoted in Ed Kilgore, "Movement Conservatives Now Prefer Trump," *New York*, Oct 27, 2017, http://nymag.com/daily/intelligencer/2017/10/movement-conservatives-now-prefer-trump.html.

17. Kristol is quoted in John Wagner and Juliet Eilperin, "Once a Populist, Trump Governs as a GOP Stalwart," *Washington Post*, Dec 6, 2017, A6.

18. Michael S. Rozeff, "Does Donald Trump Believe in Free Enterprise?" *Economic Policy Journal*, Nov 18, 2016, http://www.economicpolicyjournal.com/2016/11/does-donald-trump-believe-in-free.html; Josh Hammer, "Free Enterprise Is Intrinsically Moral. In the Age of Trump, Here's Why That Matters," *Daily Wire*, Dec 19, 2016, http://www.daily wire.com/news/11730/free-enterprise-intrinsically-moral-age-trump-josh-hammer#.

19. Noah Bierman, "Trump Aide 'Counseled' for Product Pitch," *Hartford Courant*, Feb 10, 2017, A3; Charles Lane, "Donald Trump's Contempt for the Free Market," *Washington Post*, Oct 21, 2015, https://www.washingtonpost.com/opinions/trumps-contempt-for-the-free-market/2015/10/21/2f61d87c-7815–11e5-bc80–9091021aeb69_story.html?utm_term=.5bb9445ce40c; Daniel Horowitz, "Trump Backs Price Controls—Free Enterprise in Peril," *Hill*, Feb 2, 2016, http://thehill.com/blogs/congress-blog/presidential-campaign/267831-trump-backs-price-controls-free-enterprise-in-peril; Adam K. Raymond, "Chinese Firm with Government Ties Gives Kushner Family Sweetheart Deal," *New York*, Mar 13, 2017, http://nymag.com/daily/intelligencer/2017/03/chinese-firm-give-kushner-family-sweetheart-deal.html.

20. Al Rodbell, "What Makes Trump Tick?" *New York Times*, Oct 22, 1995, F34.

21. Christopher Lehmann-Haupt, "Books of the Times," *New York Times*, Dec 7, 1987, C29.

22. George Monbiot, "Neoliberalism: The Deep Story That Lies beneath Donald Trump's Triumph," *Guardian*, Nov 14, 2016, https://www.theguardian.com/commentisfree/2016/nov/14/neoliberalsim-donald-trump-george-monbiot.

23. On the embrace of the punitive state, see Julilly Kohler-Hausmann, *Getting Tough: Welfare and Imprisonment in 1970s America* (Princeton: Princeton University Press, 2017).

24. Donald Trump, "The only problem our economy has is the Fed . . . ," Twitter, Dec 24, 2018, 10:55 a.m., https://twitter.com/realDonaldTrump/status/1077231267559755776.

25. "Free Enterprise Essential for New World of Invention Ahead, Speaker Tells Clubs," *Sheboygan Press*, Jun 2, 1943, 4.

26. "Transcript: Donald Trump's Speech Responding to Assault Accusations," *National Public Radio*, Oct 13, 2016, https://www.npr.org/2016/10/13/497857068/transcript-donald -trumps-speech-responding-to-assault-accusations.

27. John J. Faso, "Rep. John Faso Responds: Rap Music and Politics," *New York Times*, Jul 20, 2018.

28. "The Inaugural Address," Jan 20, 2017, https://www.whitehouse.gov/inaugural-address.

29. Political scientist Julia Azari has written that the "two main ideological strains of contemporary conservatism—cultural and fiscal—are closely intertwined." "Why Saying Paul Ryan and Donald Trump Belong to Different Parties Is Kinda Wrong," *Fivethirty eight.com*, Apr 26, 2018, https://fivethirtyeight.com/features/why-saying-paul-ryan-and -donald-trump-belong-to-different-parties-is-kinda-wrong/.

30. In *The Politics of Common Sense: How Social Movements Use Public Discourse to Change Politics and Win Acceptance* (New York: Oxford University Press, 2015), Deva R. Woodley examines the effectiveness of progressive common sense in political struggles.

31. In *A Commercial Republic: America's Enduring Debate over Democratic Capitalism* (Lawrence: University Press of Kansas, 2014), 5, Mike O'Connor notes that much of the public did not support the "muscular government response" to the financial crisis in 2008–9.

32. Karl Polanyi, *The Great Transformation: The Political and Economic Origins of Our Time* (Boston: Beacon, 1944), 265.